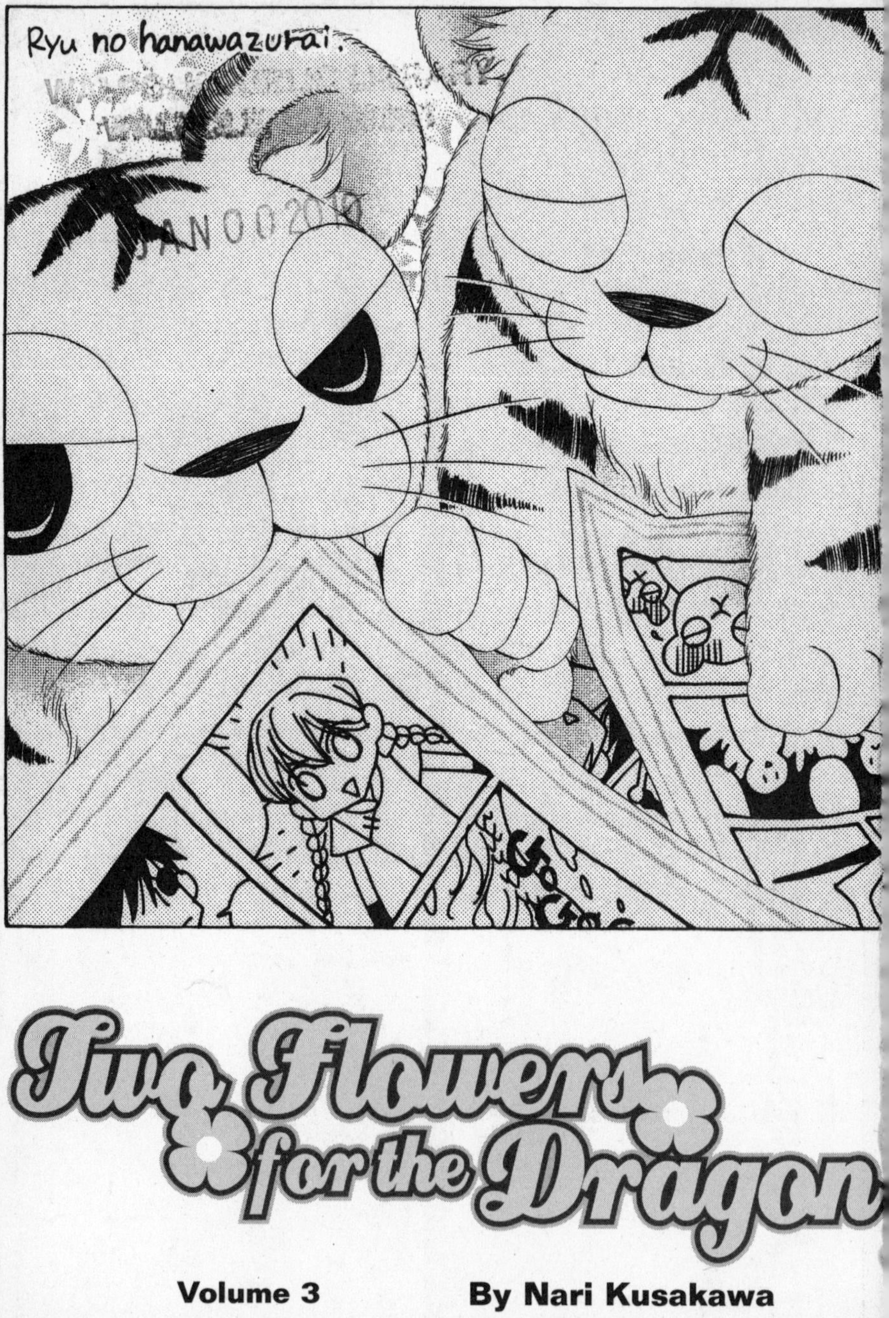
Ryu no hanawazurai.

Two Flowers for the Dragon

Volume 3

By Nari Kusakawa

CONTENTS

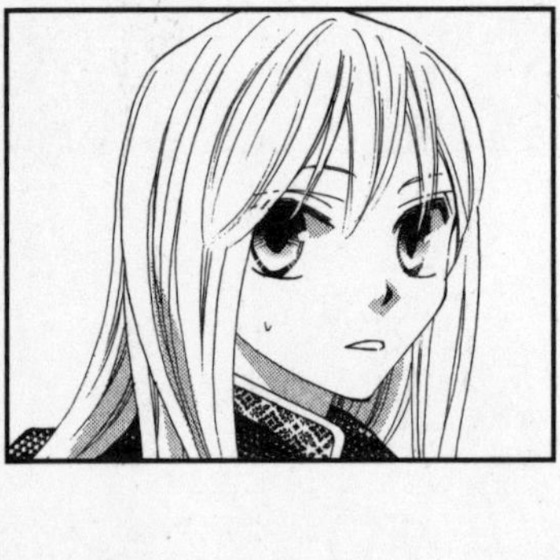

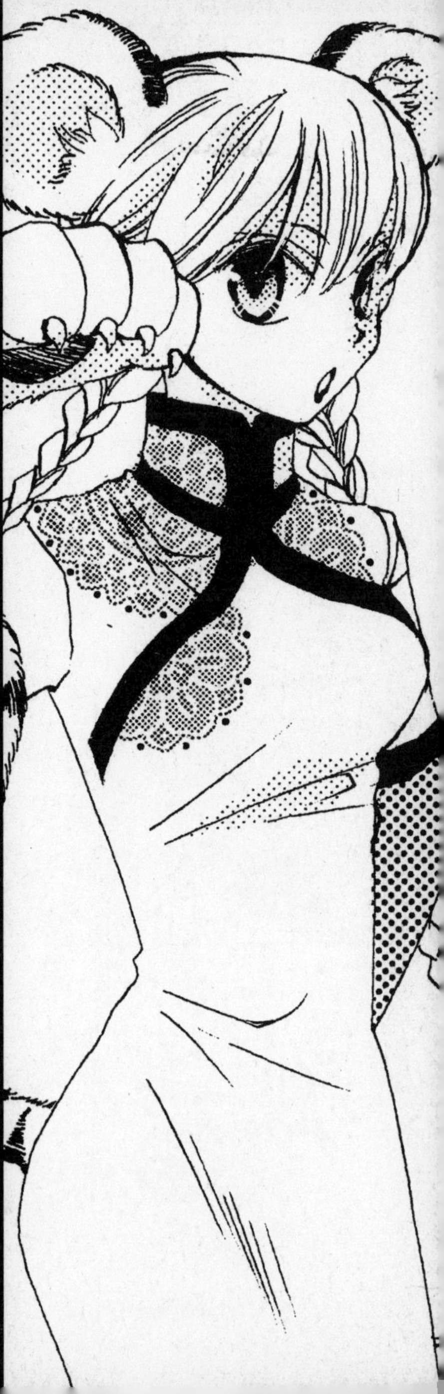

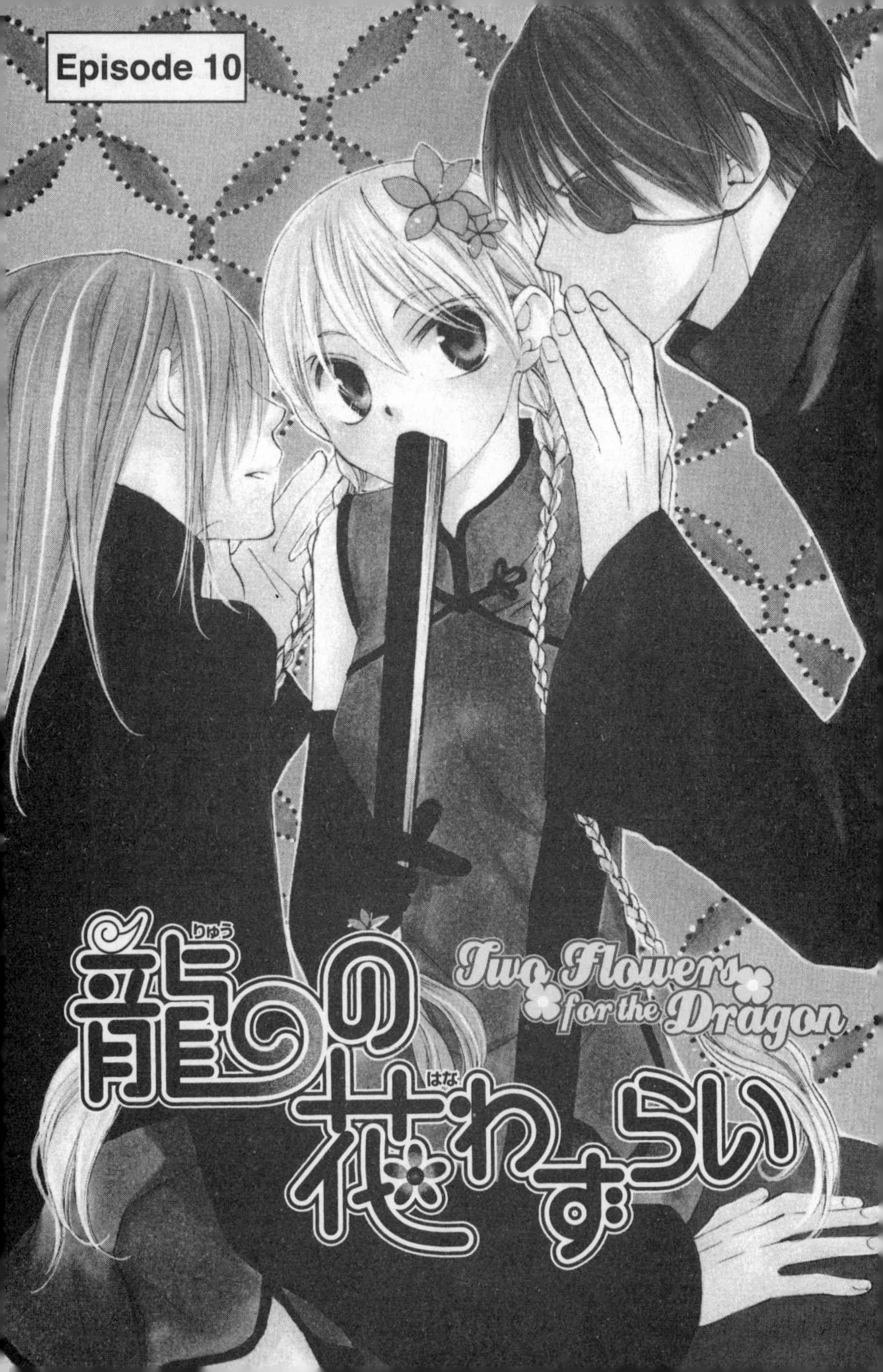
Episode 10
龍の花わずらい
Two Flowers for the Dragon

Episode 10 Preview Cut

Seems like something is hanging in the
air between them...

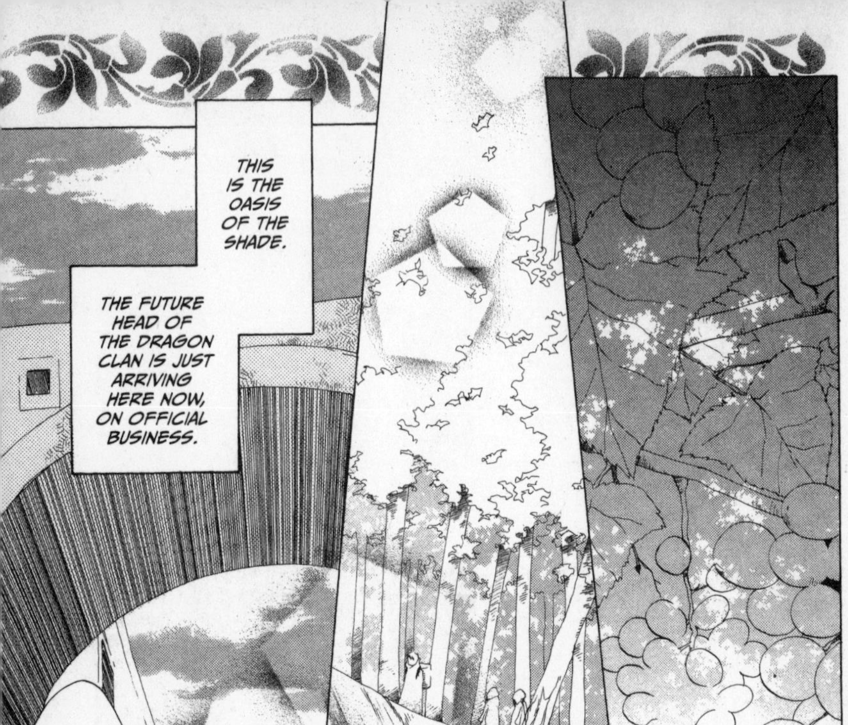
THIS IS THE OASIS OF THE SHADE.
THE FUTURE HEAD OF THE DRAGON CLAN IS JUST ARRIVING HERE NOW, ON OFFICIAL BUSINESS.
PHEW...

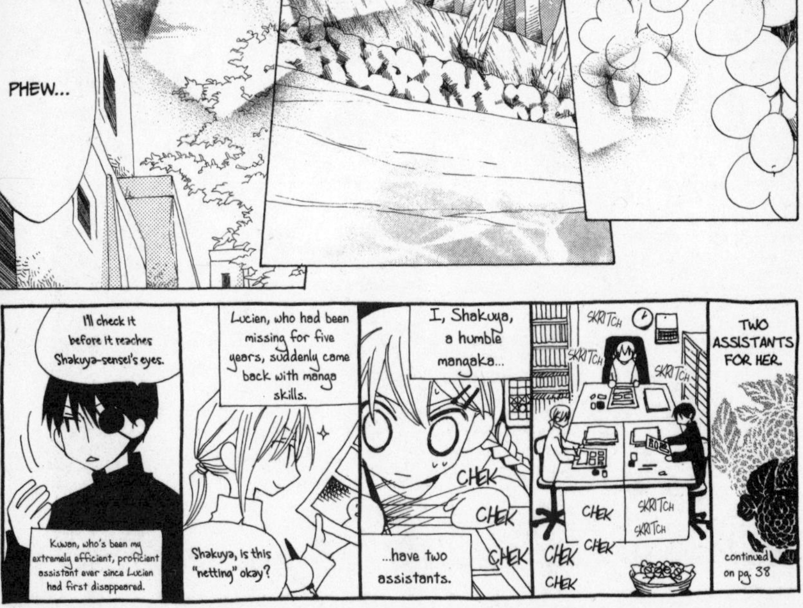
I'll check it before it reaches Shakuya-sensei's eyes.
Kuwan, who's been my extremely efficient, proficient assistant ever since Lucien had first disappeared.
Lucien, who had been missing for five years, suddenly came back with manga skills.
Shakuya, is this "netting" okay?
I, Shakuya, a humble mangaka...
CHEK
CHEK
CHEK
...have two assistants.
SKRITCH
SKRITCH
SKRITCH
CHEK
SKRITCH
SKRITCH
CHEK
CHEK
CHEK
TWO ASSISTANTS FOR HER.
continued on pg. 38

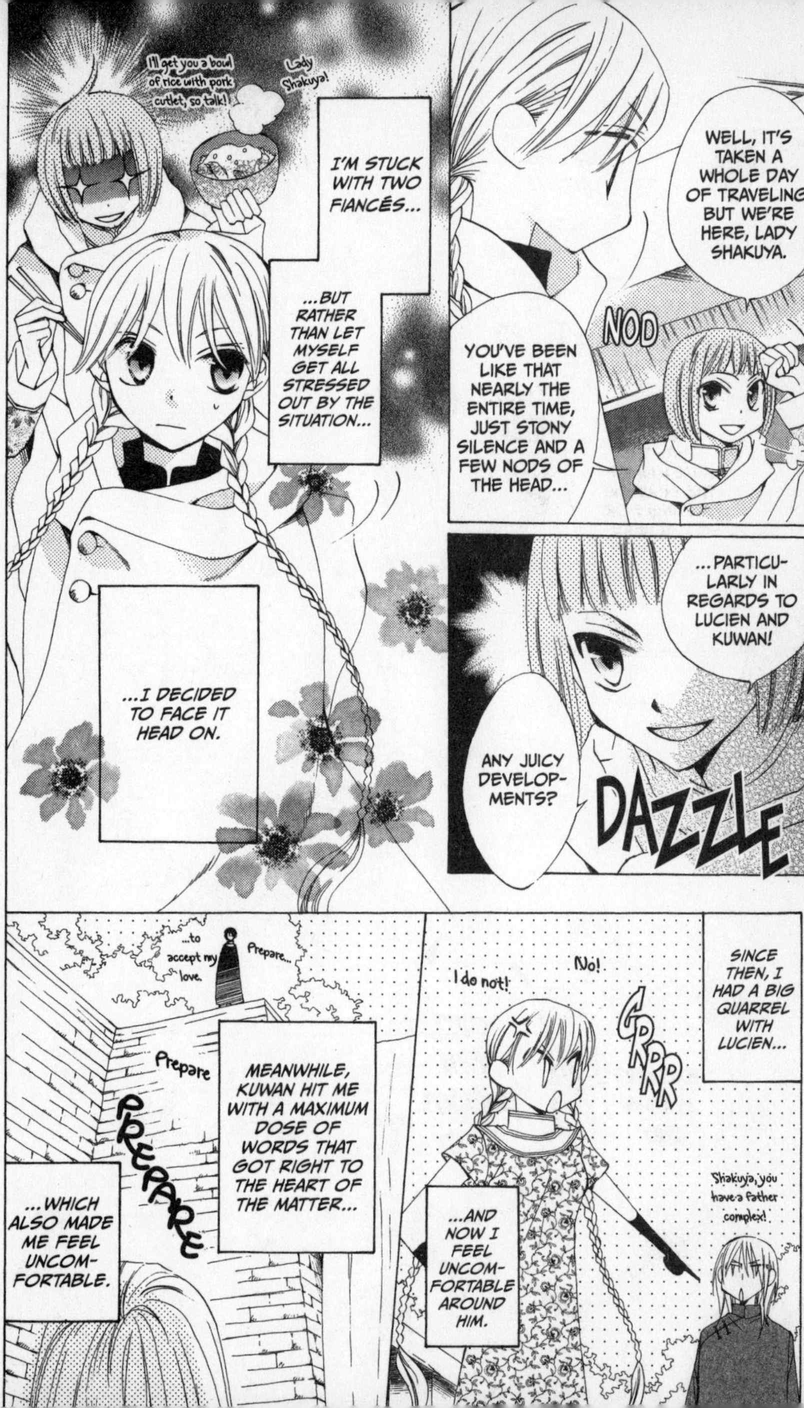
WELL, IT'S TAKEN A WHOLE DAY OF TRAVELING, BUT WE'RE HERE, LADY SHAKUYA.
NOD
YOU'VE BEEN LIKE THAT NEARLY THE ENTIRE TIME, JUST STONY SILENCE AND A FEW NODS OF THE HEAD...
...PARTICU-LARLY IN REGARDS TO LUCIEN AND KUWAN!
ANY JUICY DEVELOP-MENTS?
DAZZLE
I'll get you a bowl of rice with pork cutlet, so talk!
Lady Shakuya!
I'M STUCK WITH TWO FIANCÉS...
...BUT RATHER THAN LET MYSELF GET ALL STRESSED OUT BY THE SITUATION...
...I DECIDED TO FACE IT HEAD ON.
SINCE THEN, I HAD A BIG QUARREL WITH LUCIEN...
GRRR
No!
I do not!
Shakuya, you have a father complex!
...AND NOW I FEEL UNCOM-FORTABLE AROUND HIM.
Prepare...
...to accept my love.
Prepare
PREPARE
MEANWHILE, KUWAN HIT ME WITH A MAXIMUM DOSE OF WORDS THAT GOT RIGHT TO THE HEART OF THE MATTER...
...WHICH ALSO MADE ME FEEL UNCOM-FORTABLE.

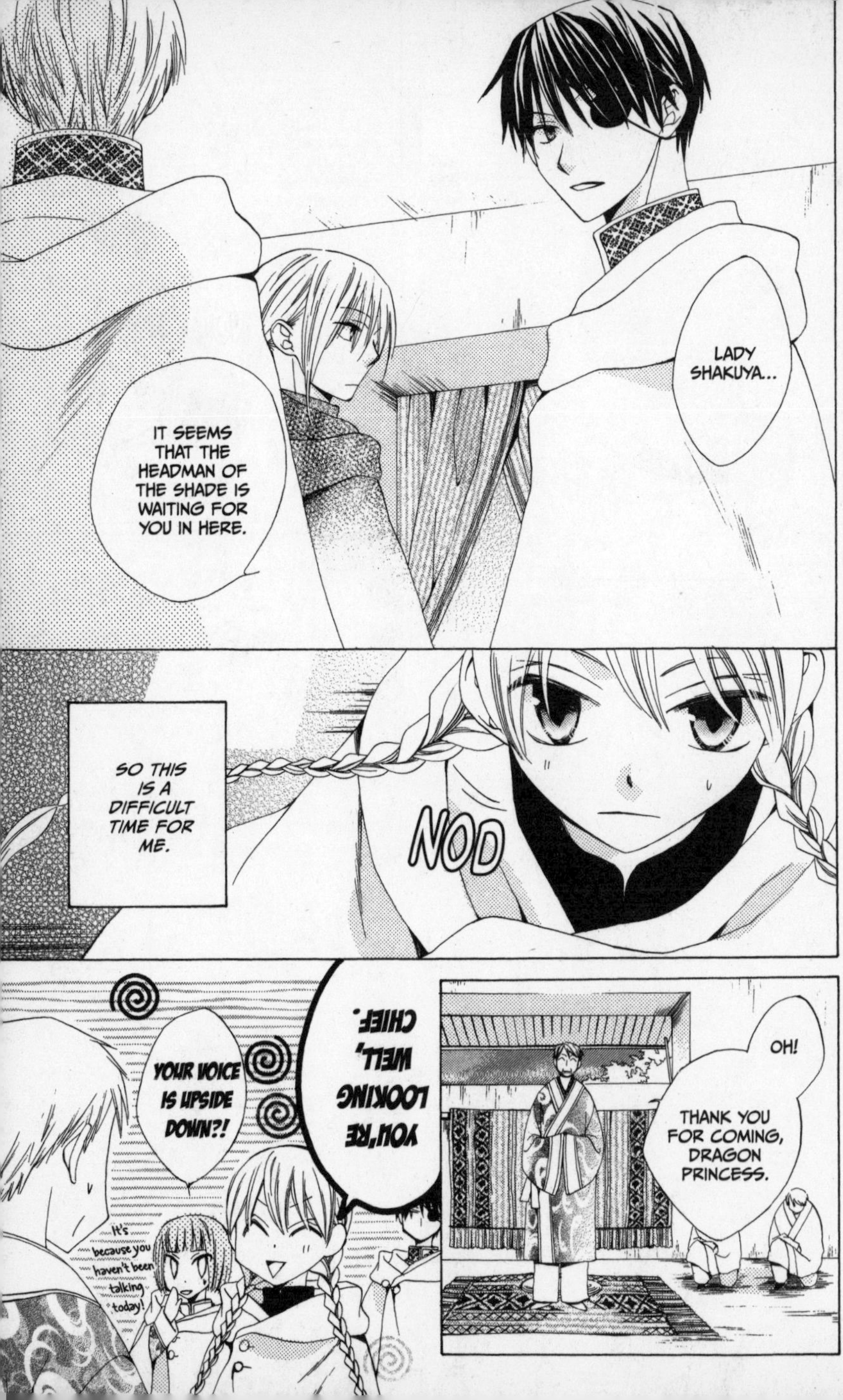
LADY SHAKUYA...
IT SEEMS THAT THE HEADMAN OF THE SHADE IS WAITING FOR YOU IN HERE.
SO THIS IS A DIFFICULT TIME FOR ME.
NOD
OH!
THANK YOU FOR COMING, DRAGON PRINCESS.
YOU'RE LOOKING WELL, CHIEF.
YOUR VOICE IS UPSIDE DOWN?!
It's because you haven't been talking today!

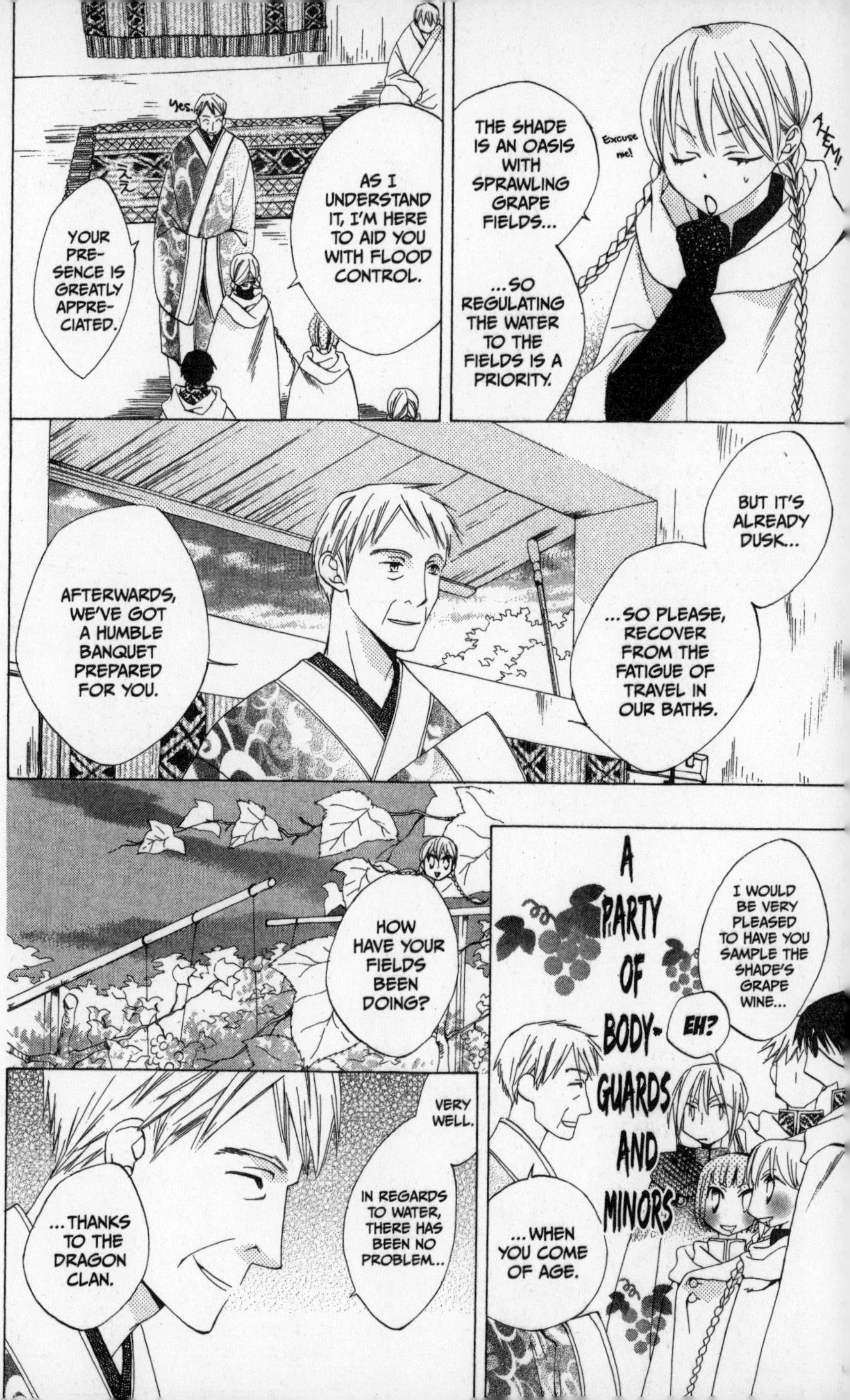
AHEM!
Excuse me!
THE SHADE IS AN OASIS WITH SPRAWLING GRAPE FIELDS...
...SO REGULATING THE WATER TO THE FIELDS IS A PRIORITY.
AS I UNDERSTAND IT, I'M HERE TO AID YOU WITH FLOOD CONTROL.
Yes.
YOUR PRE-SENCE IS GREATLY APPRE-CIATED.
BUT IT'S ALREADY DUSK...
...SO PLEASE, RECOVER FROM THE FATIGUE OF TRAVEL IN OUR BATHS.
AFTERWARDS, WE'VE GOT A HUMBLE BANQUET PREPARED FOR YOU.
A PARTY OF BODY-GUARDS AND MINORS
I WOULD BE VERY PLEASED TO HAVE YOU SAMPLE THE SHADE'S GRAPE WINE...
EH?
...WHEN YOU COME OF AGE.
HOW HAVE YOUR FIELDS BEEN DOING?
VERY WELL.
IN REGARDS TO WATER, THERE HAS BEEN NO PROBLEM...
...THANKS TO THE DRAGON CLAN.

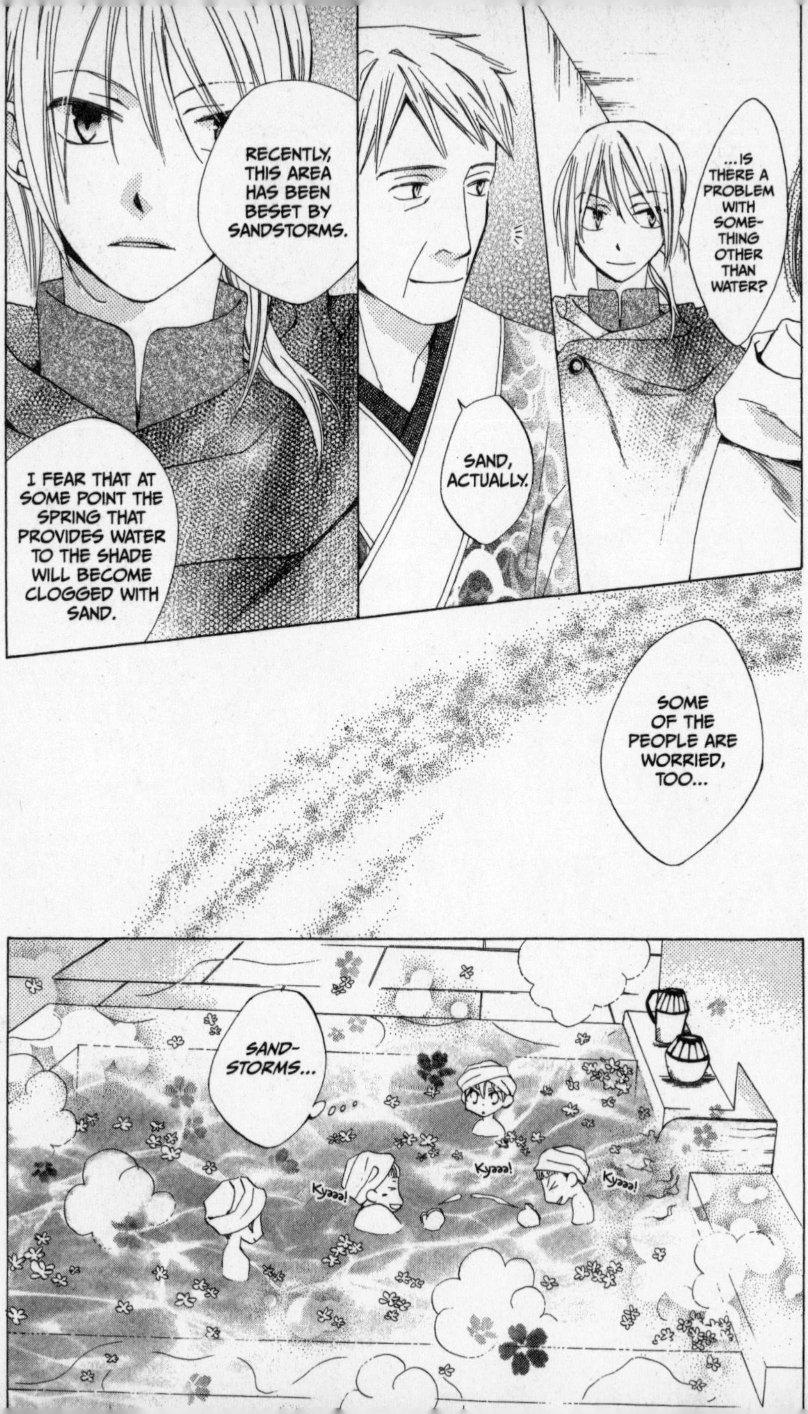
...IS THERE A PROBLEM WITH SOME-THING OTHER THAN WATER?
SAND, ACTUALLY.
RECENTLY, THIS AREA HAS BEEN BESET BY SANDSTORMS.
I FEAR THAT AT SOME POINT THE SPRING THAT PROVIDES WATER TO THE SHADE WILL BECOME CLOGGED WITH SAND.
SOME OF THE PEOPLE ARE WORRIED, TOO...
Kyaaa!
Kyaaa!
Kyaaa!
SAND-STORMS...

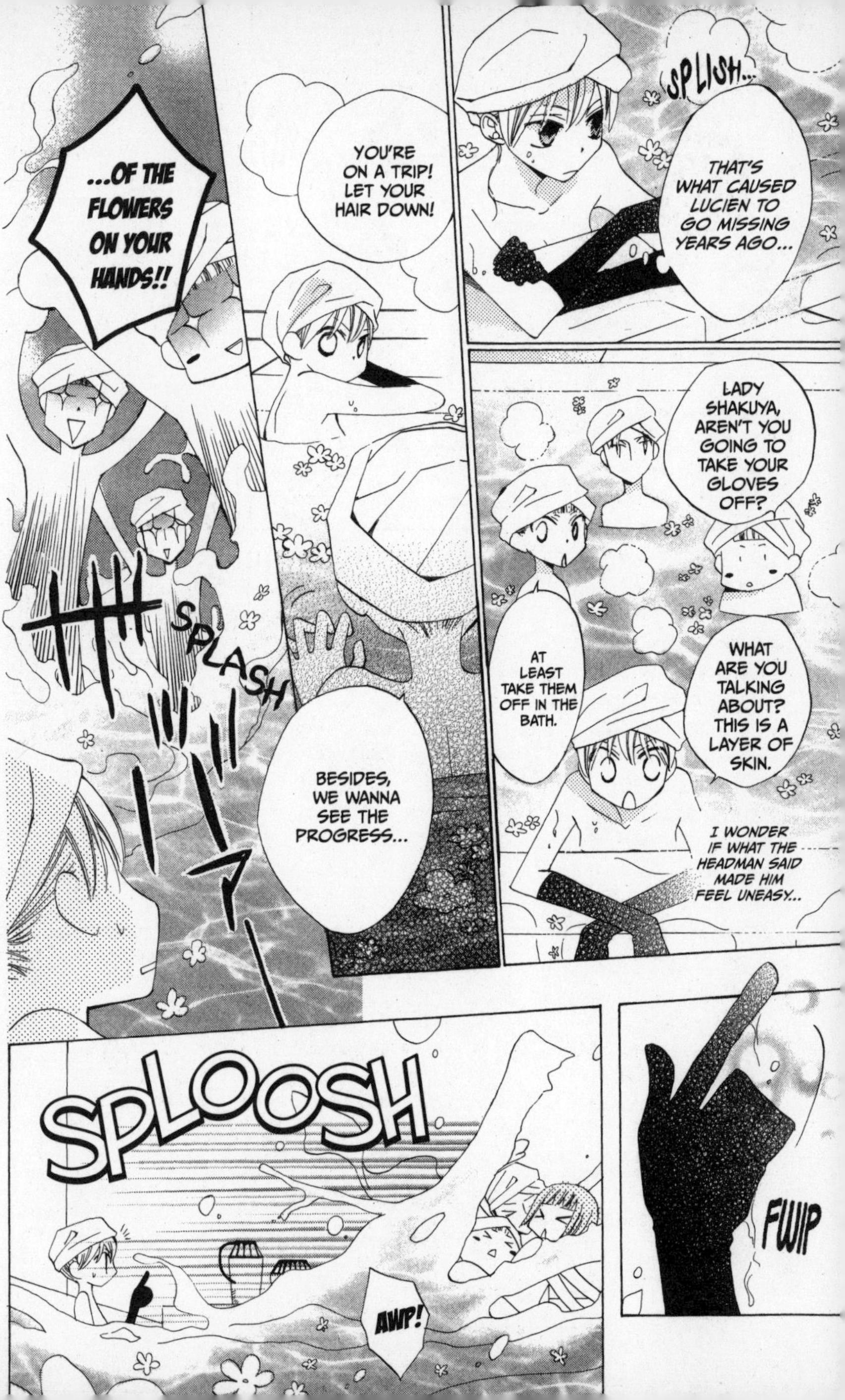
SPLISH...
THAT'S WHAT CAUSED LUCIEN TO GO MISSING YEARS AGO...
LADY SHAKUYA, AREN'T YOU GOING TO TAKE YOUR GLOVES OFF?
WHAT ARE YOU TALKING ABOUT? THIS IS A LAYER OF SKIN.
AT LEAST TAKE THEM OFF IN THE BATH.
I WONDER IF WHAT THE HEADMAN SAID MADE HIM FEEL UNEASY...
YOU'RE ON A TRIP! LET YOUR HAIR DOWN!
BESIDES, WE WANNA SEE THE PROGRESS...
...OF THE FLOWERS ON YOUR HANDS!!
SPLASH
FWIP
SPLOOSH
AWP!

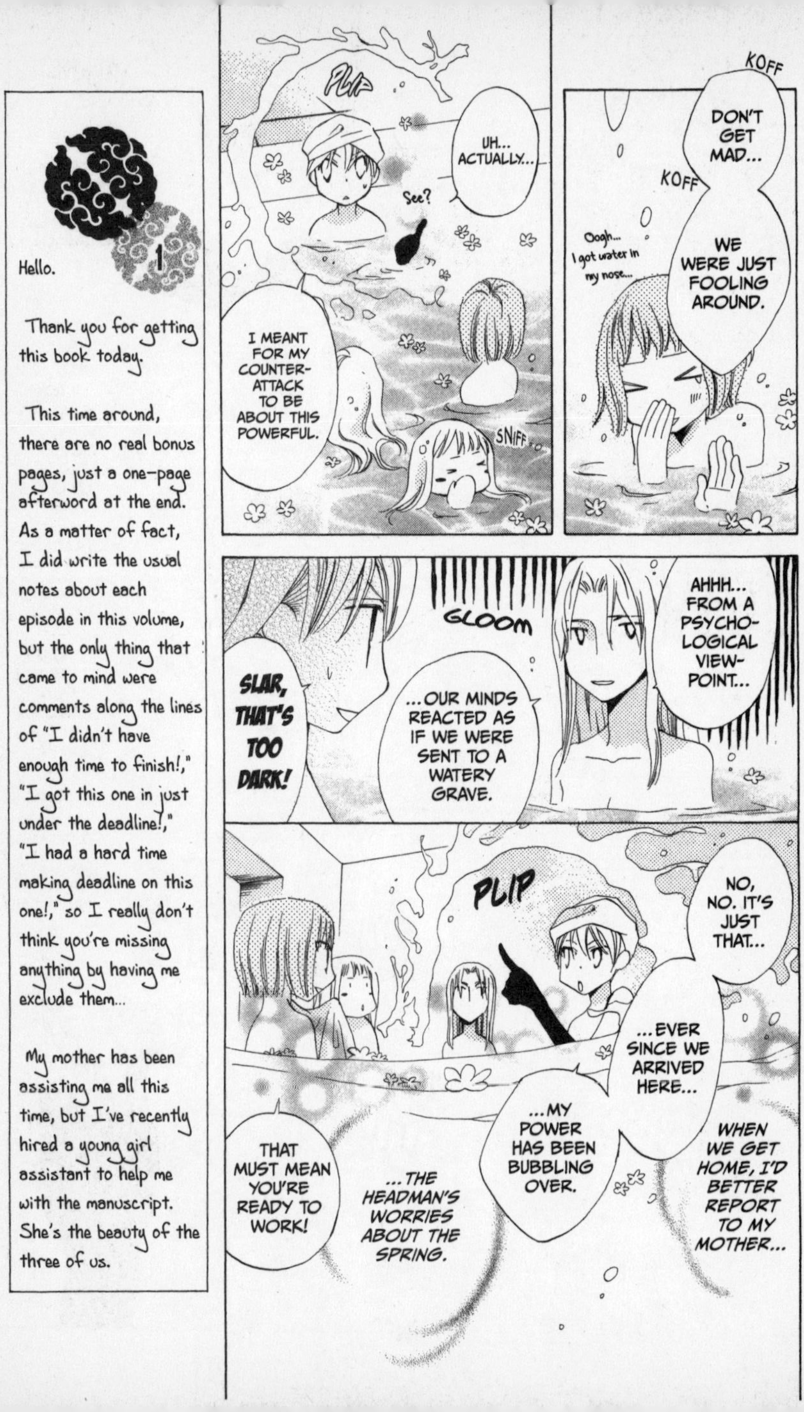
KOFF
DON'T GET MAD...
KOFF
WE WERE JUST FOOLING AROUND.
Oogh... I got water in my nose...
PLIP
UH... ACTUALLY...
See?
I MEANT FOR MY COUNTER-ATTACK TO BE ABOUT THIS POWERFUL.
SNIFF
AHHH... FROM A PSYCHO-LOGICAL VIEW-POINT...
GLOOM
...OUR MINDS REACTED AS IF WE WERE SENT TO A WATERY GRAVE.
SLAR, THAT'S TOO DARK!
NO, NO. IT'S JUST THAT...
PLIP
...EVER SINCE WE ARRIVED HERE...
WHEN WE GET HOME, I'D BETTER REPORT TO MY MOTHER...
...MY POWER HAS BEEN BUBBLING OVER.
...THE HEADMAN'S WORRIES ABOUT THE SPRING.
THAT MUST MEAN YOU'RE READY TO WORK!

1

Hello.

Thank you for getting this book today.

This time around, there are no real bonus pages, just a one-page afterword at the end. As a matter of fact, I did write the usual notes about each episode in this volume, but the only thing that came to mind were comments along the lines of "I didn't have enough time to finish!," "I got this one in just under the deadline!," "I had a hard time making deadline on this one!," so I really don't think you're missing anything by having me exclude them...

My mother has been assisting me all this time, but I've recently hired a young girl assistant to help me with the manuscript. She's the beauty of the three of us.

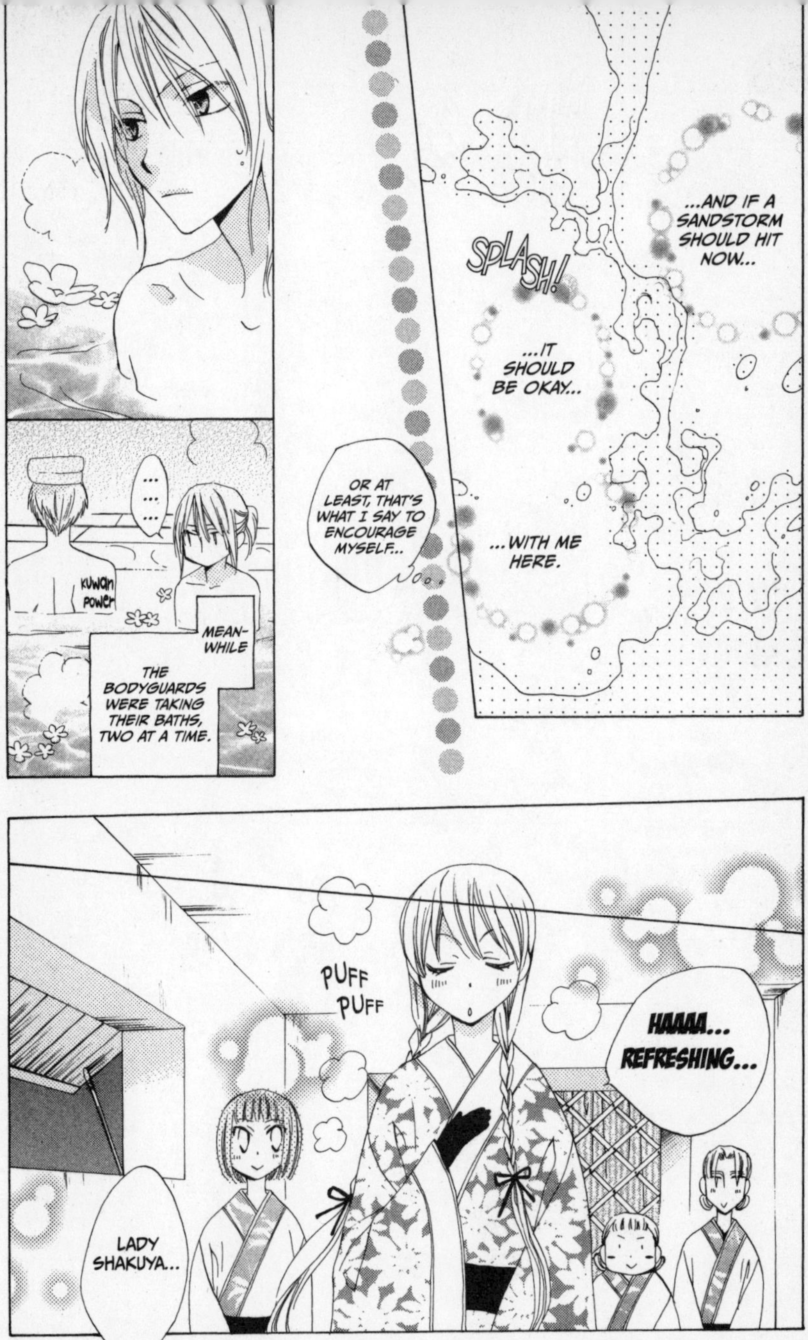
...AND IF A SANDSTORM SHOULD HIT NOW...
SPLASH!
...IT SHOULD BE OKAY...
...WITH ME HERE.
OR AT LEAST, THAT'S WHAT I SAY TO ENCOURAGE MYSELF...
MEAN-WHILE
THE BODYGUARDS WERE TAKING THEIR BATHS, TWO AT A TIME.
... ...
KUWAN POWER
HAAAA... REFRESHING...
PUFF PUFF
LADY SHAKUYA...

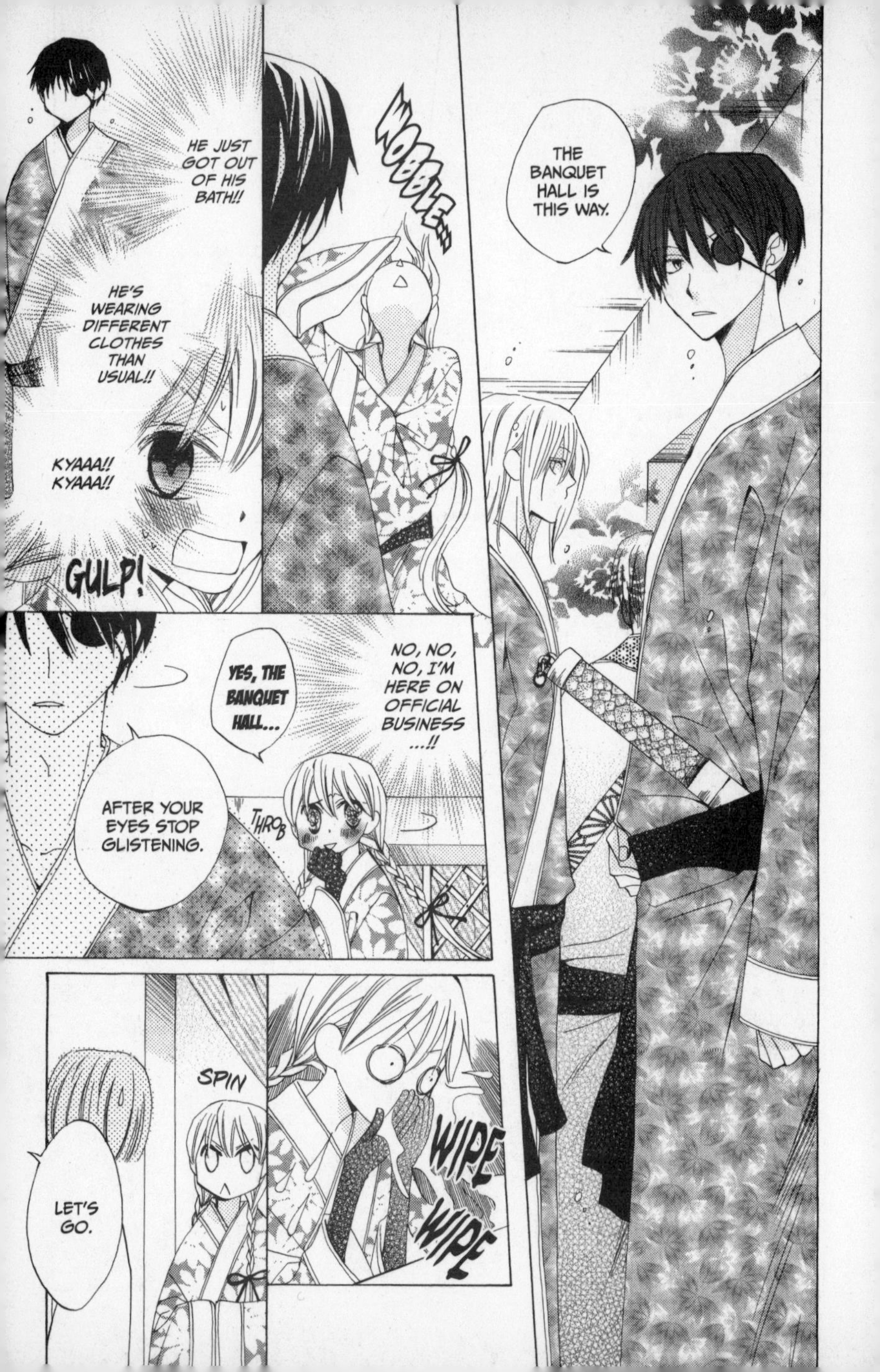
THE BANQUET HALL IS THIS WAY.
WOBBLE...!!
HE JUST GOT OUT OF HIS BATH!!
HE'S WEARING DIFFERENT CLOTHES THAN USUAL!!
KYAAA!! KYAAA!!
GULP!
NO, NO, NO, I'M HERE ON OFFICIAL BUSINESS...!!
YES, THE BANQUET HALL...
THROB
AFTER YOUR EYES STOP GLISTENING.
WIPE WIPE
SPIN
LET'S GO.

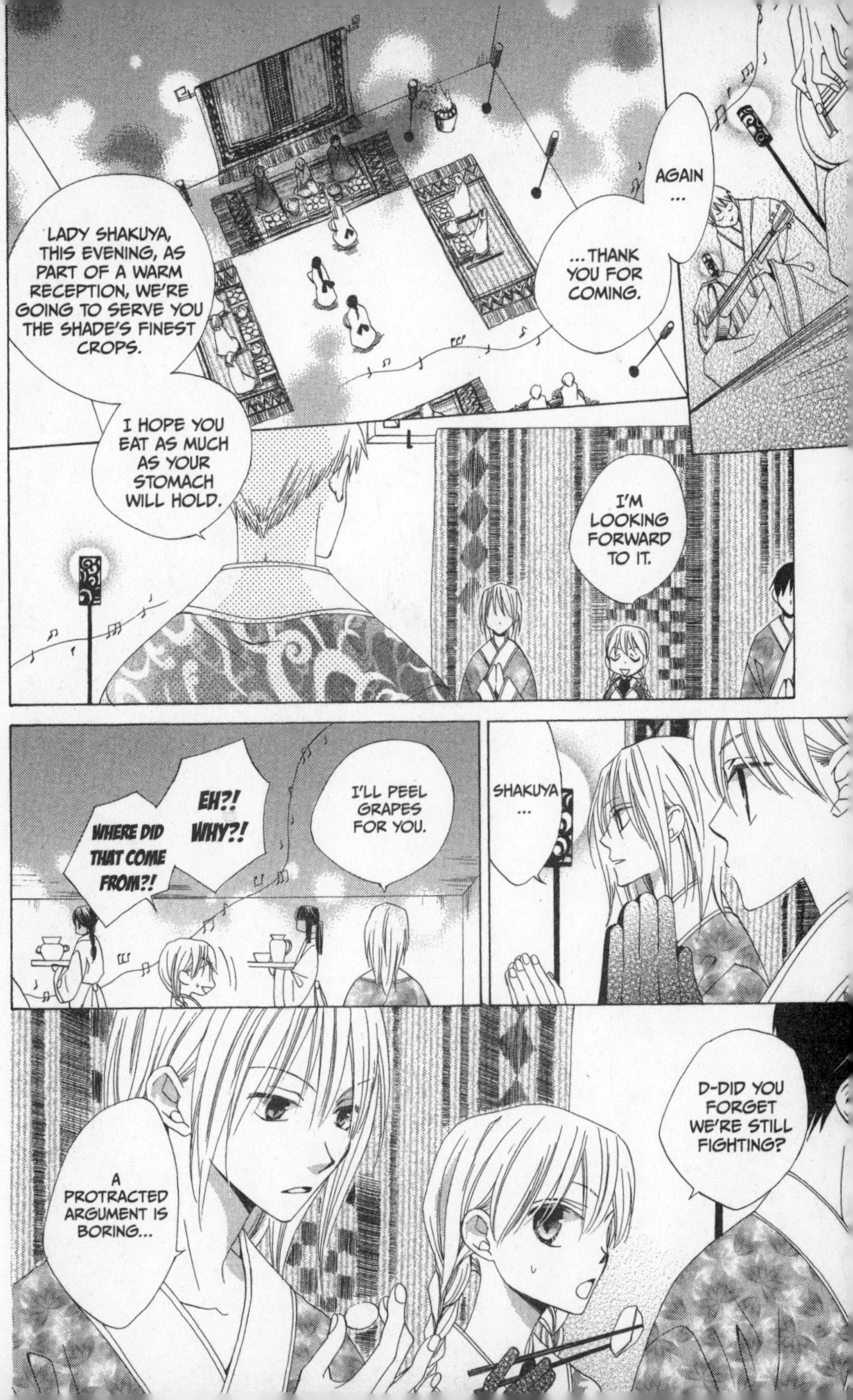
AGAIN ...
...THANK YOU FOR COMING.
LADY SHAKUYA, THIS EVENING, AS PART OF A WARM RECEPTION, WE'RE GOING TO SERVE YOU THE SHADE'S FINEST CROPS.
I HOPE YOU EAT AS MUCH AS YOUR STOMACH WILL HOLD.
I'M LOOKING FORWARD TO IT.
SHAKUYA ...
I'LL PEEL GRAPES FOR YOU.
EH?! WHY?!
WHERE DID THAT COME FROM?!
D-DID YOU FORGET WE'RE STILL FIGHTING?
A PROTRACTED ARGUMENT IS BORING...

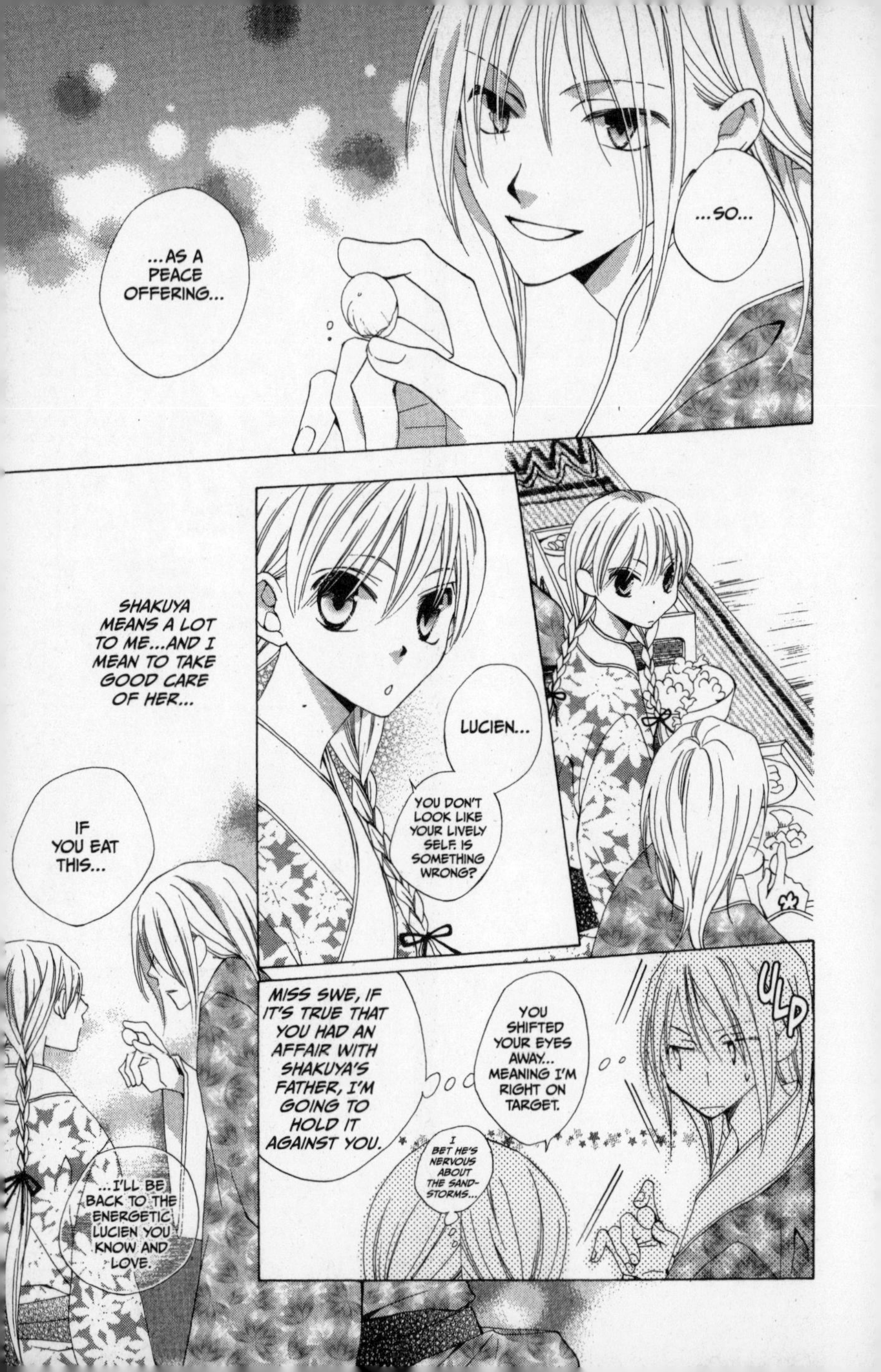
...SO...
...AS A PEACE OFFERING...
LUCIEN...
YOU DON'T LOOK LIKE YOUR LIVELY SELF. IS SOMETHING WRONG?
ULP
YOU SHIFTED YOUR EYES AWAY... MEANING I'M RIGHT ON TARGET.
MISS SWE, IF IT'S TRUE THAT YOU HAD AN AFFAIR WITH SHAKUYA'S FATHER, I'M GOING TO HOLD IT AGAINST YOU.
I BET HE'S NERVOUS ABOUT THE SAND-STORMS...
SHAKUYA MEANS A LOT TO ME...AND I MEAN TO TAKE GOOD CARE OF HER...
IF YOU EAT THIS...
...I'LL BE BACK TO THE ENERGETIC LUCIEN YOU KNOW AND LOVE.

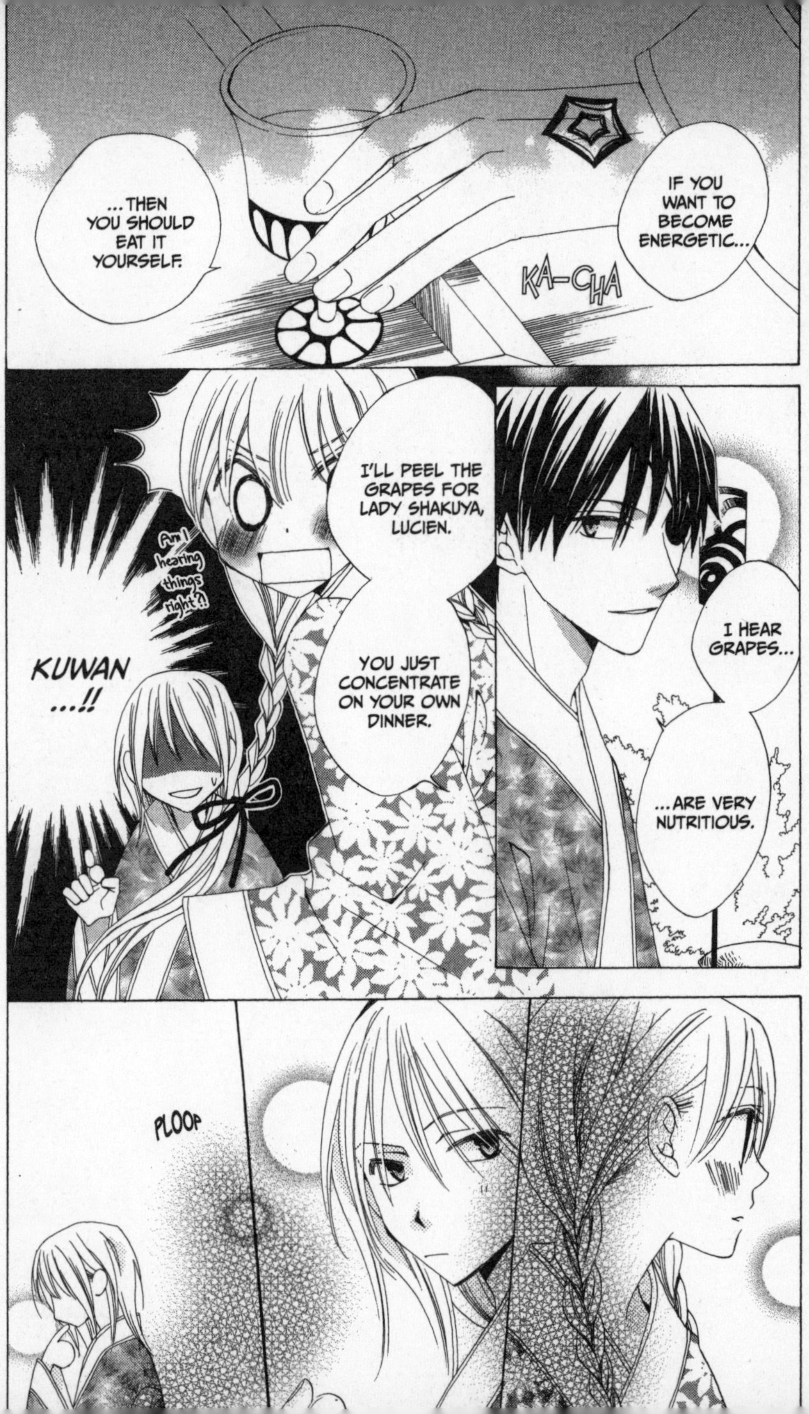
IF YOU WANT TO BECOME ENERGETIC...
KA-CHA
...THEN YOU SHOULD EAT IT YOURSELF.
I HEAR GRAPES...
...ARE VERY NUTRITIOUS.
I'LL PEEL THE GRAPES FOR LADY SHAKUYA, LUCIEN.
YOU JUST CONCENTRATE ON YOUR OWN DINNER.
Am I hearing things right?!
KUWAN ...!!
PLOOP

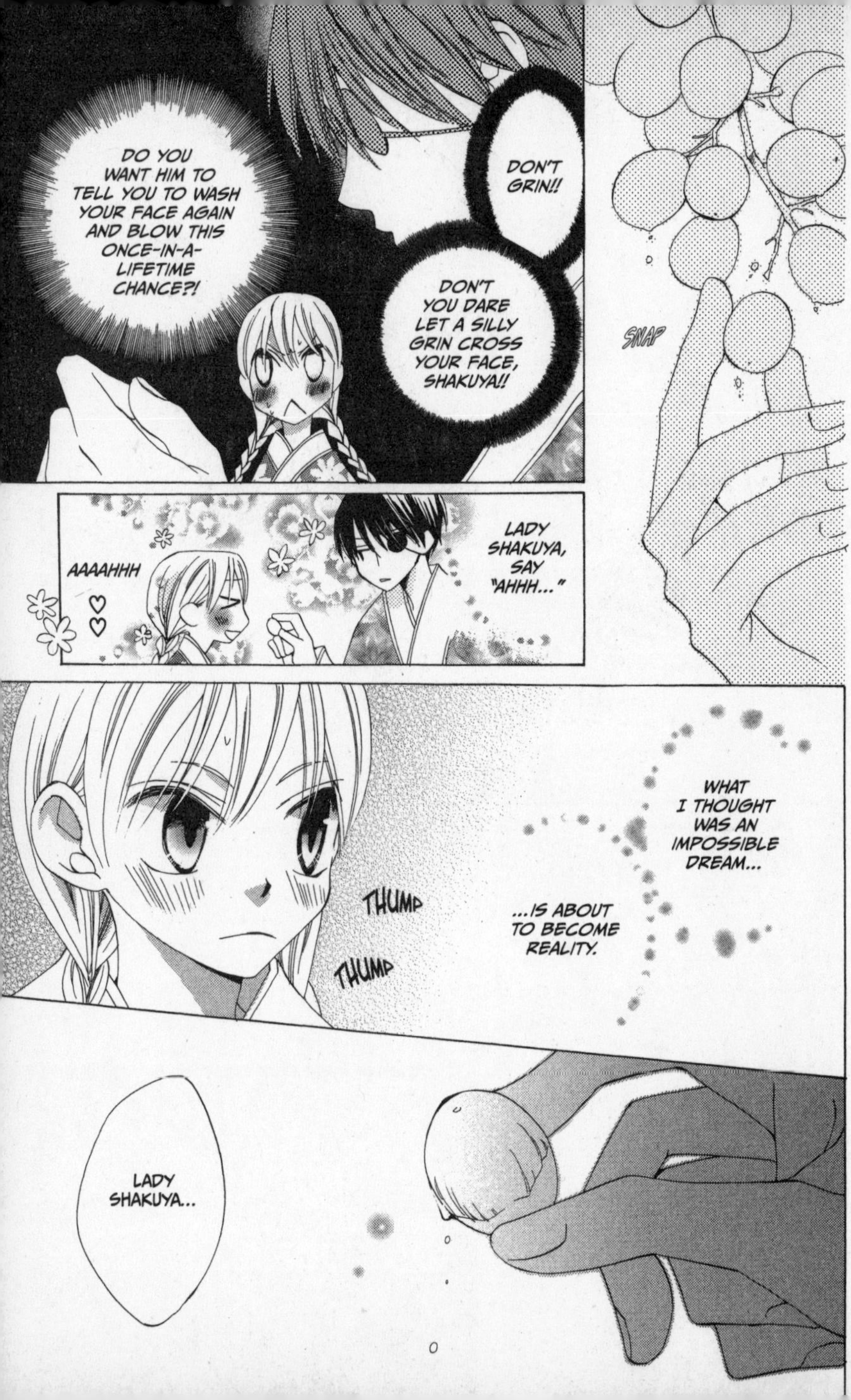
SNAP
DON'T GRIN!!
DON'T YOU DARE LET A SILLY GRIN CROSS YOUR FACE, SHAKUYA!!
DO YOU WANT HIM TO TELL YOU TO WASH YOUR FACE AGAIN AND BLOW THIS ONCE-IN-A-LIFETIME CHANCE?!
LADY SHAKUYA, SAY "AHHH..."
AAAAHHH ♡ ♡
WHAT I THOUGHT WAS AN IMPOSSIBLE DREAM...
...IS ABOUT TO BECOME REALITY.
THUMP
THUMP
LADY SHAKUYA...

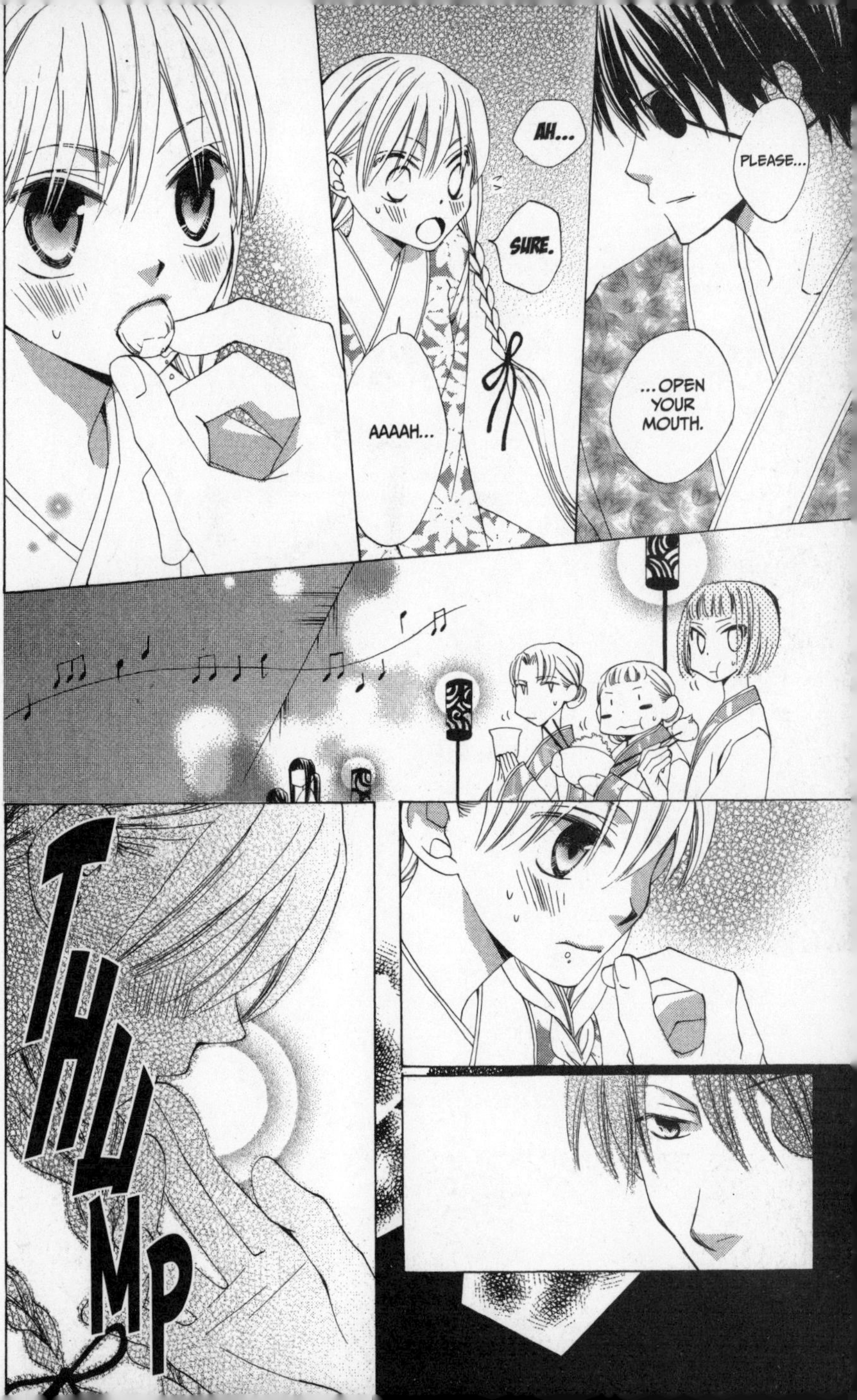
PLEASE...
...OPEN YOUR MOUTH.
AH...
SURE.
AAAAH...
THUMP

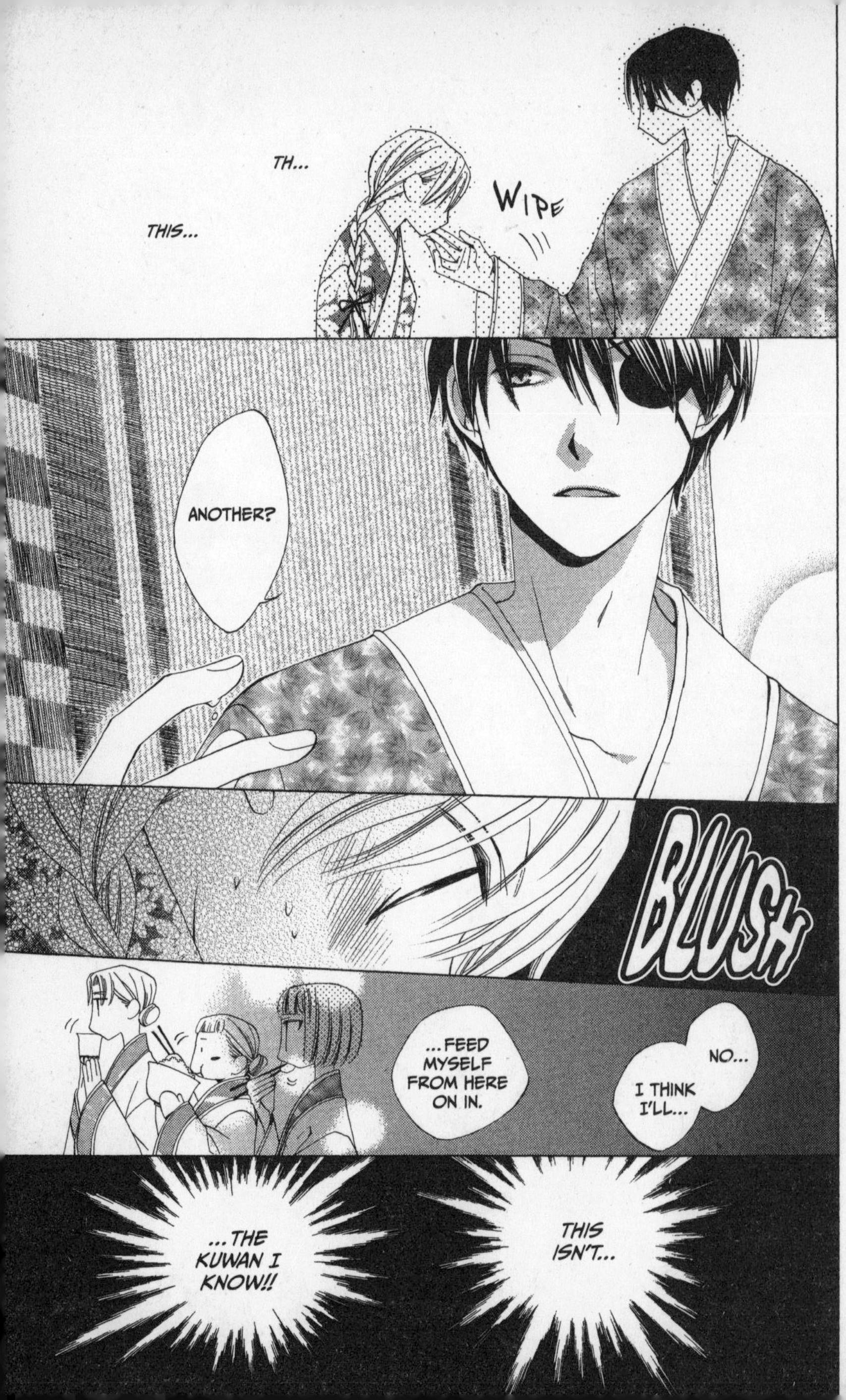
WIPE
TH...
THIS...
ANOTHER?
BLUSH
NO...
I THINK I'LL...
...FEED MYSELF FROM HERE ON IN.
THIS ISN'T...
...THE KUWAN I KNOW!!

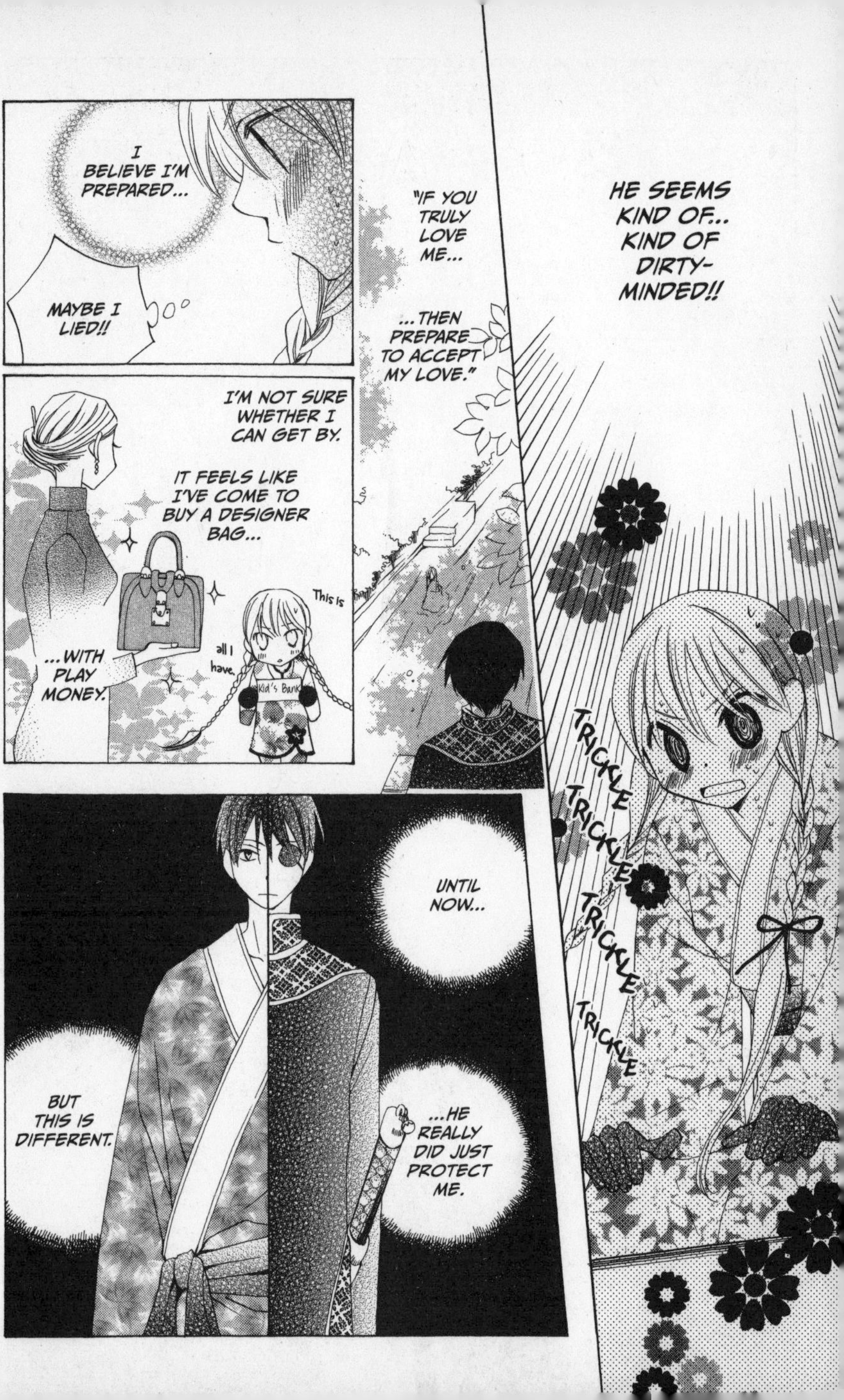
"IF YOU TRULY LOVE ME...
...THEN PREPARE TO ACCEPT MY LOVE."
I BELIEVE I'M PREPARED...
MAYBE I LIED!!
I'M NOT SURE WHETHER I CAN GET BY.
IT FEELS LIKE I'VE COME TO BUY A DESIGNER BAG...
...WITH PLAY MONEY.
This is all I have.
Kid's Bank
UNTIL NOW...
...HE REALLY DID JUST PROTECT ME.
BUT THIS IS DIFFERENT.
TRICKLE TRICKLE TRICKLE TRICKLE TRICKLE
HE SEEMS KIND OF... KIND OF DIRTY-MINDED!!

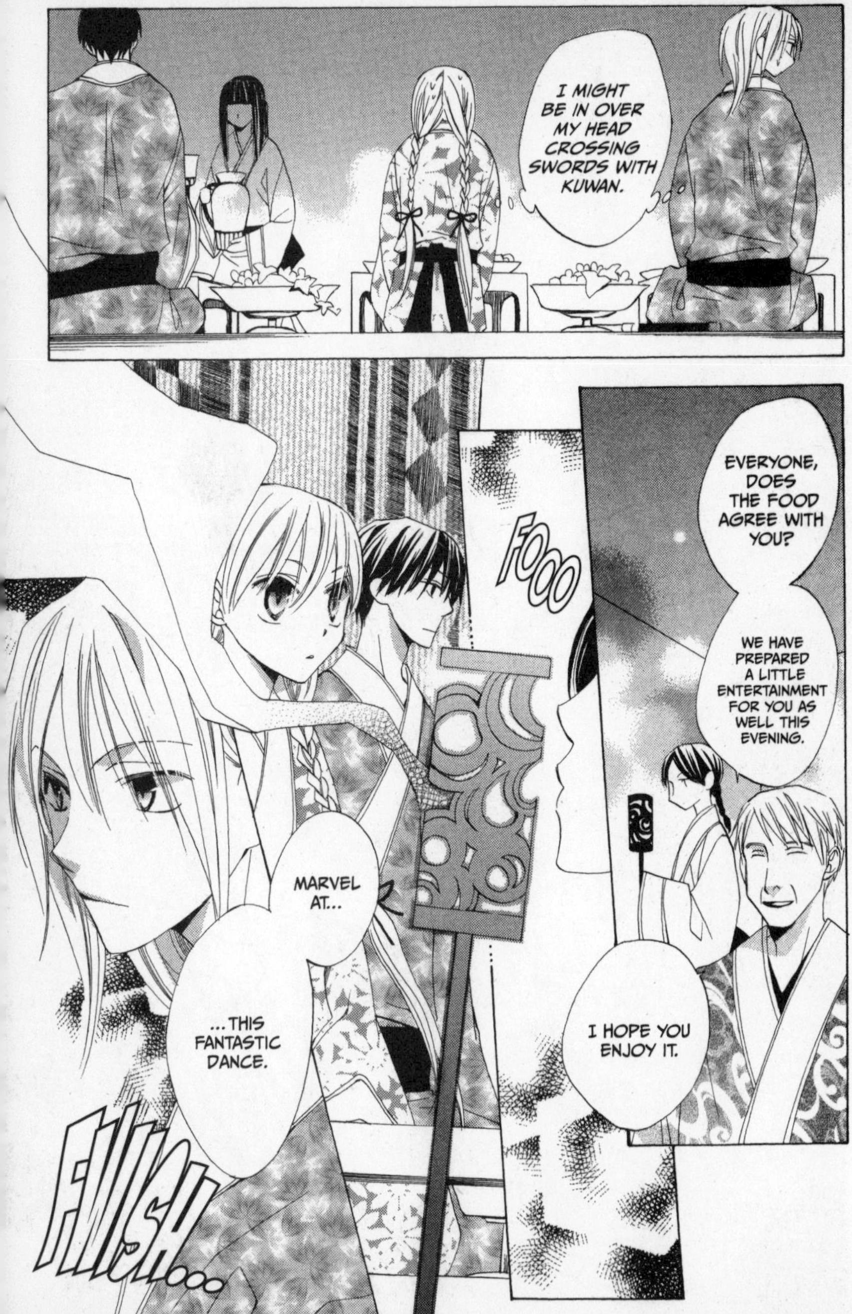
I MIGHT BE IN OVER MY HEAD CROSSING SWORDS WITH KUWAN.
EVERYONE, DOES THE FOOD AGREE WITH YOU?
WE HAVE PREPARED A LITTLE ENTERTAINMENT FOR YOU AS WELL THIS EVENING.
I HOPE YOU ENJOY IT.
FOOO
MARVEL AT...
...THIS FANTASTIC DANCE.
FWISH...

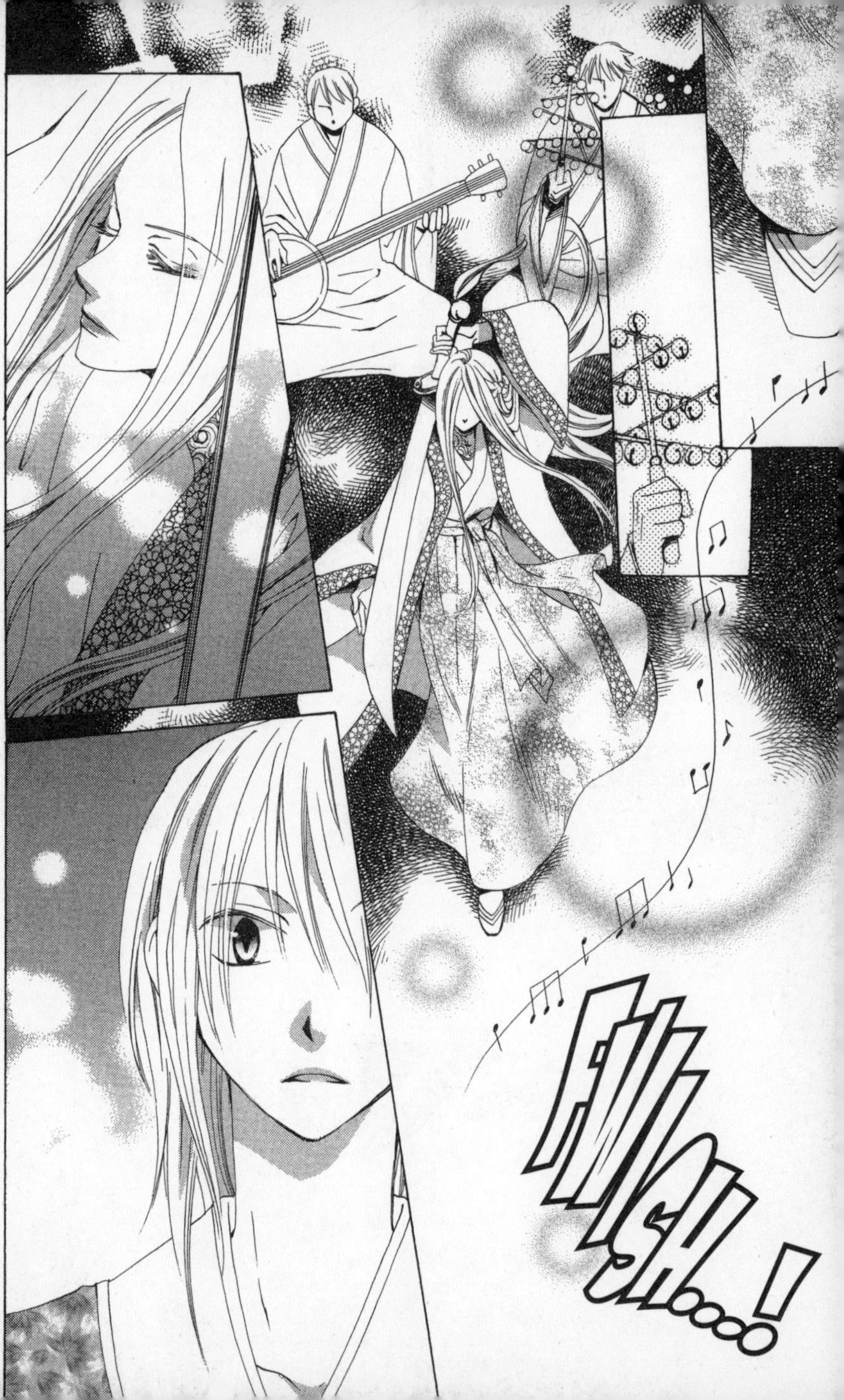
FWISHoooo!

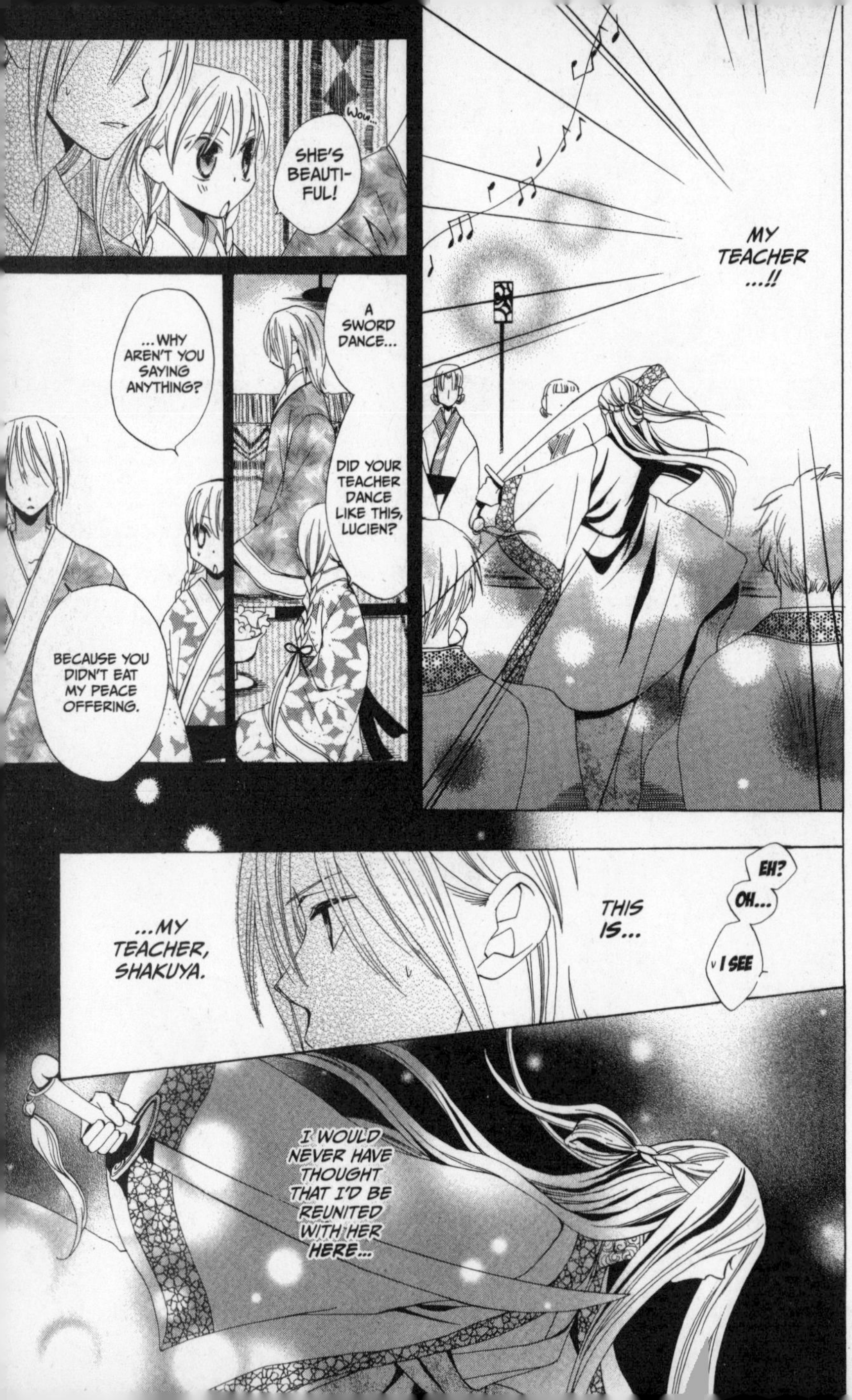
MY TEACHER ...!!
Wow...
SHE'S BEAUTI-FUL!
A SWORD DANCE...
DID YOUR TEACHER DANCE LIKE THIS, LUCIEN?
...WHY AREN'T YOU SAYING ANYTHING?
BECAUSE YOU DIDN'T EAT MY PEACE OFFERING.
EH?
OH...
I SEE
THIS IS...
...MY TEACHER, SHAKUYA.
I WOULD NEVER HAVE THOUGHT THAT I'D BE REUNITED WITH HER HERE...

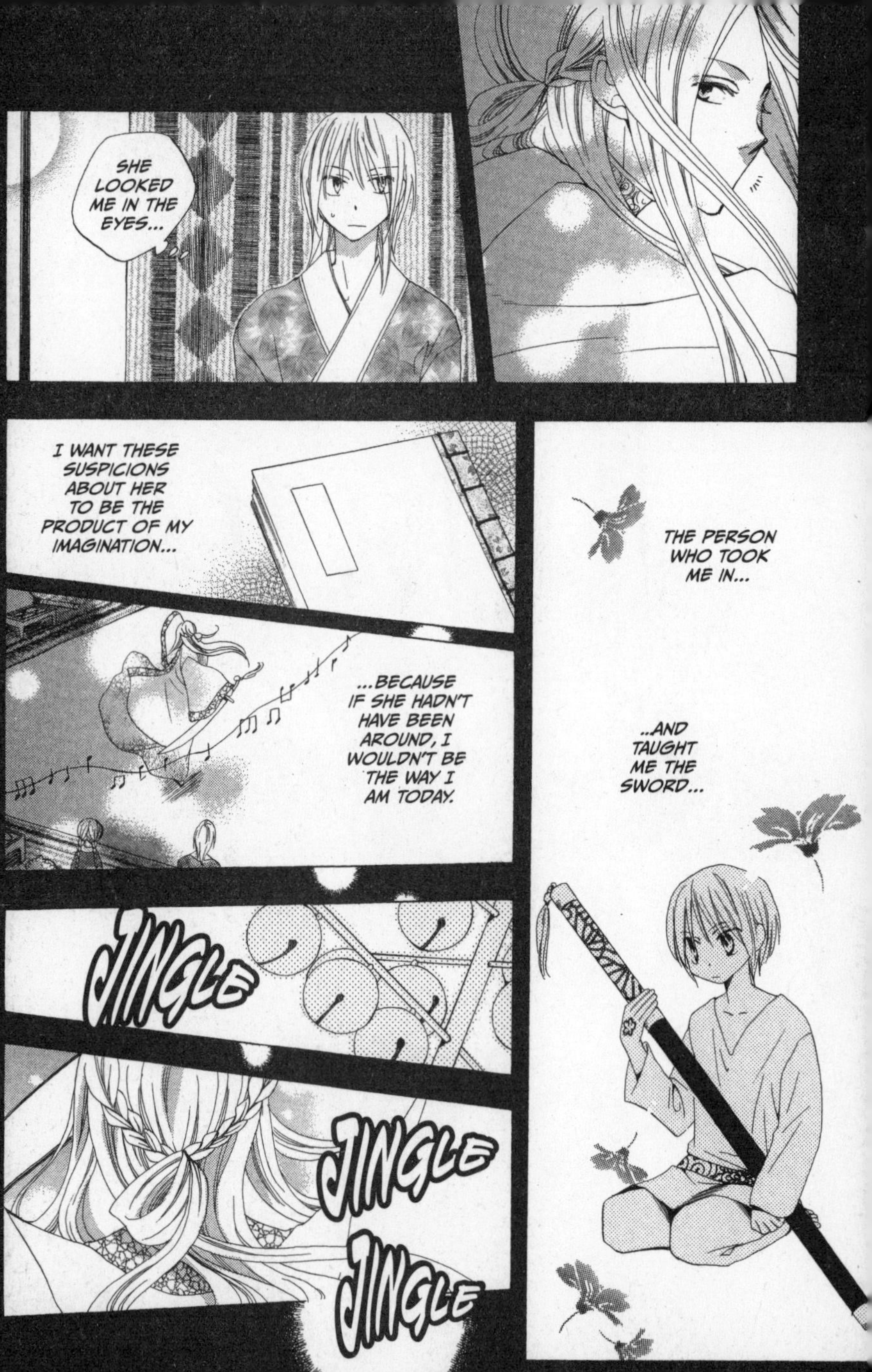
SHE LOOKED ME IN THE EYES...
THE PERSON WHO TOOK ME IN...
...AND TAUGHT ME THE SWORD...
I WANT THESE SUSPICIONS ABOUT HER TO BE THE PRODUCT OF MY IMAGINATION...
...BECAUSE IF SHE HADN'T HAVE BEEN AROUND, I WOULDN'T BE THE WAY I AM TODAY.
JINGLE
JINGLE
JINGLE

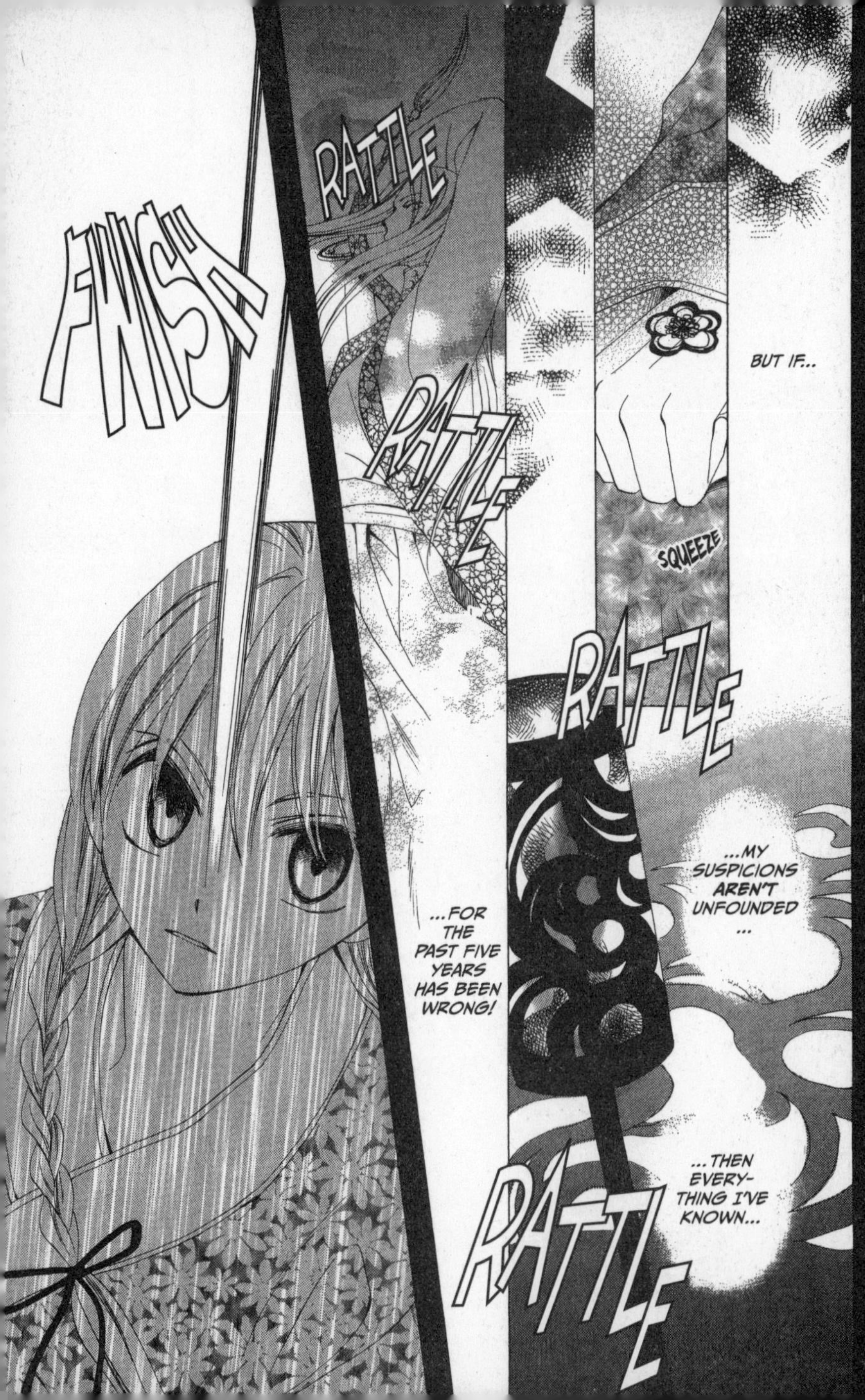
BUT IF...
SQUEEZE
RATTLE
...MY SUSPICIONS AREN'T UNFOUNDED ...
...THEN EVERY-THING I'VE KNOWN...
RATTLE
RATTLE
RATTLE
...FOR THE PAST FIVE YEARS HAS BEEN WRONG!
FWISH

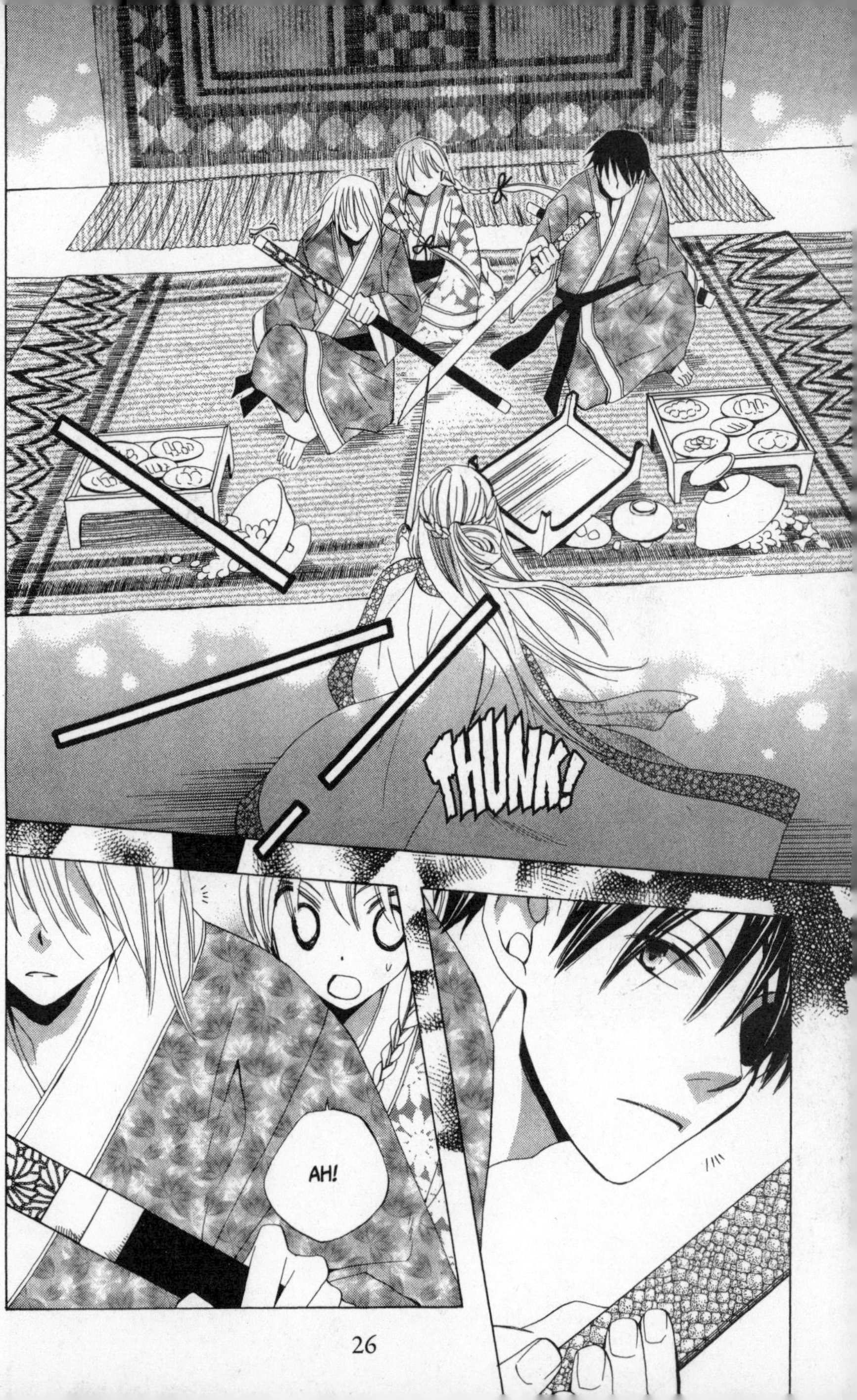
THUNK!
AH!

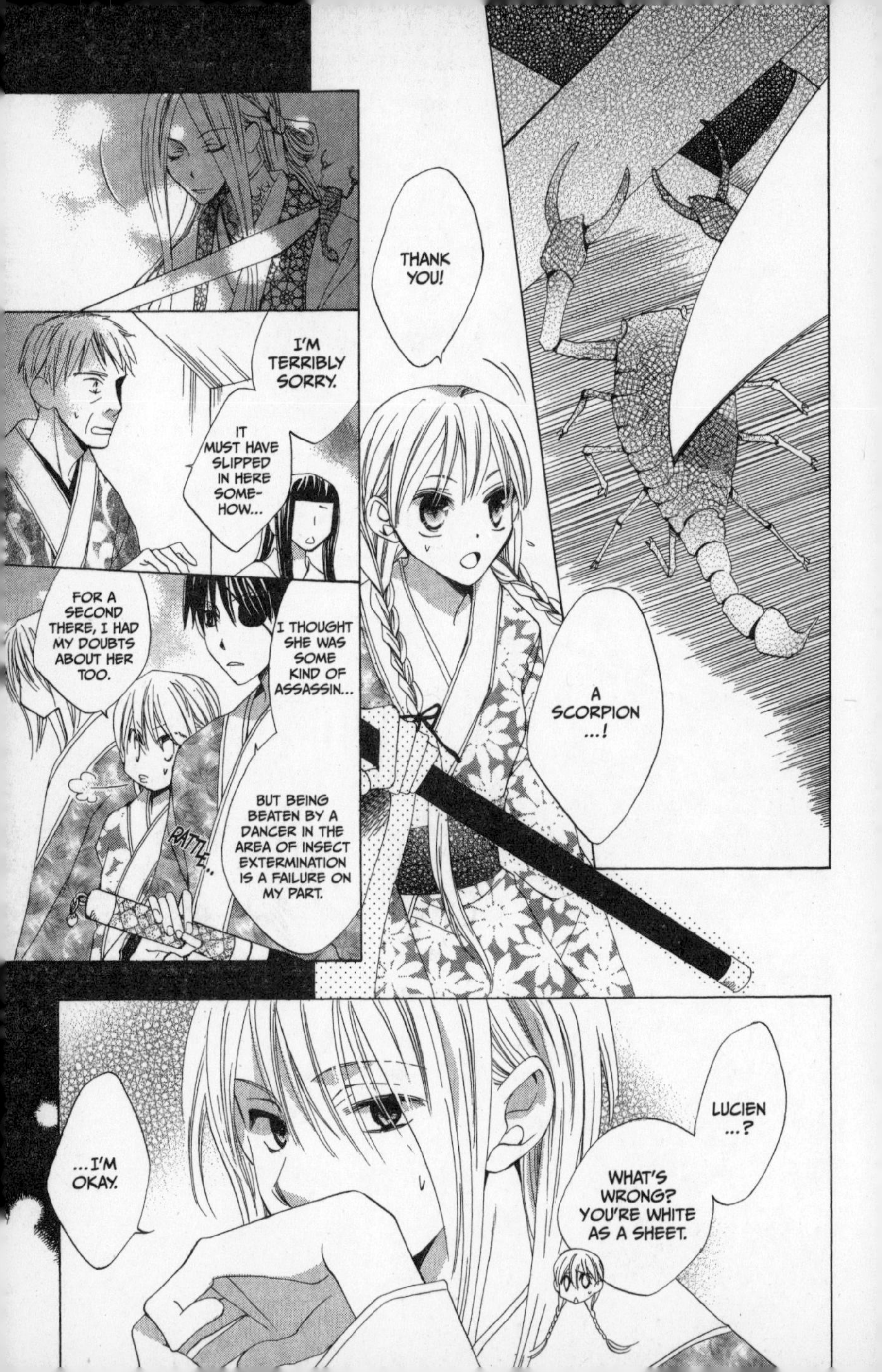
A SCORPION ...!
THANK YOU!
I'M TERRIBLY SORRY.
IT MUST HAVE SLIPPED IN HERE SOME-HOW...
I THOUGHT SHE WAS SOME KIND OF ASSASSIN...
FOR A SECOND THERE, I HAD MY DOUBTS ABOUT HER TOO.
BUT BEING BEATEN BY A DANCER IN THE AREA OF INSECT EXTERMINATION IS A FAILURE ON MY PART.
RATTLE...
LUCIEN ...?
WHAT'S WRONG? YOU'RE WHITE AS A SHEET.
...I'M OKAY.

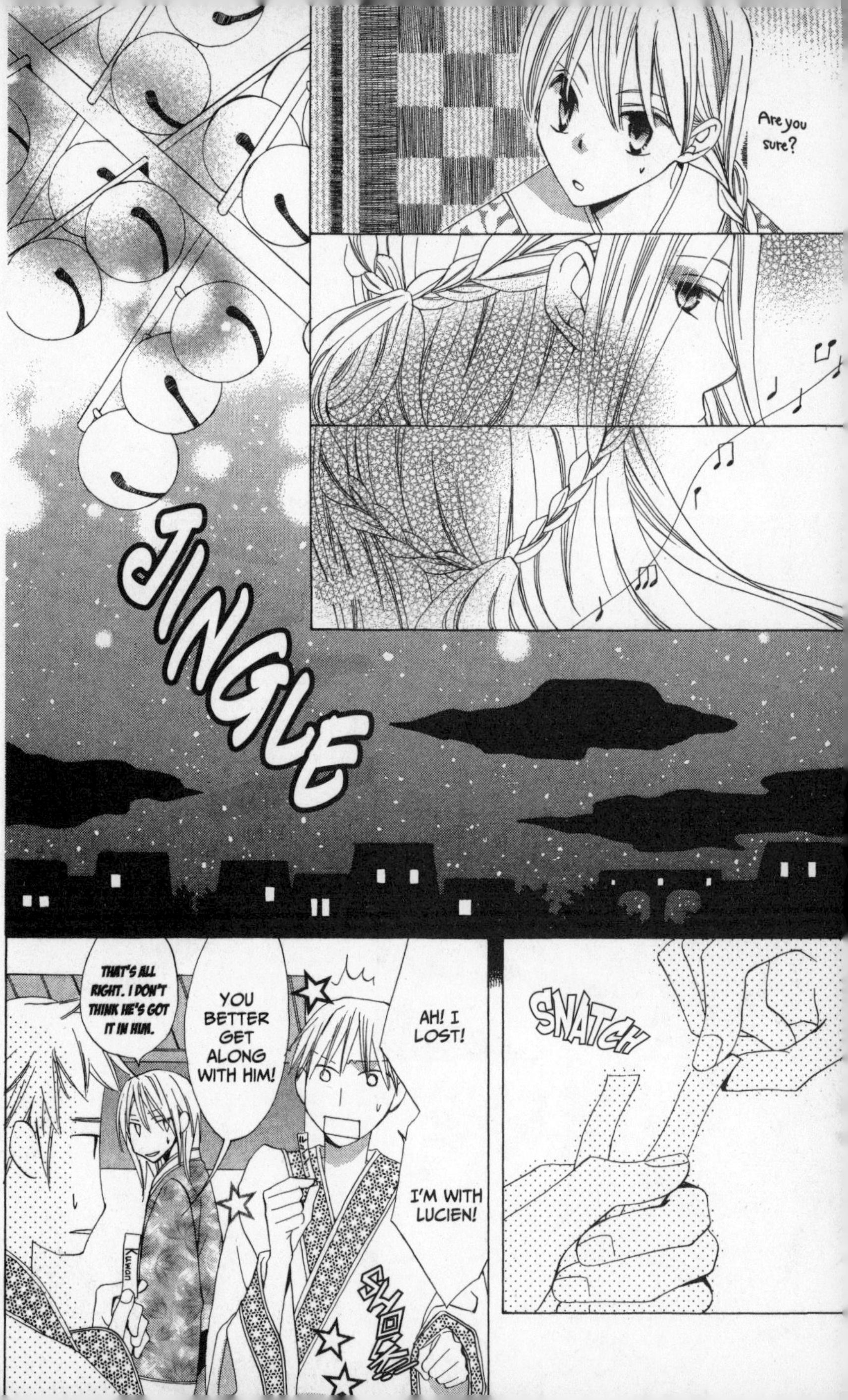
Are you sure?
JINGLE
SNATCH
AH! I LOST!
I'M WITH LUCIEN!
SHOCK!!
YOU BETTER GET ALONG WITH HIM!
THAT'S ALL RIGHT. I DON'T THINK HE'S GOT IT IN HIM.

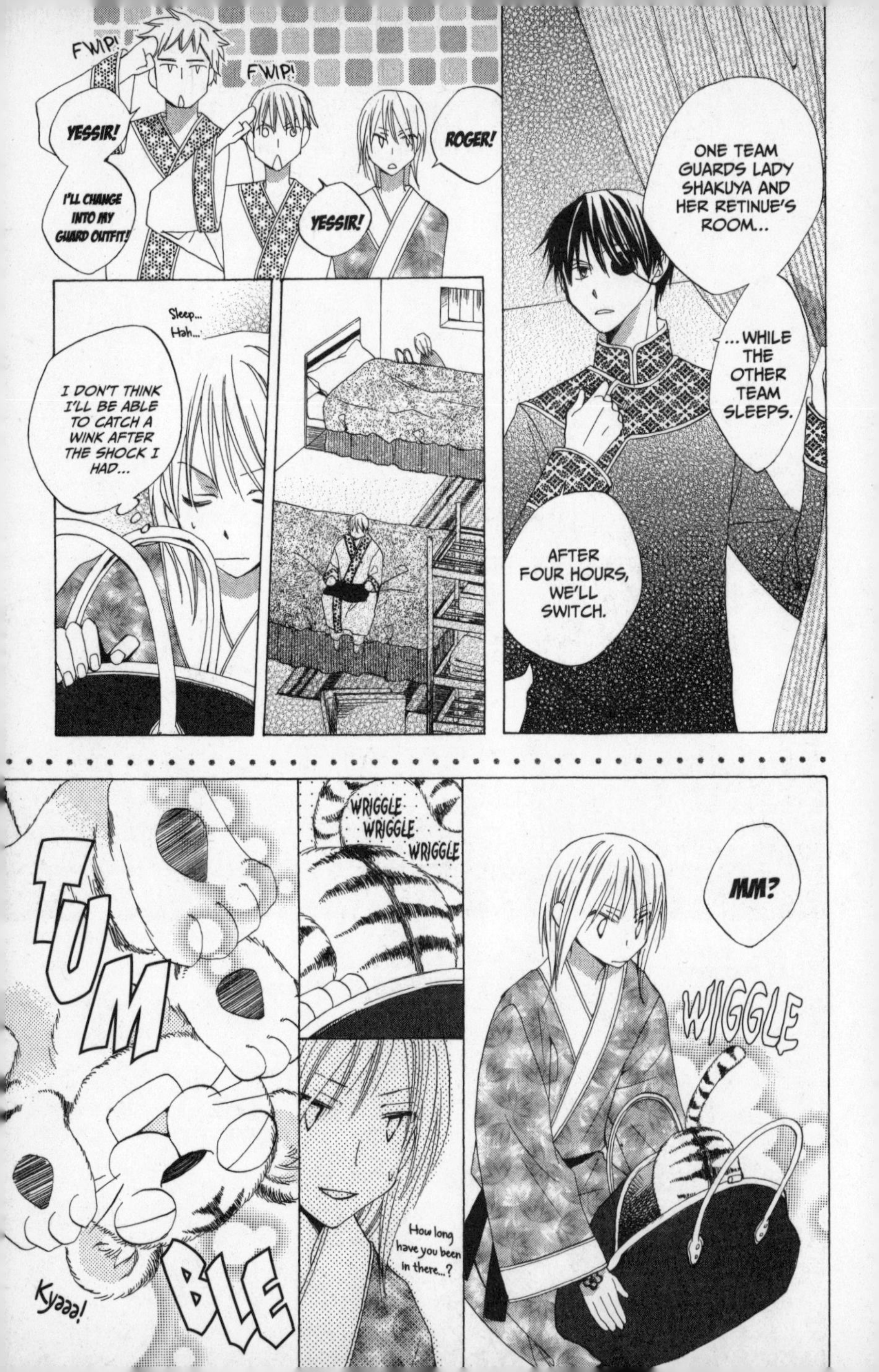
ONE TEAM GUARDS LADY SHAKUYA AND HER RETINUE'S ROOM...
...WHILE THE OTHER TEAM SLEEPS.
AFTER FOUR HOURS, WE'LL SWITCH.
ROGER!
FWIP!
YESSIR!
FWIP!
YESSIR!
I'LL CHANGE INTO MY GUARD OUTFIT!
Sleep... Hah...
I DON'T THINK I'LL BE ABLE TO CATCH A WINK AFTER THE SHOCK I HAD...
MM?
WIGGLE
WRIGGLE WRIGGLE WRIGGLE
How long have you been in there...?
TUMBLE
Kyaaa!

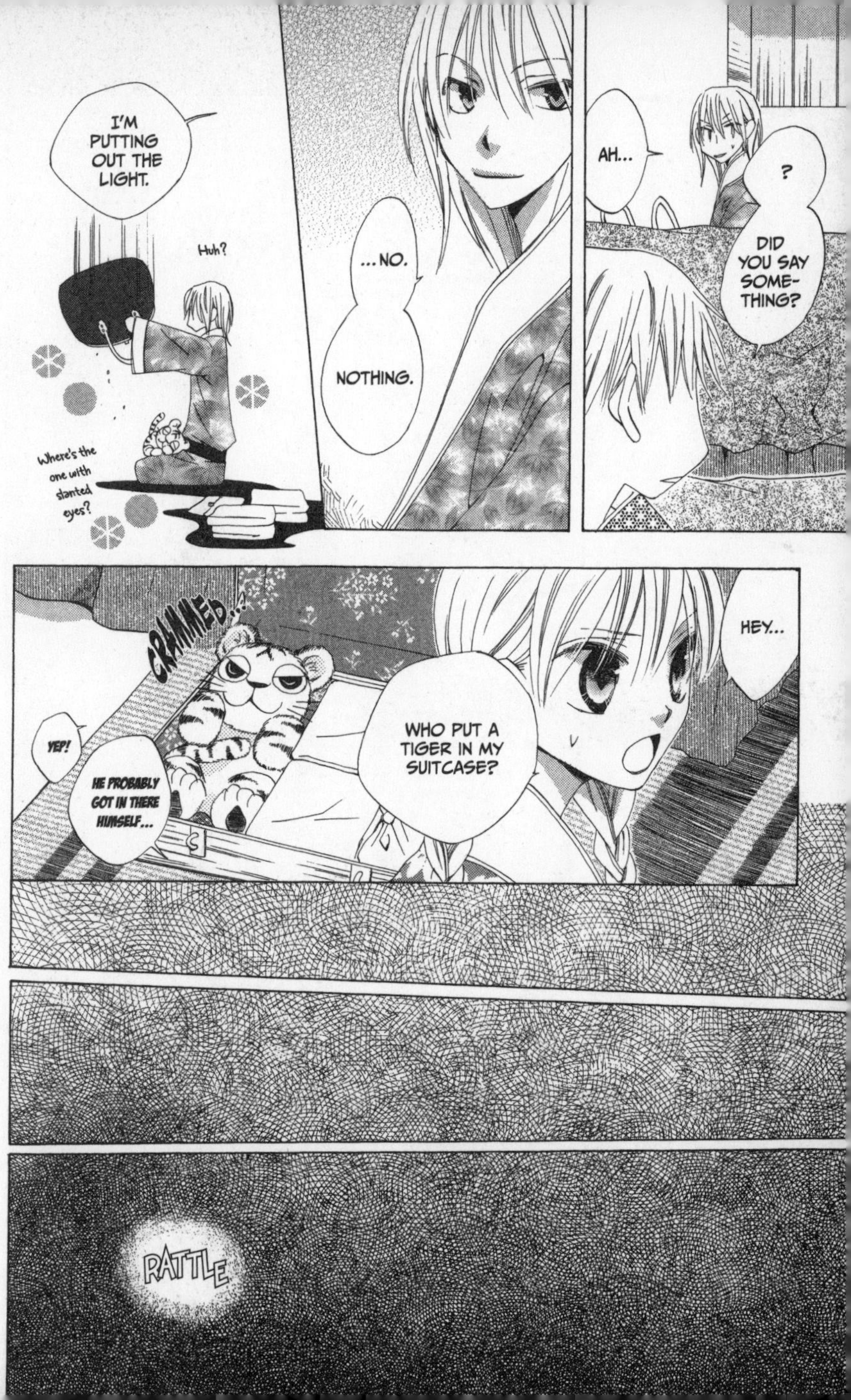
HEY...
WHO PUT A TIGER IN MY SUITCASE?
CRAMMED...
YEP!
HE PROBABLY GOT IN THERE HIMSELF...
RATTLE
DID YOU SAY SOME-THING?
?
AH...
...NO.
NOTHING.
I'M PUTTING OUT THE LIGHT.
Huh?
Where's the one with slanted eyes?

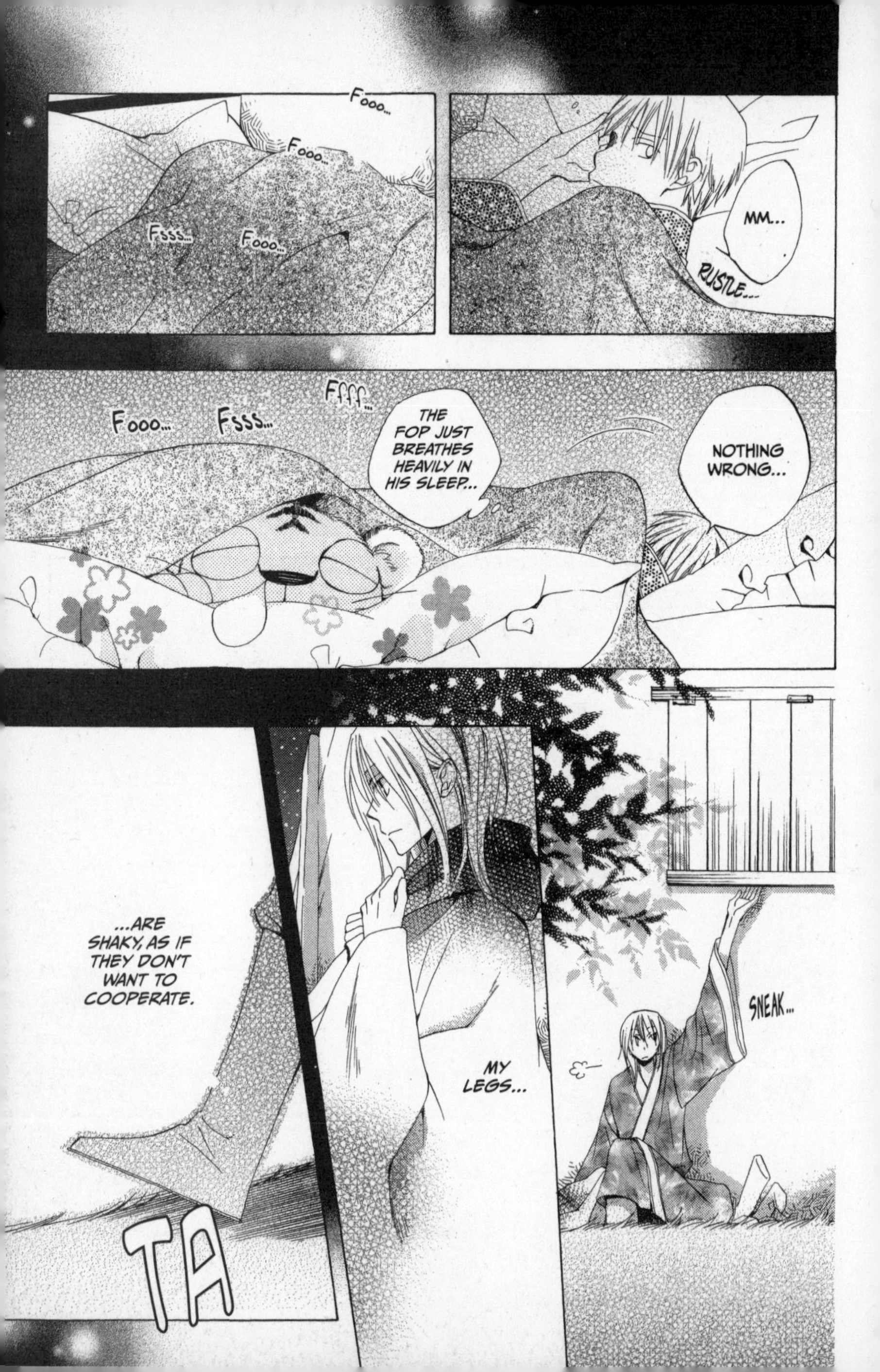
MM...
RUSTLE...
Fooo...
Fooo...
Fssss...
Fooo...
NOTHING WRONG...
THE FOP JUST BREATHES HEAVILY IN HIS SLEEP...
Ffff...
Fsss...
Fooo...
SNEAK...
MY LEGS...
...ARE SHAKY, AS IF THEY DON'T WANT TO COOPERATE.
TA

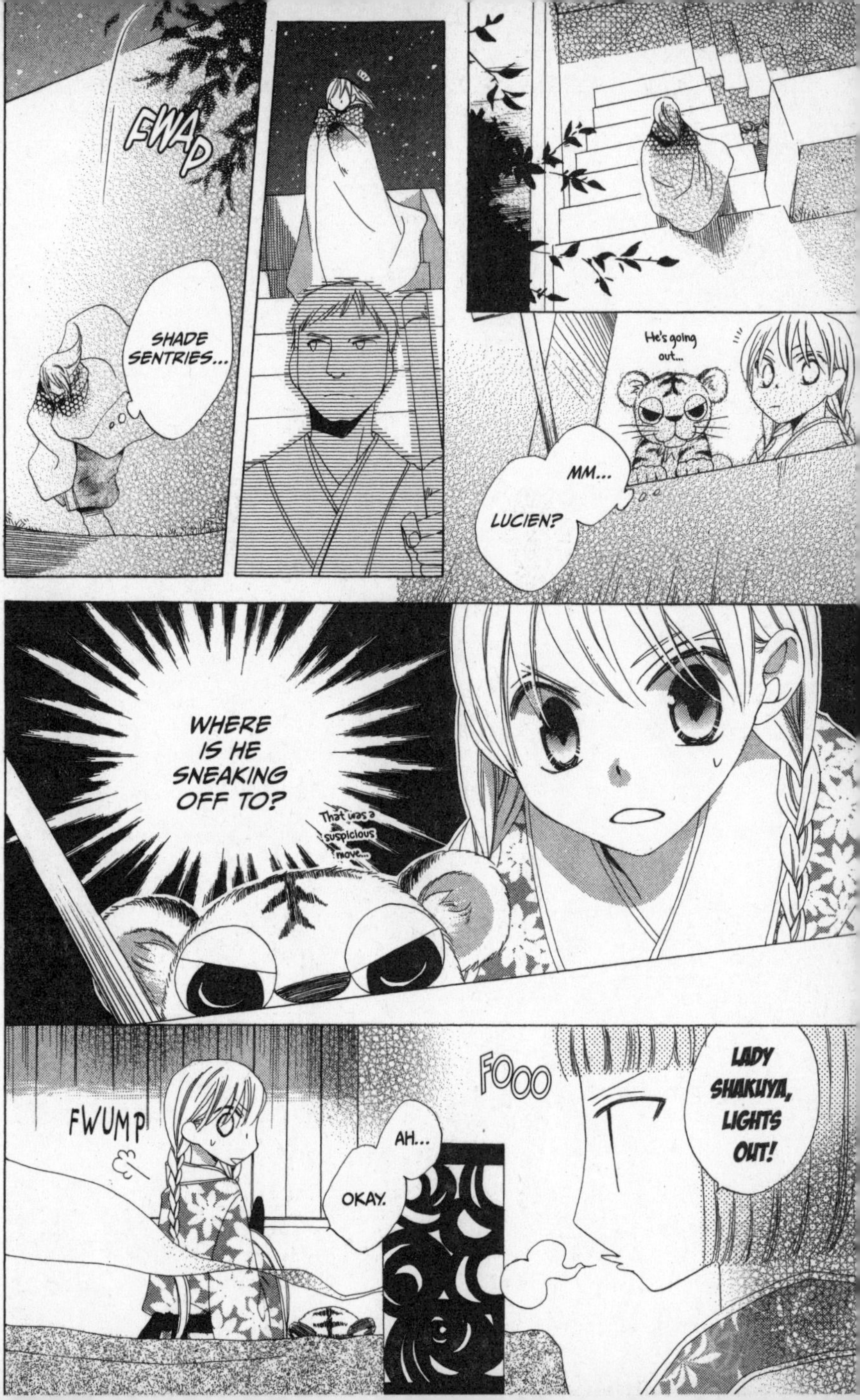
He's going out...
MM...
LUCIEN?
FWAP
SHADE SENTRIES...
WHERE IS HE SNEAKING OFF TO?
That was a suspicious move...
LADY SHAKUYA, LIGHTS OUT!
FOOO
AH...
OKAY.
FWUMP

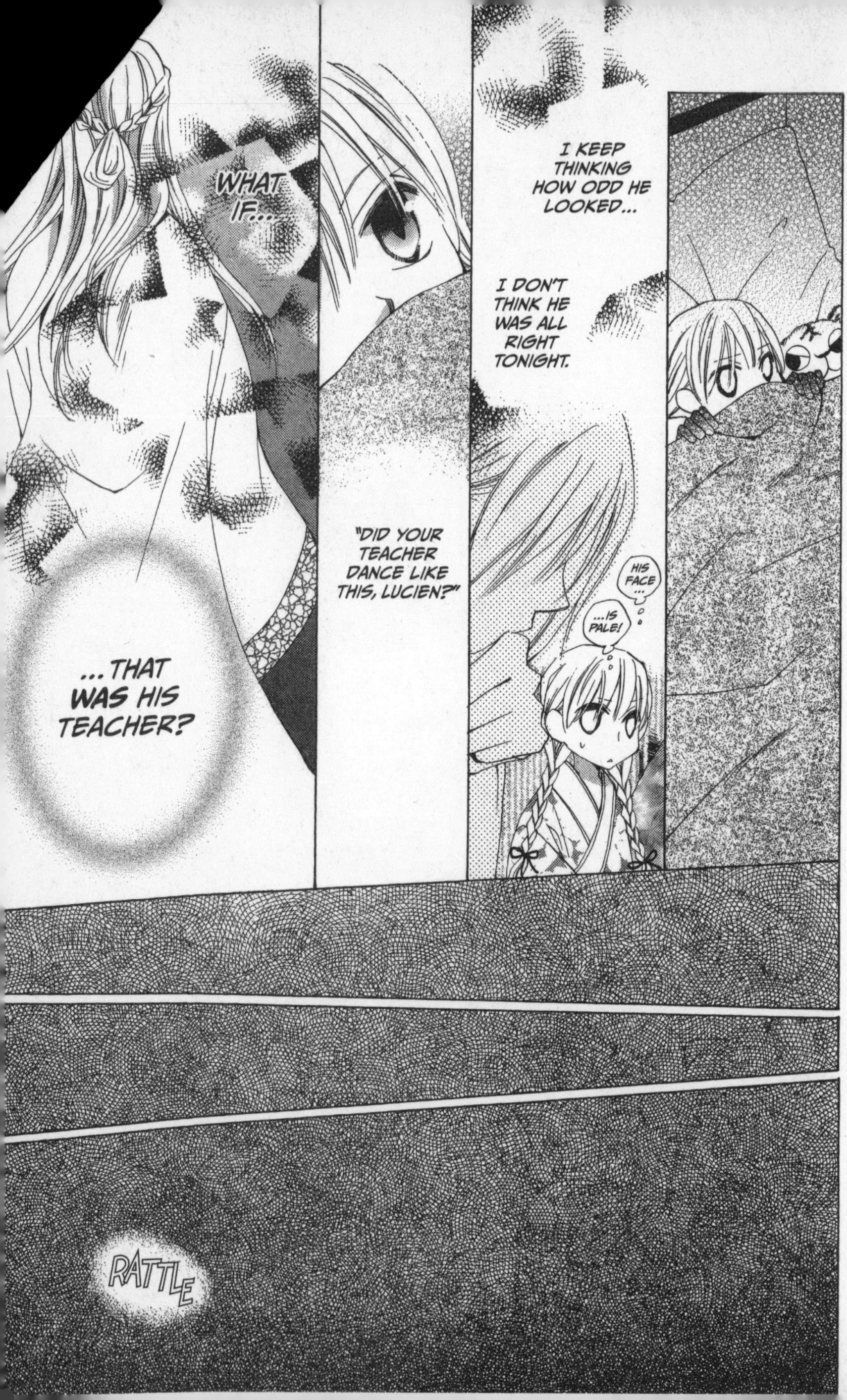
I KEEP THINKING HOW ODD HE LOOKED...
I DON'T THINK HE WAS ALL RIGHT TONIGHT.
HIS FACE...
...IS PALE!
"DID YOUR TEACHER DANCE LIKE THIS, LUCIEN?"
WHAT IF...
...THAT WAS HIS TEACHER?
RATTLE

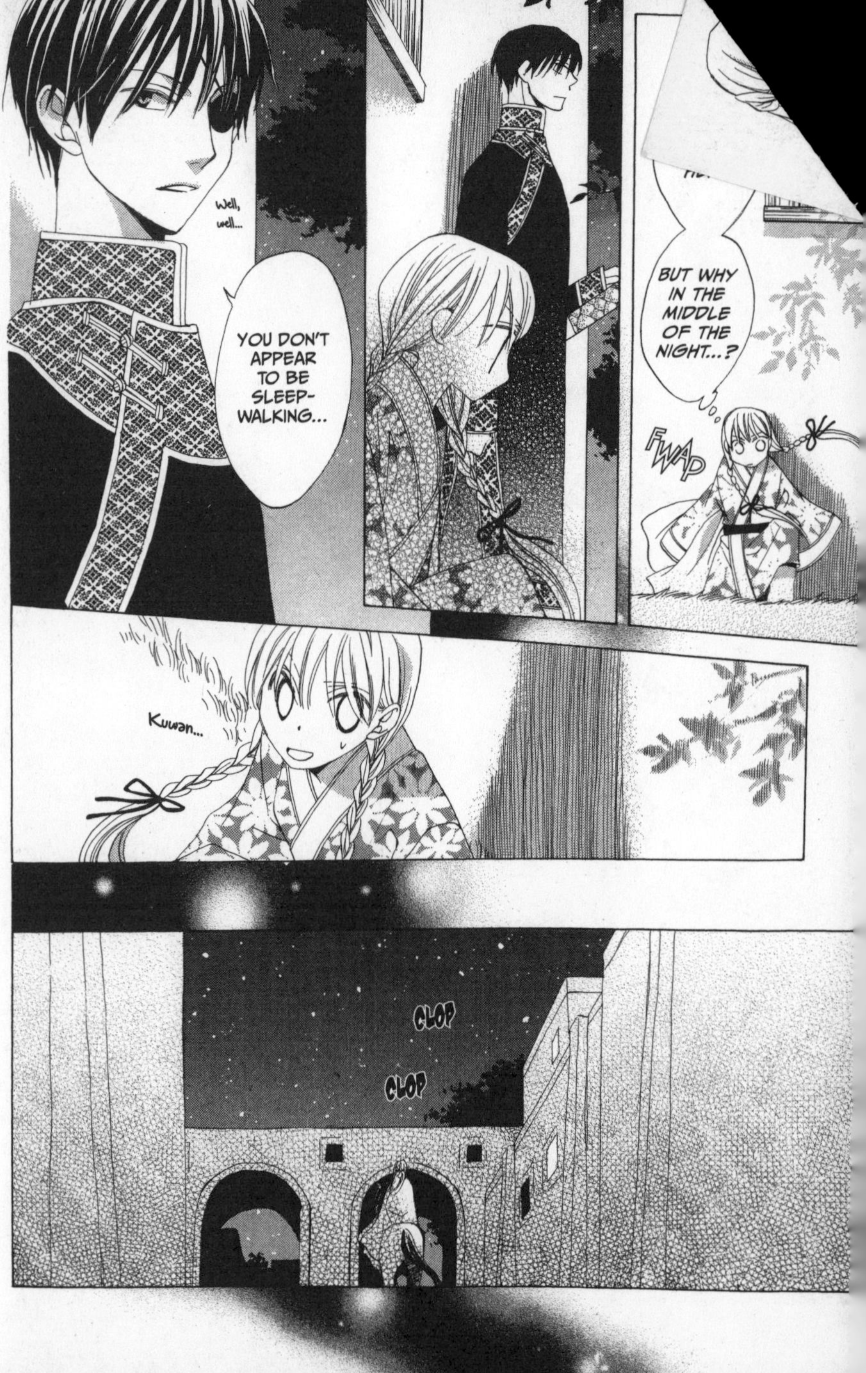
BUT WHY IN THE MIDDLE OF THE NIGHT...?
FWAP
Well, well...
YOU DON'T APPEAR TO BE SLEEP-WALKING...
Kuwan...
CLOP
CLOP

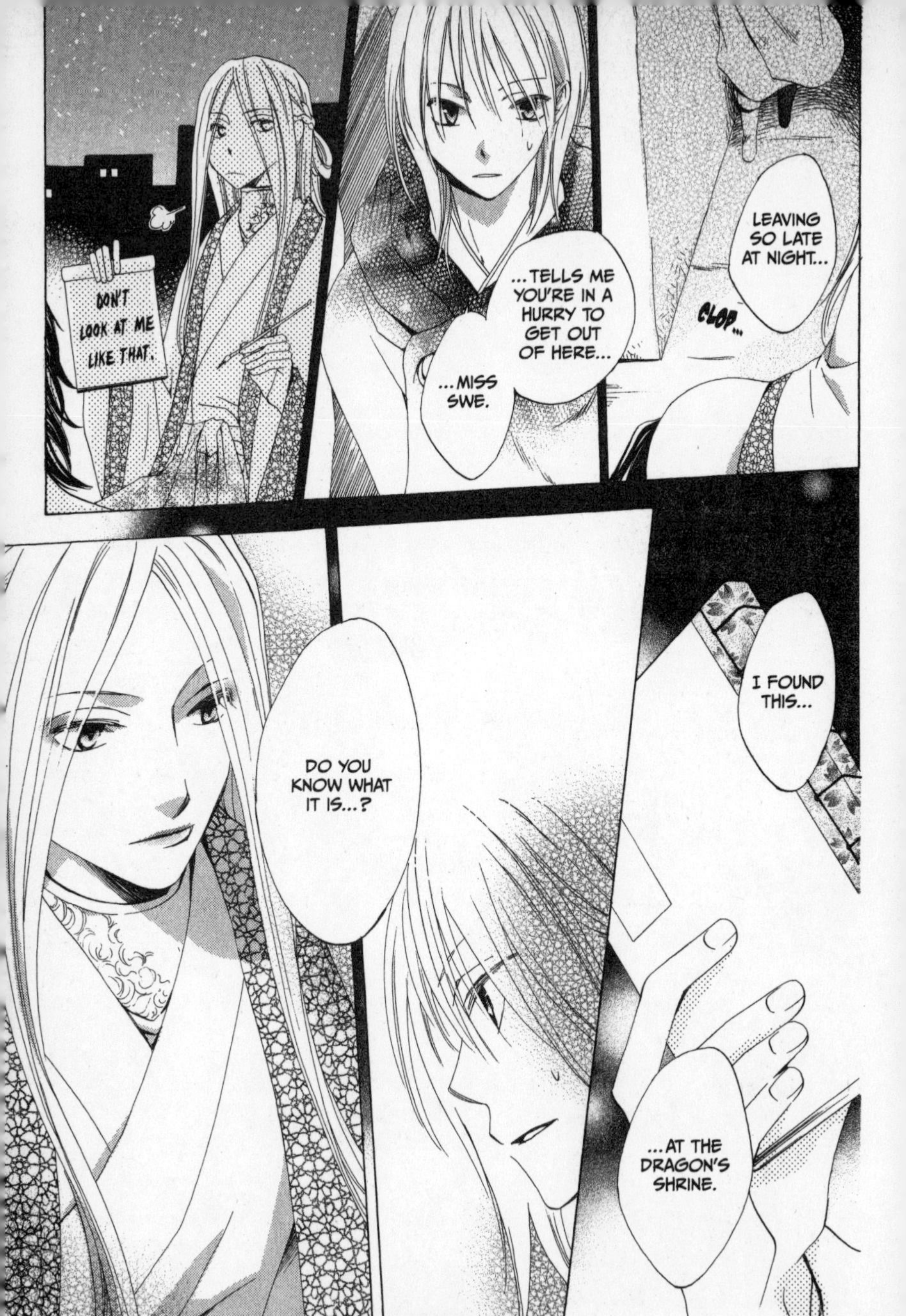
LEAVING SO LATE AT NIGHT...
CLOP...
...TELLS ME YOU'RE IN A HURRY TO GET OUT OF HERE...
...MISS SWE.
DON'T LOOK AT ME LIKE THAT.
I FOUND THIS...
...AT THE DRAGON'S SHRINE.
DO YOU KNOW WHAT IT IS...?

Episode 10: The End

Episode 11 Preview Cut

I drew Lucien, Shakuya and Kuwan alone for the preview cuts of episodes 11 to 13, but Shakuya and Kuwan share the next preview cut page. Sorry for leaving you odd man out, Lucien. When dealing with a love triangle, even little things like this have relevance.

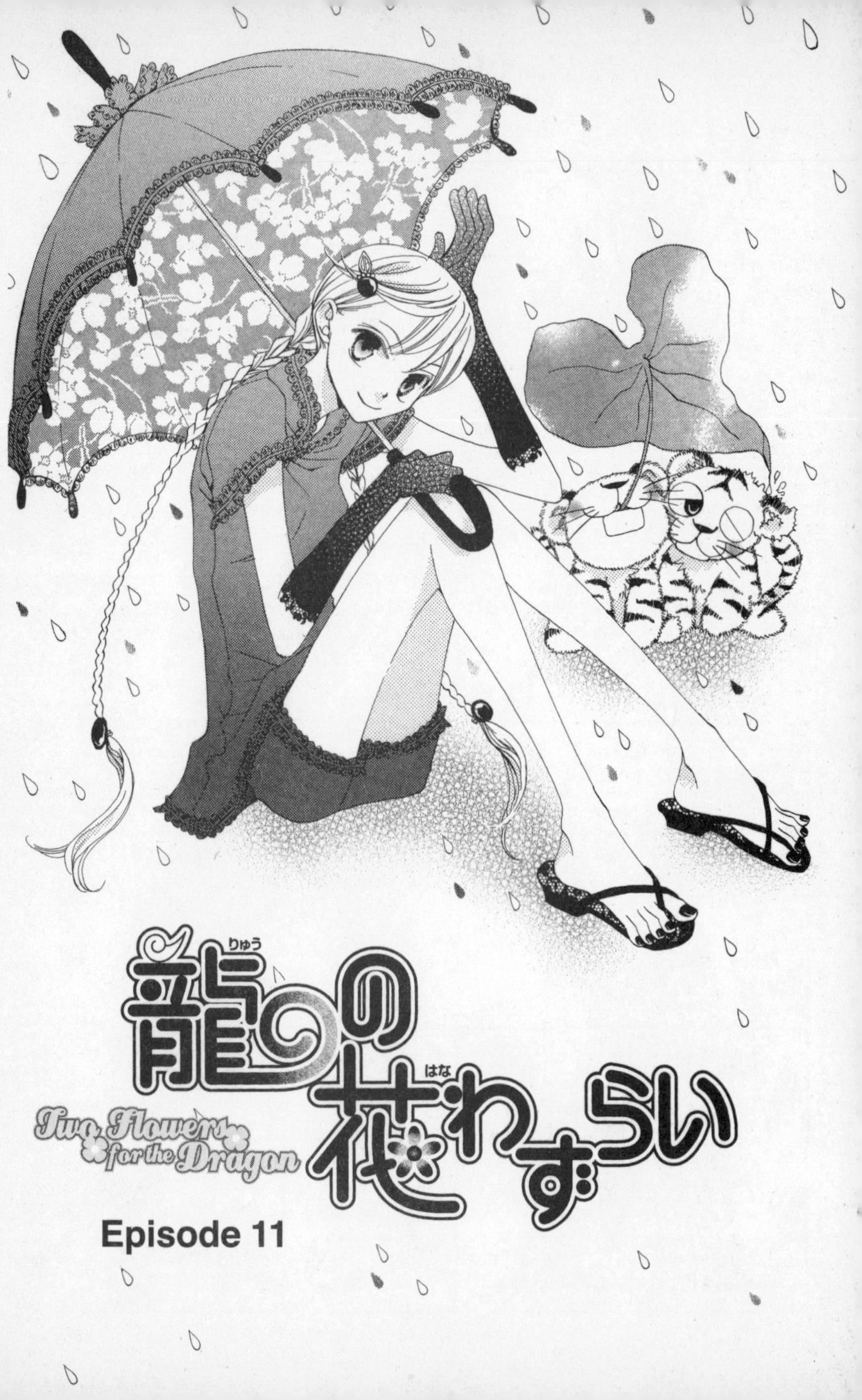
龍の花わずらい
Two Flowers for the Dragon
Episode 11

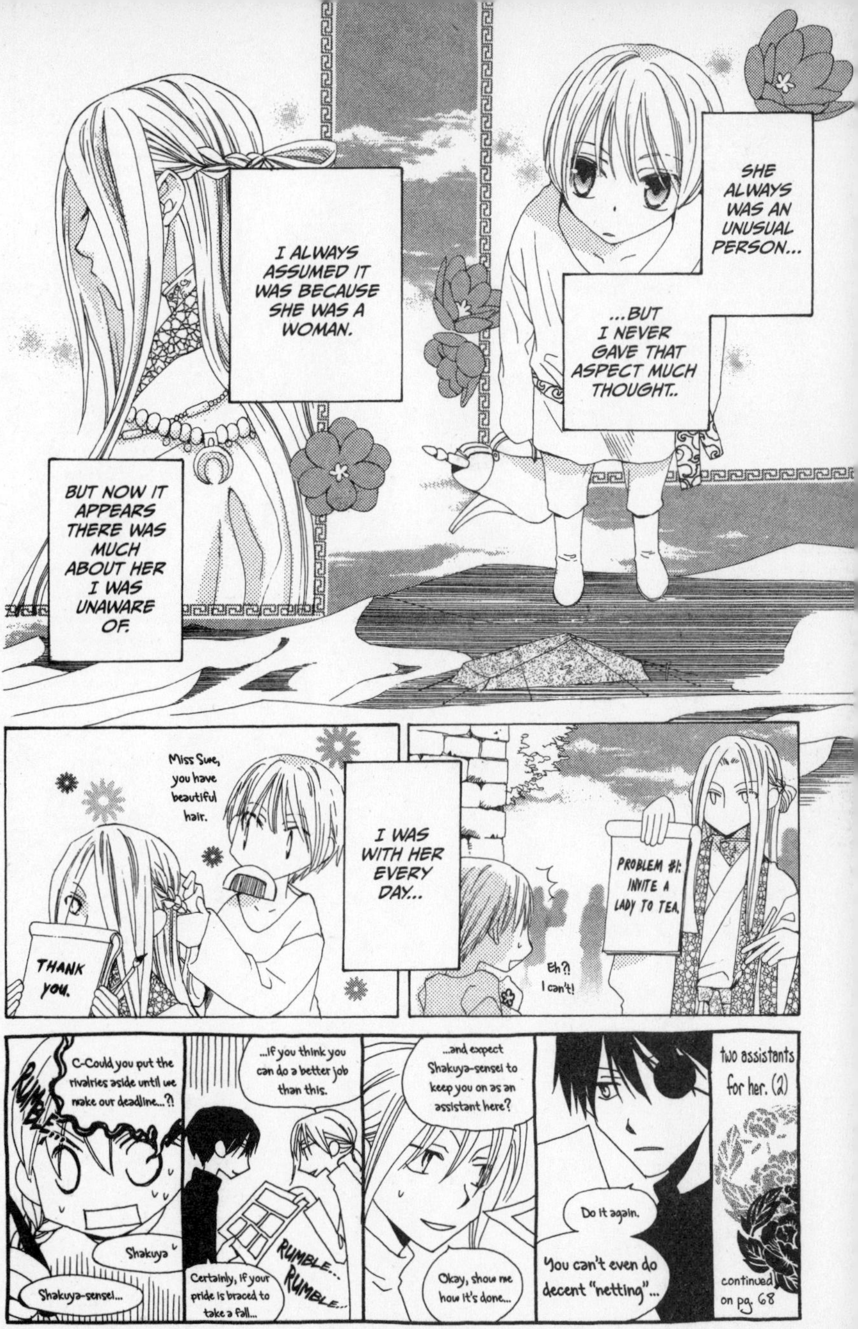
SHE ALWAYS WAS AN UNUSUAL PERSON...
...BUT I NEVER GAVE THAT ASPECT MUCH THOUGHT..
I ALWAYS ASSUMED IT WAS BECAUSE SHE WAS A WOMAN.
BUT NOW IT APPEARS THERE WAS MUCH ABOUT HER I WAS UNAWARE OF.
PROBLEM #1: INVITE A LADY TO TEA.
Eh?! I can't!
I WAS WITH HER EVERY DAY...
Miss Sue, you have beautiful hair.
THANK YOU.
two assistants for her. (2)
continued on pg. 68
Do it again.
You can't even do decent "netting"...
...and expect Shakuya-sensei to keep you on as an assistant here?
Okay, show me how it's done...
...If you think you can do a better job than this.
Certainly, if your pride is braced to take a fall...
RUMBLE... RUMBLE...
C-Could you put the rivalries aside until we make our deadline...?!
RUMBLE...
Shakuya
Shakuya-sensei...

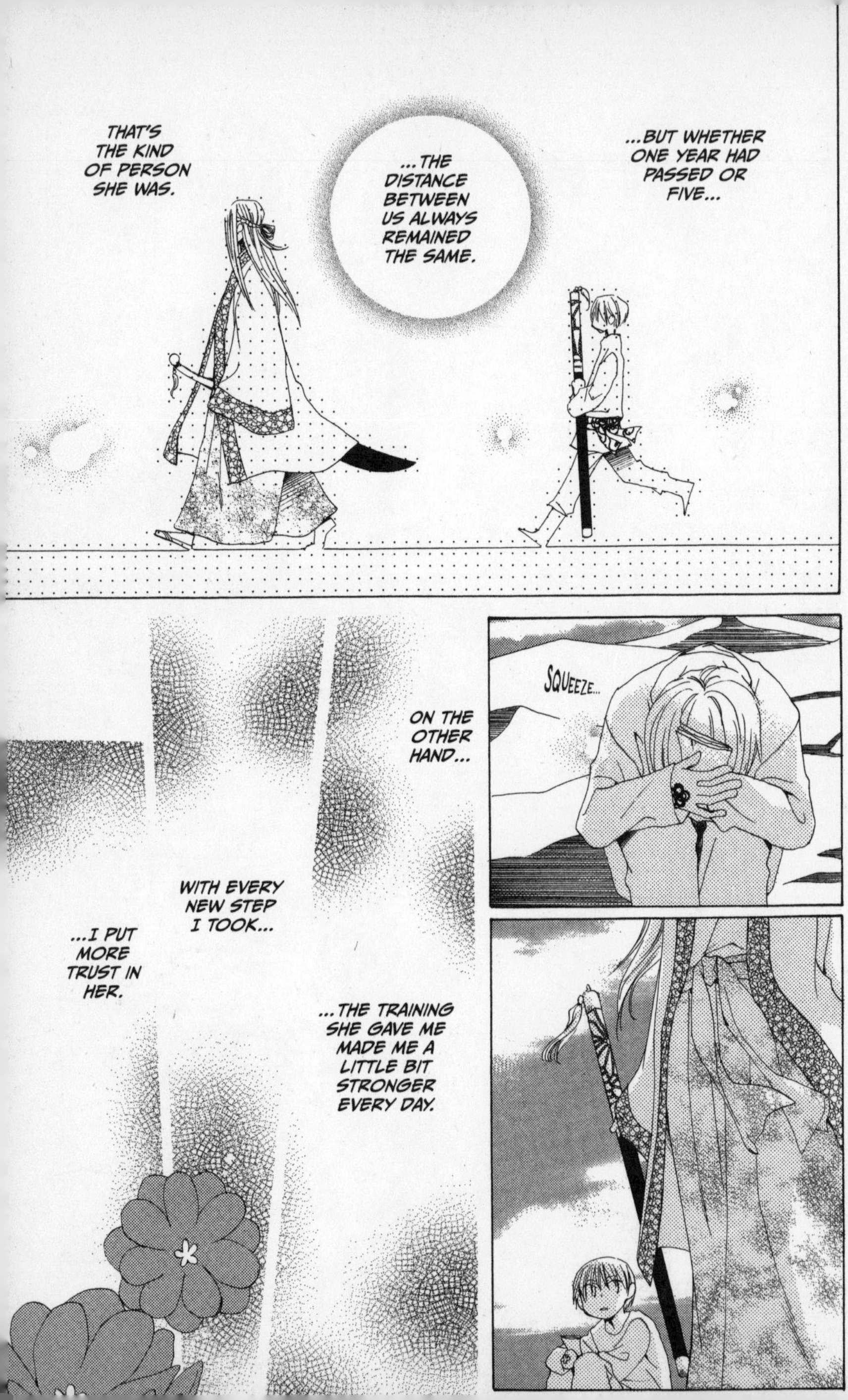
...BUT WHETHER ONE YEAR HAD PASSED OR FIVE...
...THE DISTANCE BETWEEN US ALWAYS REMAINED THE SAME.
THAT'S THE KIND OF PERSON SHE WAS.
SQUEEZE...
ON THE OTHER HAND...
WITH EVERY NEW STEP I TOOK...
...I PUT MORE TRUST IN HER.
...THE TRAINING SHE GAVE ME MADE ME A LITTLE BIT STRONGER EVERY DAY.

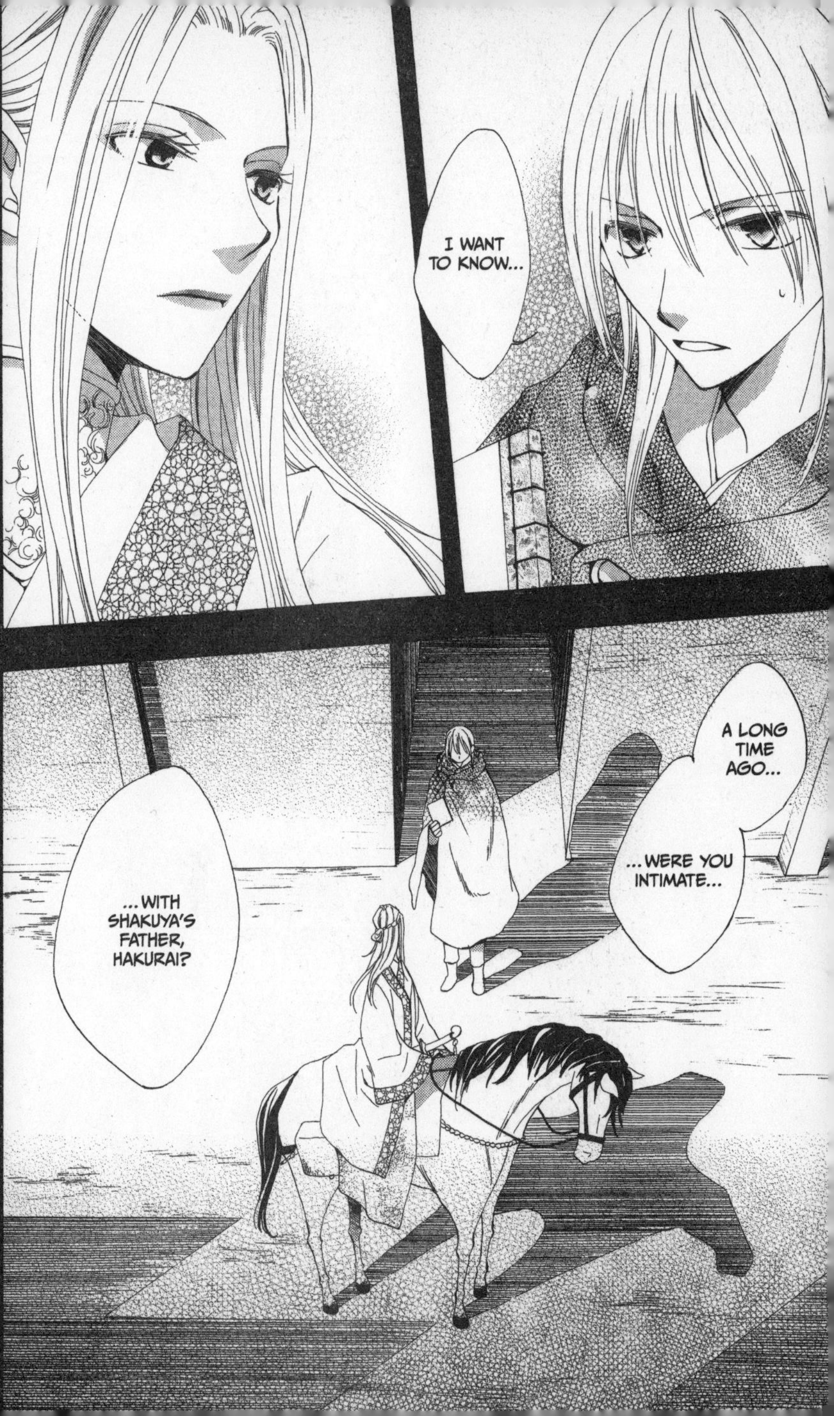
I WANT TO KNOW...
A LONG TIME AGO...
...WERE YOU INTIMATE...
...WITH SHAKUYA'S FATHER, HAKURAI?

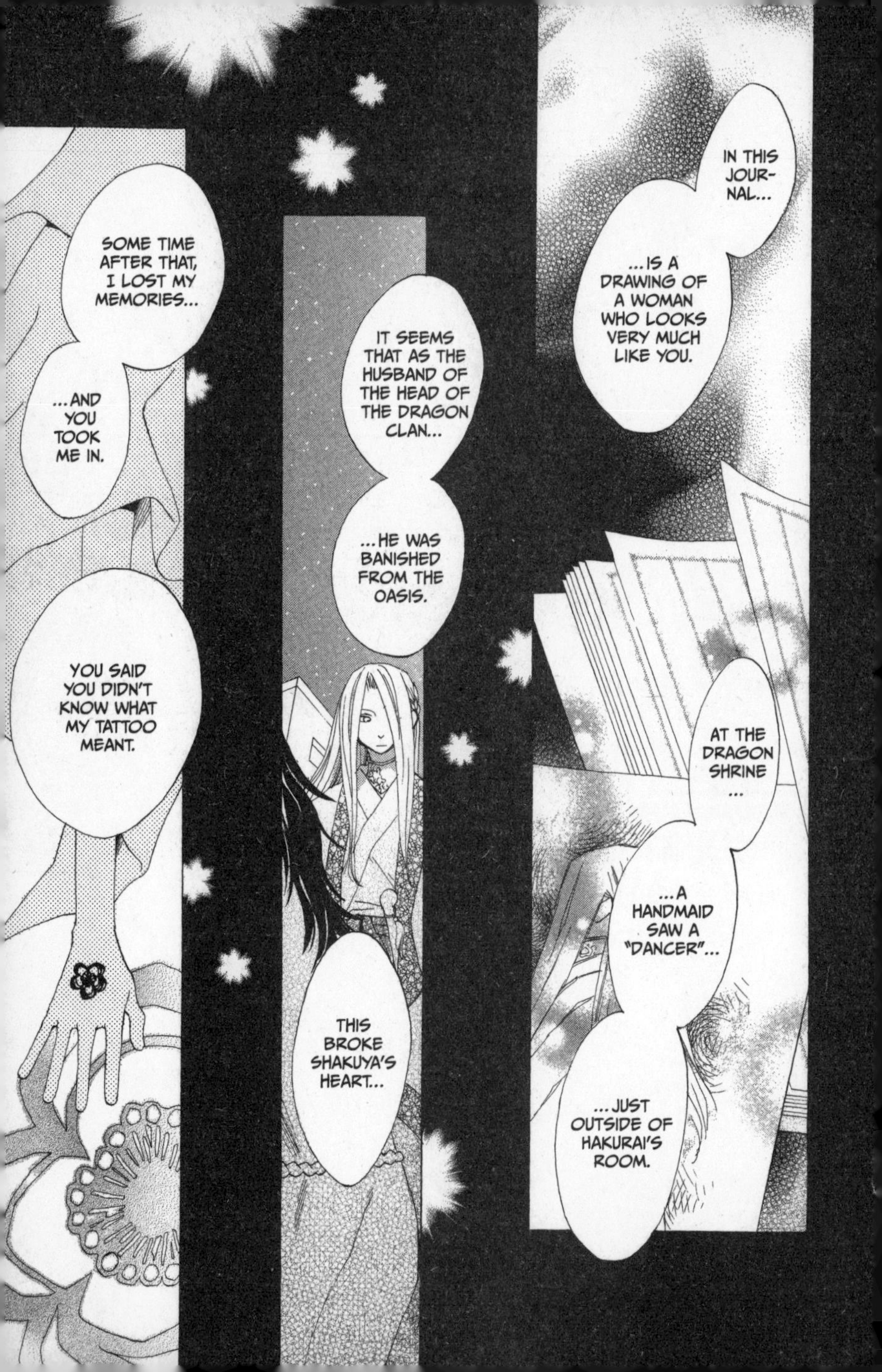
IN THIS JOURNAL...
...IS A DRAWING OF A WOMAN WHO LOOKS VERY MUCH LIKE YOU.
AT THE DRAGON SHRINE ...
...A HANDMAID SAW A "DANCER"...
...JUST OUTSIDE OF HAKURAI'S ROOM.
IT SEEMS THAT AS THE HUSBAND OF THE HEAD OF THE DRAGON CLAN...
...HE WAS BANISHED FROM THE OASIS.
THIS BROKE SHAKUYA'S HEART...
SOME TIME AFTER THAT, I LOST MY MEMORIES...
...AND YOU TOOK ME IN.
YOU SAID YOU DIDN'T KNOW WHAT MY TATTOO MEANT.

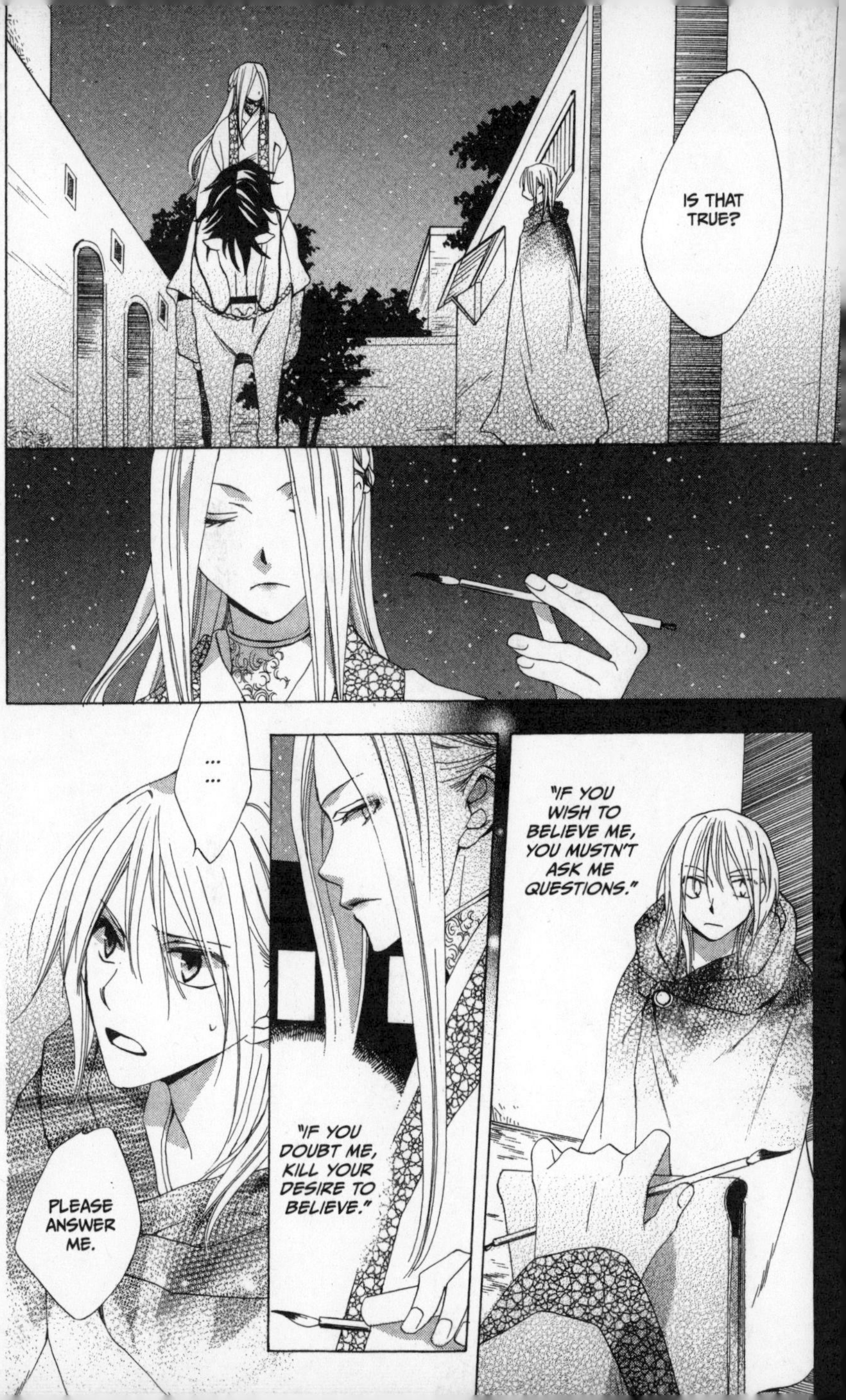
IS THAT TRUE?
"IF YOU WISH TO BELIEVE ME, YOU MUSTN'T ASK ME QUESTIONS."
"IF YOU DOUBT ME, KILL YOUR DESIRE TO BELIEVE."
... ...
PLEASE ANSWER ME.

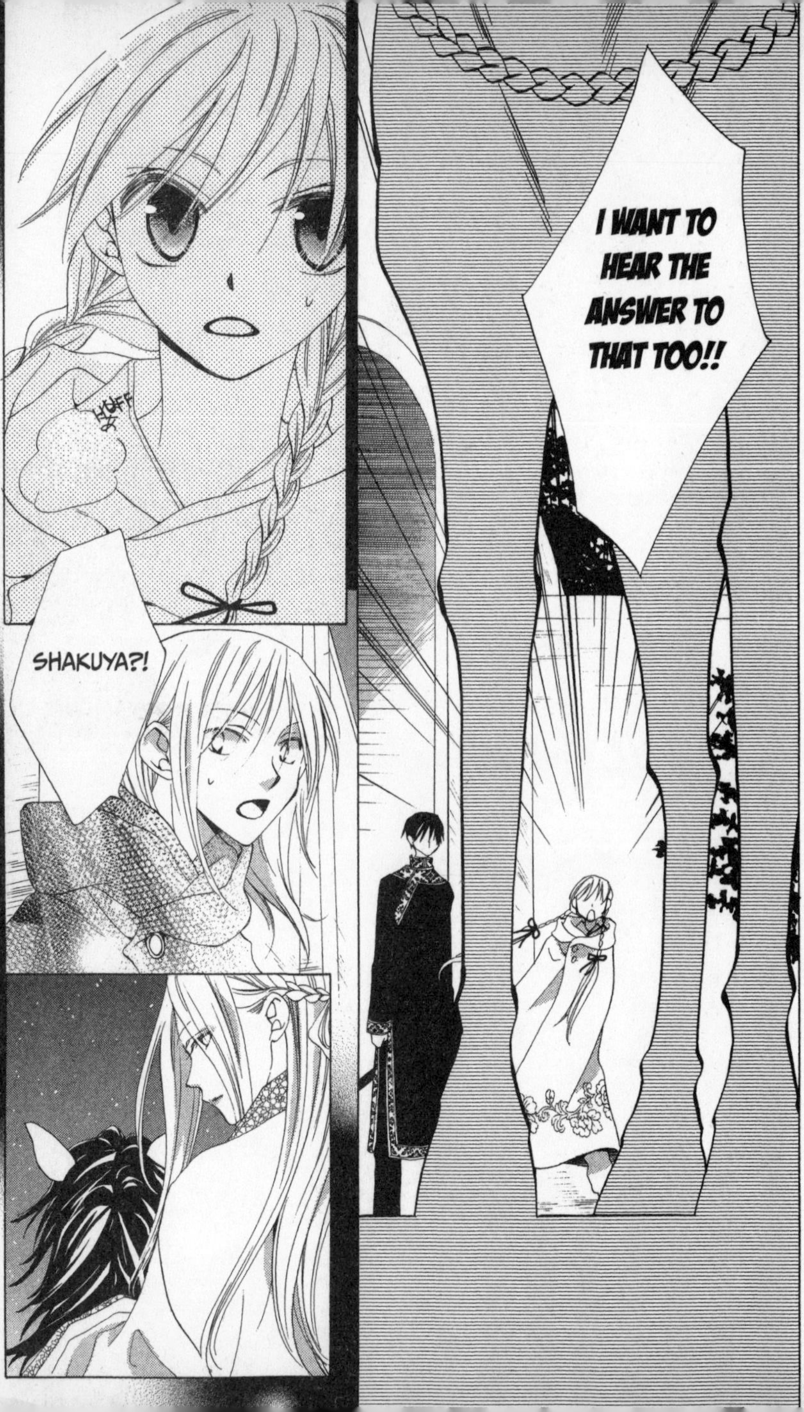
I WANT TO HEAR THE ANSWER TO THAT TOO!!
HUFF
SHAKUYA?!

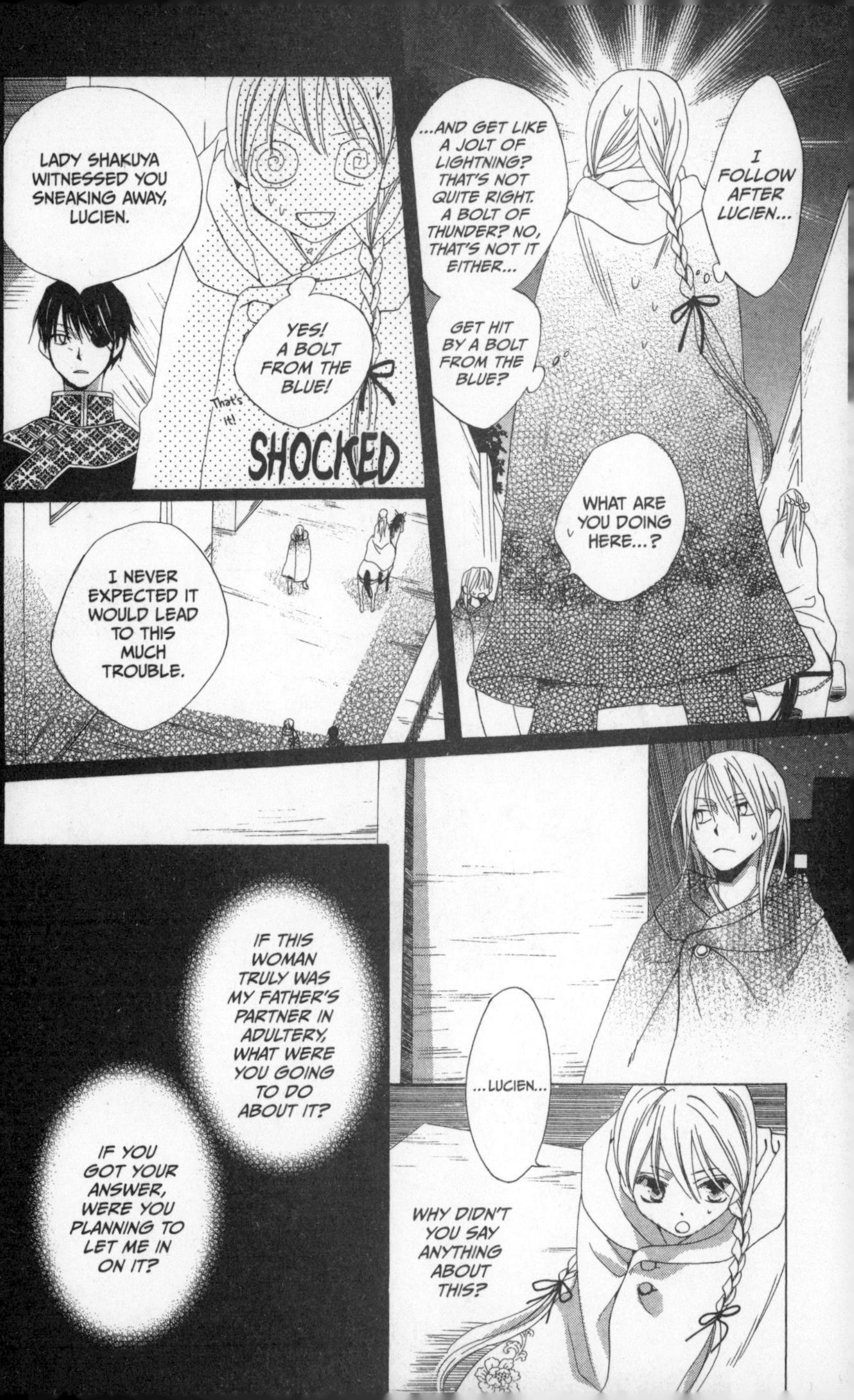
I FOLLOW AFTER LUCIEN...
...AND GET LIKE A JOLT OF LIGHTNING? THAT'S NOT QUITE RIGHT. A BOLT OF THUNDER? NO, THAT'S NOT IT EITHER...
GET HIT BY A BOLT FROM THE BLUE?
WHAT ARE YOU DOING HERE...?
YES! A BOLT FROM THE BLUE!
That's it!
SHOCKED
LADY SHAKUYA WITNESSED YOU SNEAKING AWAY, LUCIEN.
I NEVER EXPECTED IT WOULD LEAD TO THIS MUCH TROUBLE.
...LUCIEN...
WHY DIDN'T YOU SAY ANYTHING ABOUT THIS?
IF THIS WOMAN TRULY WAS MY FATHER'S PARTNER IN ADULTERY, WHAT WERE YOU GOING TO DO ABOUT IT?
IF YOU GOT YOUR ANSWER, WERE YOU PLANNING TO LET ME IN ON IT?

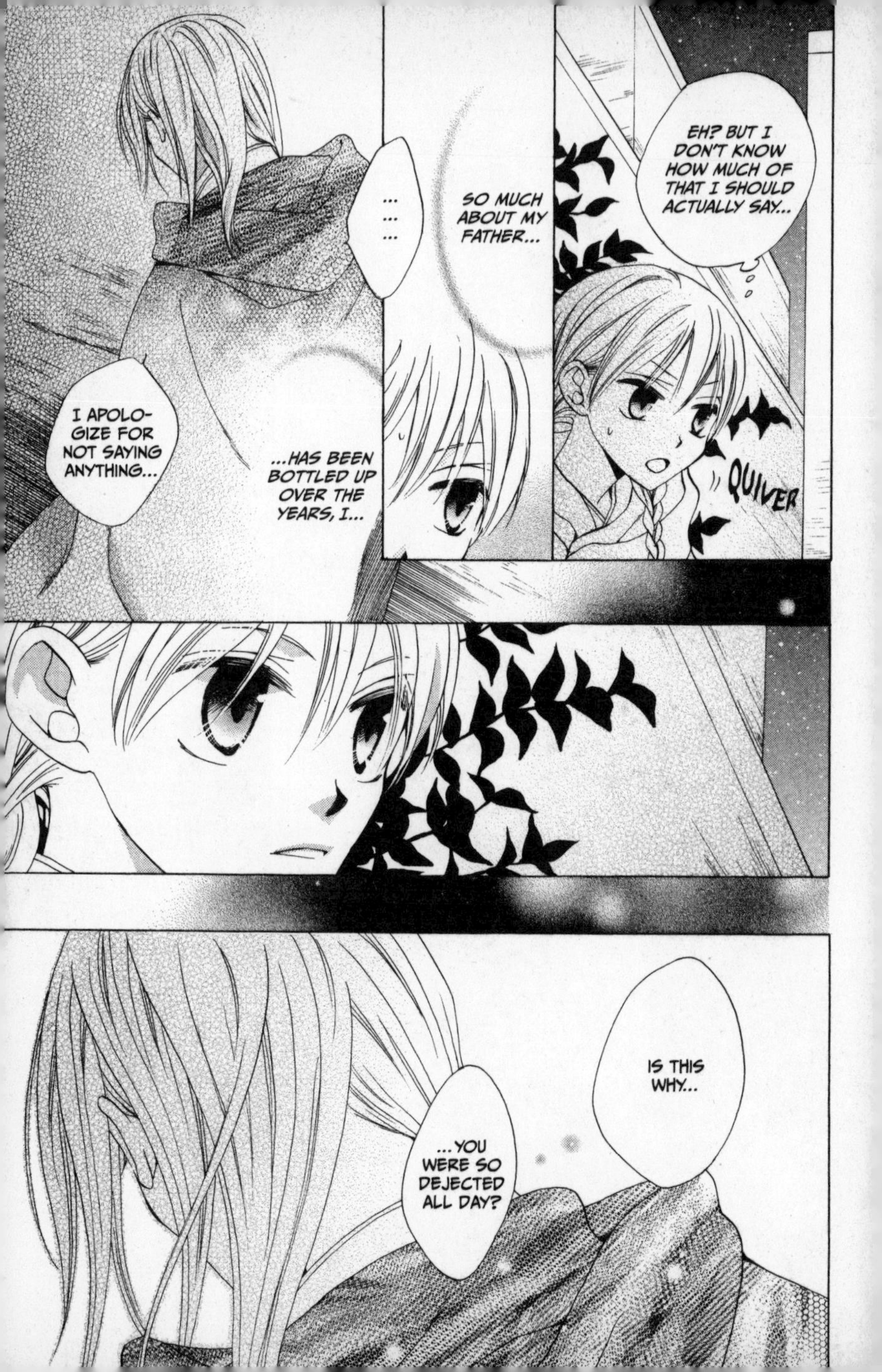
EH? BUT I DON'T KNOW HOW MUCH OF THAT I SHOULD ACTUALLY SAY...
QUIVER
SO MUCH ABOUT MY FATHER...
...HAS BEEN BOTTLED UP OVER THE YEARS, I...
... ...
I APOLOGIZE FOR NOT SAYING ANYTHING...
IS THIS WHY...
...YOU WERE SO DEJECTED ALL DAY?

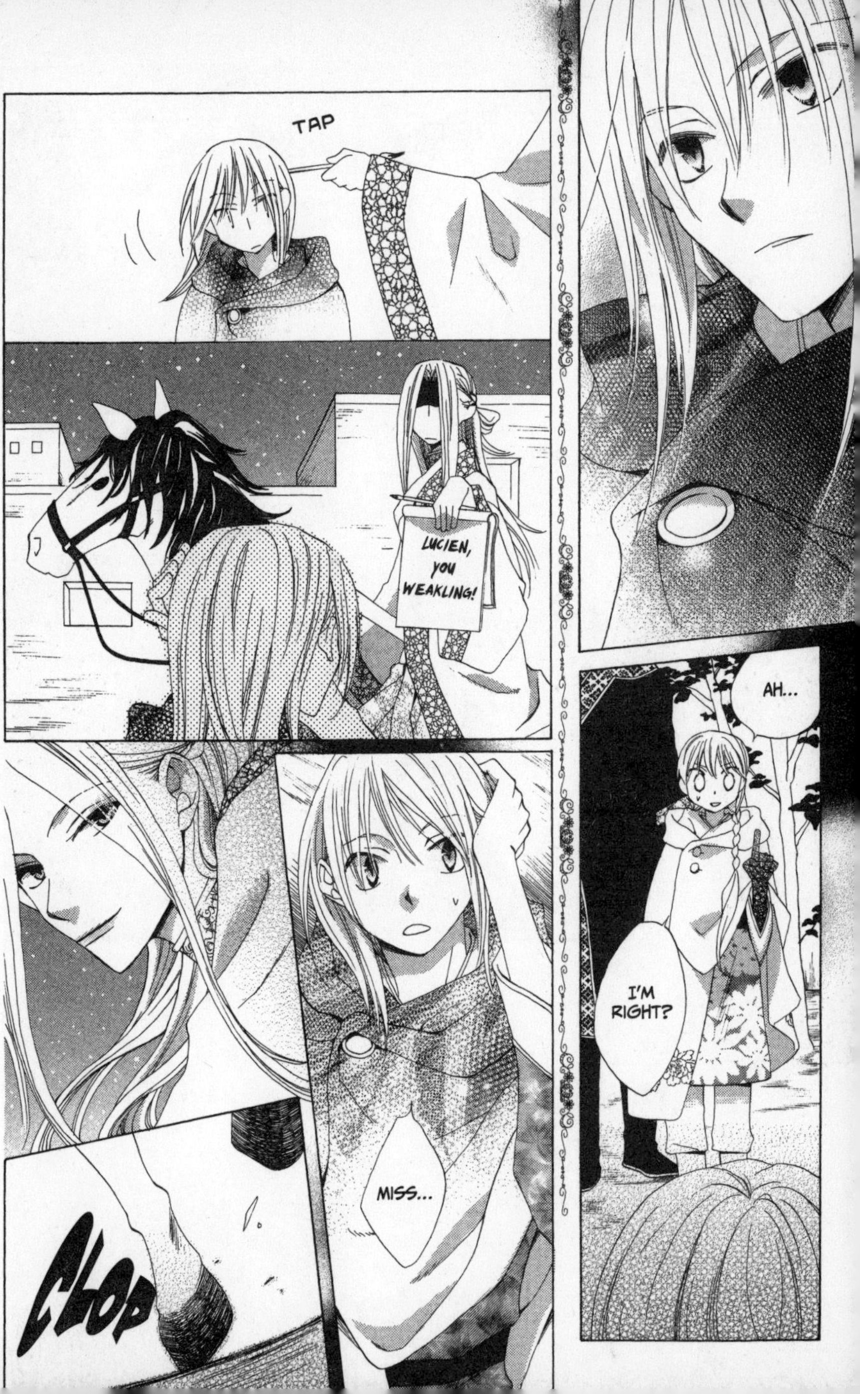
AH...
I'M RIGHT?
TAP
LUCIEN, YOU WEAKLING!
MISS...
CLOP

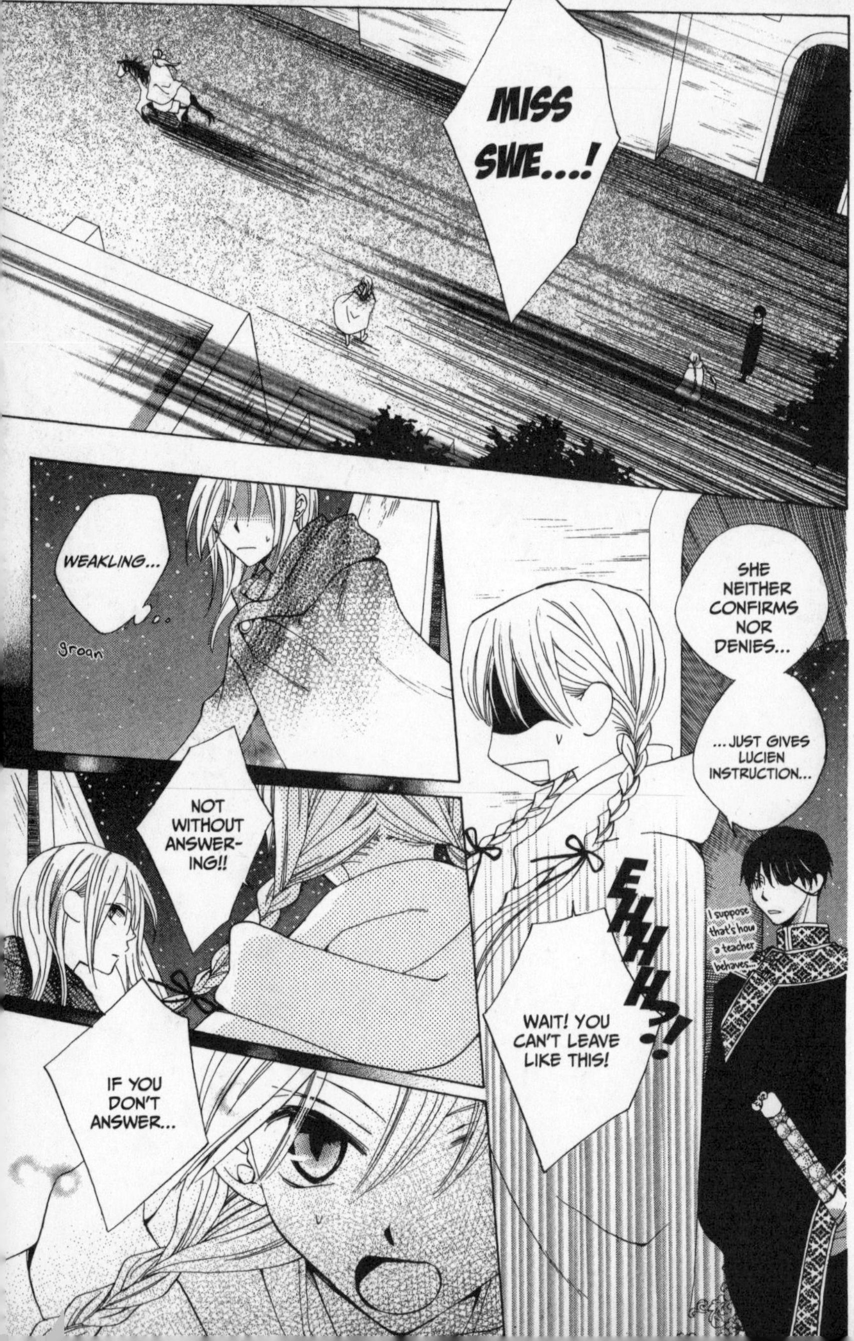
MISS SWE...!
SHE NEITHER CONFIRMS NOR DENIES...
...JUST GIVES LUCIEN INSTRUCTION...
I suppose that's how a teacher behaves...
EHHH?!
WAIT! YOU CAN'T LEAVE LIKE THIS!
WEAKLING...
groan
NOT WITHOUT ANSWERING!!
IF YOU DON'T ANSWER...

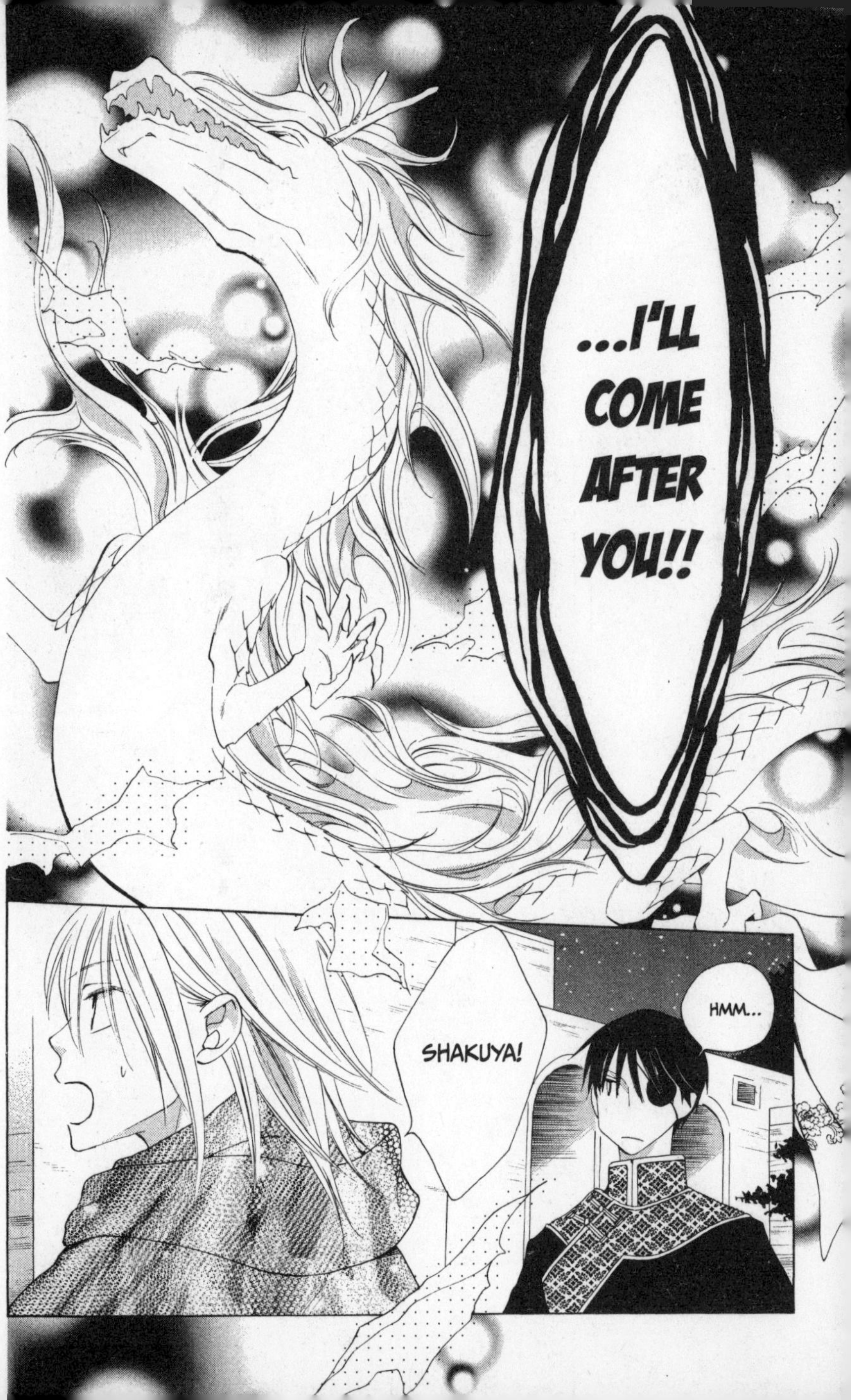
...I'LL COME AFTER YOU!!
HMM...
SHAKUYA!

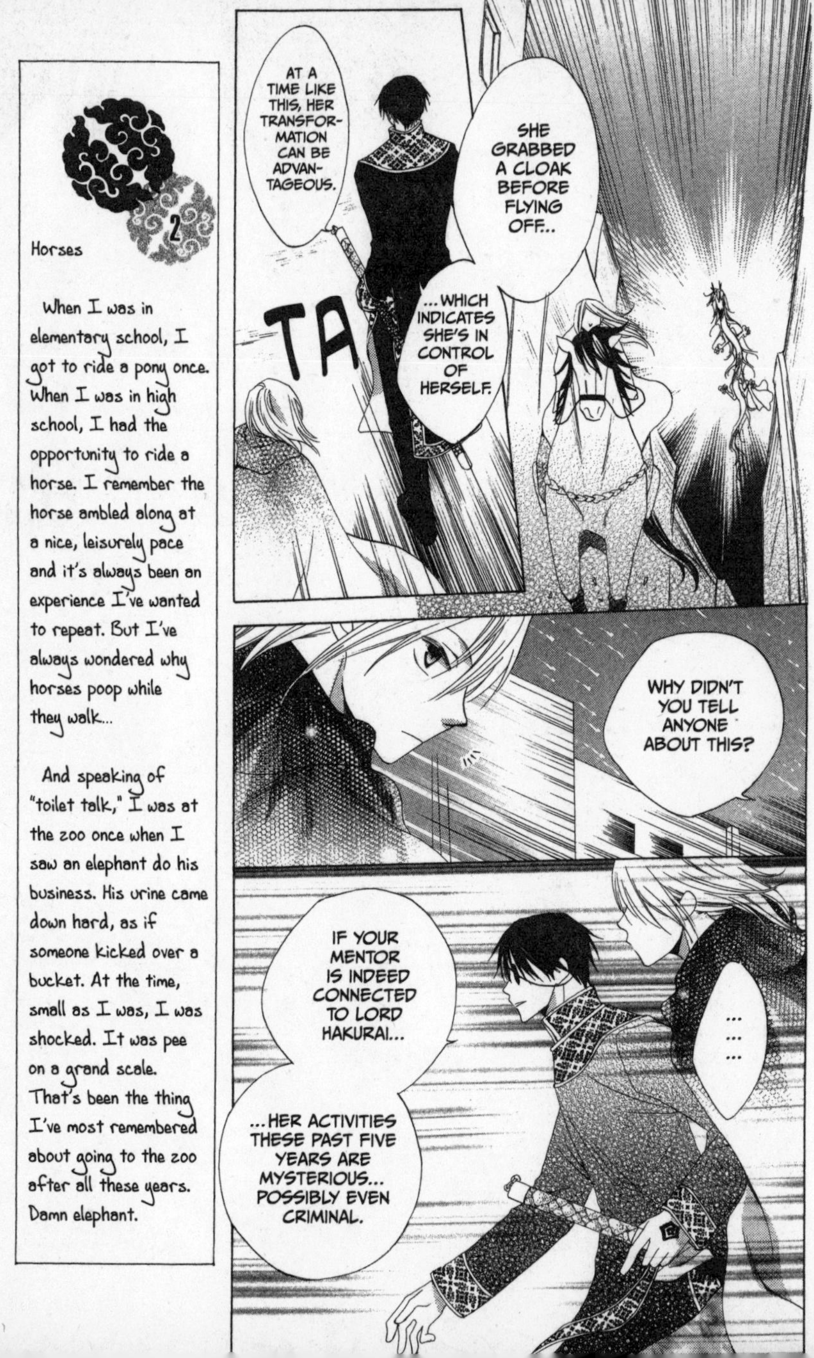
SHE GRABBED A CLOAK BEFORE FLYING OFF...
...WHICH INDICATES SHE'S IN CONTROL OF HERSELF.
AT A TIME LIKE THIS, HER TRANSFORMATION CAN BE ADVANTAGEOUS.
TA
WHY DIDN'T YOU TELL ANYONE ABOUT THIS?
...
...
...
IF YOUR MENTOR IS INDEED CONNECTED TO LORD HAKURAI...
...HER ACTIVITIES THESE PAST FIVE YEARS ARE MYSTERIOUS... POSSIBLY EVEN CRIMINAL.

2

Horses

When I was in elementary school, I got to ride a pony once. When I was in high school, I had the opportunity to ride a horse. I remember the horse ambled along at a nice, leisurely pace and it's always been an experience I've wanted to repeat. But I've always wondered why horses poop while they walk...

And speaking of "toilet talk," I was at the zoo once when I saw an elephant do his business. His urine came down hard, as if someone kicked over a bucket. At the time, small as I was, I was shocked. It was pee on a grand scale. That's been the thing I've most remembered about going to the zoo after all these years. Damn elephant.

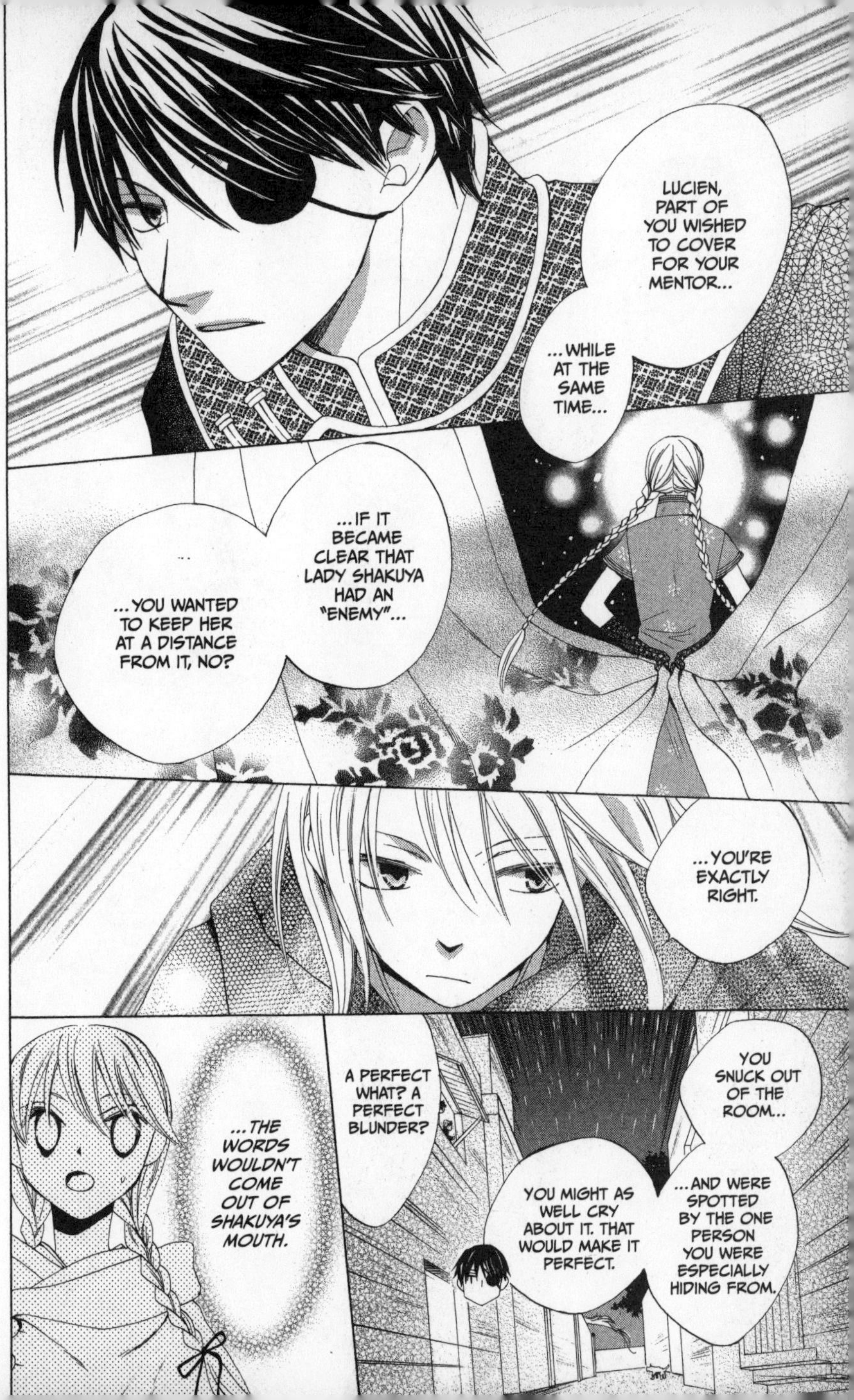
LUCIEN, PART OF YOU WISHED TO COVER FOR YOUR MENTOR...
...WHILE AT THE SAME TIME...
...IF IT BECAME CLEAR THAT LADY SHAKUYA HAD AN "ENEMY"...
...YOU WANTED TO KEEP HER AT A DISTANCE FROM IT, NO?
...
...YOU'RE EXACTLY RIGHT.
YOU SNUCK OUT OF THE ROOM...
...AND WERE SPOTTED BY THE ONE PERSON YOU WERE ESPECIALLY HIDING FROM.
YOU MIGHT AS WELL CRY ABOUT IT. THAT WOULD MAKE IT PERFECT.
A PERFECT WHAT? A PERFECT BLUNDER?
...THE WORDS WOULDN'T COME OUT OF SHAKUYA'S MOUTH.

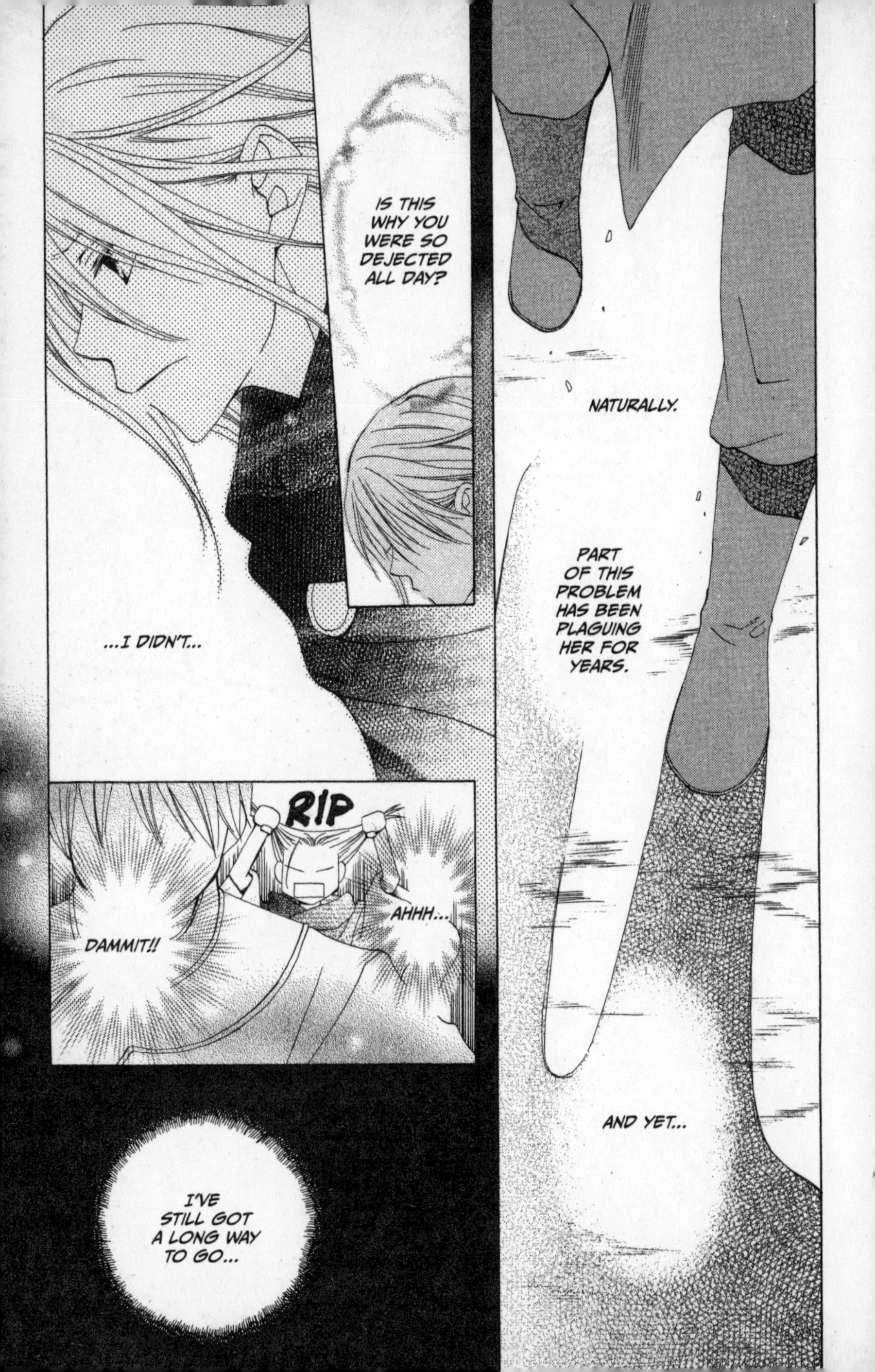
NATURALLY.
PART OF THIS PROBLEM HAS BEEN PLAGUING HER FOR YEARS.
AND YET...
IS THIS WHY YOU WERE SO DEJECTED ALL DAY?
...I DIDN'T...
RIP
AHHH...
DAMMIT!!
I'VE STILL GOT A LONG WAY TO GO...

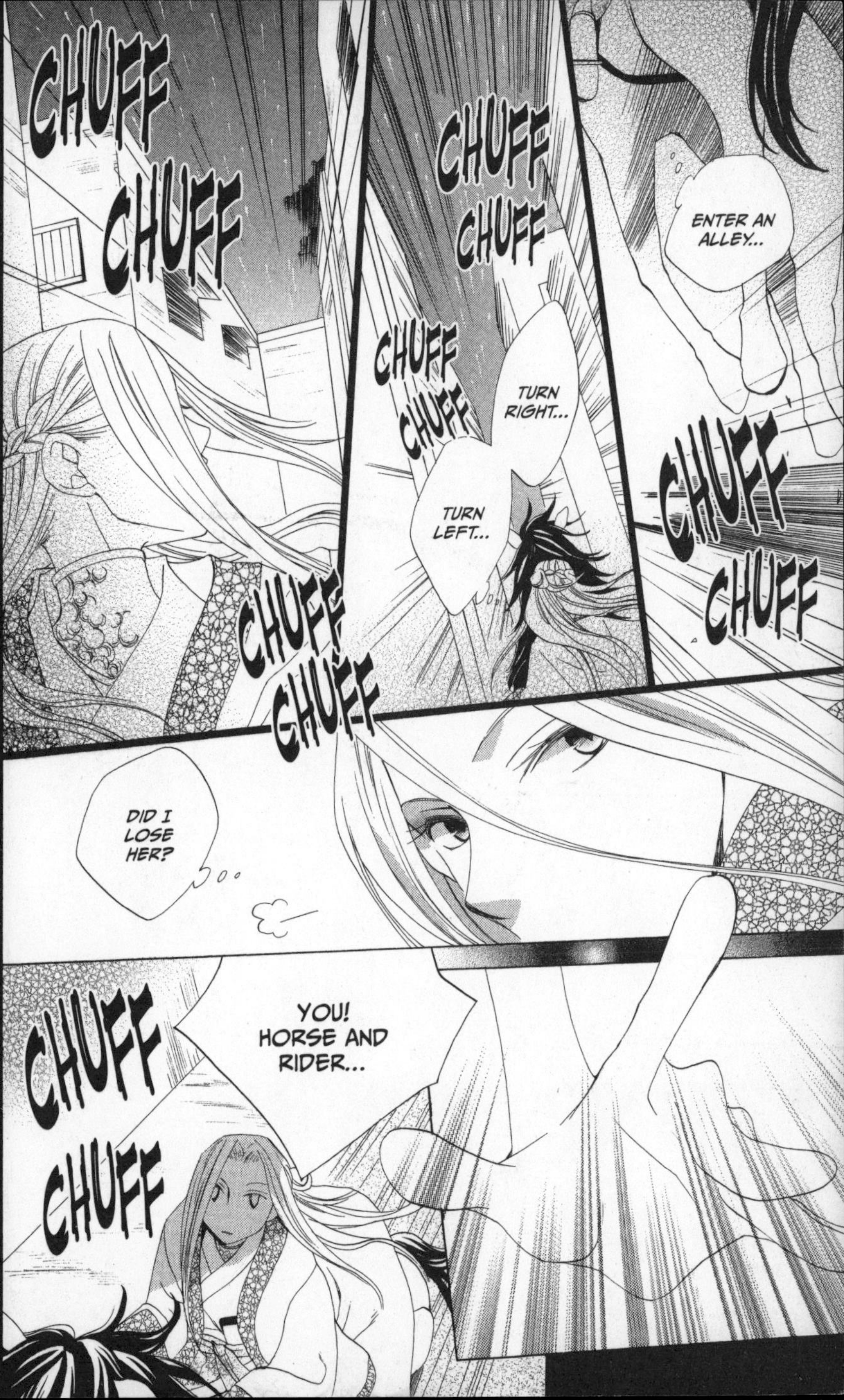
ENTER AN ALLEY...
CHUFF CHUFF
CHUFF CHUFF
CHUFF CHUFF
TURN RIGHT...
TURN LEFT...
CHUFF CHUFF
CHUFF CHUFF
DID I LOSE HER?
YOU! HORSE AND RIDER...
CHUFF CHUFF

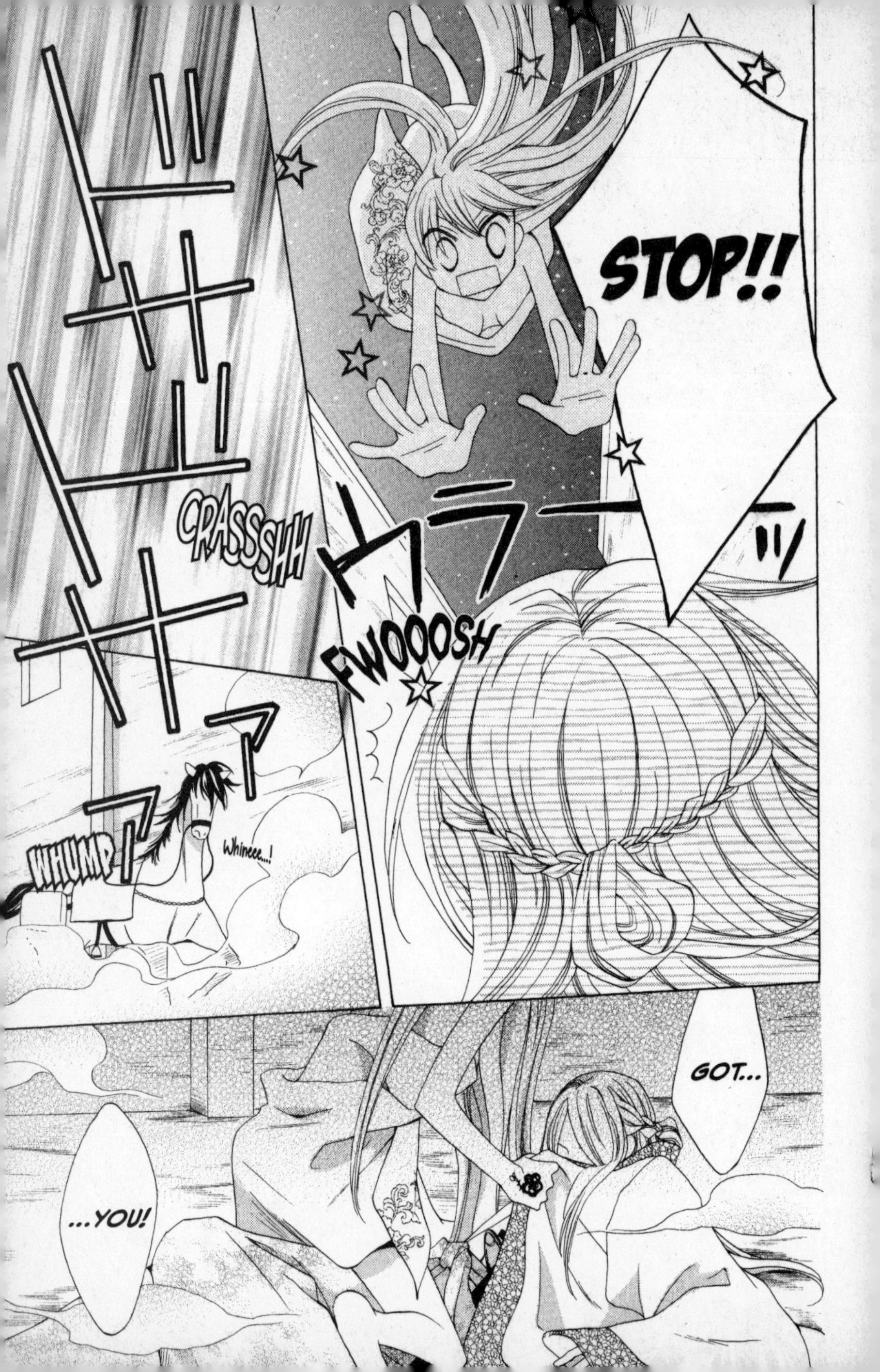
STOP!!
FWOOOSH
CRASSSHH
WHUMP
Whineee...!
GOT...
...YOU!

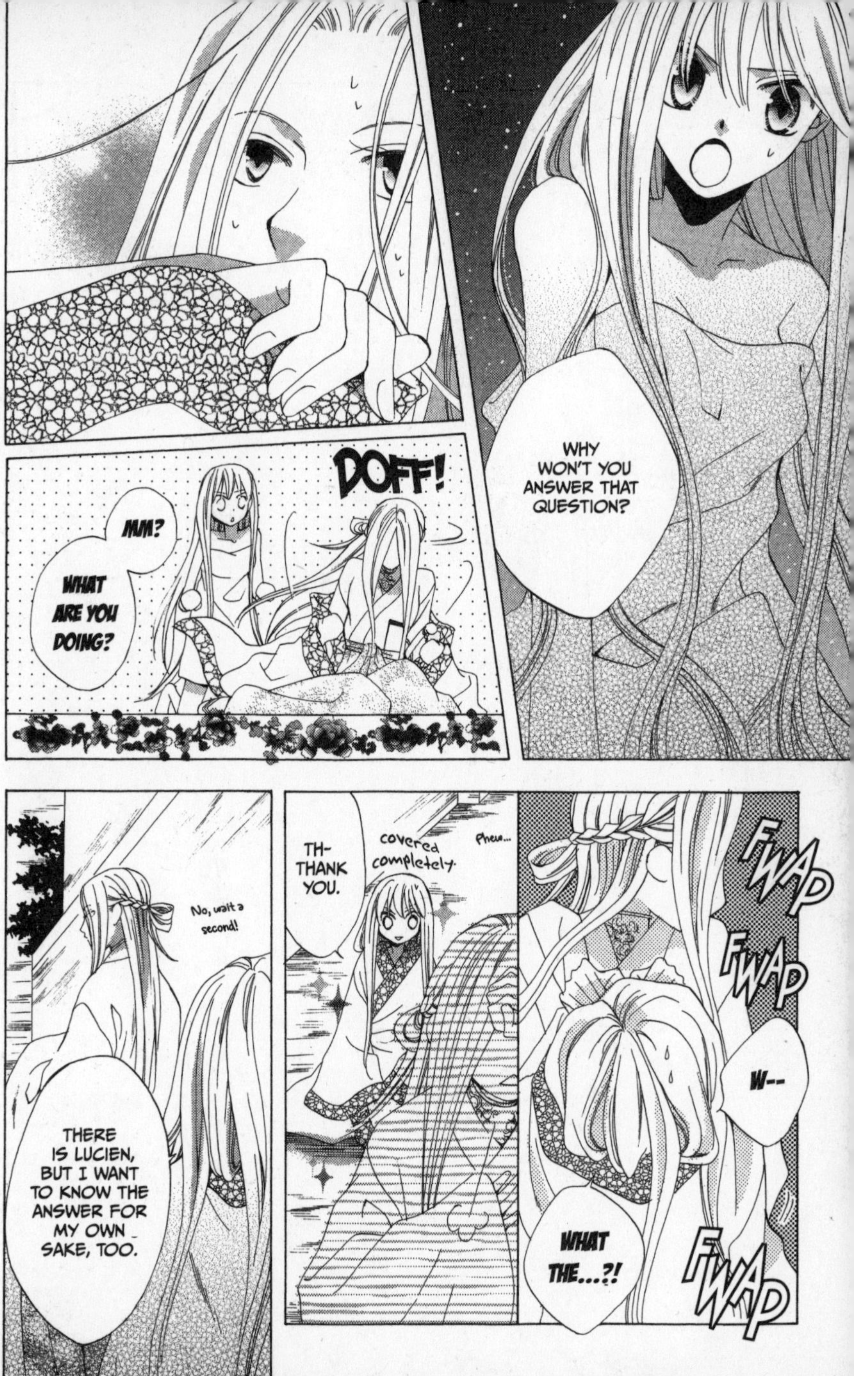
WHY WON'T YOU ANSWER THAT QUESTION?
DOFF!
MM?
WHAT ARE YOU DOING?
FWAP
FWAP
W--
WHAT THE...?!
FWAP
Phew...
covered completely.
TH- THANK YOU.
No, wait a second!
THERE IS LUCIEN, BUT I WANT TO KNOW THE ANSWER FOR MY OWN SAKE, TOO.

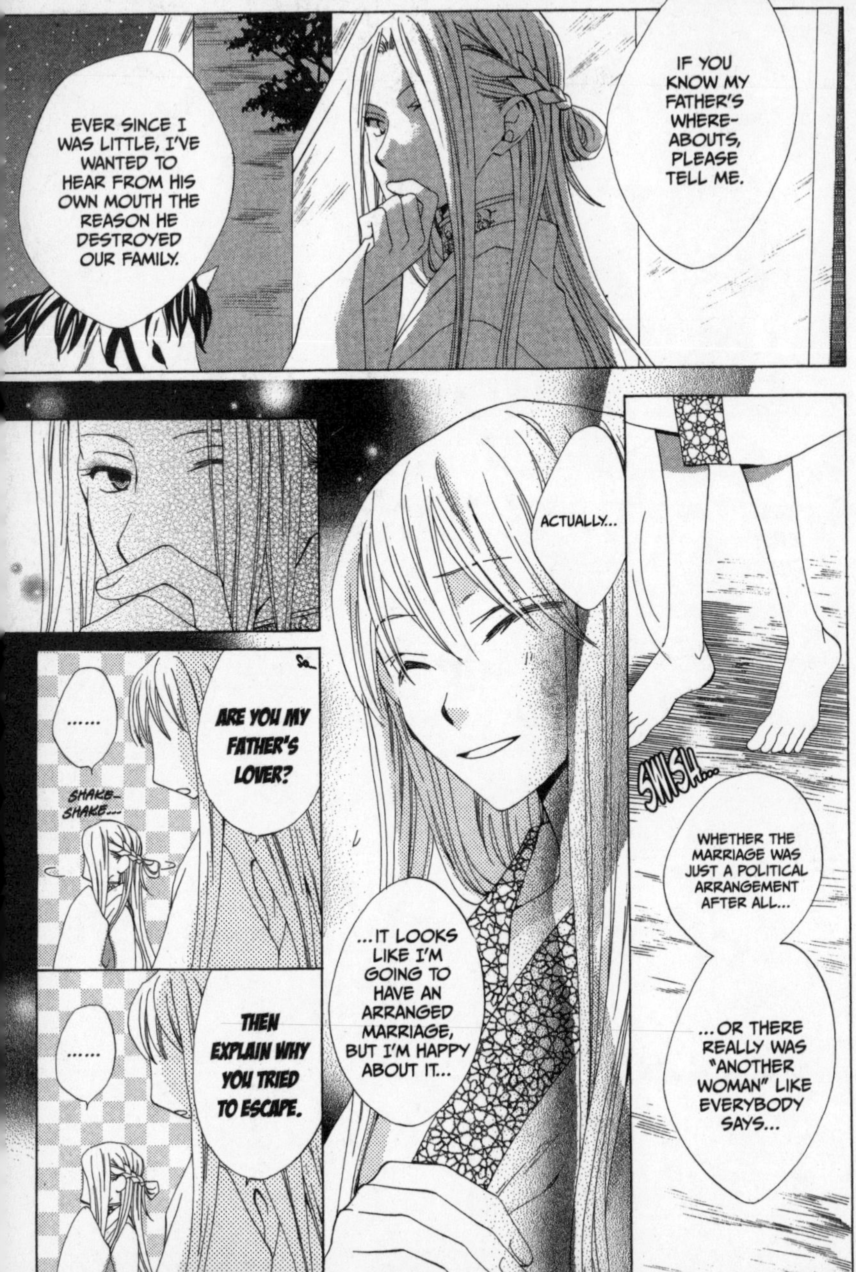
IF YOU KNOW MY FATHER'S WHERE-ABOUTS, PLEASE TELL ME.
EVER SINCE I WAS LITTLE, I'VE WANTED TO HEAR FROM HIS OWN MOUTH THE REASON HE DESTROYED OUR FAMILY.
SWISH...
WHETHER THE MARRIAGE WAS JUST A POLITICAL ARRANGEMENT AFTER ALL...
...OR THERE REALLY WAS "ANOTHER WOMAN" LIKE EVERYBODY SAYS...
ACTUALLY...
...IT LOOKS LIKE I'M GOING TO HAVE AN ARRANGED MARRIAGE, BUT I'M HAPPY ABOUT IT...
ARE YOU MY FATHER'S LOVER?
......
SHAKE-SHAKE...
THEN EXPLAIN WHY YOU TRIED TO ESCAPE.
......

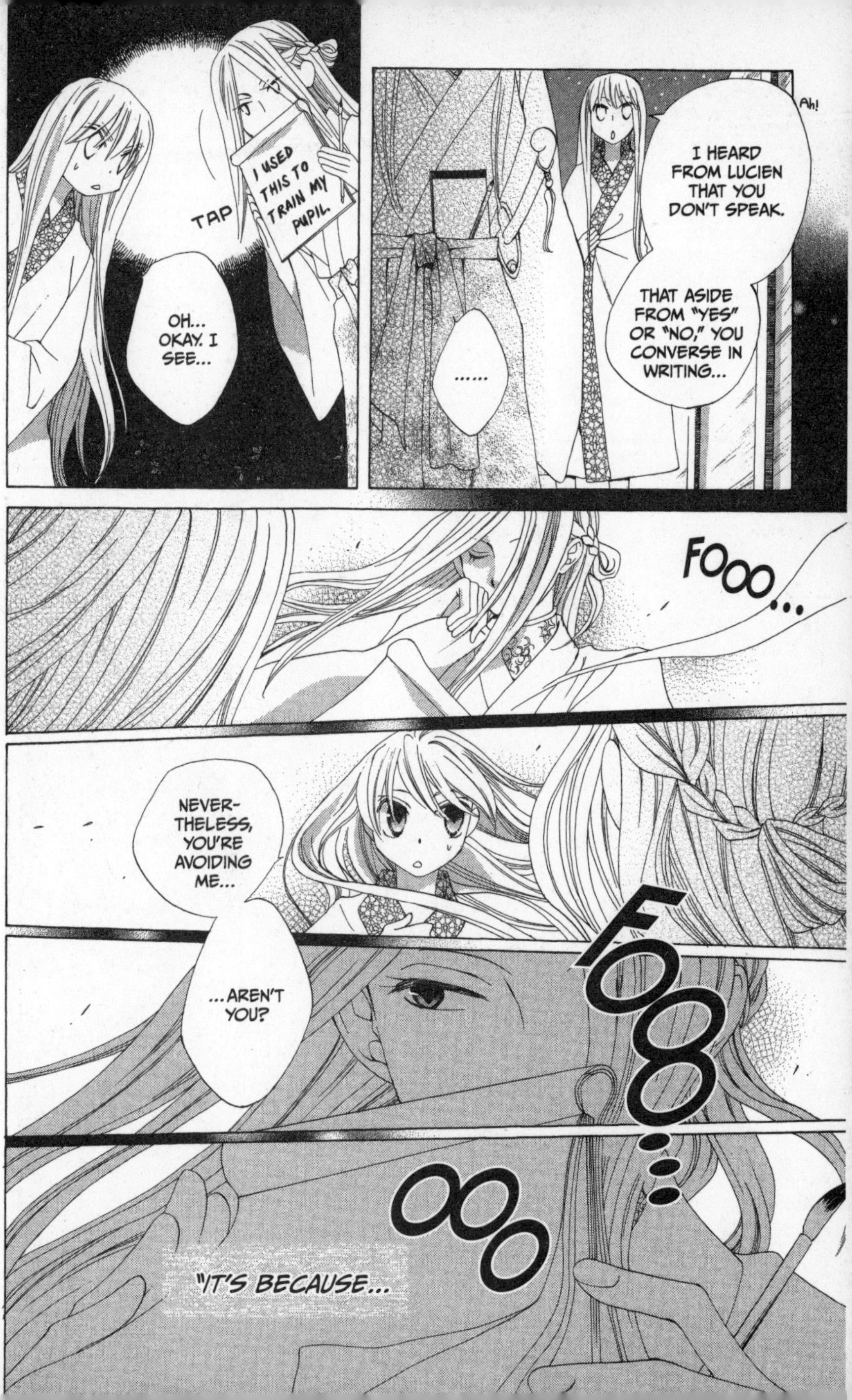
Ah!
I HEARD FROM LUCIEN THAT YOU DON'T SPEAK.
THAT ASIDE FROM "YES" OR "NO," YOU CONVERSE IN WRITING...
......
I USED THIS TO TRAIN MY PUPIL.
TAP
OH... OKAY. I SEE...
FOOO...
NEVER-THELESS, YOU'RE AVOIDING ME...
FOOO...
...AREN'T YOU?
OOO
"IT'S BECAUSE...

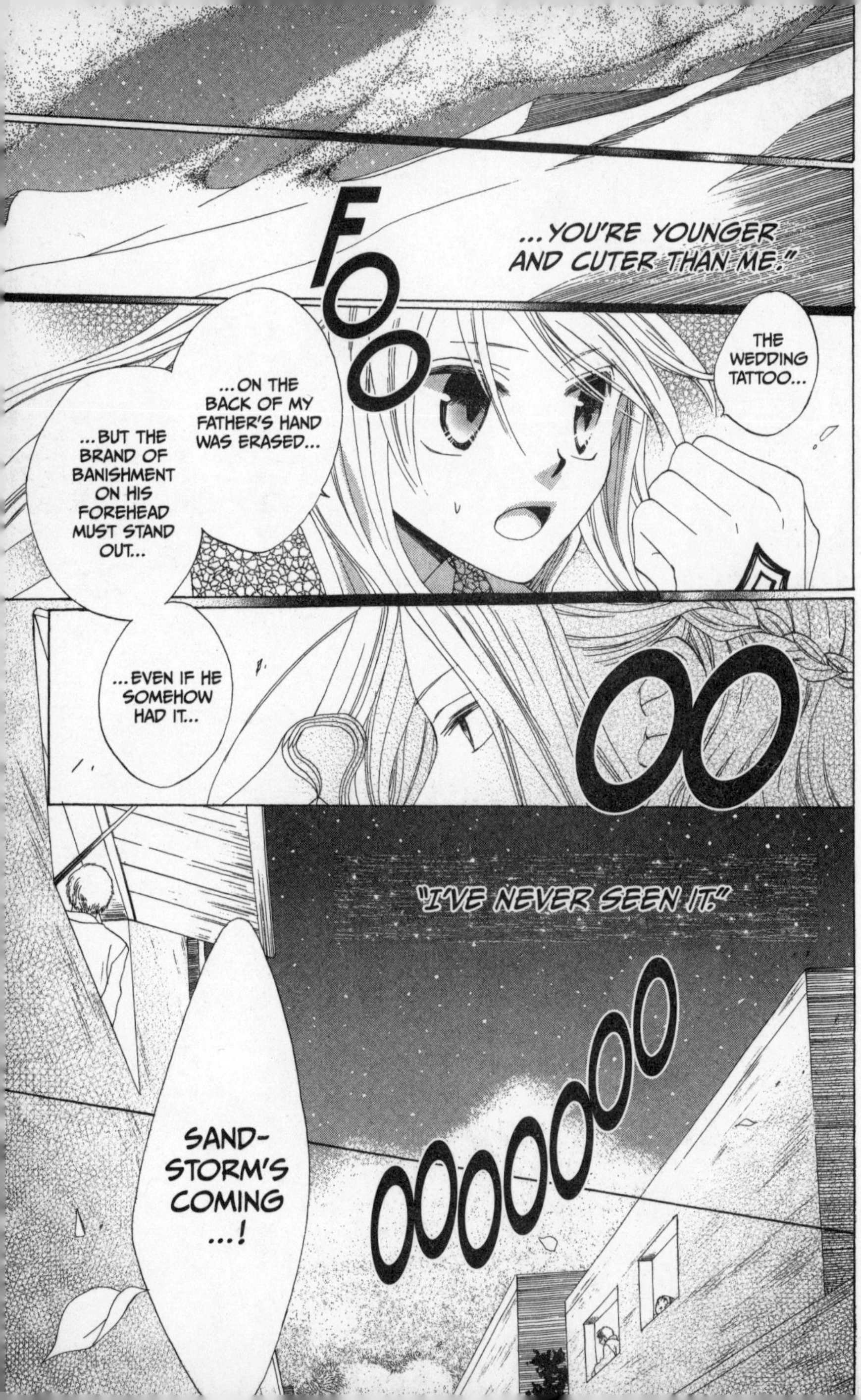
...YOU'RE YOUNGER AND CUTER THAN ME."
FOO
THE WEDDING TATTOO...
...ON THE BACK OF MY FATHER'S HAND WAS ERASED...
...BUT THE BRAND OF BANISHMENT ON HIS FOREHEAD MUST STAND OUT...
...EVEN IF HE SOMEHOW HAD IT...
OO
"I'VE NEVER SEEN IT."
OOOOOOO
SAND-STORM'S COMING ...!

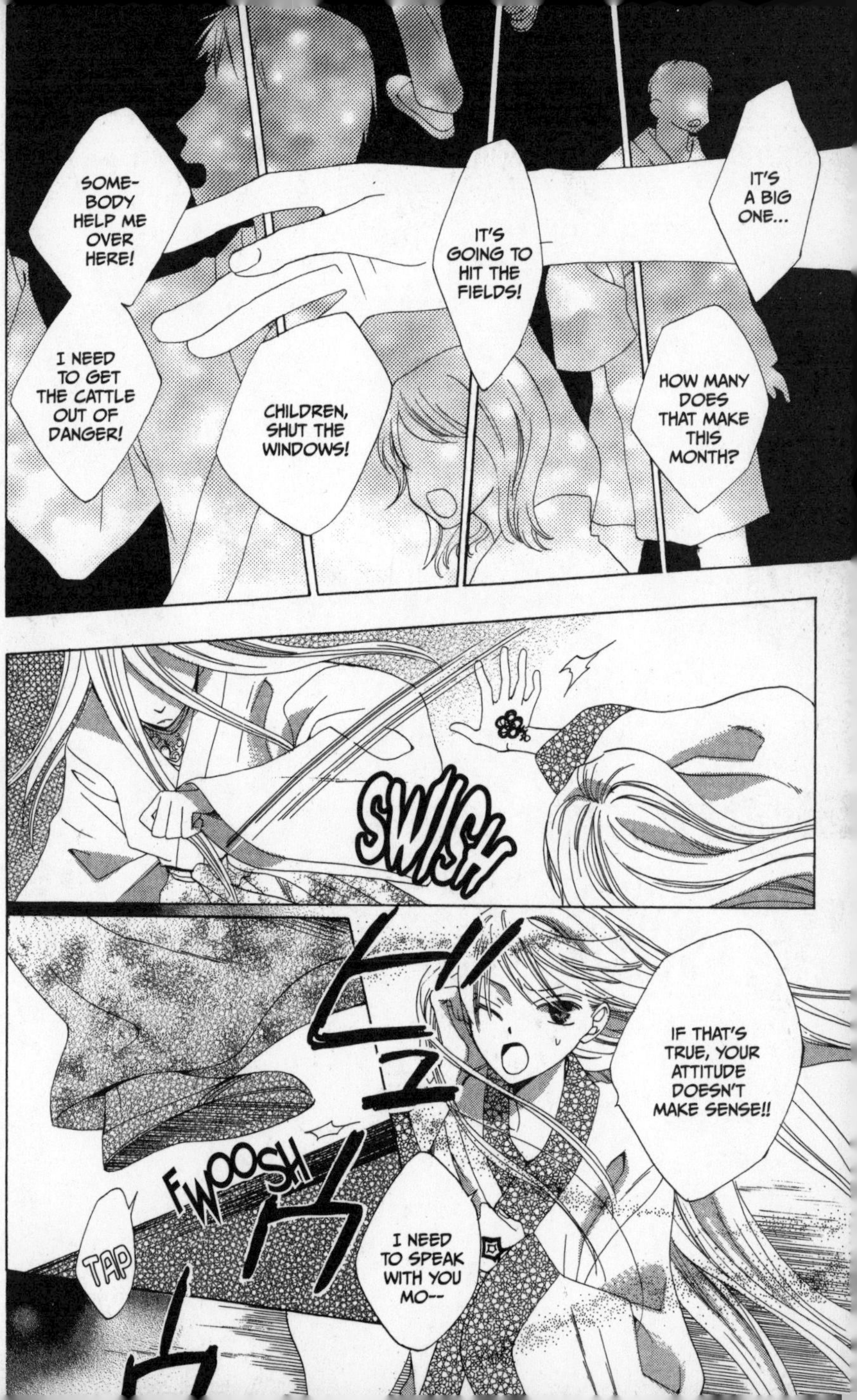
IT'S A BIG ONE...
IT'S GOING TO HIT THE FIELDS!
SOME-BODY HELP ME OVER HERE!
HOW MANY DOES THAT MAKE THIS MONTH?
CHILDREN, SHUT THE WINDOWS!
I NEED TO GET THE CATTLE OUT OF DANGER!
SWISH
IF THAT'S TRUE, YOUR ATTITUDE DOESN'T MAKE SENSE!!
I NEED TO SPEAK WITH YOU MO--
FWOOSH
TAP

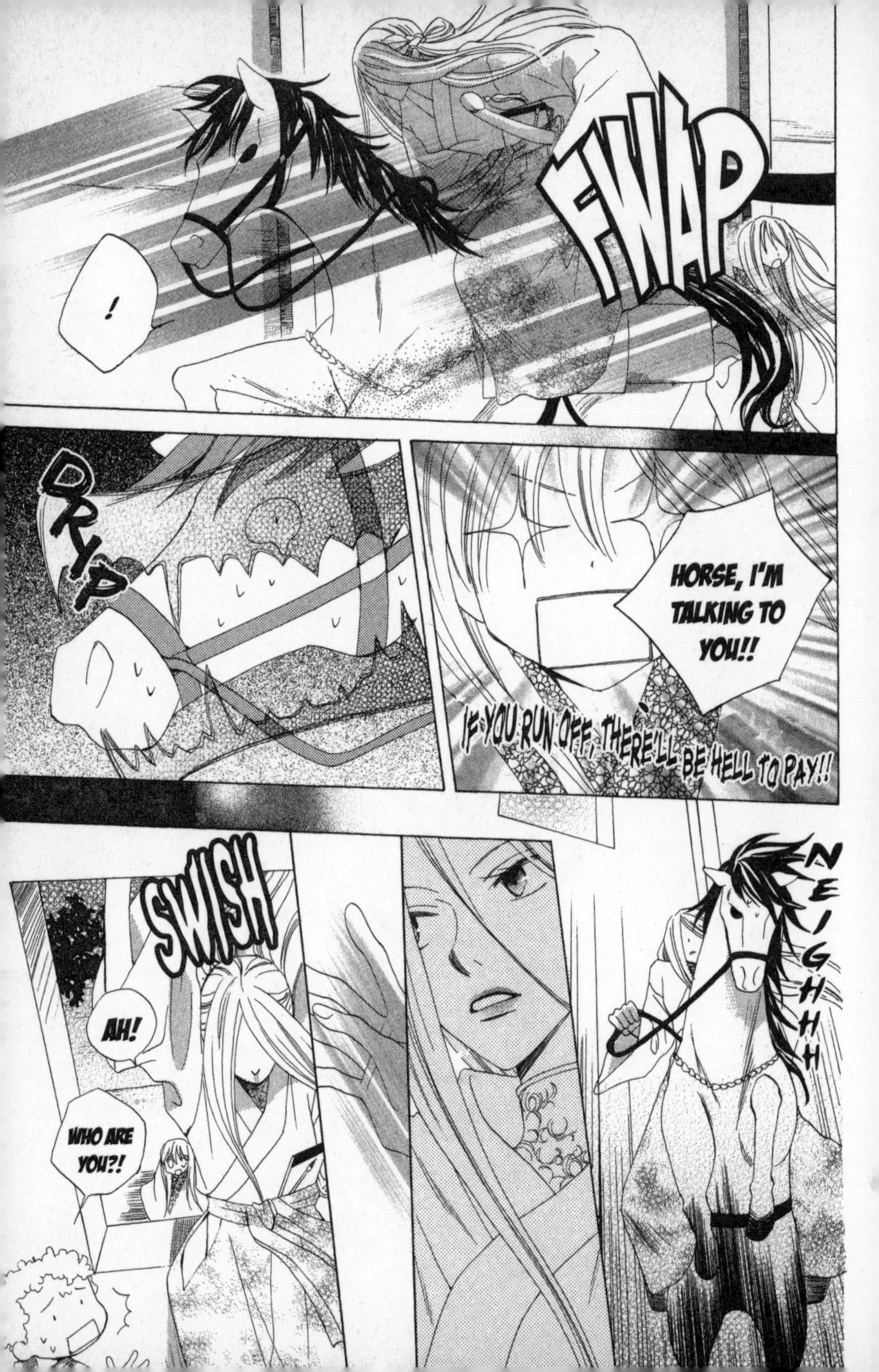
FWAP
!
HORSE, I'M TALKING TO YOU!!
IF YOU RUN OFF, THERE'LL BE HELL TO PAY!!
DRYP
NEIGHHHH
SWISH
AH!
WHO ARE YOU?!

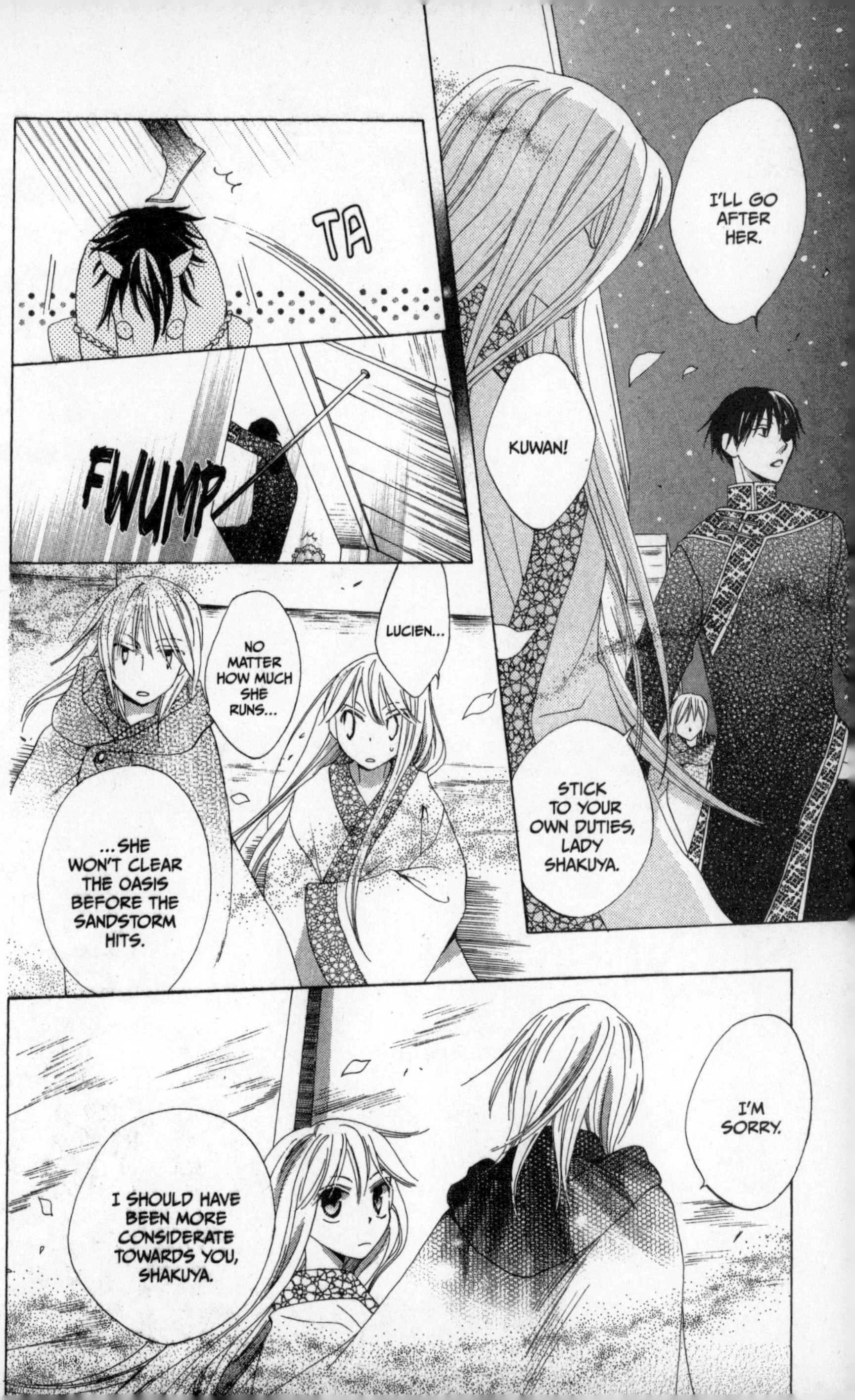
I'LL GO AFTER HER.
KUWAN!
STICK TO YOUR OWN DUTIES, LADY SHAKUYA.
TA
FWUMP
LUCIEN...
NO MATTER HOW MUCH SHE RUNS...
...SHE WON'T CLEAR THE OASIS BEFORE THE SANDSTORM HITS.
I'M SORRY.
I SHOULD HAVE BEEN MORE CONSIDERATE TOWARDS YOU, SHAKUYA.

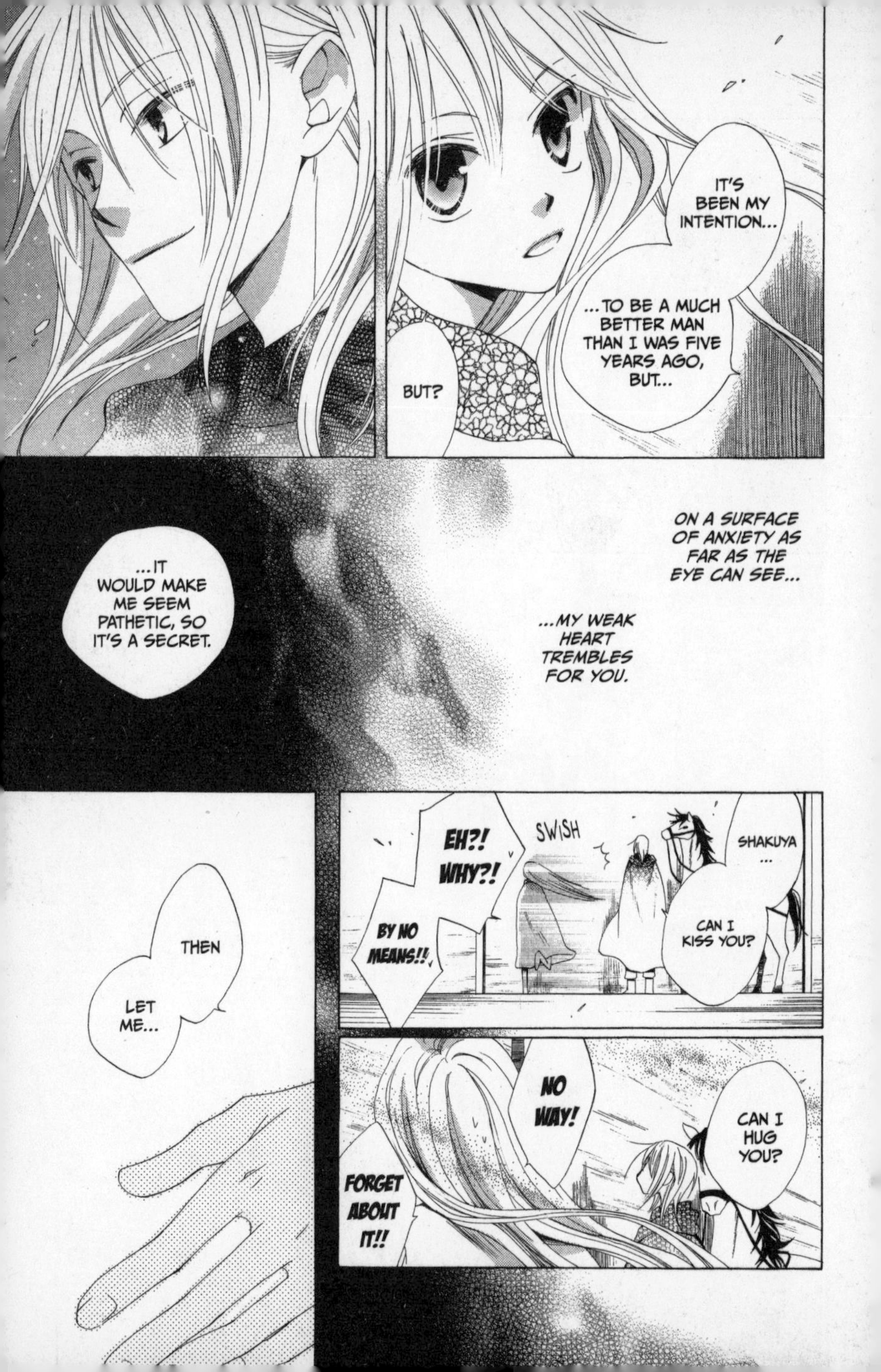
IT'S BEEN MY INTENTION...
...TO BE A MUCH BETTER MAN THAN I WAS FIVE YEARS AGO, BUT...
BUT?
ON A SURFACE OF ANXIETY AS FAR AS THE EYE CAN SEE...
...MY WEAK HEART TREMBLES FOR YOU.
...IT WOULD MAKE ME SEEM PATHETIC, SO IT'S A SECRET.
SHAKUYA...
CAN I KISS YOU?
SWISH
EH?! WHY?!
BY NO MEANS!!
CAN I HUG YOU?
NO WAY!
FORGET ABOUT IT!!
THEN
LET ME...

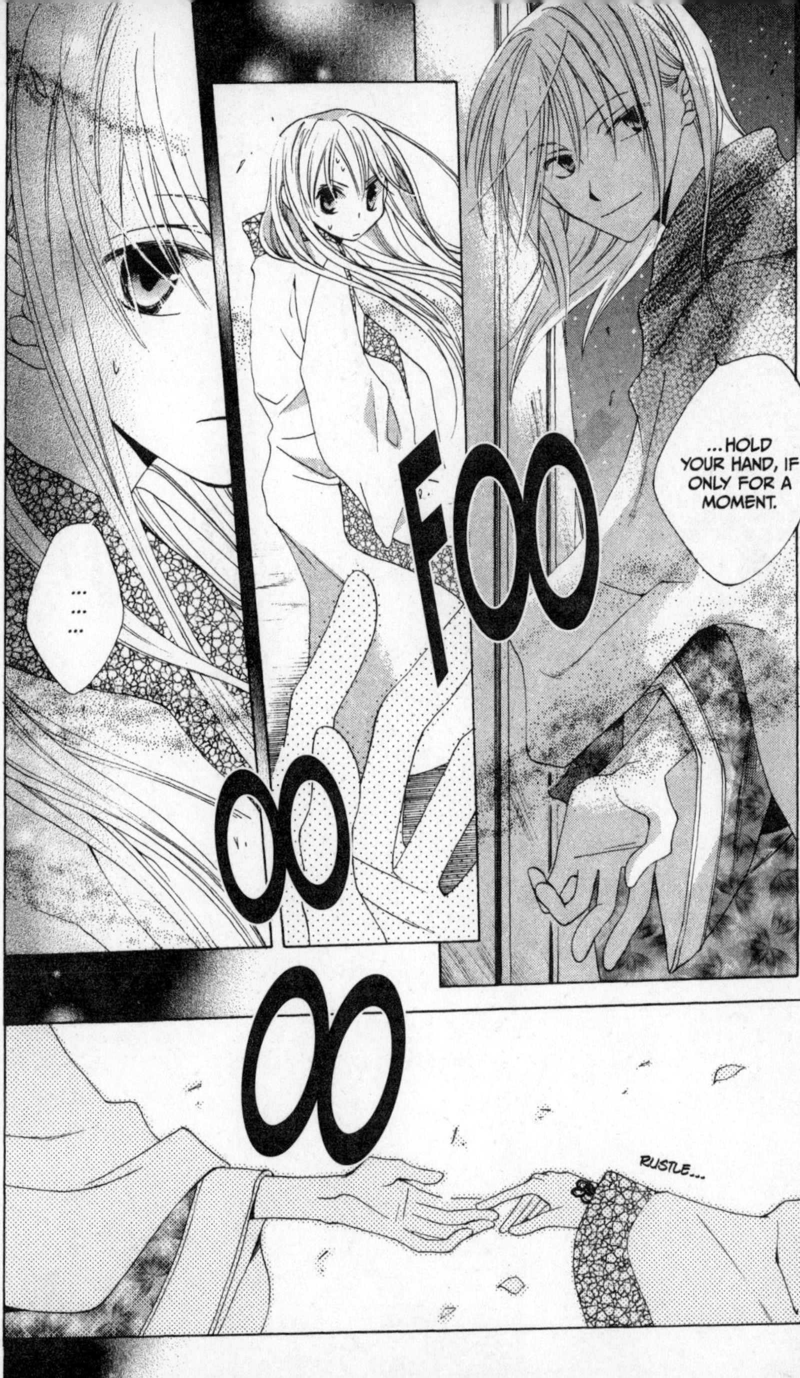
...HOLD YOUR HAND, IF ONLY FOR A MOMENT.
FOO
OO
OO
...
...
...
RUSTLE...

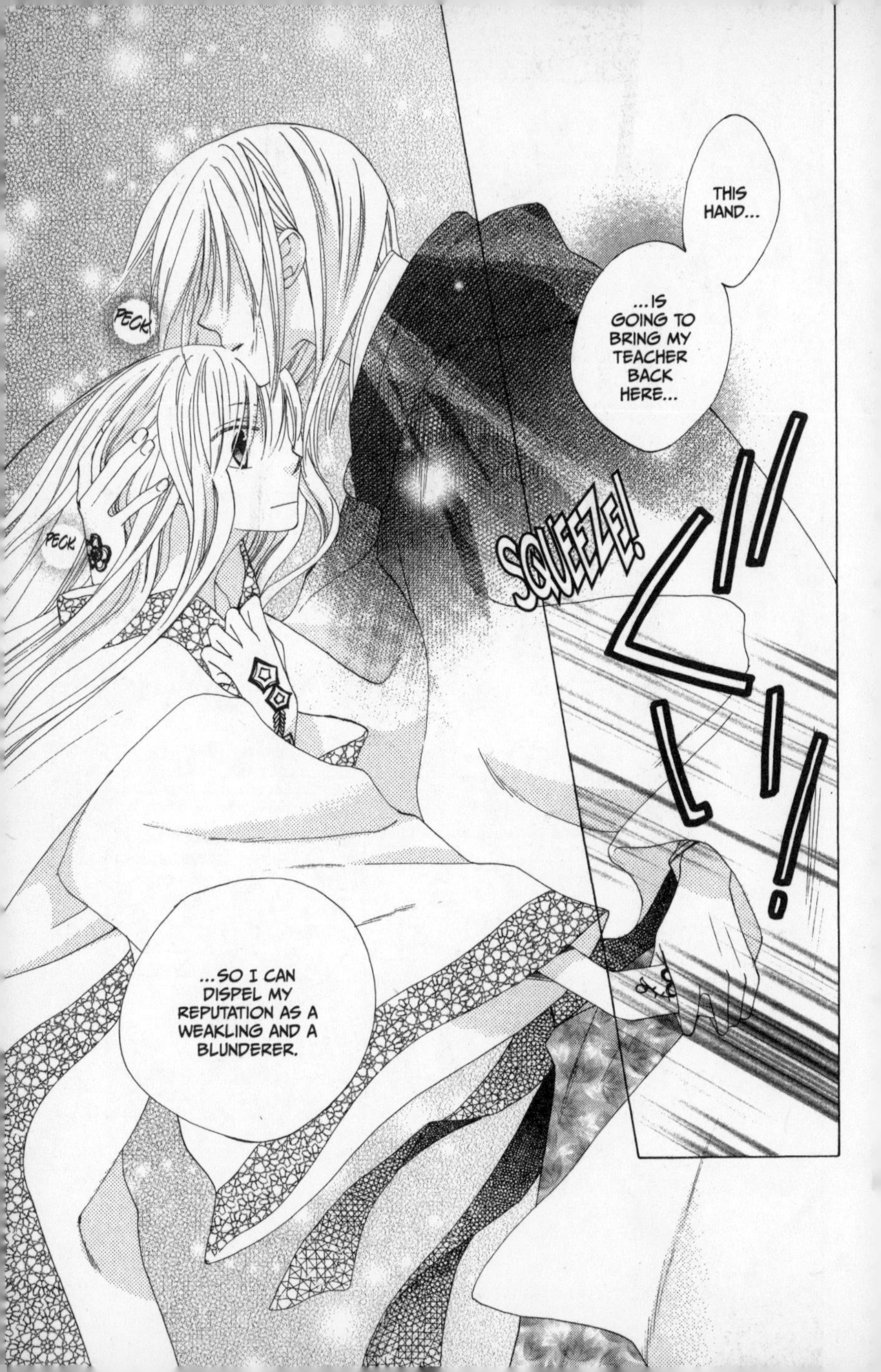
THIS HAND...
...IS GOING TO BRING MY TEACHER BACK HERE...
SQUEEZE!
PECK
PECK
...SO I CAN DISPEL MY REPUTATION AS A WEAKLING AND A BLUNDERER.

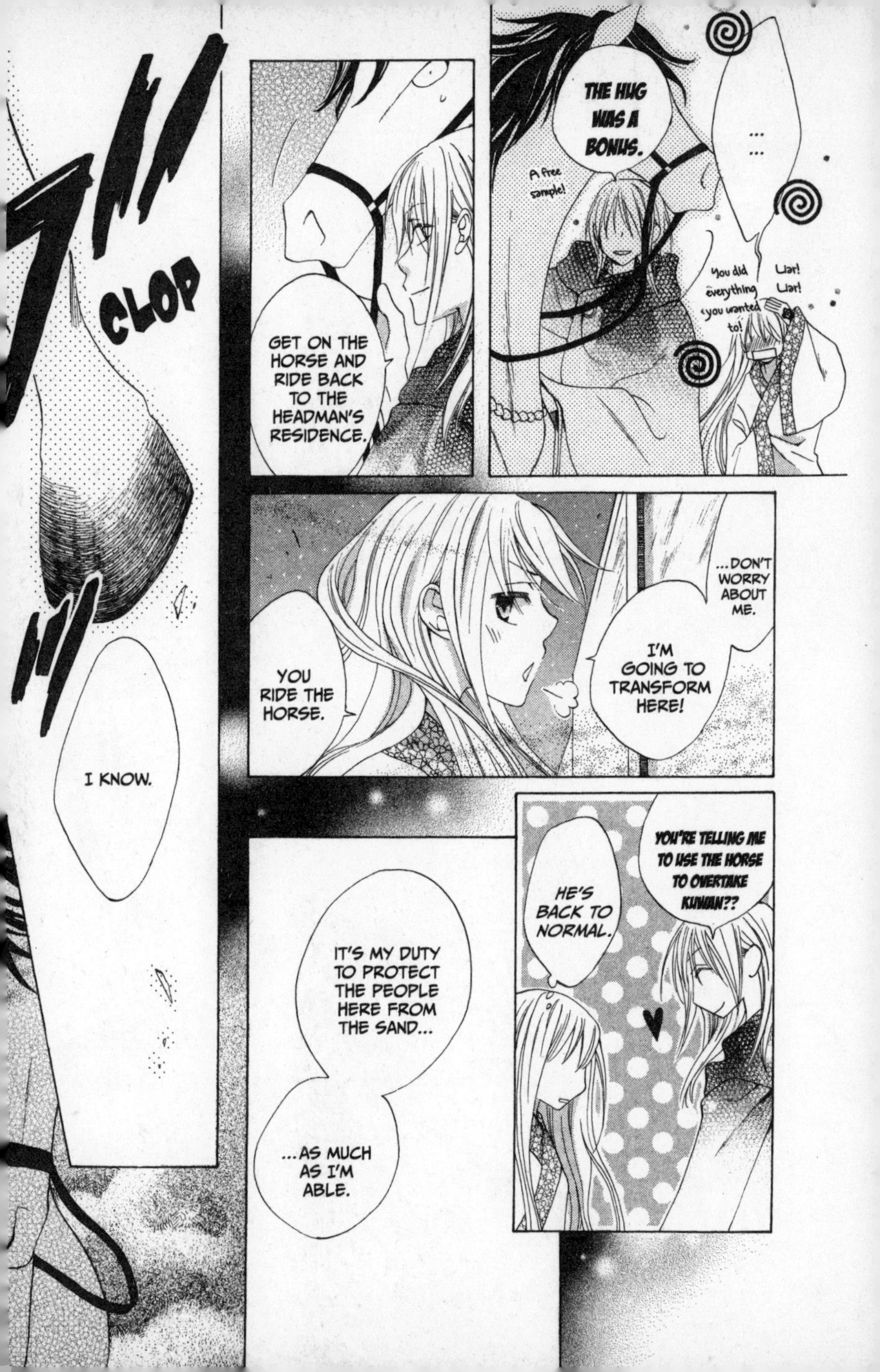
THE HUG WAS A BONUS.
A free sample!
...
...
Liar! Liar!
You did everything you wanted to!
GET ON THE HORSE AND RIDE BACK TO THE HEADMAN'S RESIDENCE.
...DON'T WORRY ABOUT ME.
I'M GOING TO TRANSFORM HERE!
YOU RIDE THE HORSE.
YOU'RE TELLING ME TO USE THE HORSE TO OVERTAKE KUWAN??
HE'S BACK TO NORMAL.
IT'S MY DUTY TO PROTECT THE PEOPLE HERE FROM THE SAND...
...AS MUCH AS I'M ABLE.
CLOP
I KNOW.

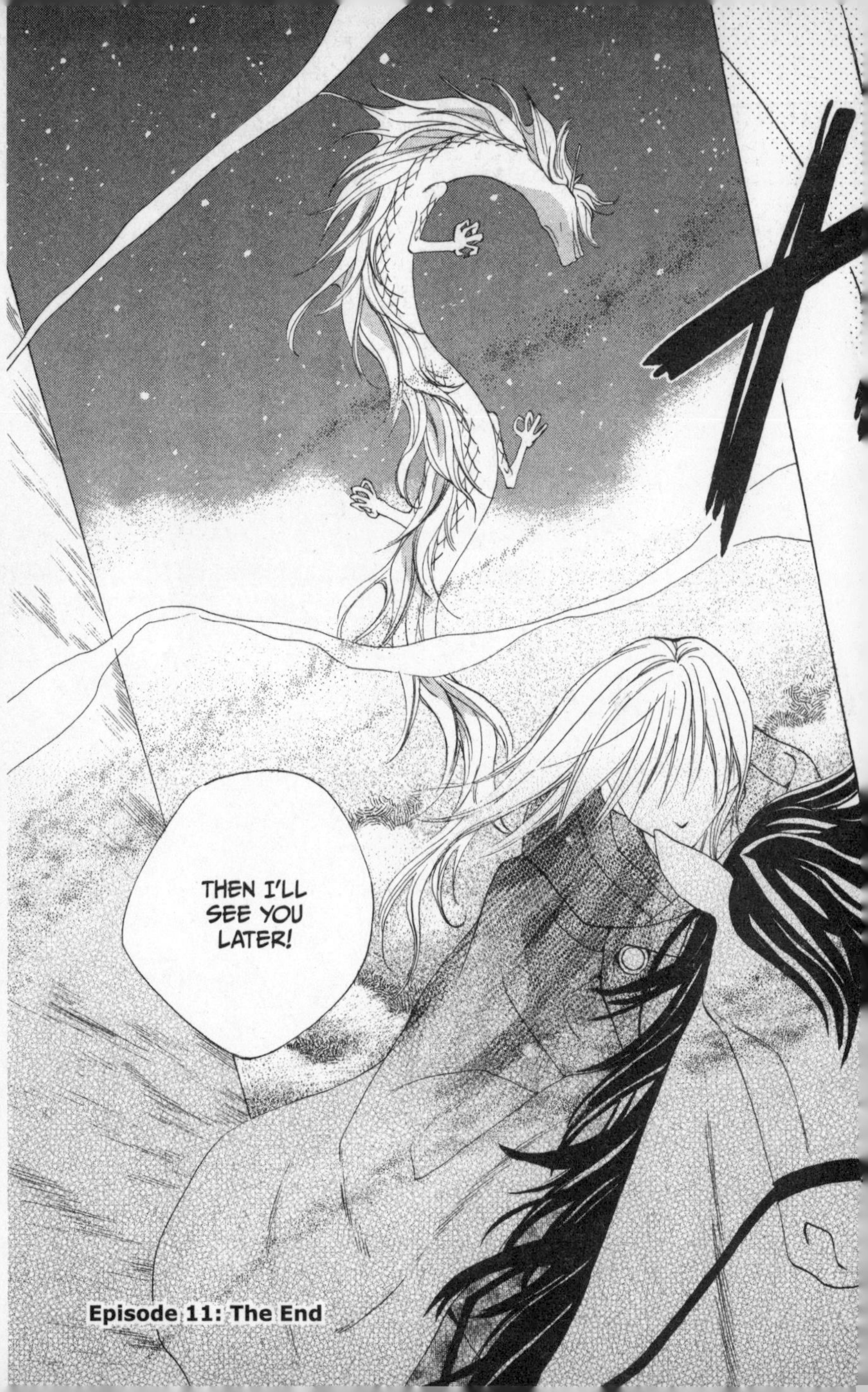
THEN I'LL SEE YOU LATER!
Episode 11: The End

Episode 12 Preview Cut

This didn't turn out that cute, especially the tiger ears and tail.

Episode 13 Preview Cut

Yes, I left his pants open.

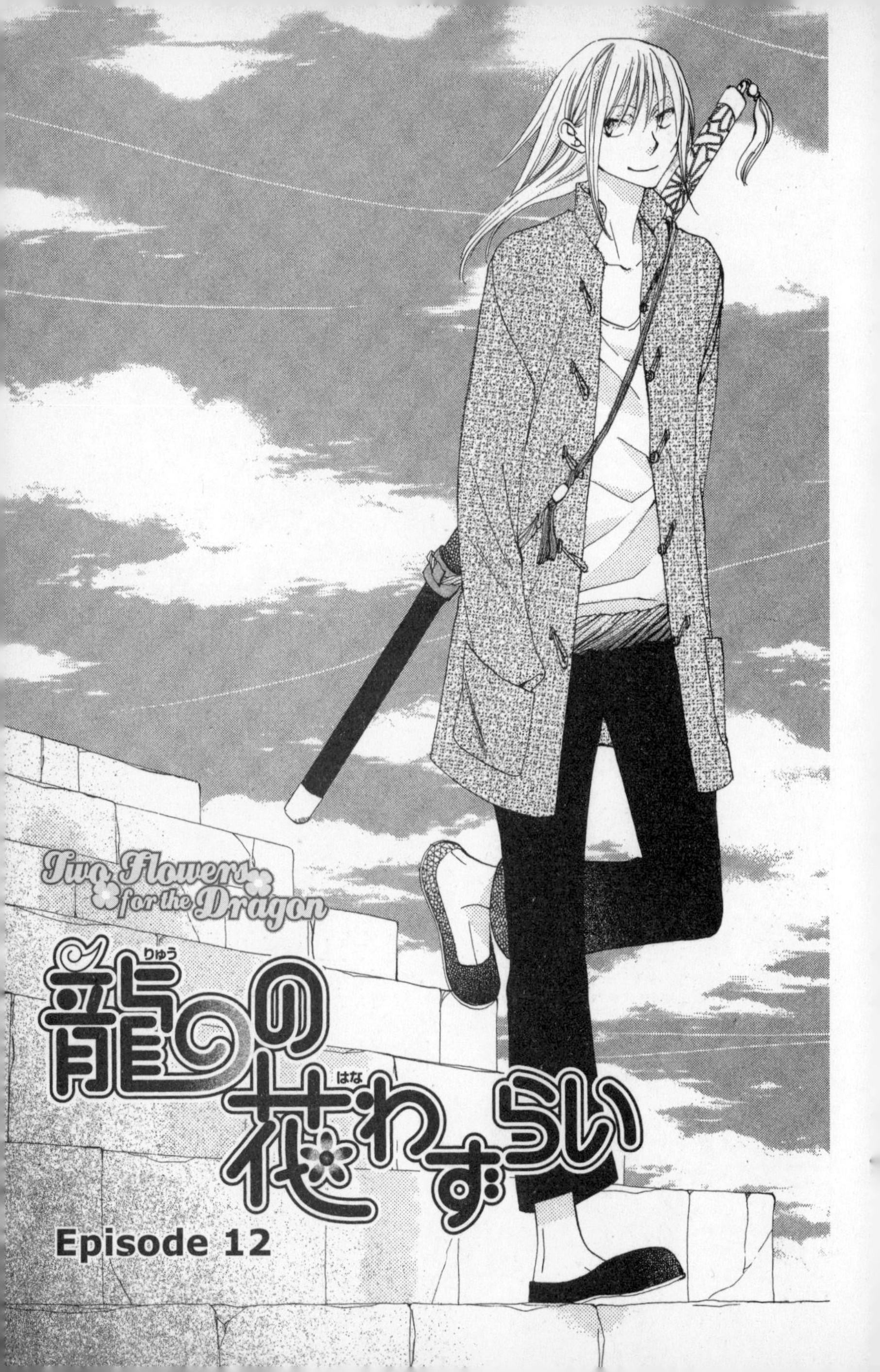
Two Flowers for the Dragon
龍(りゅう)の花(はな)わずらい
Episode 12

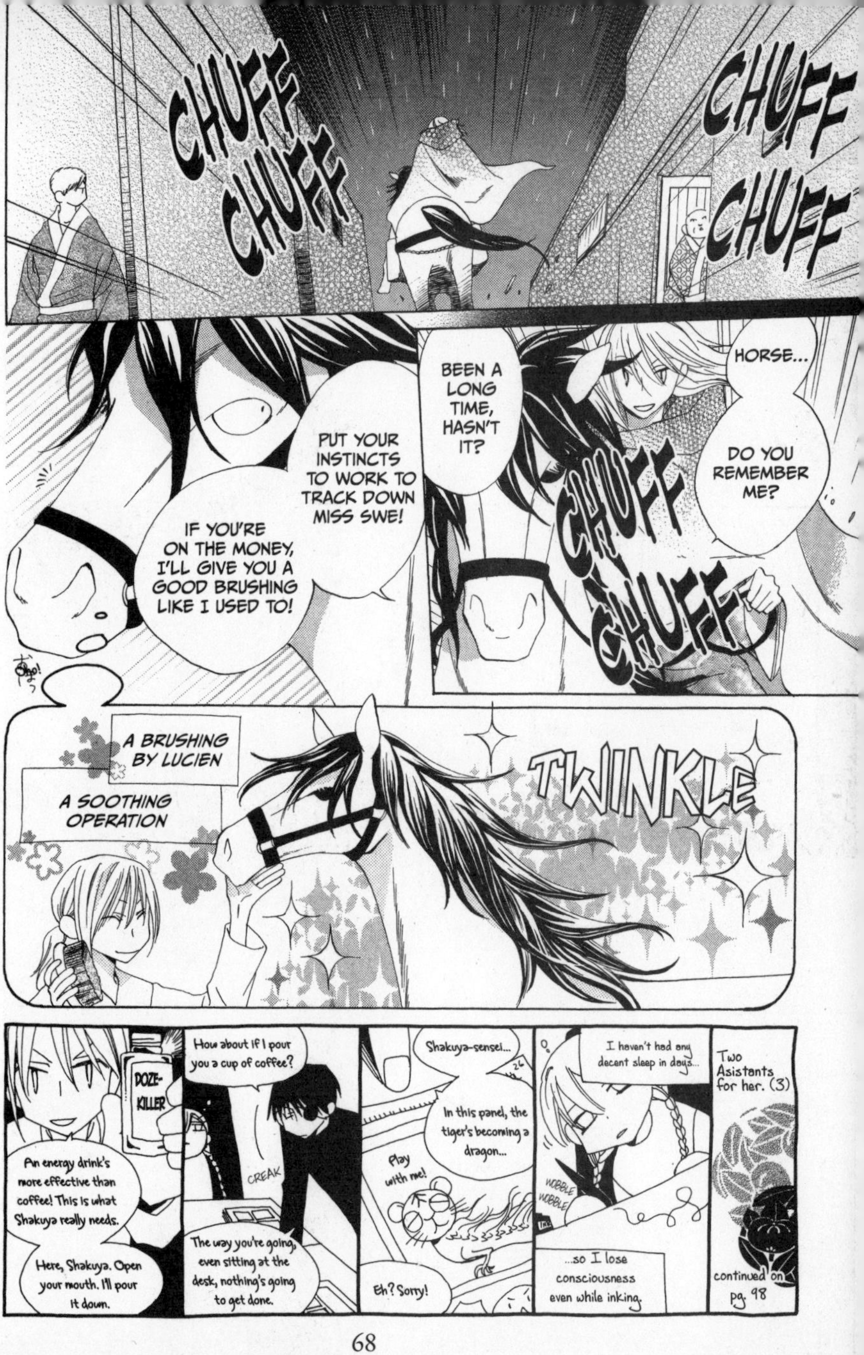
CHUFF CHUFF
CHUFF CHUFF
HORSE...
DO YOU REMEMBER ME?
BEEN A LONG TIME, HASN'T IT?
CHUFF CHUFF
PUT YOUR INSTINCTS TO WORK TO TRACK DOWN MISS SWE!
IF YOU'RE ON THE MONEY, I'LL GIVE YOU A GOOD BRUSHING LIKE I USED TO!
TWINKLE
A BRUSHING BY LUCIEN
A SOOTHING OPERATION
Two Asistants for her. (3)
continued on pg. 98
I haven't had any decent sleep in days...
WOBBLE WOBBLE
...so I lose consciousness even while inking.
Shakuya-sensei...
In this panel, the tiger's becoming a dragon...
Play with me!
Eh? Sorry!
How about if I pour you a cup of coffee?
CREAK
The way you're going, even sitting at the desk, nothing's going to get done.
DOZE-KILLER
An energy drink's more effective than coffee! This is what Shakuya really needs.
Here, Shakuya. Open your mouth. I'll pour it down.

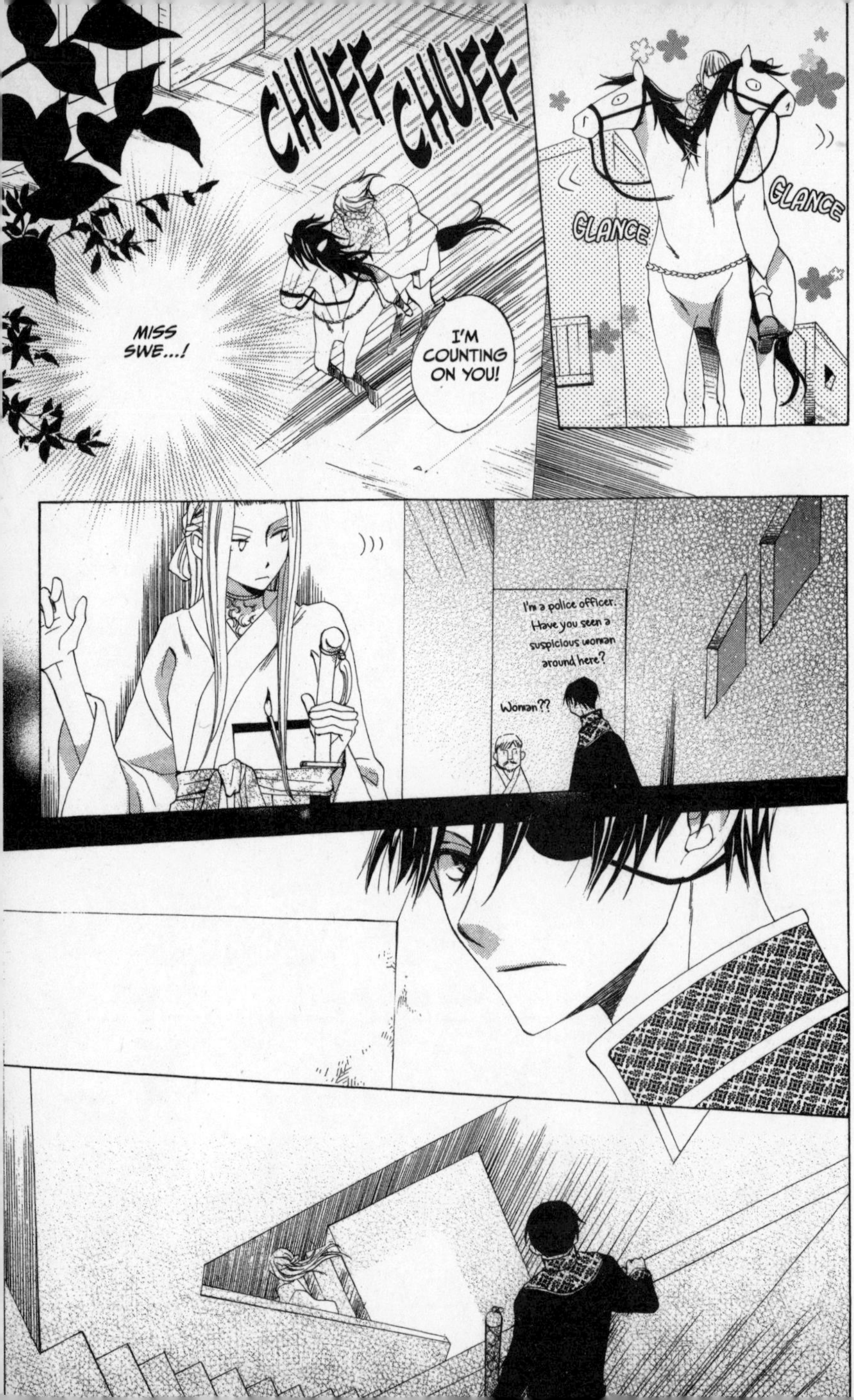
GLANCE
GLANCE
CHUFF CHUFF
I'M COUNTING ON YOU!
MISS SWE...!
I'm a police officer. Have you seen a suspicious woman around here?
Woman??

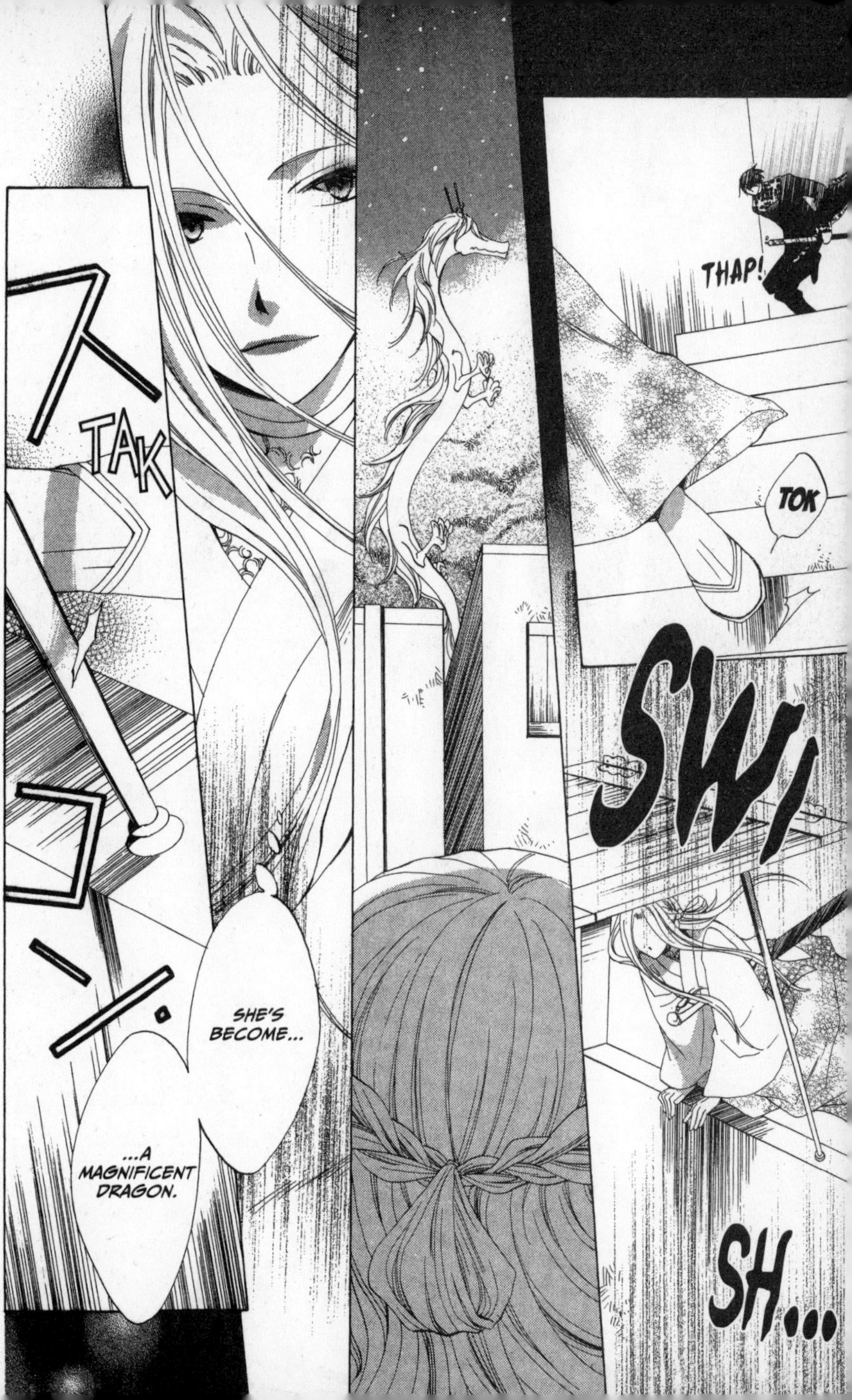
THAP!
TOK
SWI
SH...
TAK
SHE'S BECOME...
...A MAGNIFICENT DRAGON.

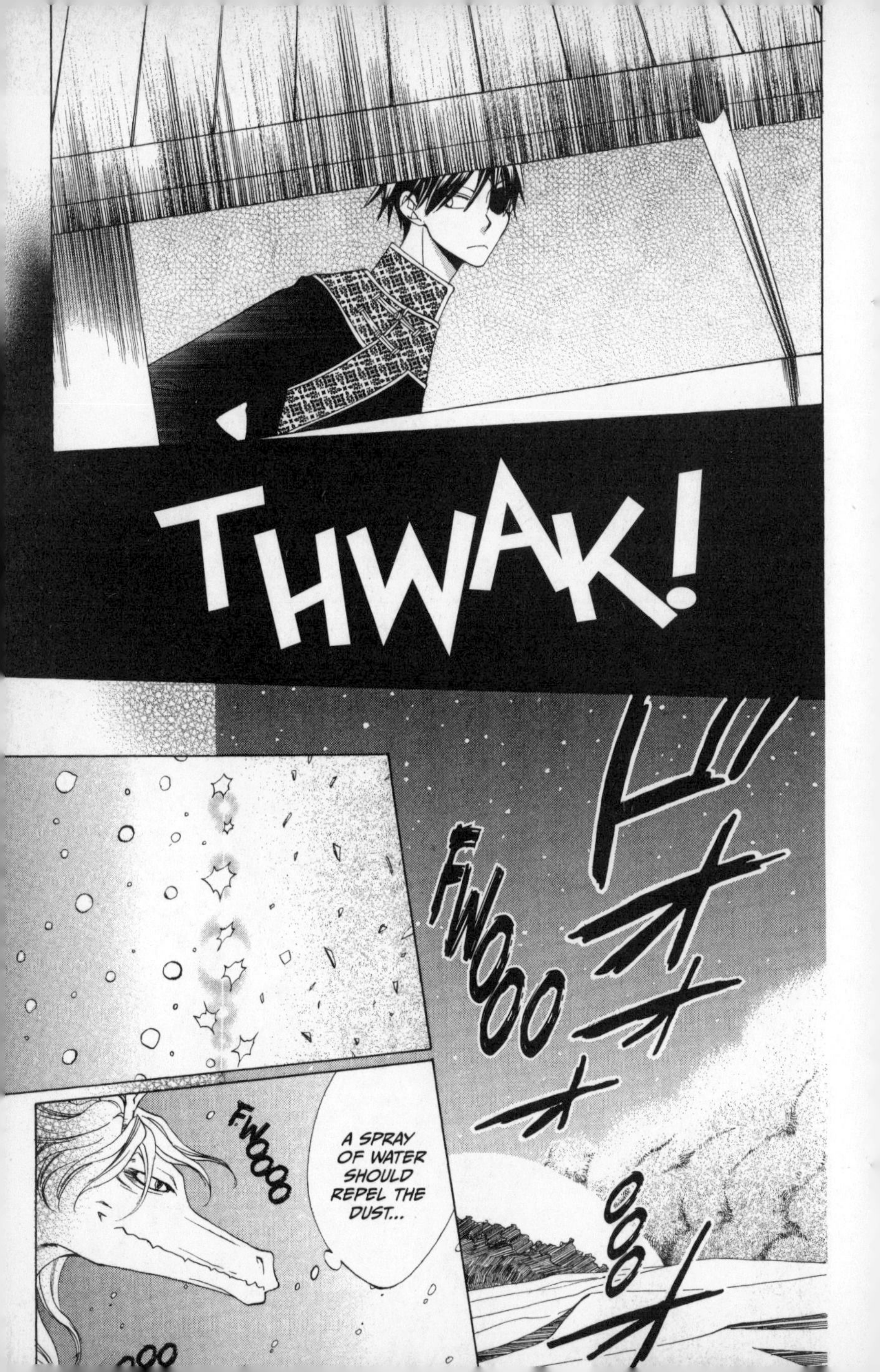
THWAK!
FWOOOO
FWOOOO
A SPRAY OF WATER SHOULD REPEL THE DUST...

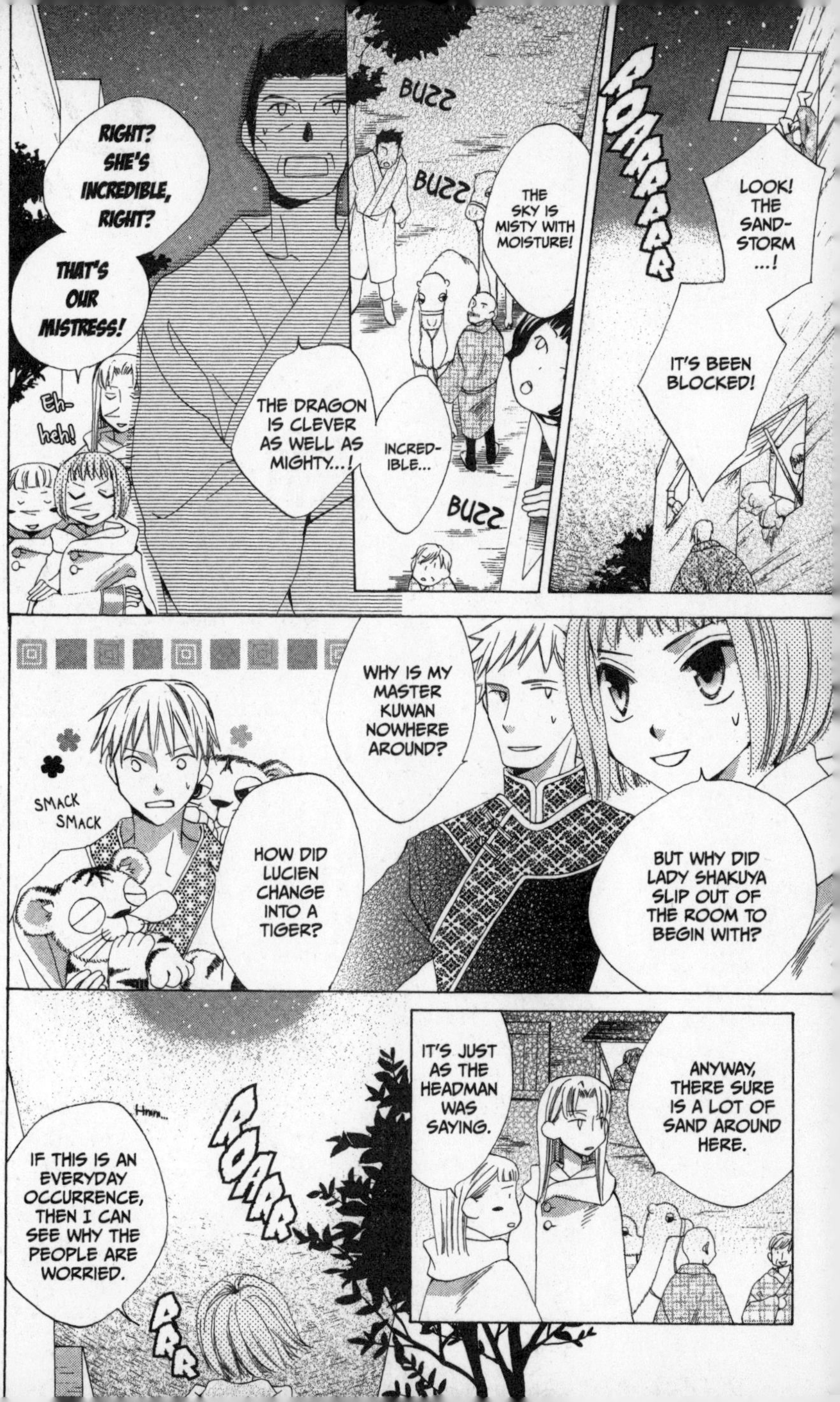
ROARRRAR
LOOK! THE SANDSTORM ...!
IT'S BEEN BLOCKED!
BUZZ
BUZZ
THE SKY IS MISTY WITH MOISTURE!
BUZZ
INCREDIBLE...
THE DRAGON IS CLEVER AS WELL AS MIGHTY...!
RIGHT? SHE'S INCREDIBLE, RIGHT?
THAT'S OUR MISTRESS!
Eh-heh!
BUT WHY DID LADY SHAKUYA SLIP OUT OF THE ROOM TO BEGIN WITH?
WHY IS MY MASTER KUWAN NOWHERE AROUND?
HOW DID LUCIEN CHANGE INTO A TIGER?
SMACK SMACK
ANYWAY, THERE SURE IS A LOT OF SAND AROUND HERE.
IT'S JUST AS THE HEADMAN WAS SAYING.
ROARR
Hmm...
IF THIS IS AN EVERYDAY OCCURRENCE, THEN I CAN SEE WHY THE PEOPLE ARE WORRIED.
ARR

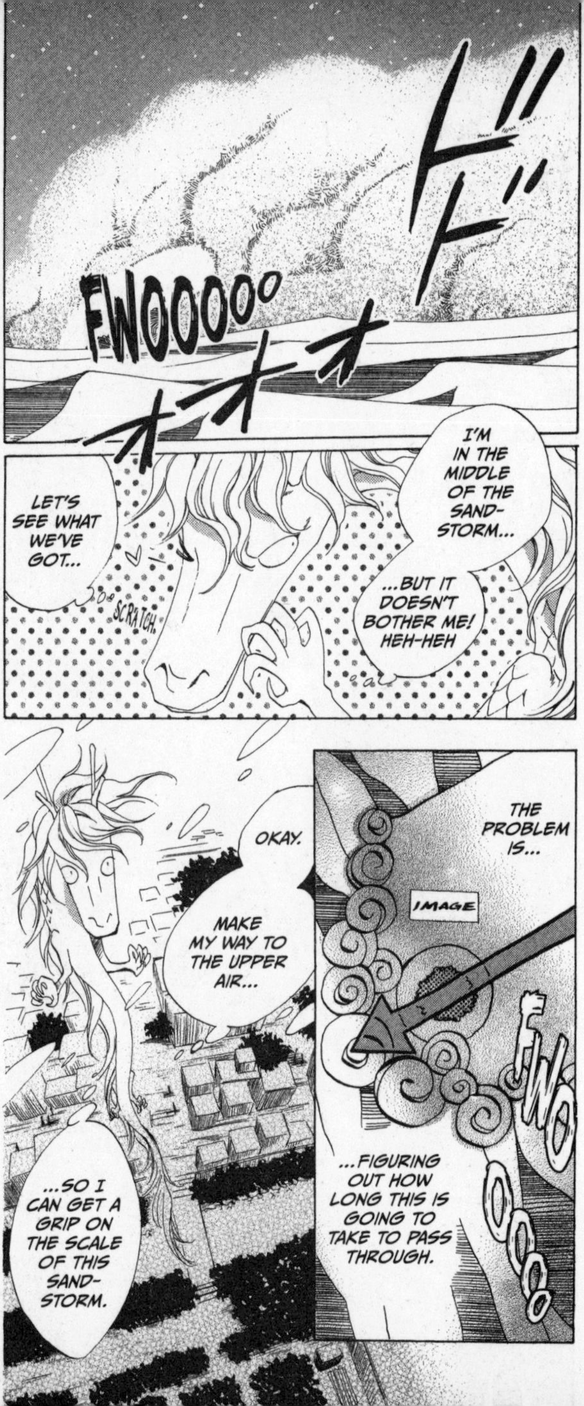
FWOOOOO
I'M IN THE MIDDLE OF THE SAND-STORM...
...BUT IT DOESN'T BOTHER ME! HEH-HEH
LET'S SEE WHAT WE'VE GOT...
SCRATCH.
THE PROBLEM IS...
IMAGE
FWOOOOO
...FIGURING OUT HOW LONG THIS IS GOING TO TAKE TO PASS THROUGH.
OKAY.
MAKE MY WAY TO THE UPPER AIR...
...SO I CAN GET A GRIP ON THE SCALE OF THIS SAND-STORM.

3

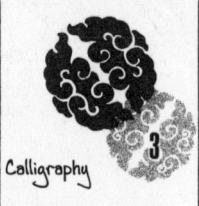

Calligraphy

I used to study it as a kid.

The inkstone that I used for a long time had a black ink-stained, crusty surface that I thought gave me "calligraphy cred," so I used the entire stone, even to its edges, to give it even more of a "used" quality. And I didn't hate doing the actual writing either.

At some point, I received a paperweight that was modeled on an abacus (and now I think, "Why an abacus?"). I painted it with ink and now it serves to hold the manuscript down.

A disappointing result when it comes to studying calligraphy, but forgive me!

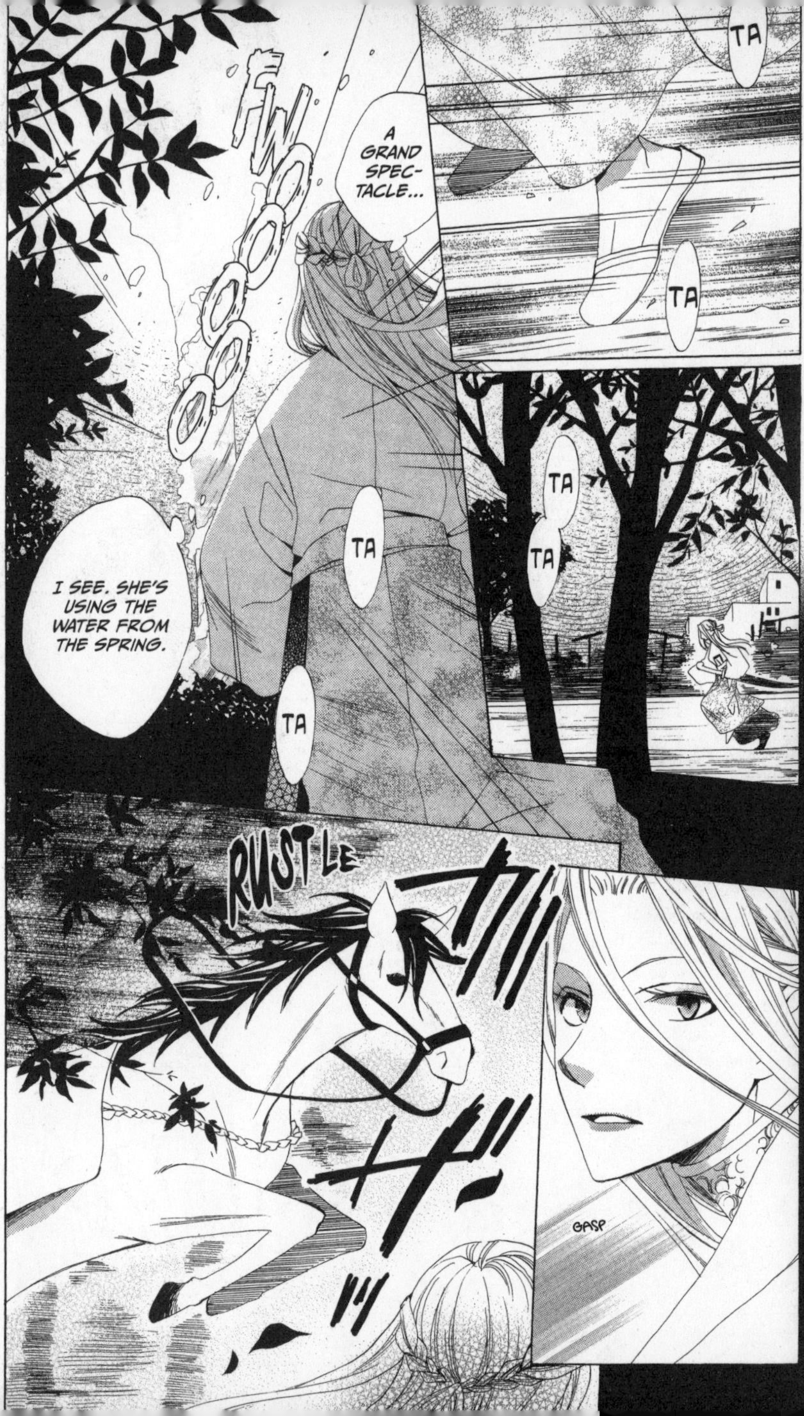
TA
TA
A GRAND SPEC-TACLE...
FWOOOOOO
TA
TA
TA
I SEE. SHE'S USING THE WATER FROM THE SPRING.
TA
RUSTLE
GASP

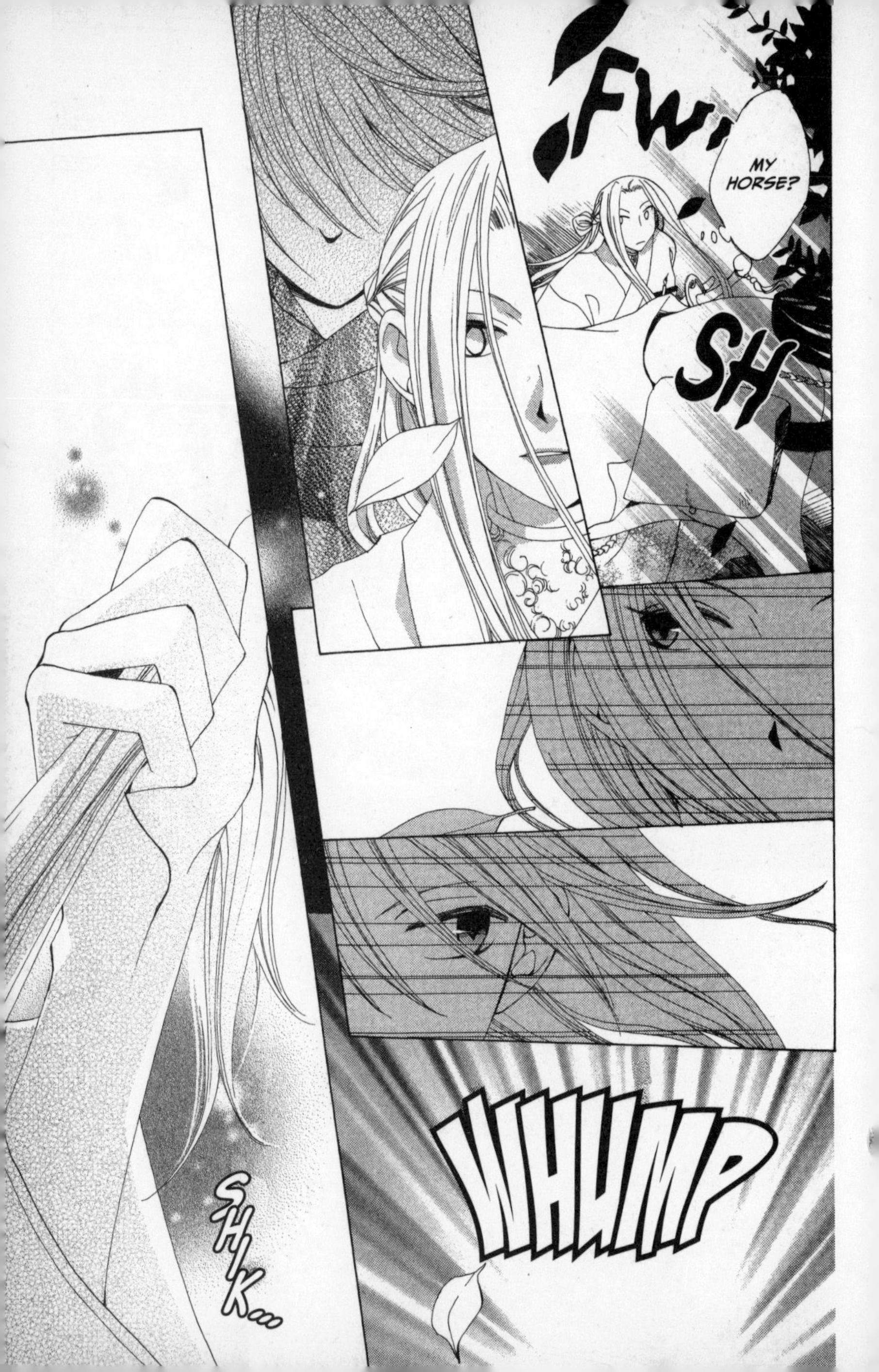
FWI
MY HORSE?
SH
WHUMP
SHHK...

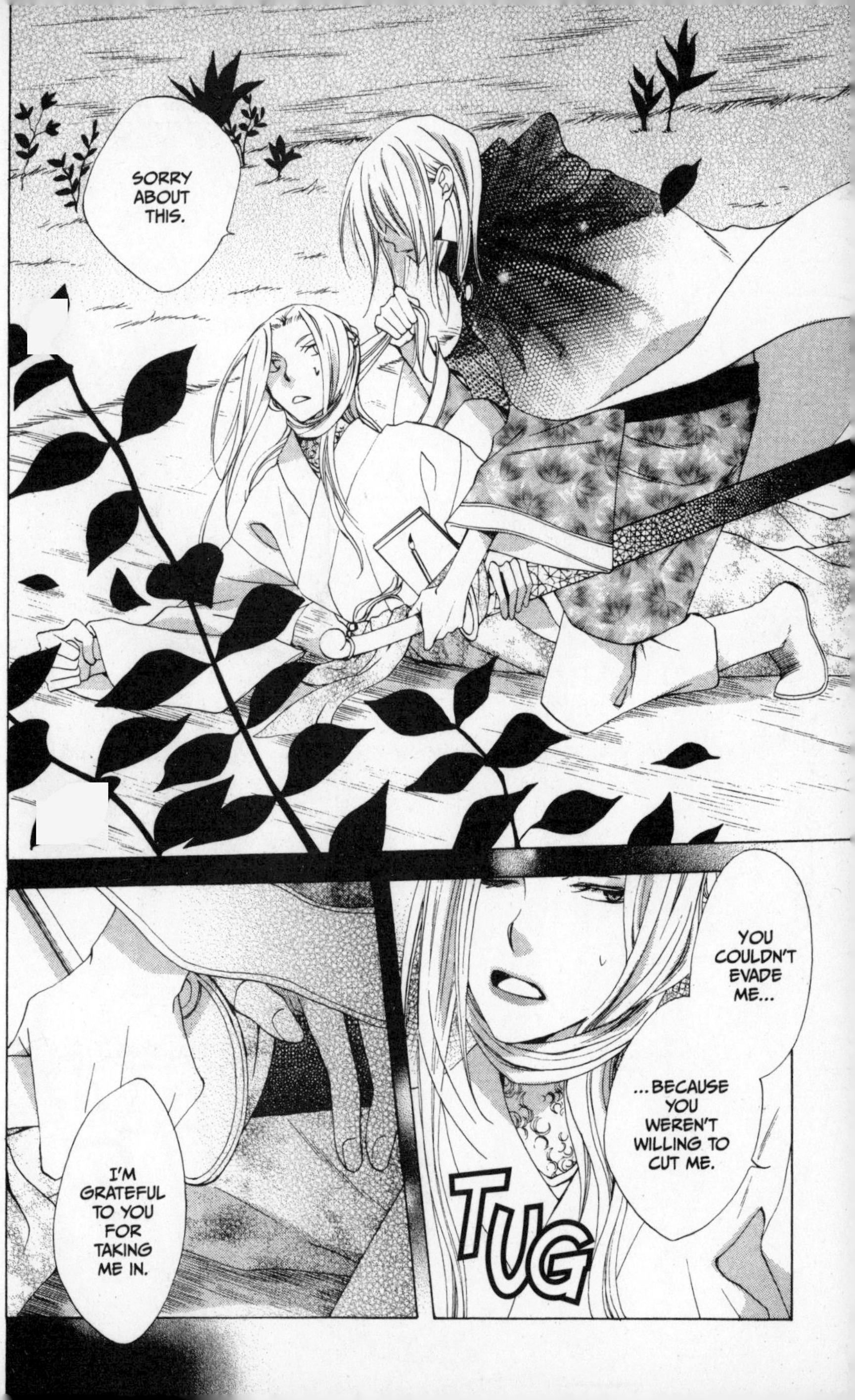
SORRY ABOUT THIS.
YOU COULDN'T EVADE ME...
...BECAUSE YOU WEREN'T WILLING TO CUT ME.
TUG
I'M GRATEFUL TO YOU FOR TAKING ME IN.

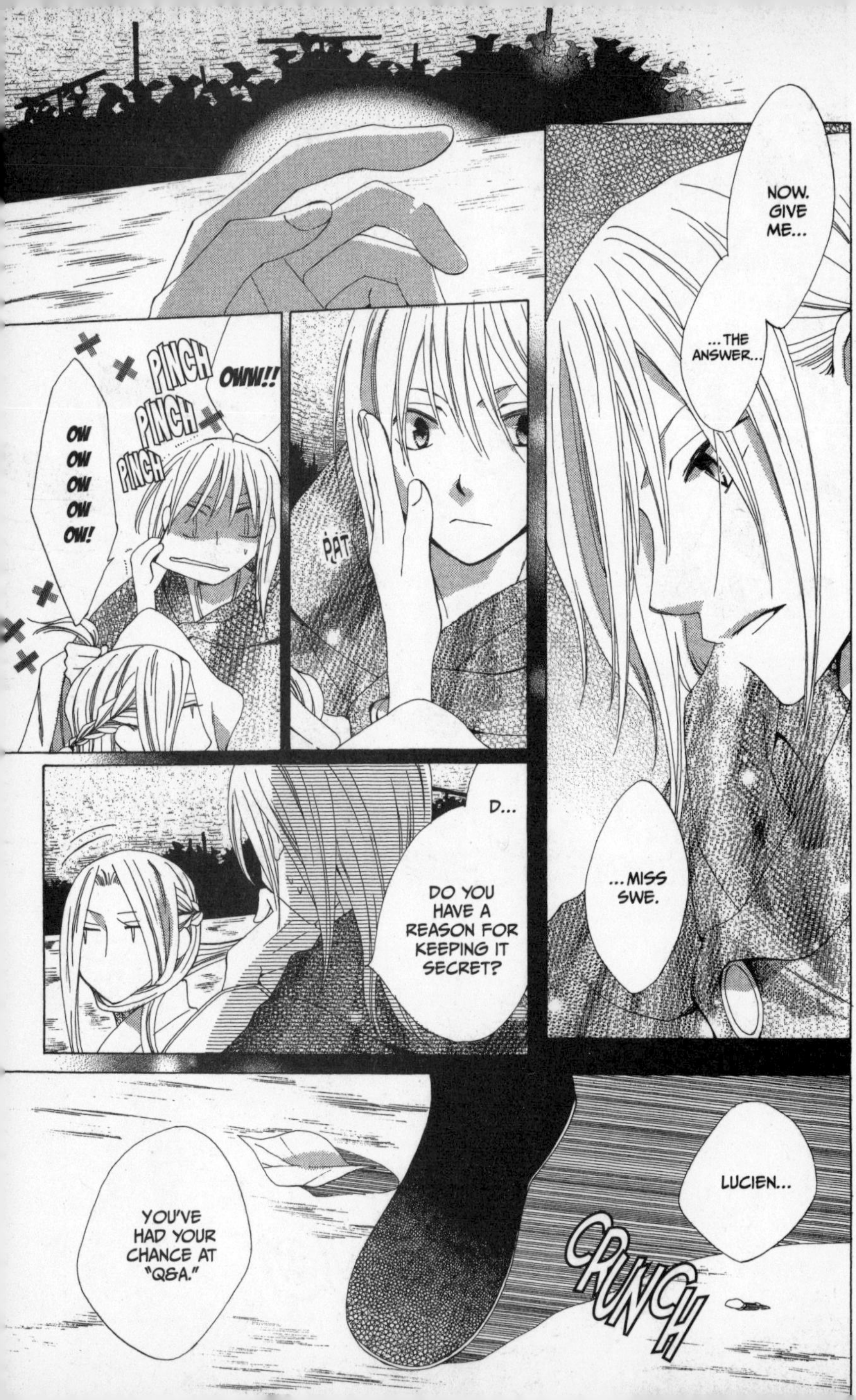
NOW. GIVE ME...
...THE ANSWER...
...MISS SWE.
PAT
OW OW OW OW OW!
PINCH PINCH PINCH
OWW!!
D...
DO YOU HAVE A REASON FOR KEEPING IT SECRET?
LUCIEN...
CRUNCH
YOU'VE HAD YOUR CHANCE AT "Q&A."

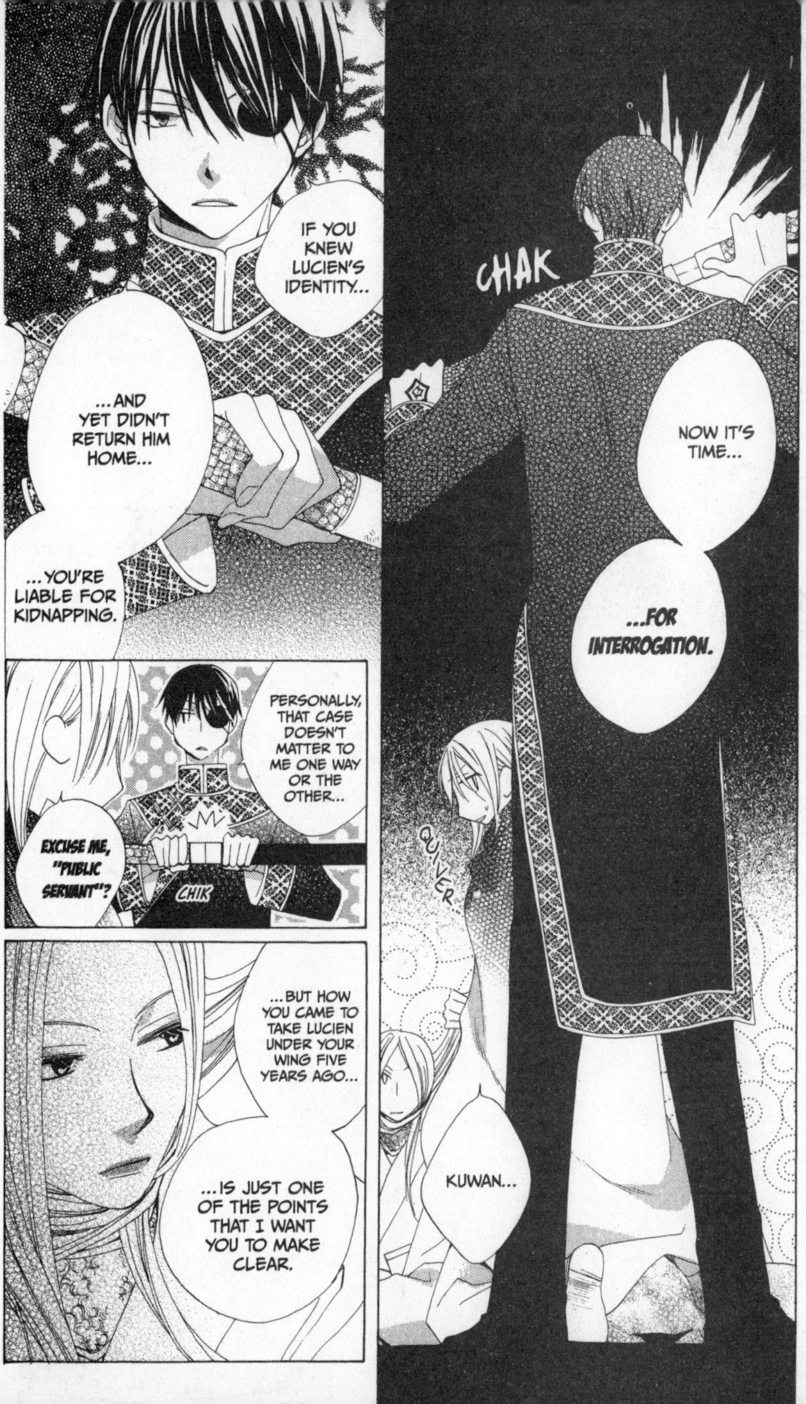
CHAK
NOW IT'S TIME...
...FOR INTERROGATION.
QUIVER
KUWAN...
IF YOU KNEW LUCIEN'S IDENTITY...
...AND YET DIDN'T RETURN HIM HOME...
...YOU'RE LIABLE FOR KIDNAPPING.
PERSONALLY, THAT CASE DOESN'T MATTER TO ME ONE WAY OR THE OTHER...
EXCUSE ME, "PUBLIC SERVANT"?
CHIK
...BUT HOW YOU CAME TO TAKE LUCIEN UNDER YOUR WING FIVE YEARS AGO...
...IS JUST ONE OF THE POINTS THAT I WANT YOU TO MAKE CLEAR.

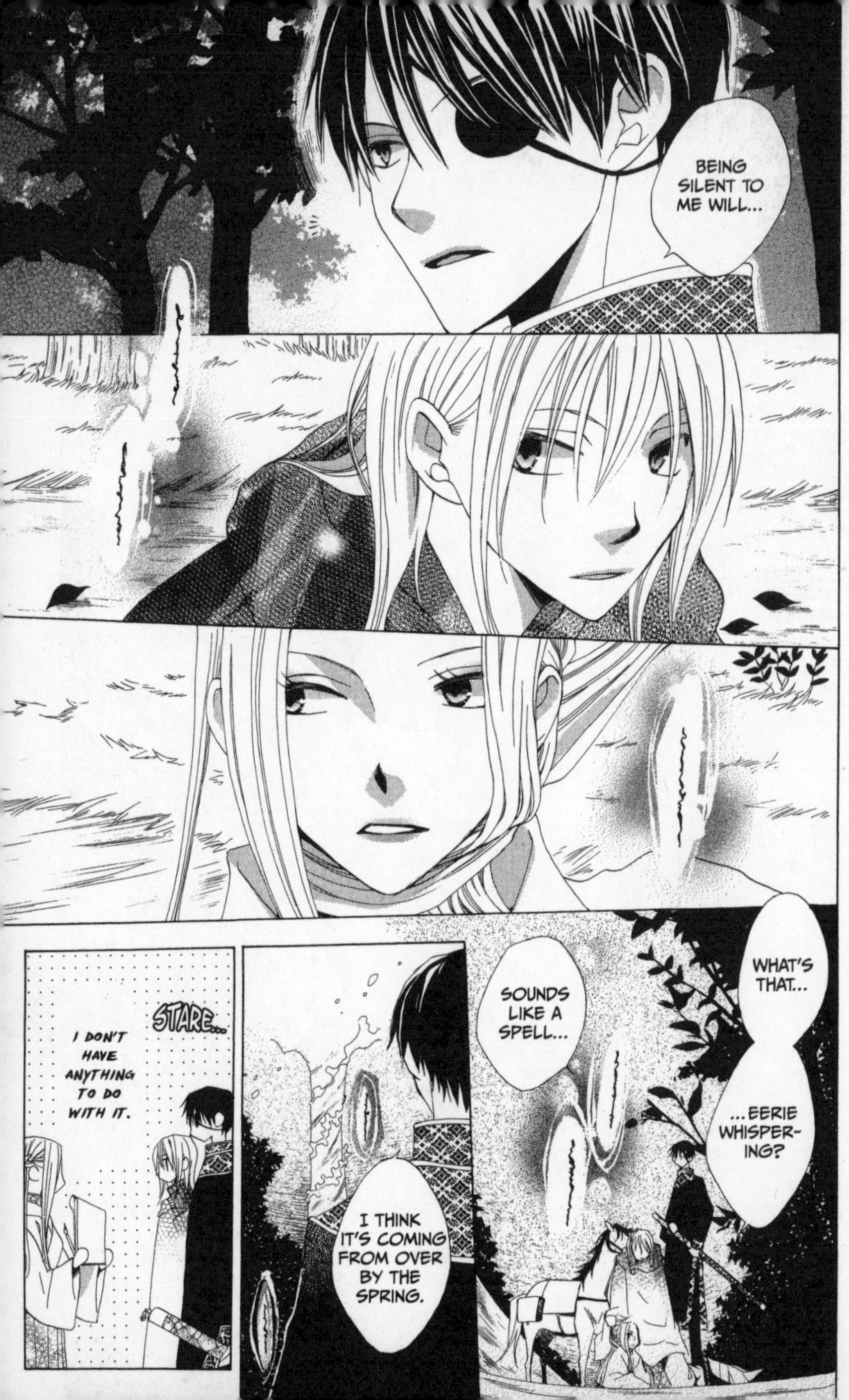
BEING SILENT TO ME WILL...
WHAT'S THAT...
...EERIE WHISPERING?
SOUNDS LIKE A SPELL...
I THINK IT'S COMING FROM OVER BY THE SPRING.
STARE...
I DON'T HAVE ANYTHING TO DO WITH IT.

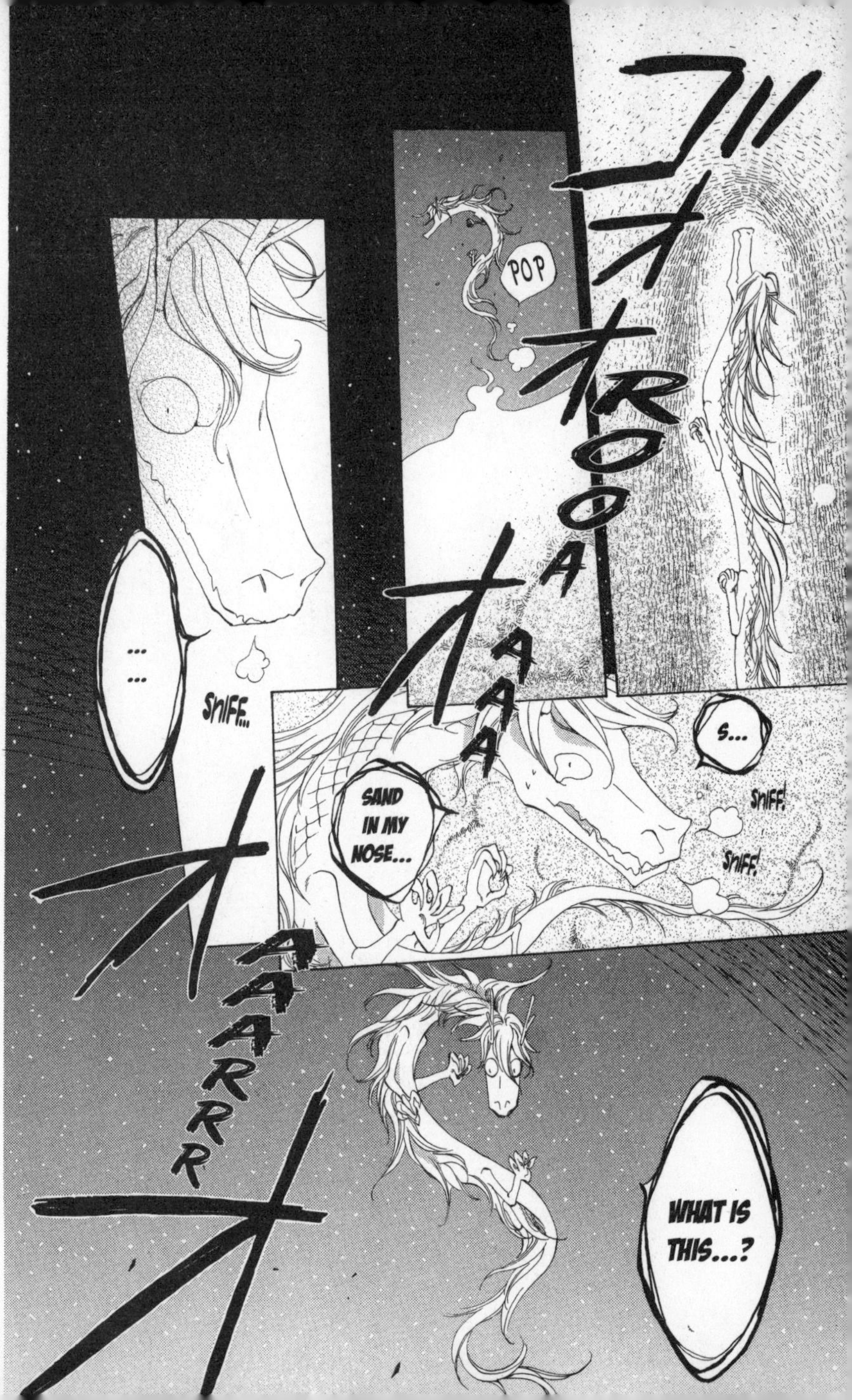
ブオROOAAAA
POP
......
SNIFF...
S...
SNIFF!
SNIFF!
SAND IN MY NOSE...
オAAARRRRオ
WHAT IS THIS...?

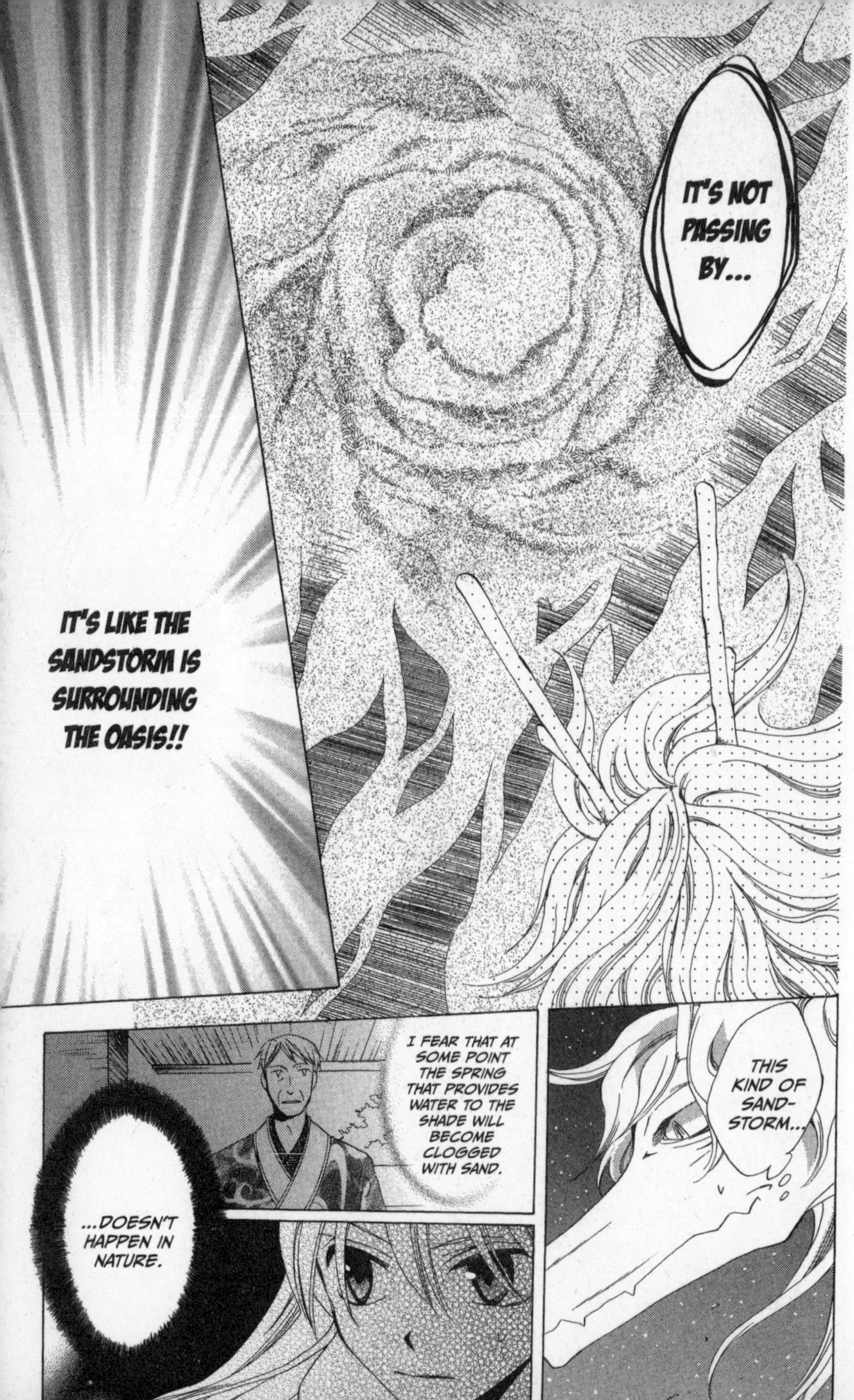
IT'S NOT PASSING BY...
IT'S LIKE THE SANDSTORM IS SURROUNDING THE OASIS!!
THIS KIND OF SAND-STORM...
I FEAR THAT AT SOME POINT THE SPRING THAT PROVIDES WATER TO THE SHADE WILL BECOME CLOGGED WITH SAND.
...DOESN'T HAPPEN IN NATURE.

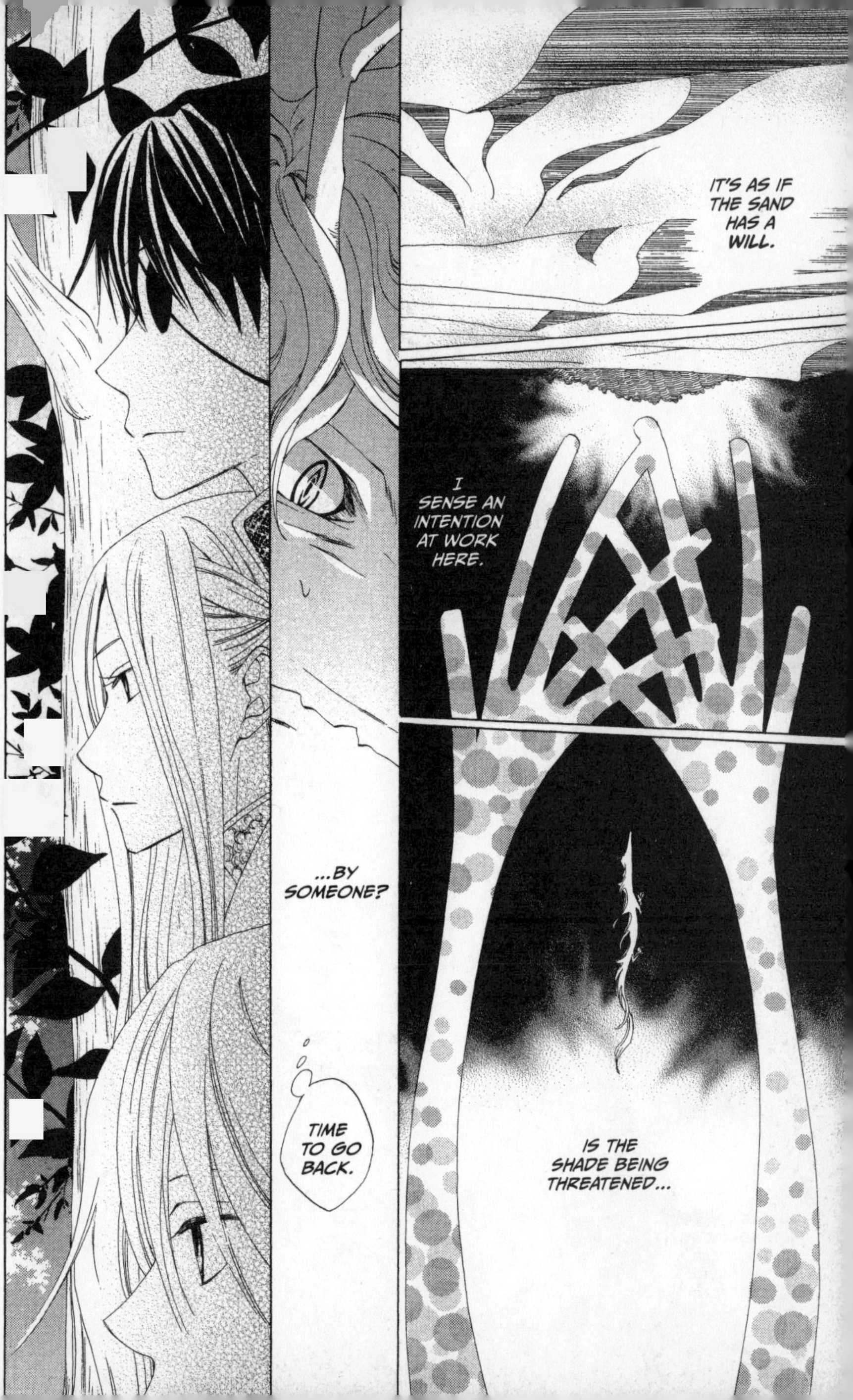
IT'S AS IF THE SAND HAS A WILL.
I SENSE AN INTENTION AT WORK HERE.
IS THE SHADE BEING THREATENED...
...BY SOMEONE?
TIME TO GO BACK.

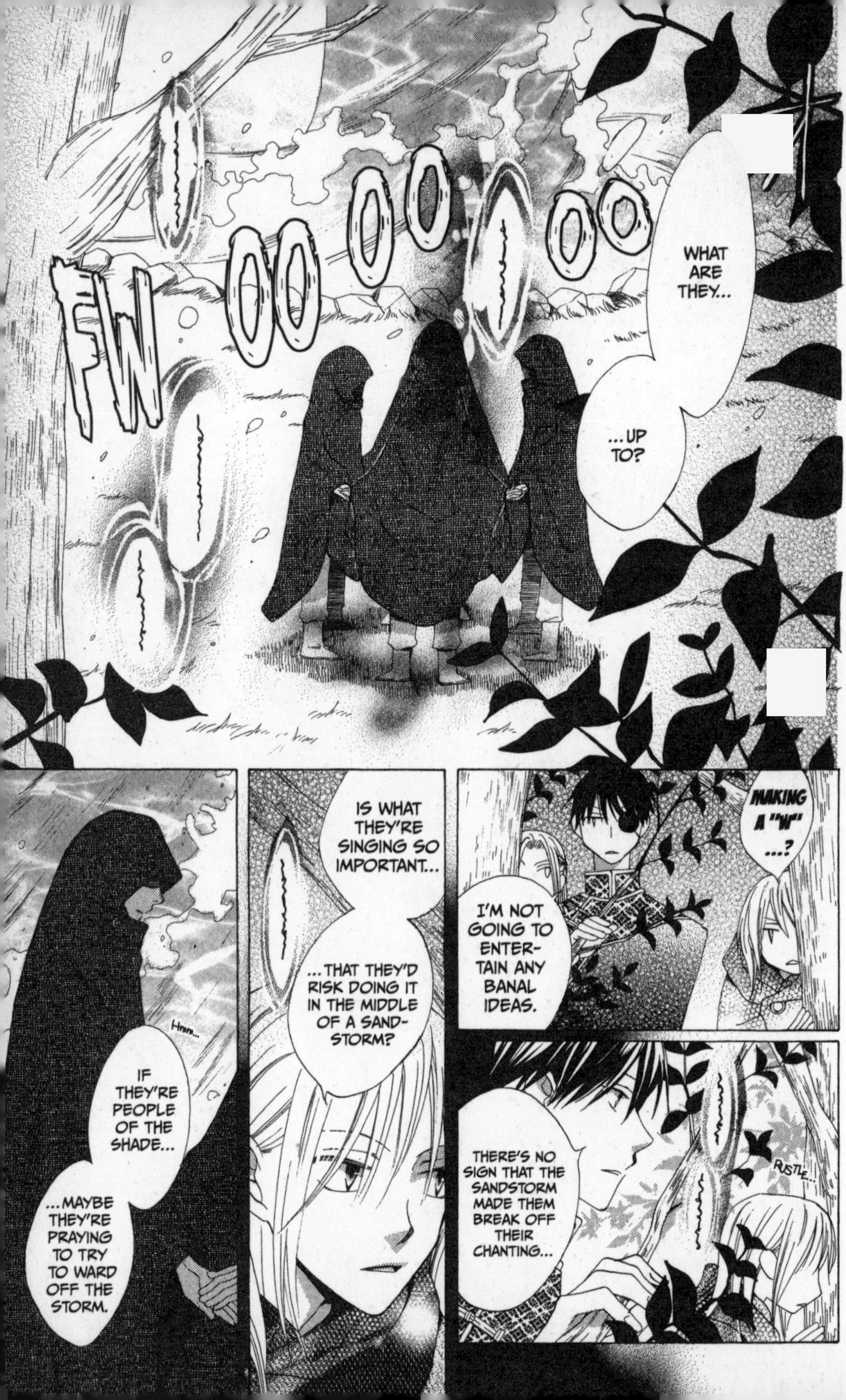
WHAT ARE THEY...
...UP TO?
FWOOOOOOO
MAKING A "W" ...?
I'M NOT GOING TO ENTERTAIN ANY BANAL IDEAS.
THERE'S NO SIGN THAT THE SANDSTORM MADE THEM BREAK OFF THEIR CHANTING...
RUSTLE...
IS WHAT THEY'RE SINGING SO IMPORTANT...
...THAT THEY'D RISK DOING IT IN THE MIDDLE OF A SANDSTORM?
Hmm...
IF THEY'RE PEOPLE OF THE SHADE...
...MAYBE THEY'RE PRAYING TO TRY TO WARD OFF THE STORM.

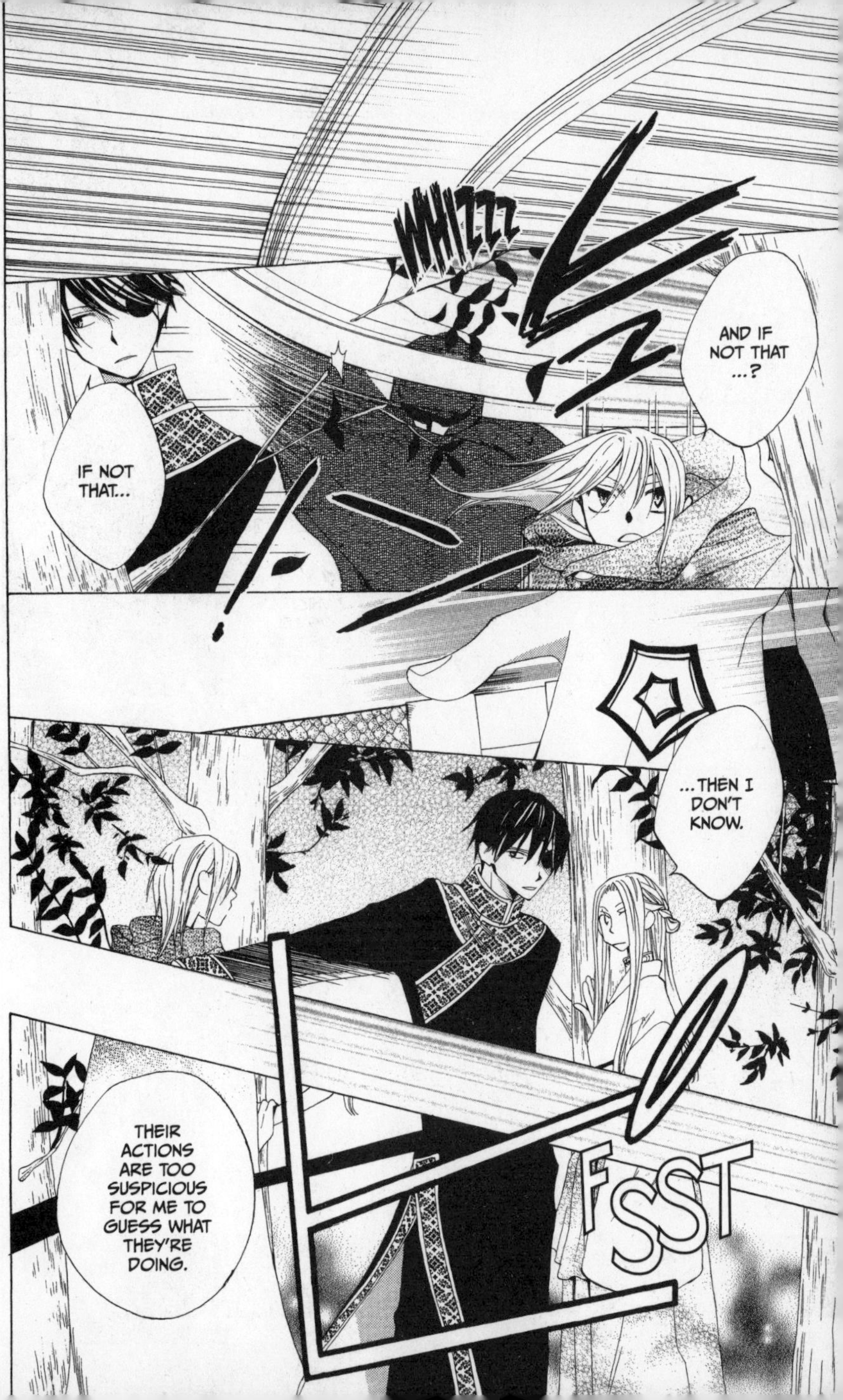
WHIZZZ
AND IF NOT THAT ...?
IF NOT THAT...
...THEN I DON'T KNOW.
FSST
THEIR ACTIONS ARE TOO SUSPICIOUS FOR ME TO GUESS WHAT THEY'RE DOING.

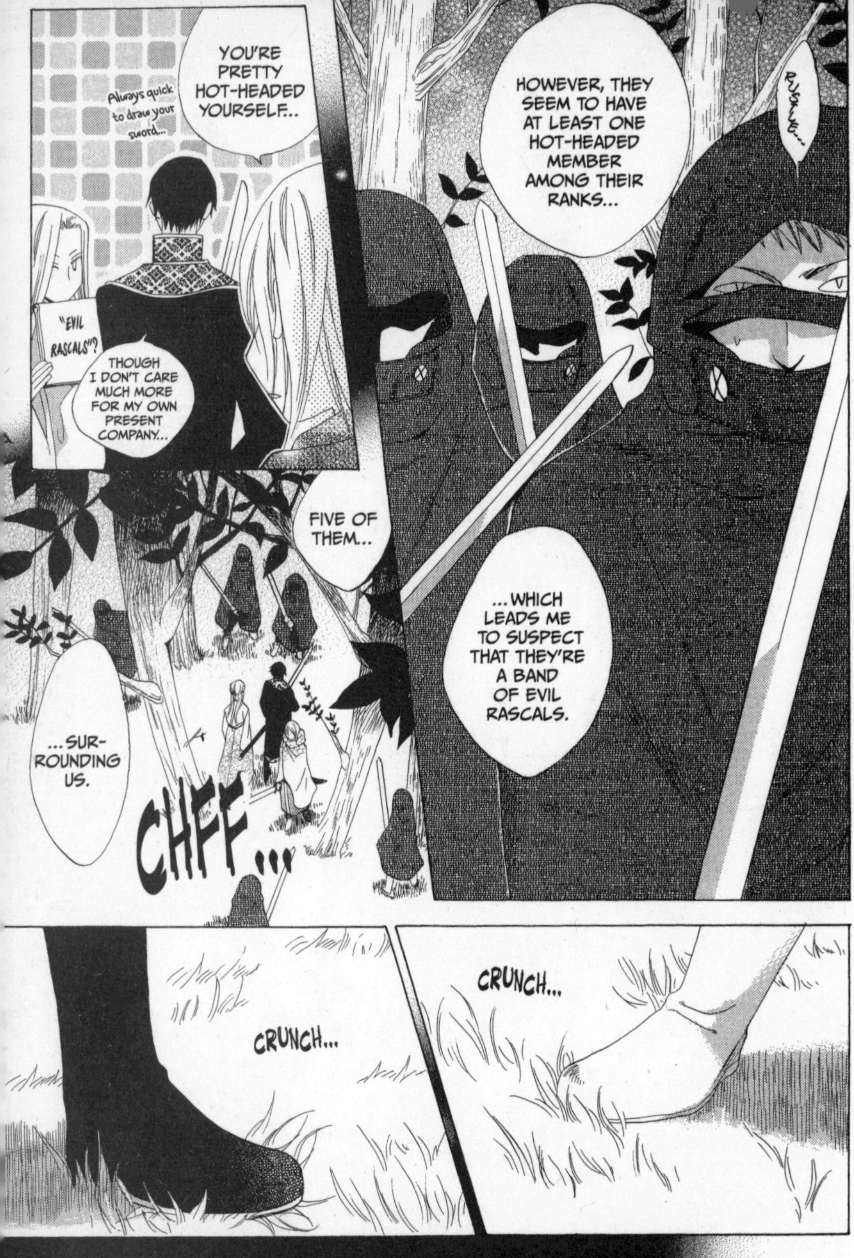
RUSTLE...
HOWEVER, THEY SEEM TO HAVE AT LEAST ONE HOT-HEADED MEMBER AMONG THEIR RANKS...
...WHICH LEADS ME TO SUSPECT THAT THEY'RE A BAND OF EVIL RASCALS.
YOU'RE PRETTY HOT-HEADED YOURSELF...
Always quick to draw your sword...
"EVIL RASCALS"?
THOUGH I DON'T CARE MUCH MORE FOR MY OWN PRESENT COMPANY...
FIVE OF THEM...
...SUR-ROUNDING US.
CHFF...
CRUNCH...
CRUNCH...

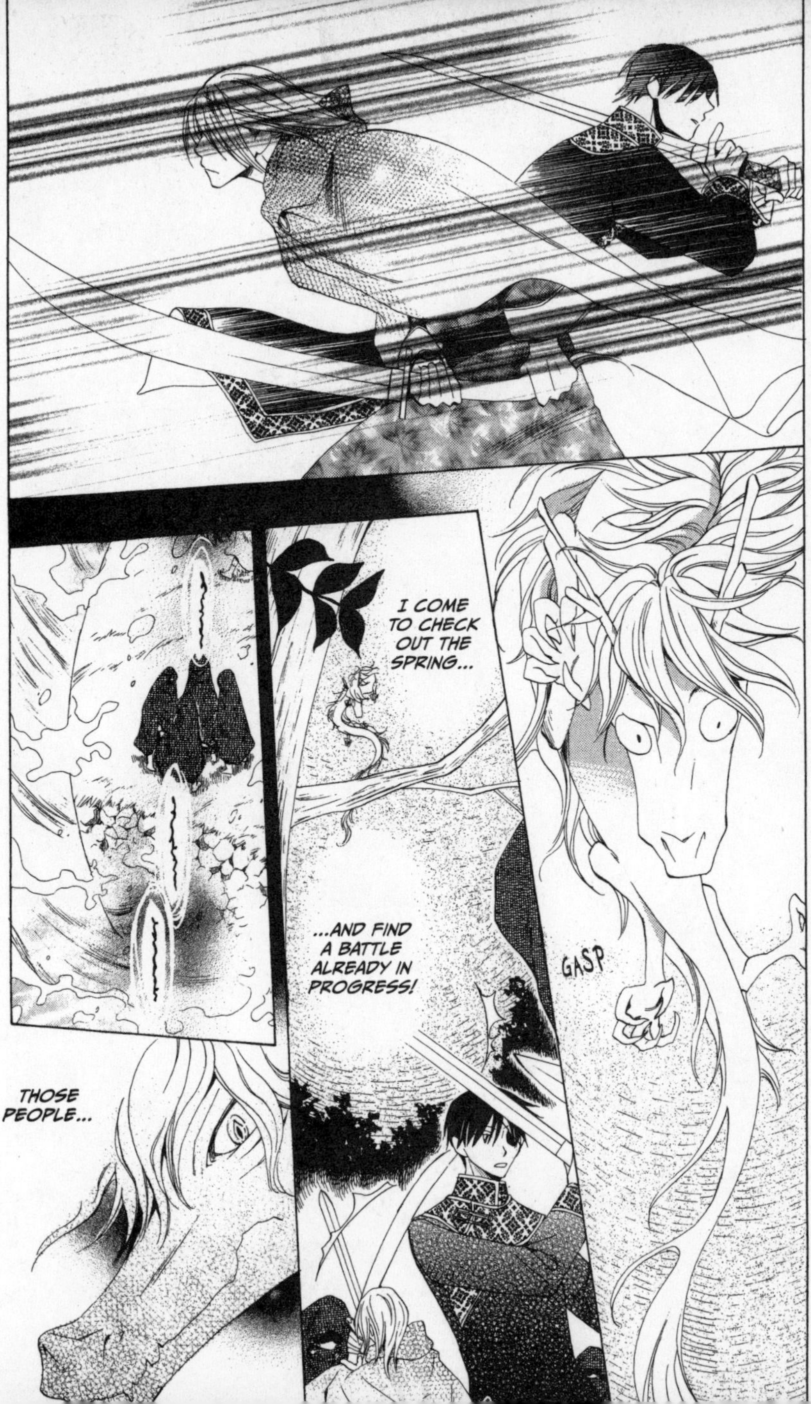
GASP
I COME TO CHECK OUT THE SPRING...
...AND FIND A BATTLE ALREADY IN PROGRESS!
THOSE PEOPLE...

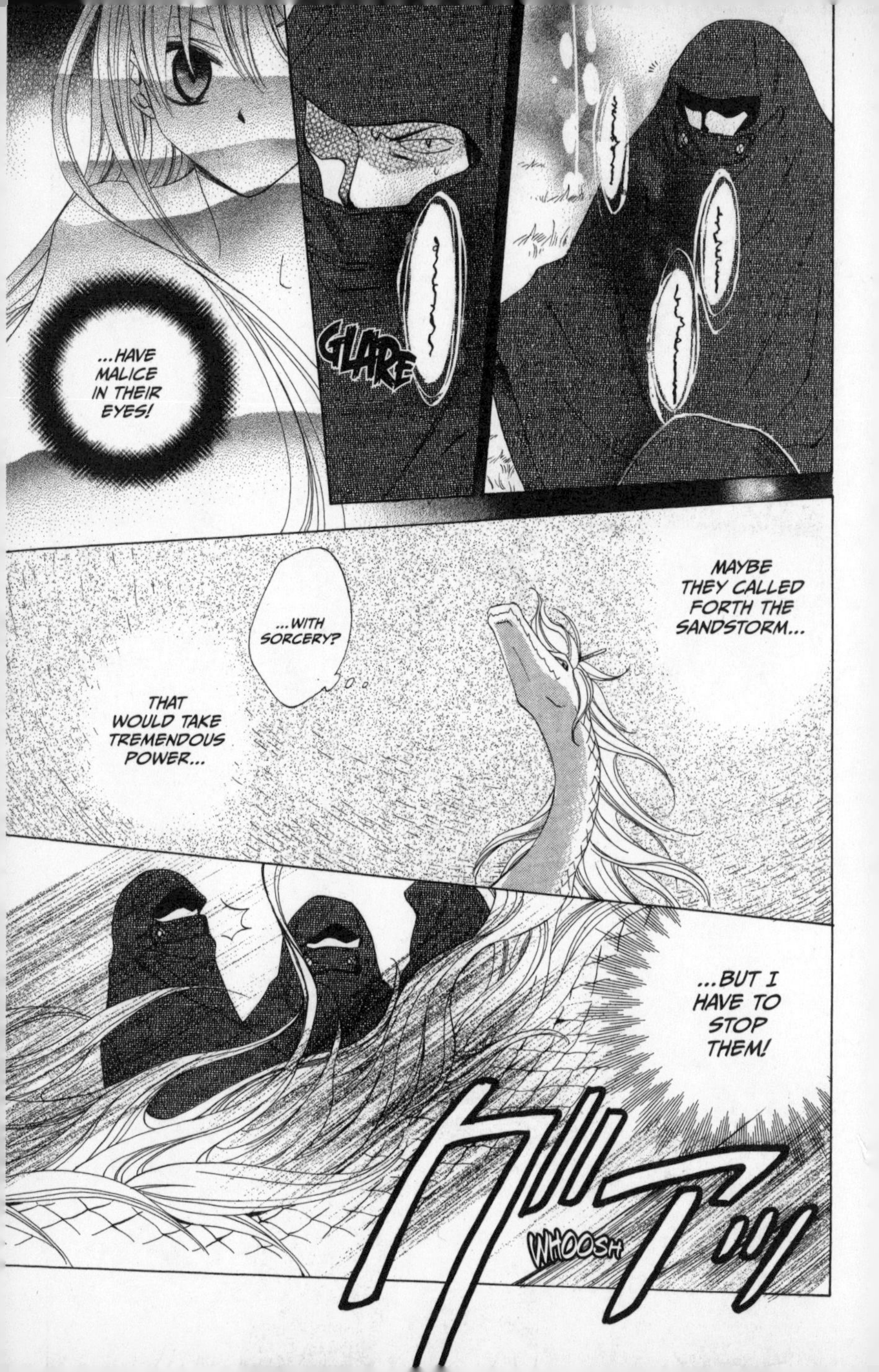
GLARE
...HAVE MALICE IN THEIR EYES!
MAYBE THEY CALLED FORTH THE SANDSTORM...
...WITH SORCERY?
THAT WOULD TAKE TREMENDOUS POWER...
...BUT I HAVE TO STOP THEM!
WHOOSH

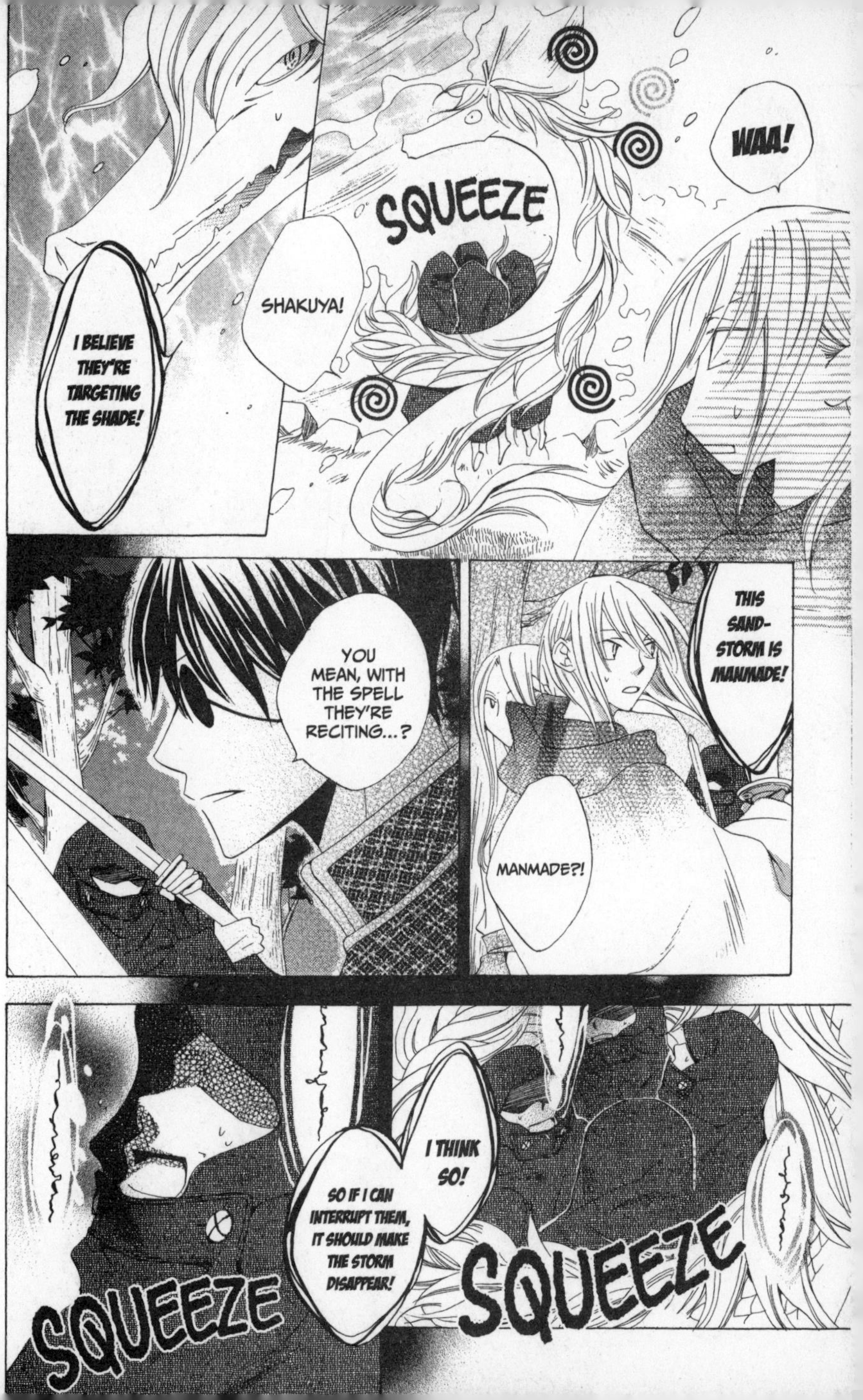
WAA!
SQUEEZE
SHAKUYA!
I BELIEVE THEY'RE TARGETING THE SHADE!
THIS SAND-STORM IS MANMADE!
MANMADE?!
YOU MEAN, WITH THE SPELL THEY'RE RECITING...?
I THINK SO!
SO IF I CAN INTERRUPT THEM, IT SHOULD MAKE THE STORM DISAPPEAR!
SQUEEZE
SQUEEZE

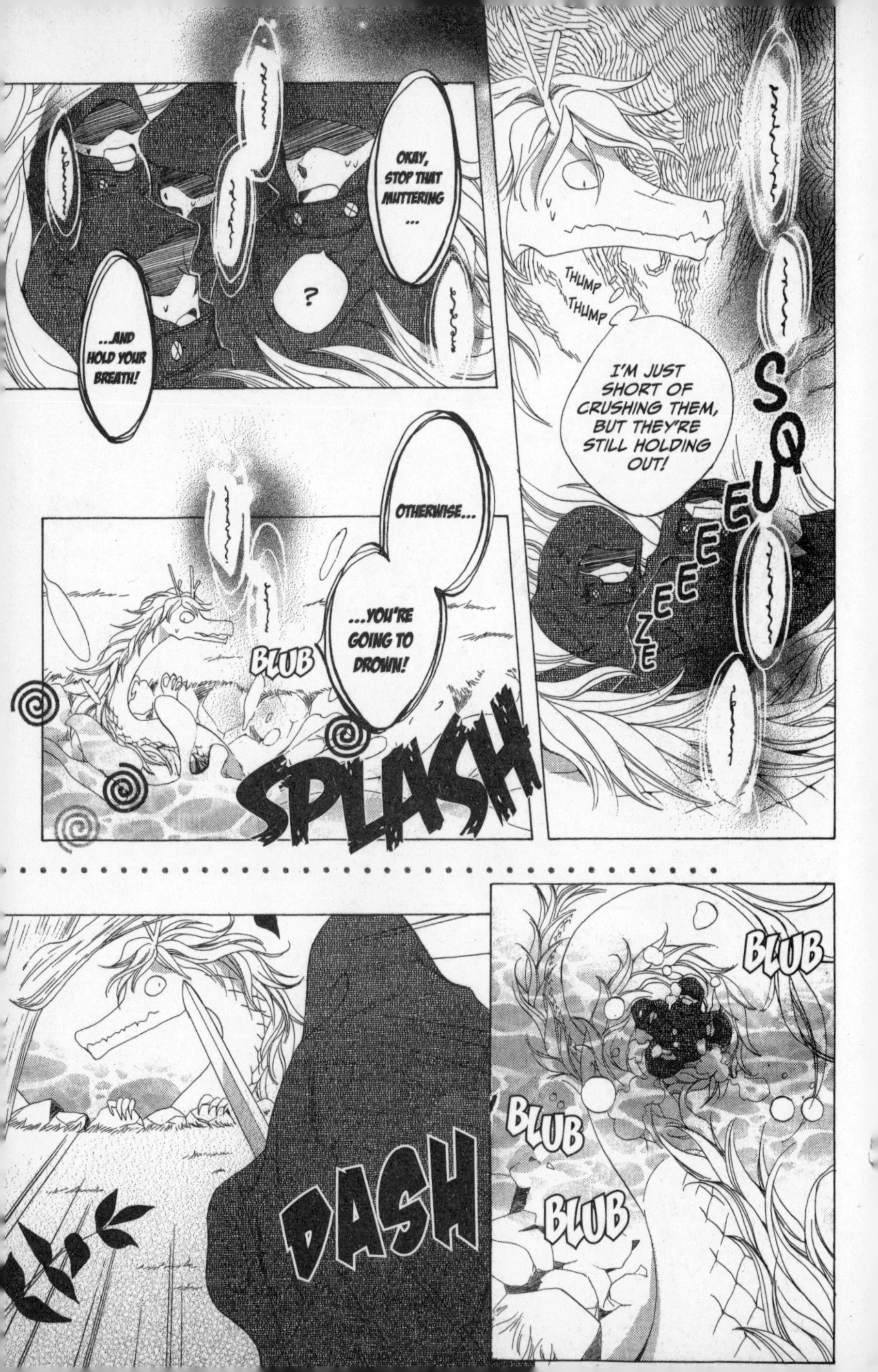
THUMP
THUMP
I'M JUST SHORT OF CRUSHING THEM, BUT THEY'RE STILL HOLDING OUT!
SQUEEEEEZE
OKAY, STOP THAT MUTTERING...
?
...AND HOLD YOUR BREATH!
OTHERWISE...
...YOU'RE GOING TO DROWN!
BLUB
SPLASH
BLUB
BLUB
BLUB
DASH

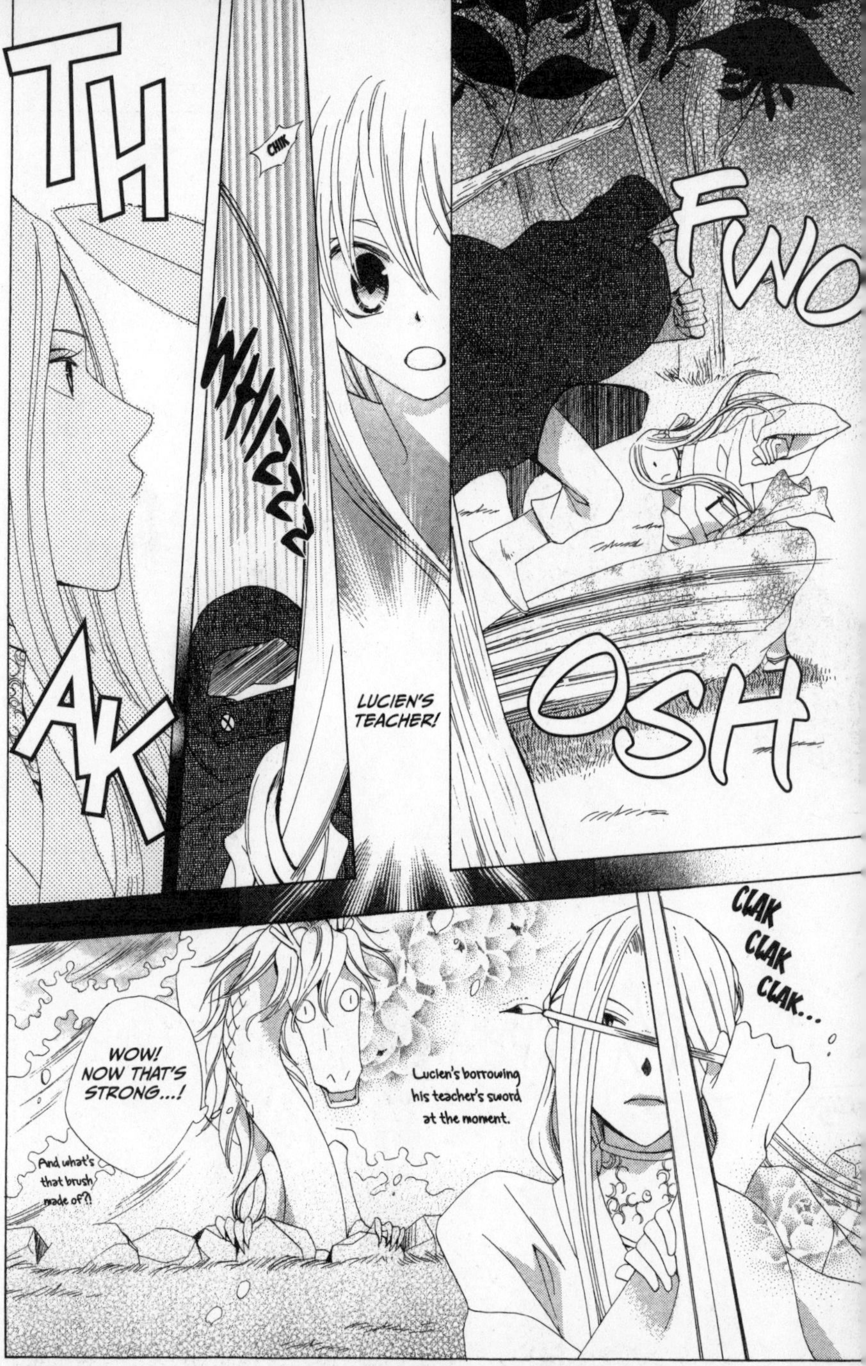
FWOOSH
CHIK
WHIZZZ
LUCIEN'S TEACHER!
THWAK
CLAK CLAK CLAK...
Lucien's borrowing his teacher's sword at the moment.
WOW! NOW THAT'S STRONG...!
And what's that brush made of?!

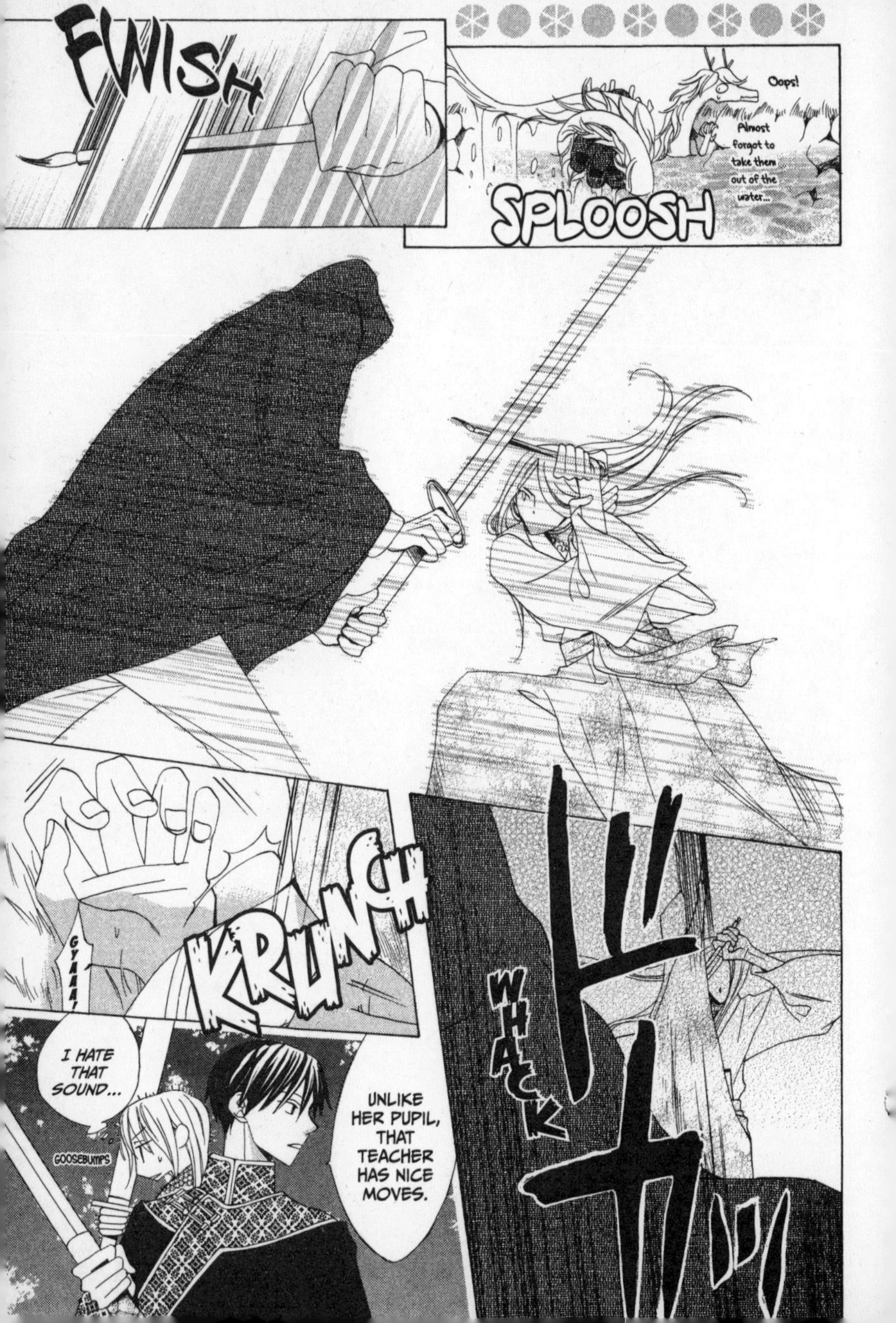
Oops!
Almost forgot to take them out of the water...
SPLOOSH
FWISH
WHACK
KRUNCH
GYAAA!
I HATE THAT SOUND...
GOOSEBUMPS
UNLIKE HER PUPIL, THAT TEACHER HAS NICE MOVES.

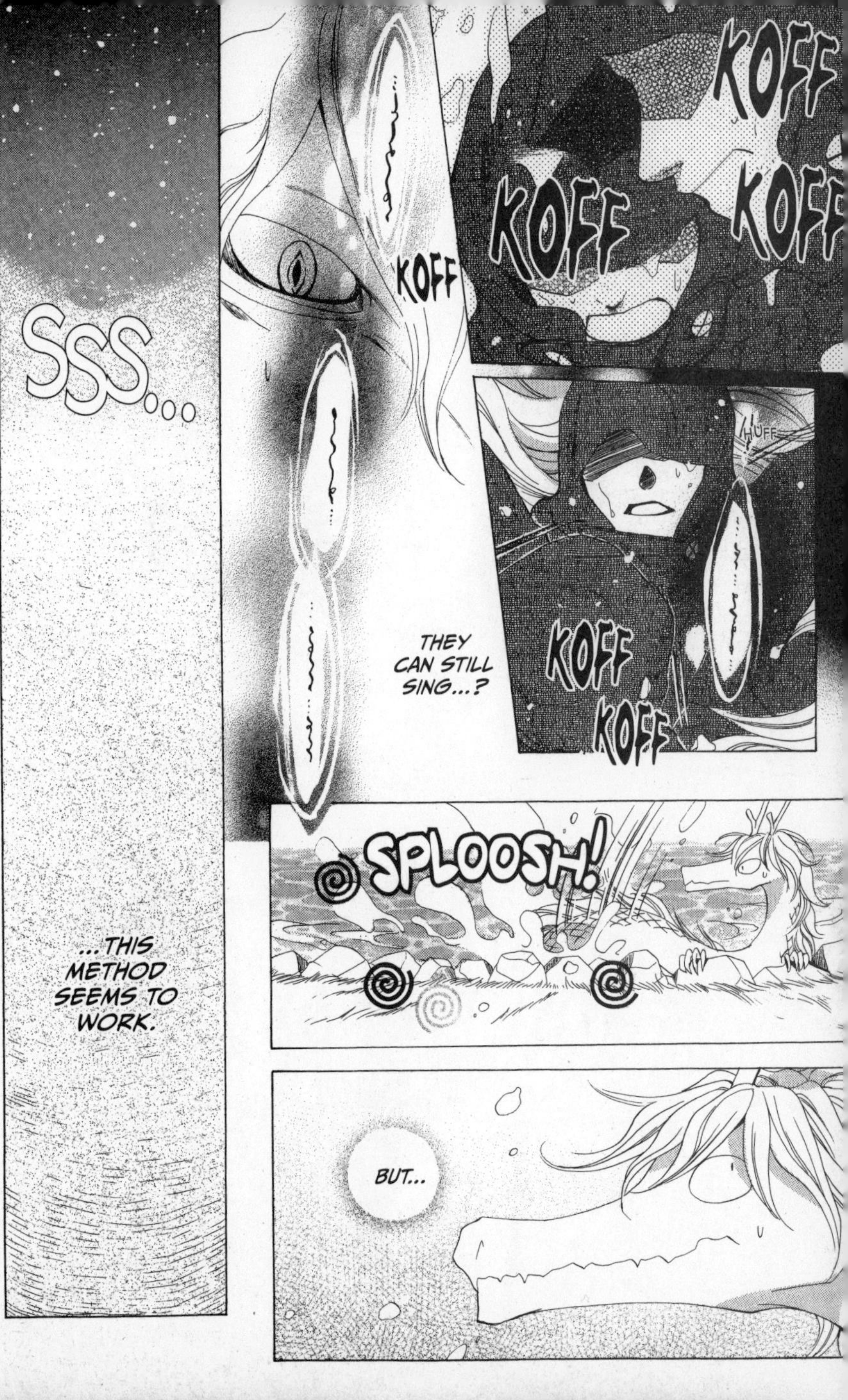
KOFF
KOFF
KOFF
KOFF
HUFF
KOFF
KOFF
THEY CAN STILL SING...?
SPLOOSH!
BUT...
SSS...
...THIS METHOD SEEMS TO WORK.

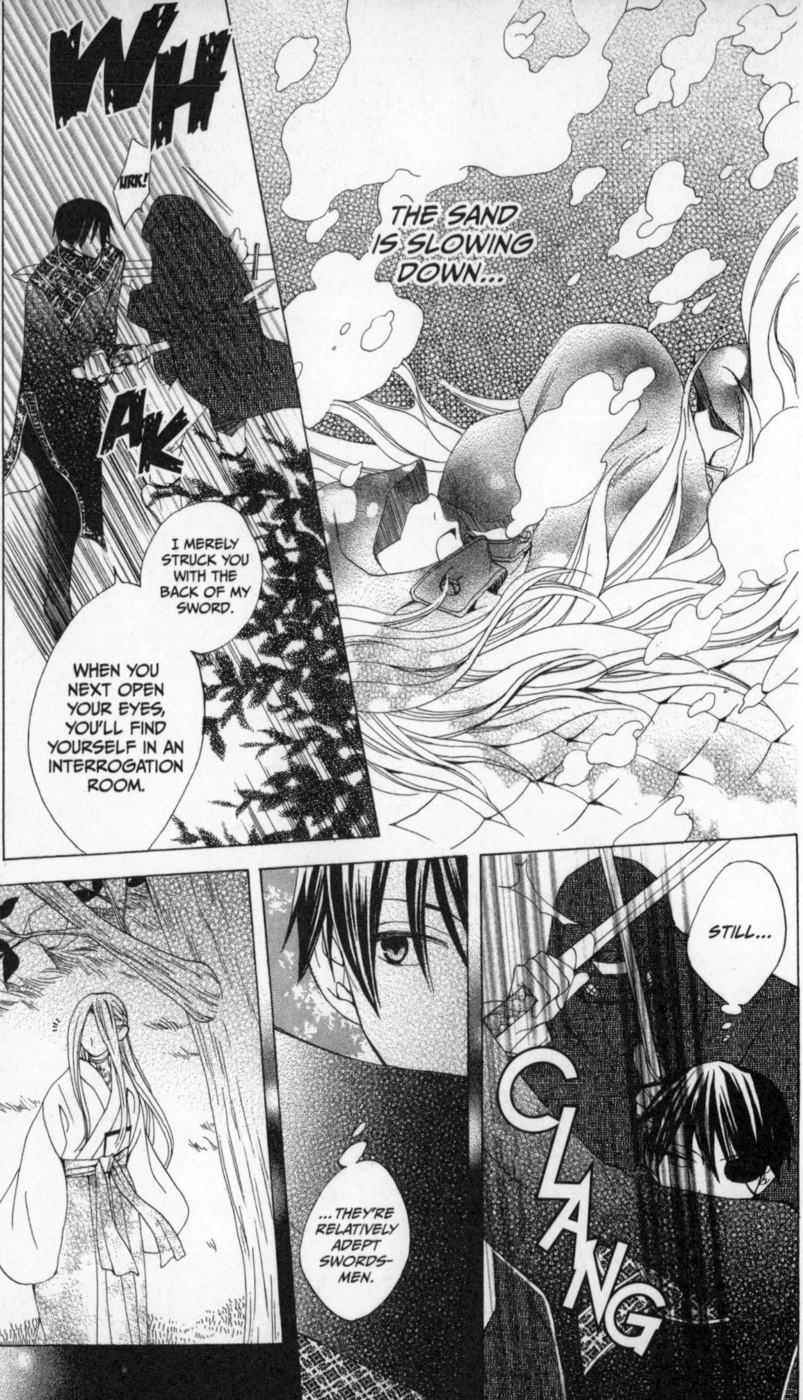
THE SAND IS SLOWING DOWN...
WH
URK!
AK
I MERELY STRUCK YOU WITH THE BACK OF MY SWORD.
WHEN YOU NEXT OPEN YOUR EYES, YOU'LL FIND YOURSELF IN AN INTERROGATION ROOM.
STILL...
CLANG
...THEY'RE RELATIVELY ADEPT SWORDS-MEN.

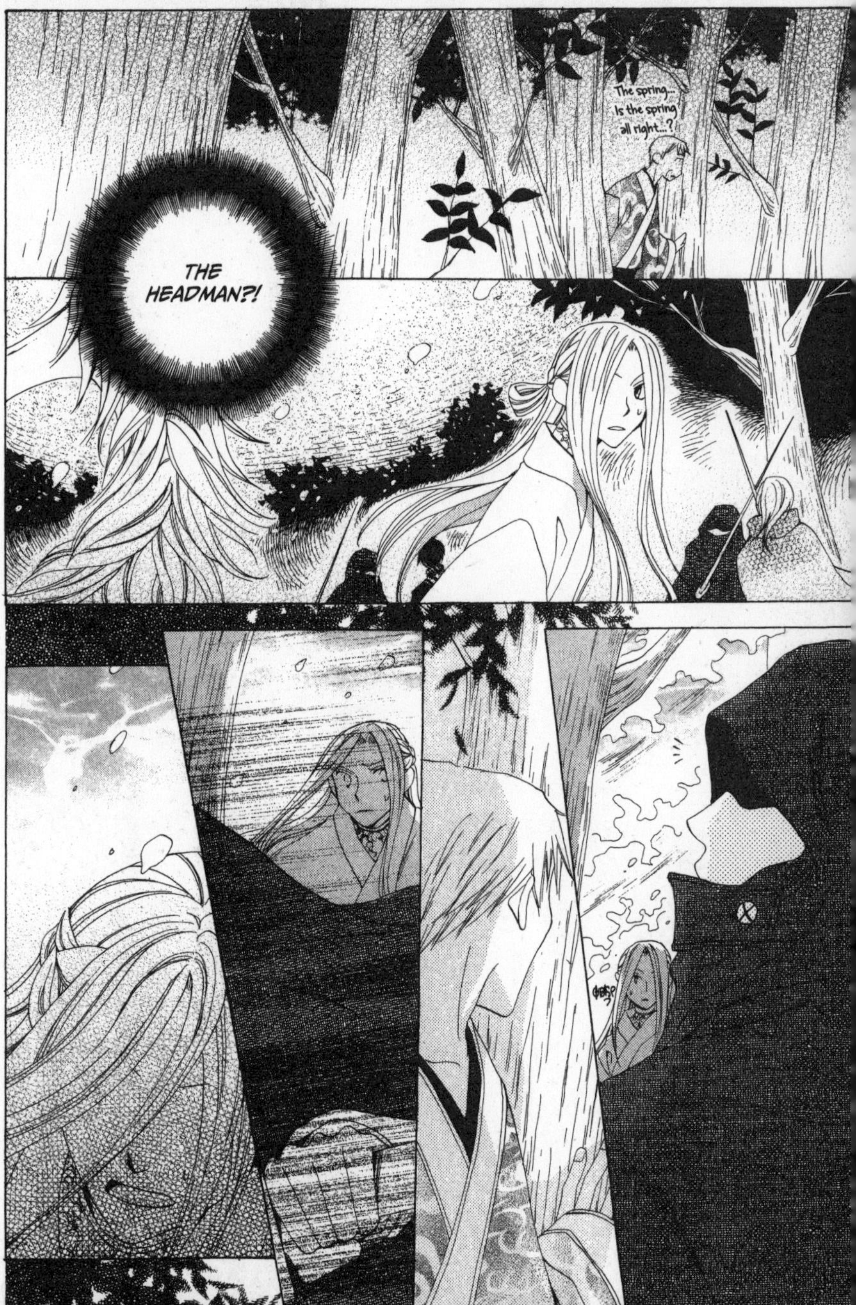
The spring... Is the spring all right...?
THE HEADMAN?!

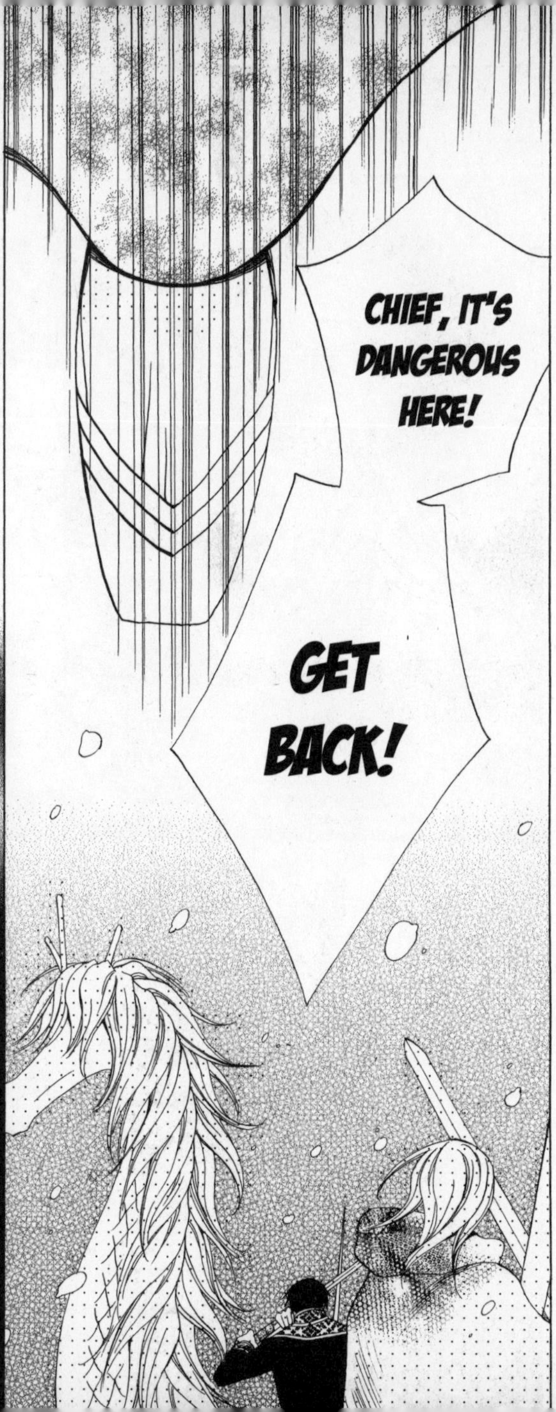
CHIEF, IT'S DANGEROUS HERE!
GET BACK!
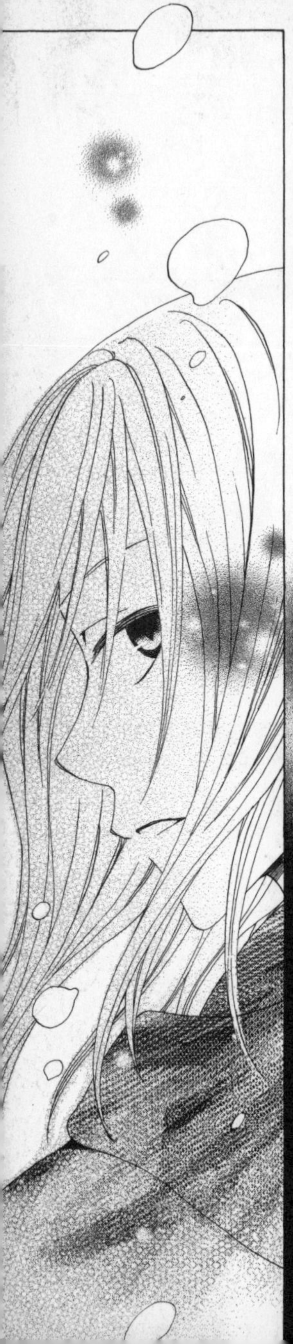

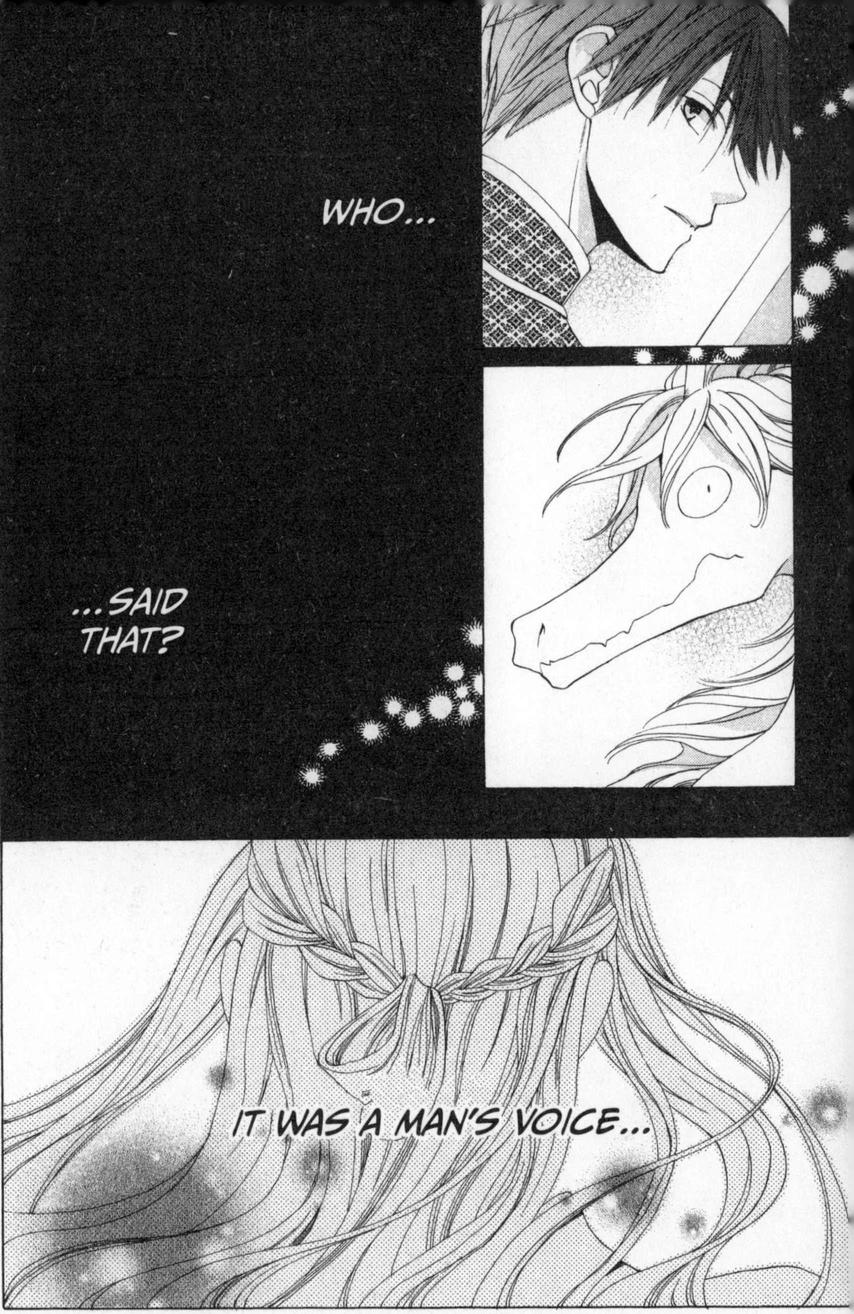
WHO...
...SAID THAT?
IT WAS A MAN'S VOICE...

Episode 12: The End

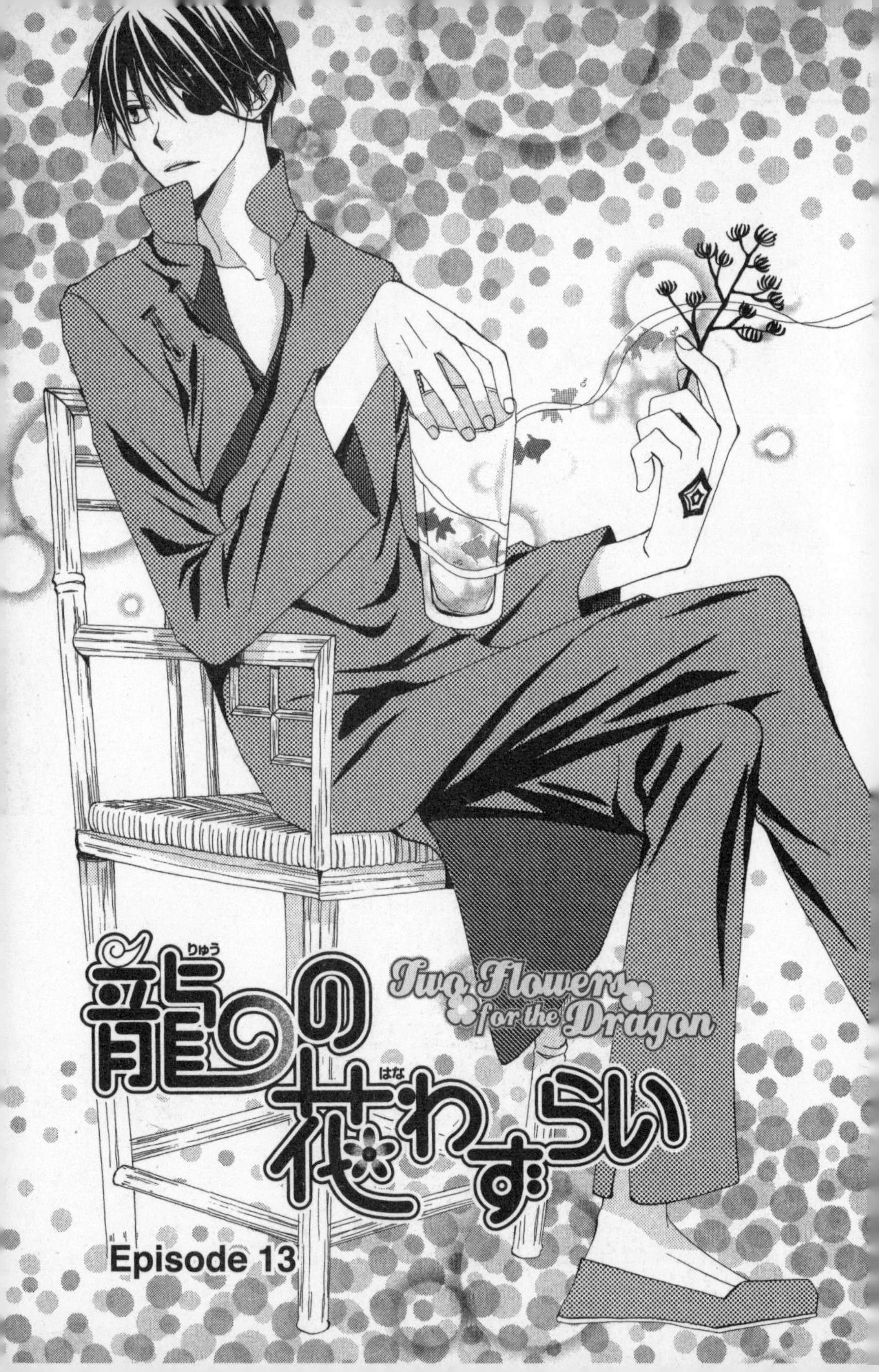
龍の花わずらい
りゅう
はな
Two Flowers for the Dragon
Episode 13

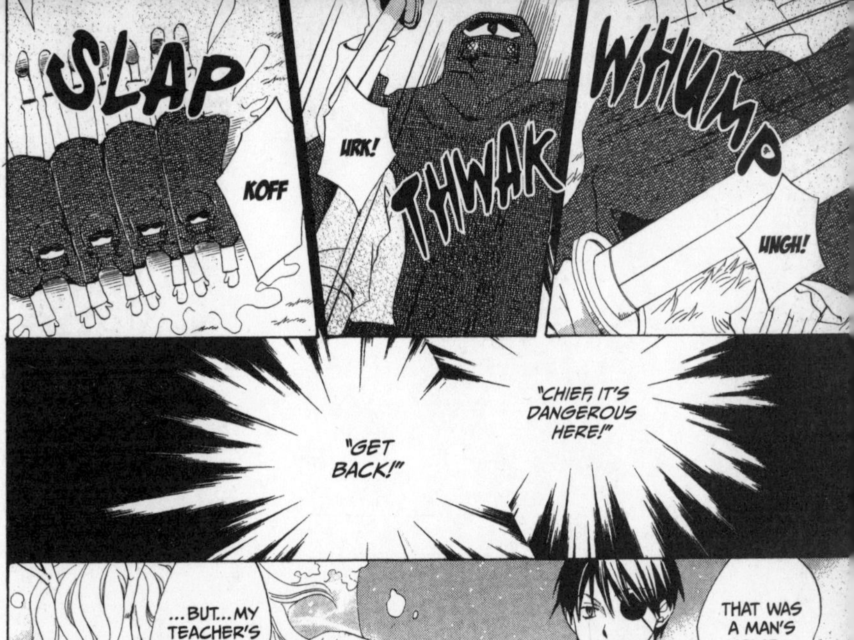
WHUMP
UNGH!
THWAK
URK!
SLAP
KOFF
"CHIEF, IT'S DANGEROUS HERE!"
"GET BACK!"
THAT WAS A MAN'S VOICE...
...COMING OUT OF YOUR TEACHER'S THROAT, LUCIEN?
HUH. WHAT A COINCIDENCE.
I THOUGHT I HEARD IT FROM THE SAME DIRECTION, TOO...
...BUT...MY TEACHER'S A WOMAN!
HAVE YOU EVER SEEN HER...IN THE ALTOGETHER?
WELL, NO, BUT...

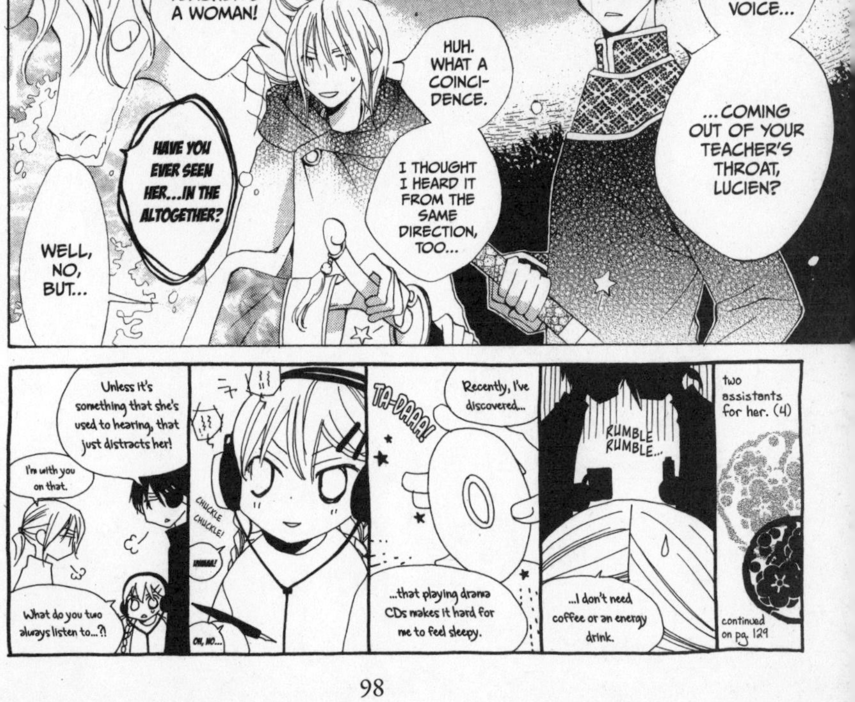
What do you two always listen to...?!
I'm with you on that.
Unless it's something that she's used to hearing, that just distracts her!
OH, NO...
CHUCKLE CHUCKLE!
Recently, I've discovered...
TA-DAAA!
...that playing drama CDs makes it hard for me to feel sleepy.
RUMBLE RUMBLE...
...I don't need coffee or an energy drink.
two assistants for her. (4)
continued on pg. 129

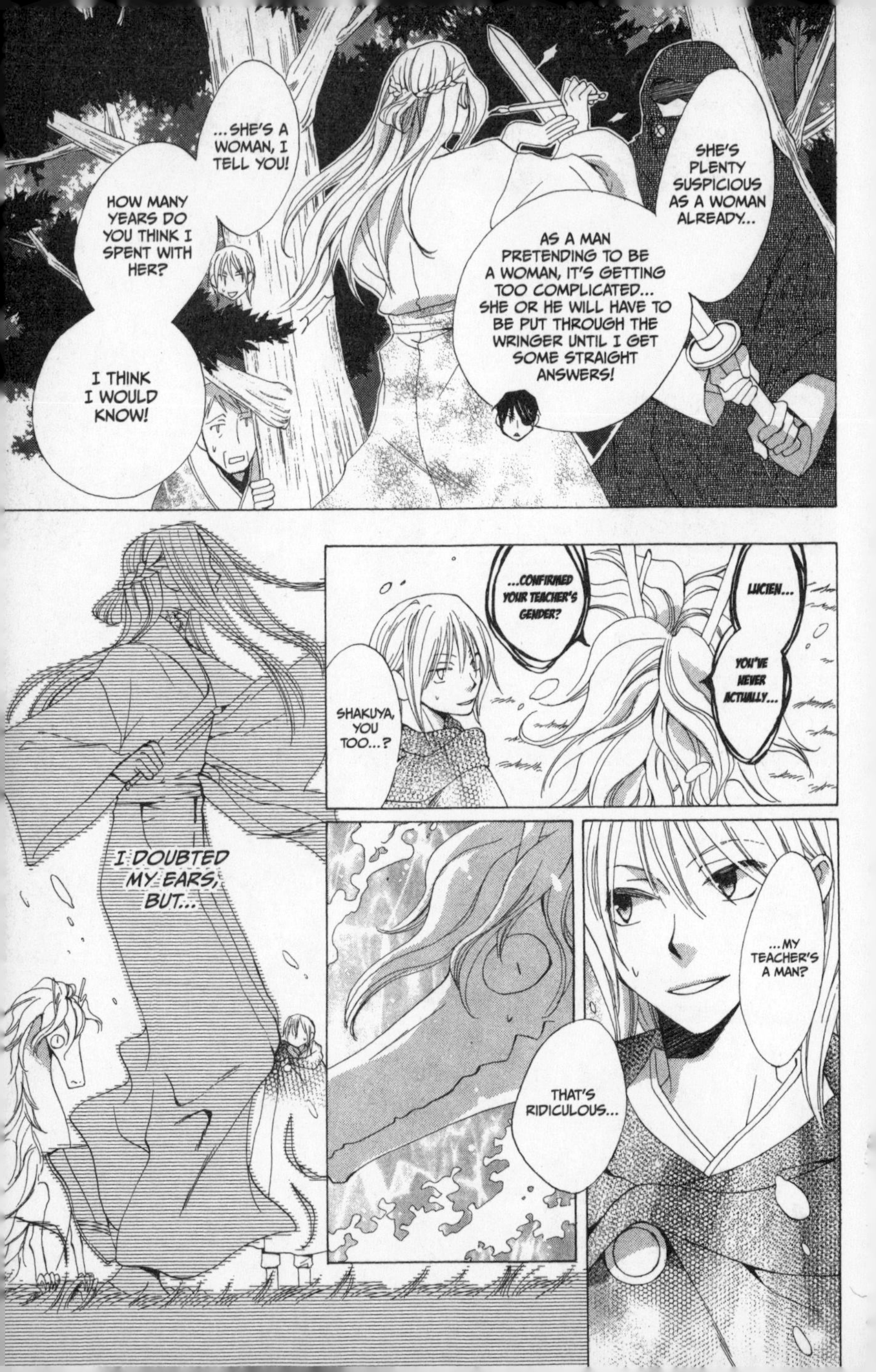
SHE'S PLENTY SUSPICIOUS AS A WOMAN ALREADY...
AS A MAN PRETENDING TO BE A WOMAN, IT'S GETTING TOO COMPLICATED... SHE OR HE WILL HAVE TO BE PUT THROUGH THE WRINGER UNTIL I GET SOME STRAIGHT ANSWERS!
...SHE'S A WOMAN, I TELL YOU!
HOW MANY YEARS DO YOU THINK I SPENT WITH HER?
I THINK I WOULD KNOW!
LUCIEN...
YOU'VE NEVER ACTUALLY...
...CONFIRMED YOUR TEACHER'S GENDER?
SHAKUYA, YOU TOO...?
...MY TEACHER'S A MAN?
THAT'S RIDICULOUS...
I DOUBTED MY EARS, BUT...

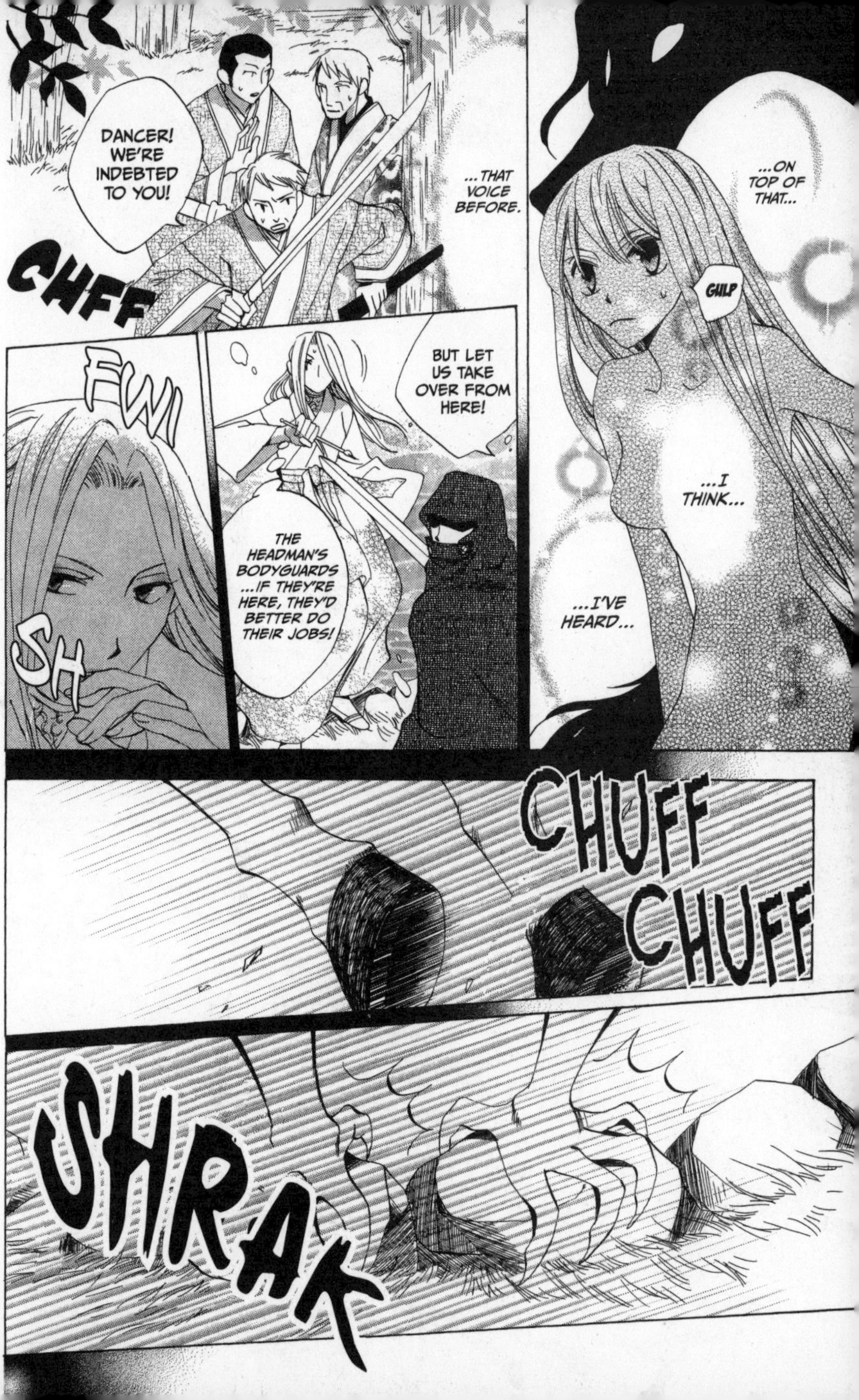
...ON TOP OF THAT...
GULP
...I THINK...
...I'VE HEARD...
...THAT VOICE BEFORE.
DANCER! WE'RE INDEBTED TO YOU!
CHFF
BUT LET US TAKE OVER FROM HERE!
THE HEADMAN'S BODYGUARDS ...IF THEY'RE HERE, THEY'D BETTER DO THEIR JOBS!
FWI
SH
CHUFF CHUFF
SHRAK

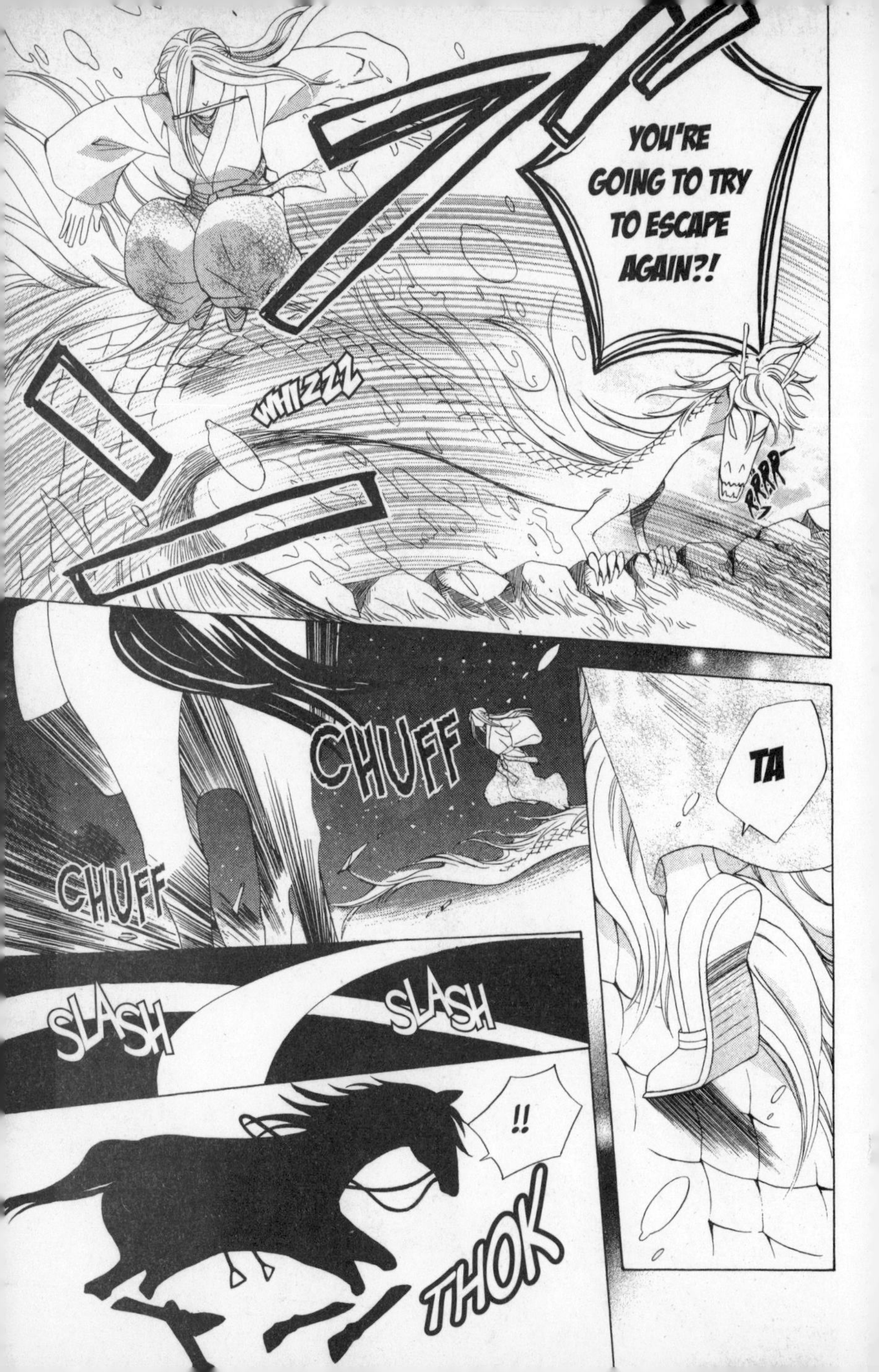
YOU'RE GOING TO TRY TO ESCAPE AGAIN?!
WHI-Z-Z-Z
R-R-R-R
TA
CHUFF
CHUFF
SLASH
SLASH
!!
THOK

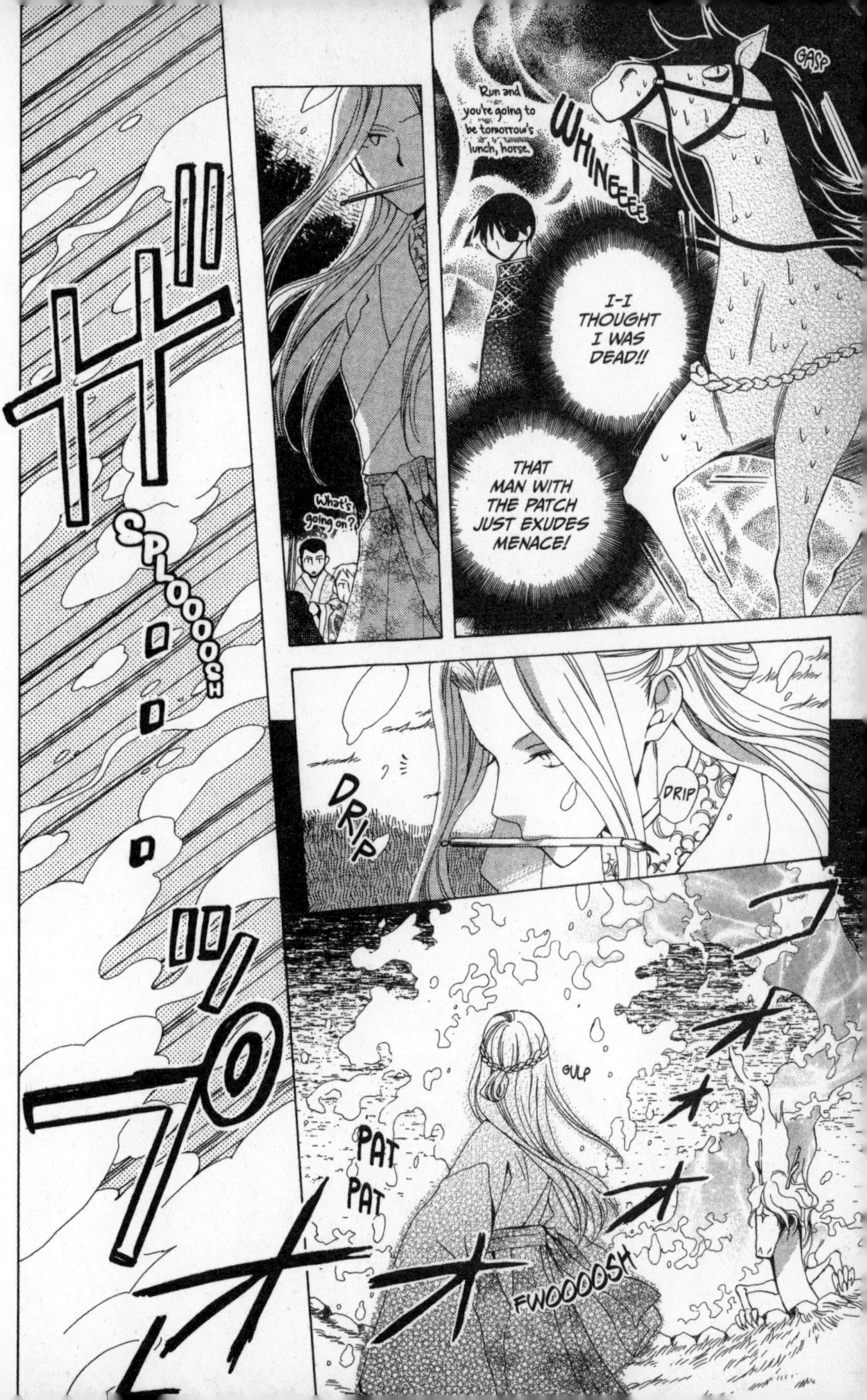
GASP
WHINEEEEE
Run and you're going to be tomorrow's lunch, horse.
I-I THOUGHT I WAS DEAD!!
THAT MAN WITH THE PATCH JUST EXUDES MENACE!
What's going on?
SPLOOOOSH
DRIP
DRIP
GULP
PAT PAT
FWOOOOSH

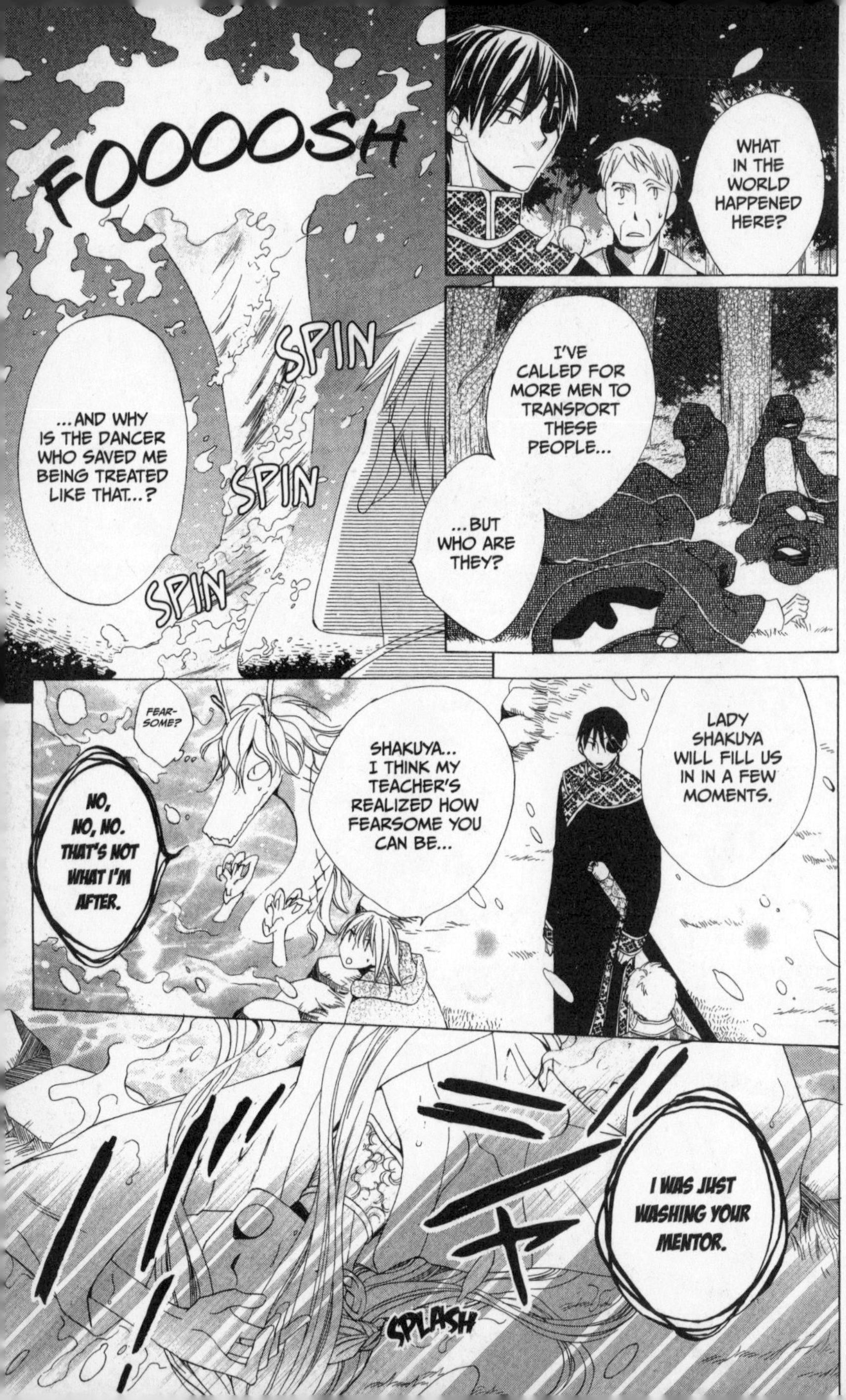
WHAT IN THE WORLD HAPPENED HERE?
I'VE CALLED FOR MORE MEN TO TRANSPORT THESE PEOPLE...
...BUT WHO ARE THEY?
FOOOOSH
SPIN
SPIN
SPIN
...AND WHY IS THE DANCER WHO SAVED ME BEING TREATED LIKE THAT...?
LADY SHAKUYA WILL FILL US IN IN A FEW MOMENTS.
SHAKUYA... I THINK MY TEACHER'S REALIZED HOW FEARSOME YOU CAN BE...
FEAR-SOME?
NO, NO, NO. THAT'S NOT WHAT I'M AFTER.
I WAS JUST WASHING YOUR MENTOR.
SPLASH

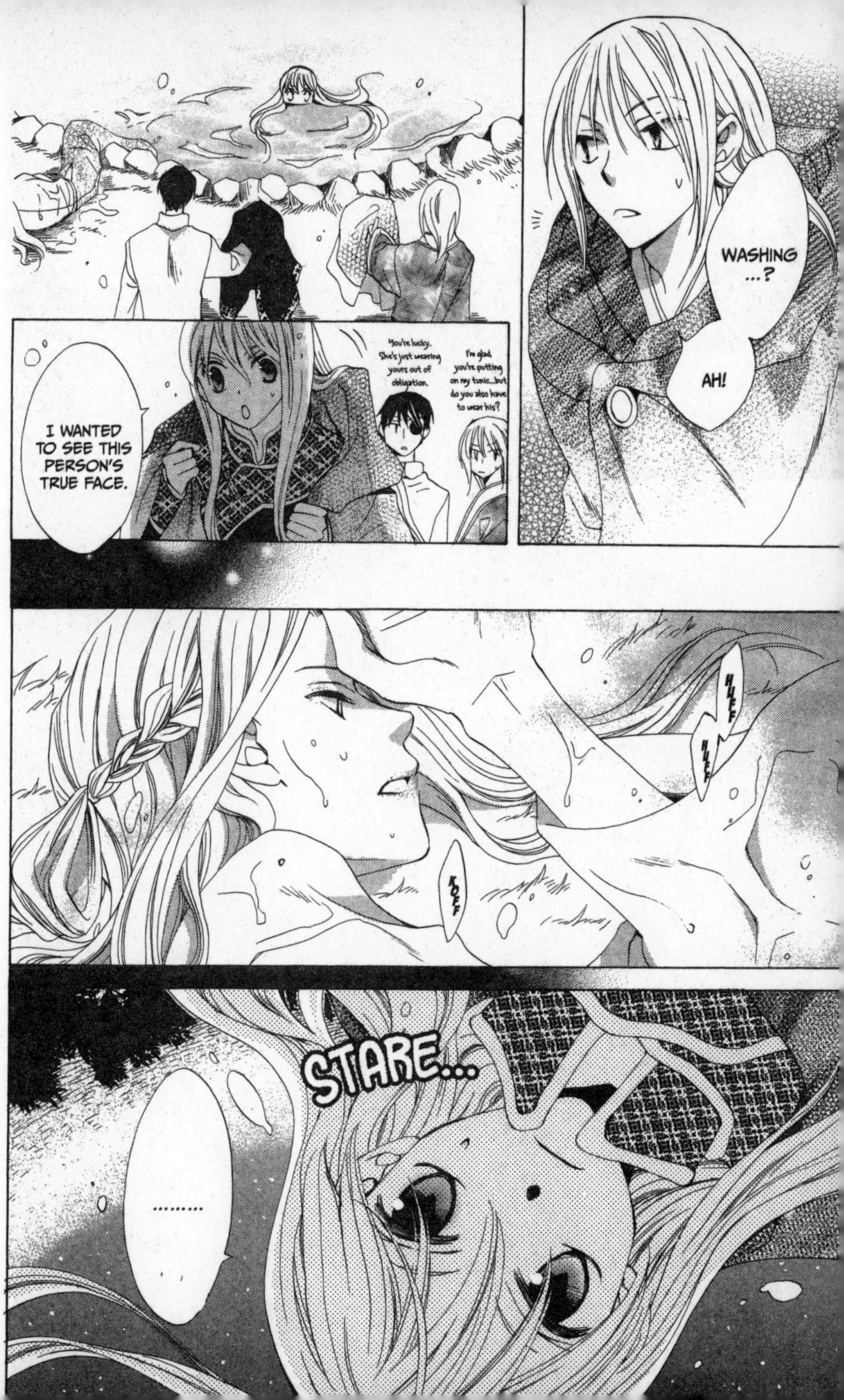
WASHING ...?
AH!
I WANTED TO SEE THIS PERSON'S TRUE FACE.
I'm glad you're putting on my tunic...but do you also have to wear his?
You're lucky. She's just wearing yours out of obligation.
HUFF HUFF
KOFF
STARE...
....

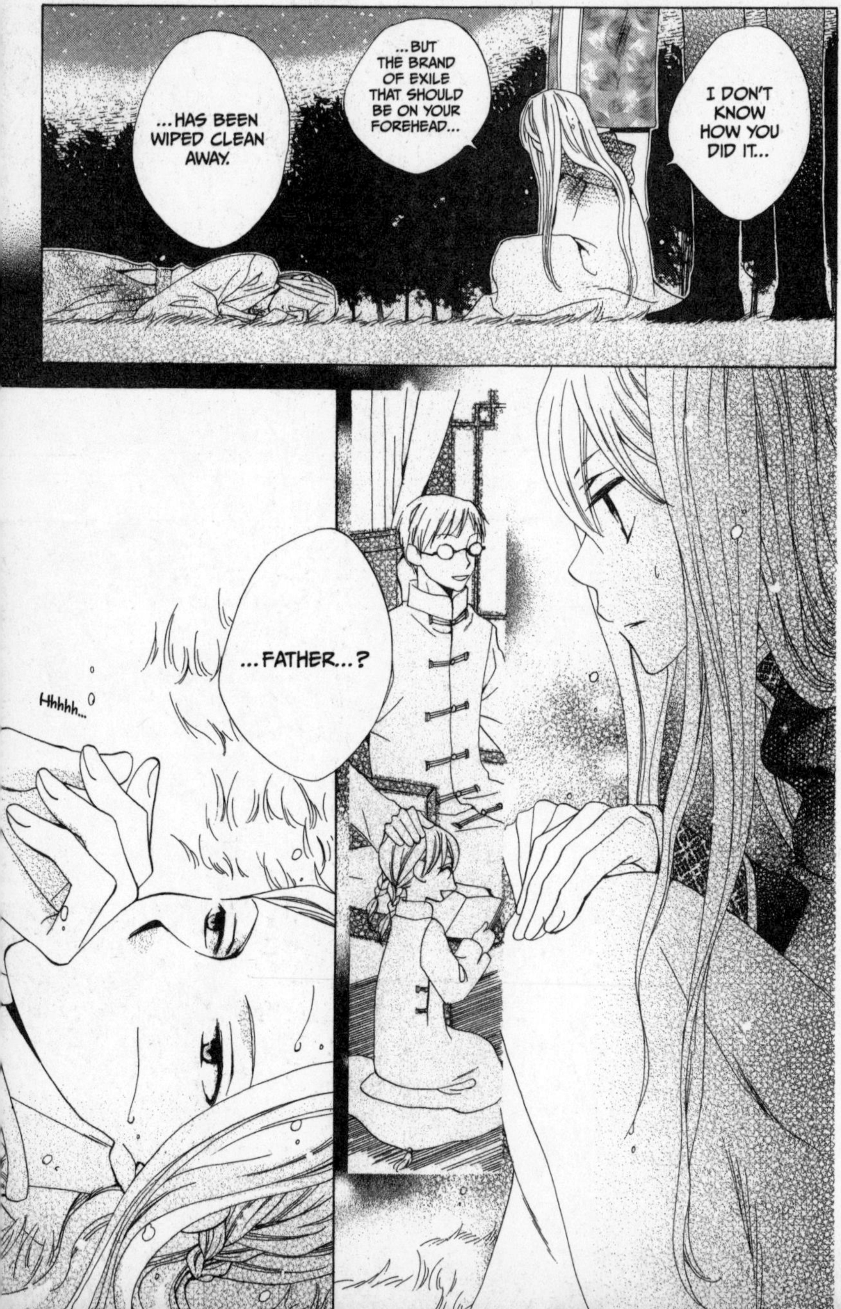
I DON'T KNOW HOW YOU DID IT...
...BUT THE BRAND OF EXILE THAT SHOULD BE ON YOUR FOREHEAD...
...HAS BEEN WIPED CLEAN AWAY.
...FATHER...?
Hhhhh...

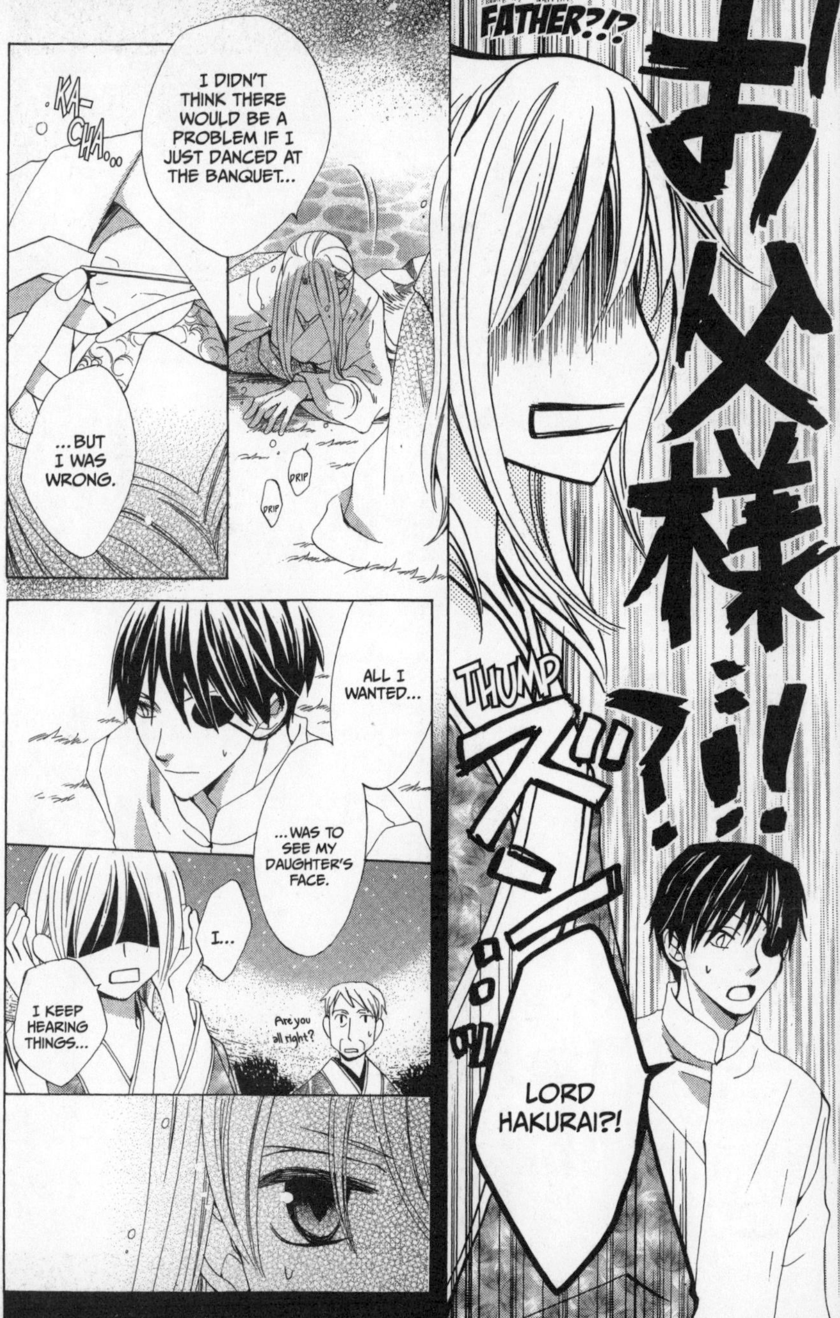
FATHER?!?
お父様?!
THUMP
LORD HAKURAI?!
KA-CHA...
I DIDN'T THINK THERE WOULD BE A PROBLEM IF I JUST DANCED AT THE BANQUET...
...BUT I WAS WRONG.
DRIP
DRIP
ALL I WANTED...
...WAS TO SEE MY DAUGHTER'S FACE.
I...
I KEEP HEARING THINGS...
Are you all right?

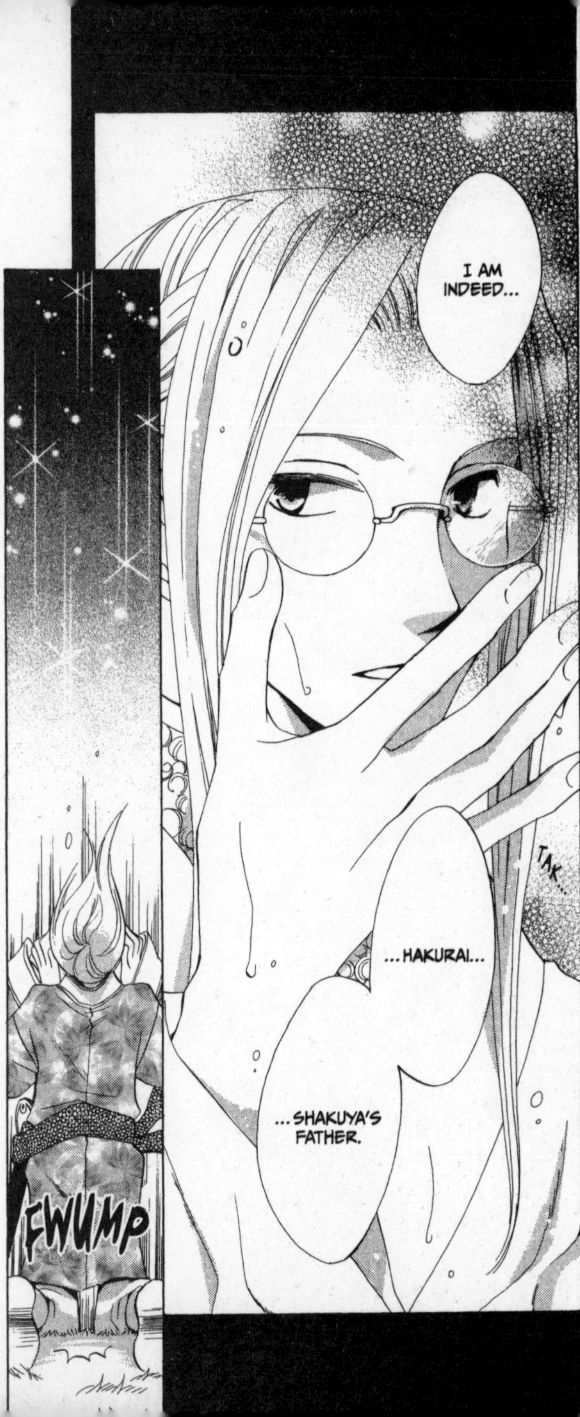
I AM INDEED...
TAK...
...HAKURAI...
...SHAKUYA'S FATHER.
FWUMP

4

Washing

When the washing machine is full, I pour in baking soda to try to dispel any odors. After the clothes are washed, they come out smelling pleasant and it's a smell that makes me feel nostalgic, but I haven't been able to remember where or when I smelled it before. It's a scent that makes me feel as if all is well... The face soap that I use these days also makes me feel nostalgic and I have a certain memory associated with it. It reminds me of the plastic bag I used to always take to the pool with me when I was in elementary school, though I know the bag back then had a more "plastic-y" smell to it. No, there's something else, something closer to the actual smell of the soap...but what is it? What is it?! This kind of thing happens to me on a fairly regular basis.

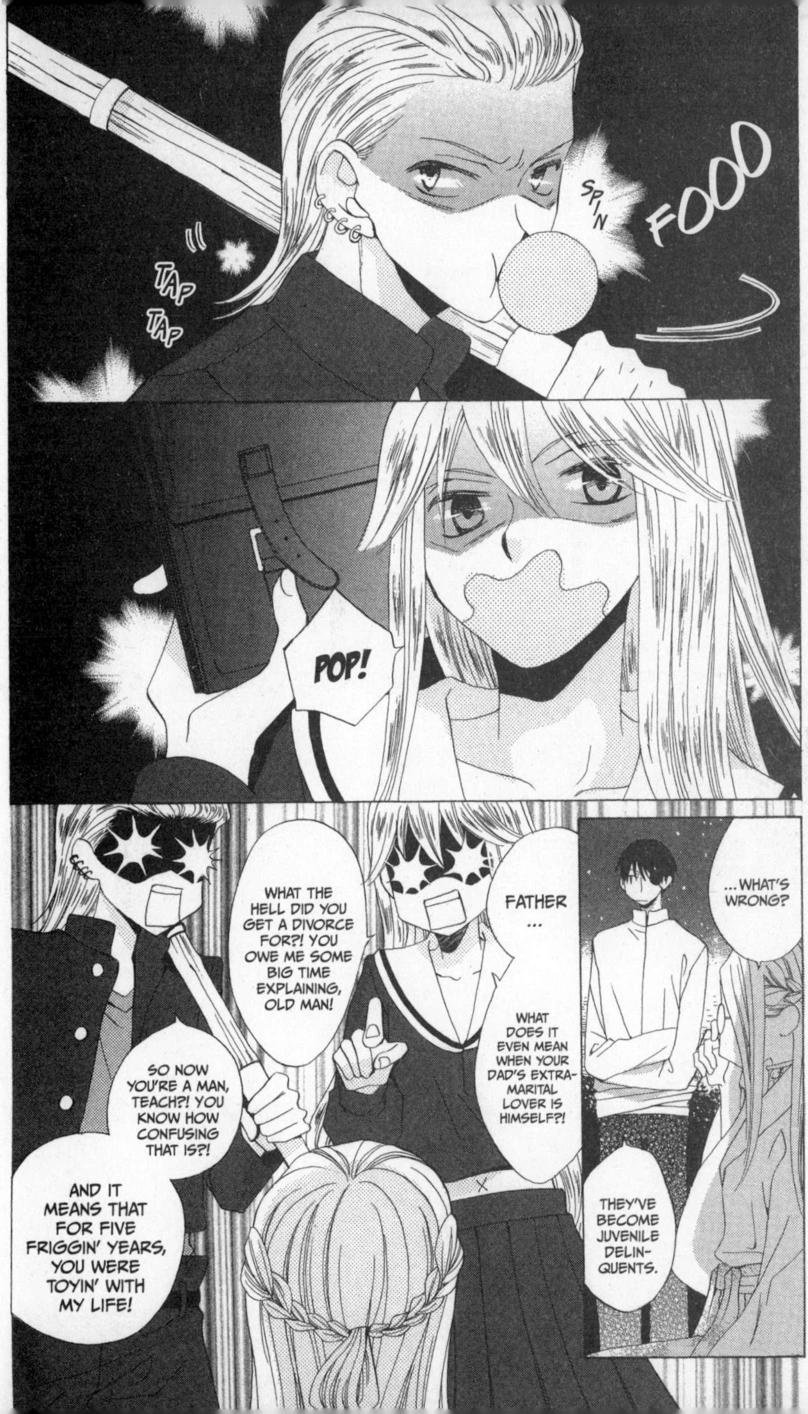
FOOO
SPIN
TAP TAP
POP!
...WHAT'S WRONG?
THEY'VE BECOME JUVENILE DELIN-QUENTS.
FATHER ...
WHAT THE HELL DID YOU GET A DIVORCE FOR?! YOU OWE ME SOME BIG TIME EXPLAINING, OLD MAN!
WHAT DOES IT EVEN MEAN WHEN YOUR DAD'S EXTRA-MARITAL LOVER IS HIMSELF?!
SO NOW YOU'RE A MAN, TEACH?! YOU KNOW HOW CONFUSING THAT IS?!
AND IT MEANS THAT FOR FIVE FRIGGIN' YEARS, YOU WERE TOYIN' WITH MY LIFE!

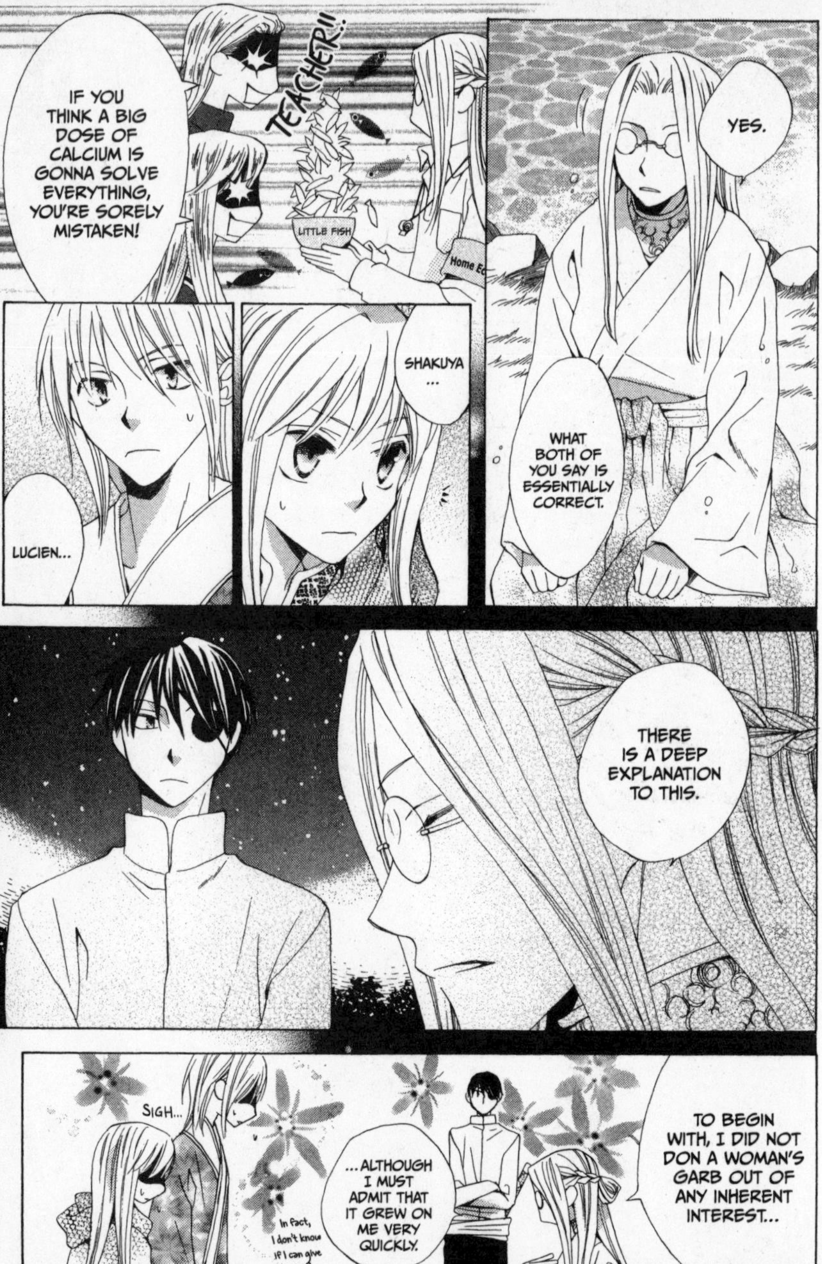
YES.
WHAT BOTH OF YOU SAY IS ESSENTIALLY CORRECT.
IF YOU THINK A BIG DOSE OF CALCIUM IS GONNA SOLVE EVERYTHING, YOU'RE SORELY MISTAKEN!
TEACHER!!
LITTLE FISH
Home Ec
SHAKUYA...
LUCIEN...
THERE IS A DEEP EXPLANATION TO THIS.
TO BEGIN WITH, I DID NOT DON A WOMAN'S GARB OUT OF ANY INHERENT INTEREST...
...ALTHOUGH I MUST ADMIT THAT IT GREW ON ME VERY QUICKLY.
In fact, I don't know if I can give it up?
SIGH...

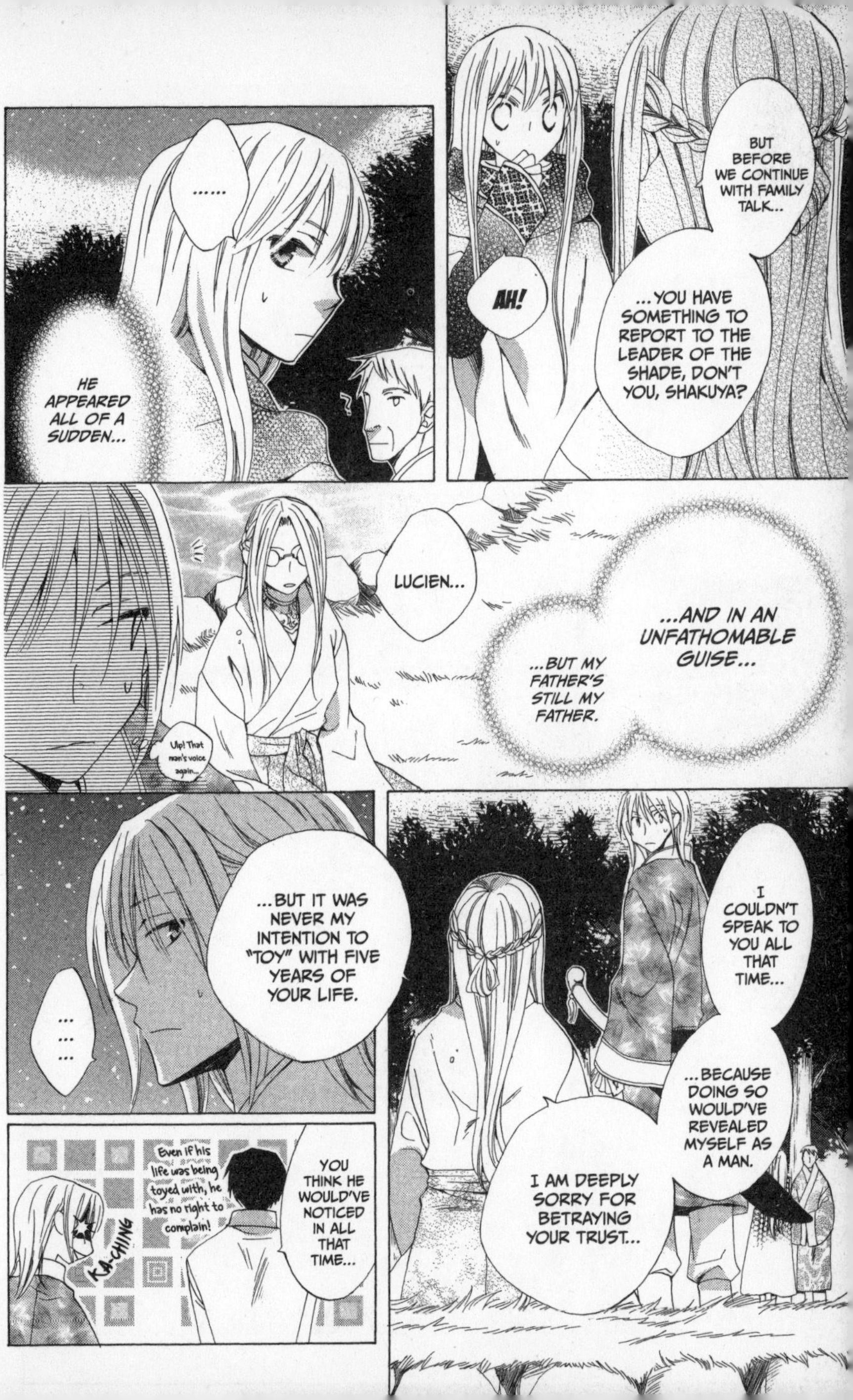
BUT BEFORE WE CONTINUE WITH FAMILY TALK...
...YOU HAVE SOMETHING TO REPORT TO THE LEADER OF THE SHADE, DON'T YOU, SHAKUYA?
AH!
......
HE APPEARED ALL OF A SUDDEN...
...AND IN AN UNFATHOMABLE GUISE...
...BUT MY FATHER'S STILL MY FATHER.
LUCIEN...
Ulp! That man's voice again...
I COULDN'T SPEAK TO YOU ALL THAT TIME...
...BECAUSE DOING SO WOULD'VE REVEALED MYSELF AS A MAN.
I AM DEEPLY SORRY FOR BETRAYING YOUR TRUST...
...BUT IT WAS NEVER MY INTENTION TO "TOY" WITH FIVE YEARS OF YOUR LIFE.
...
...
...
YOU THINK HE WOULD'VE NOTICED IN ALL THAT TIME...
Even if his life was being toyed with, he has no right to complain!
KA-CHING

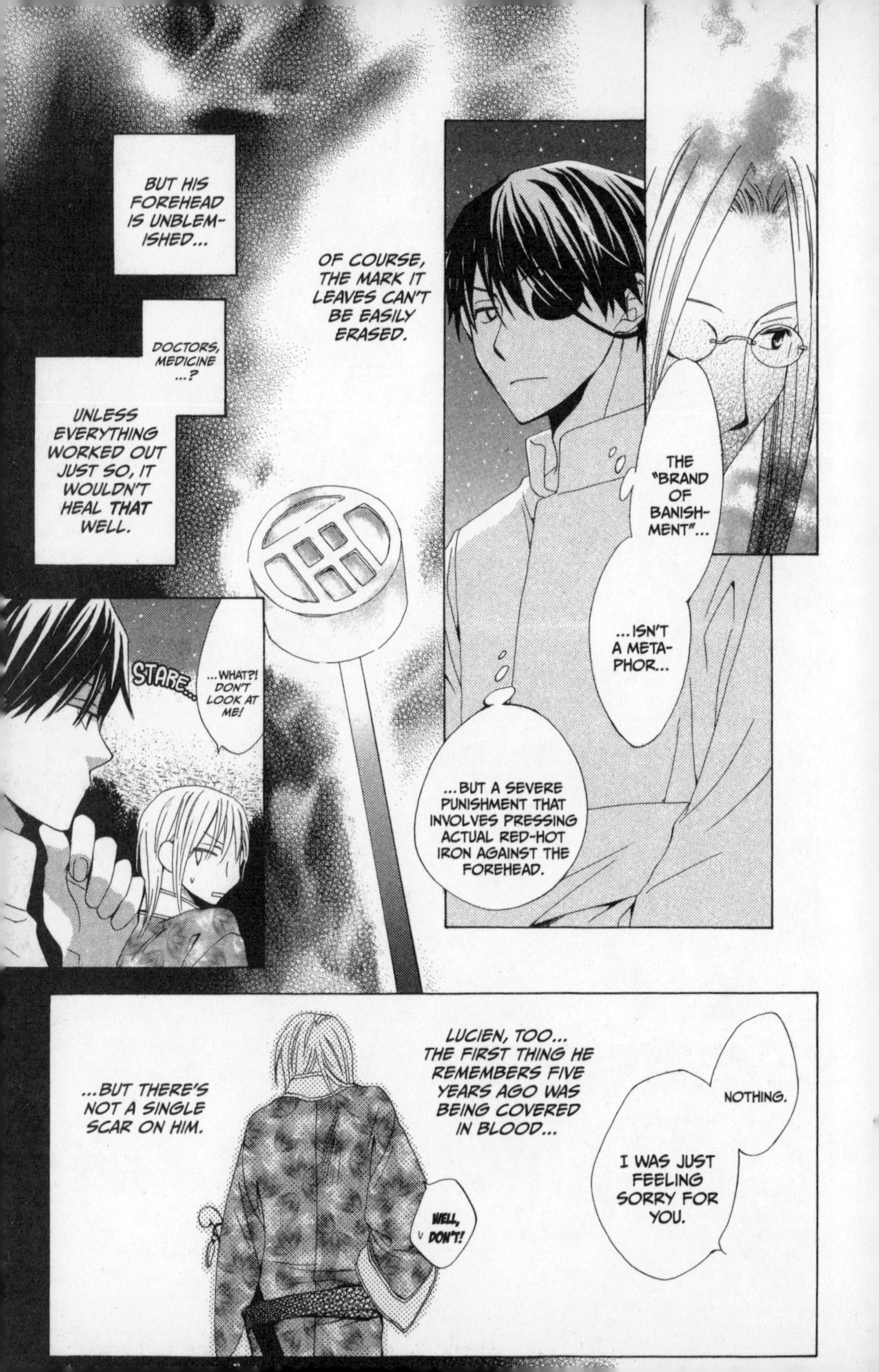
THE "BRAND OF BANISHMENT"...
...ISN'T A METAPHOR...
...BUT A SEVERE PUNISHMENT THAT INVOLVES PRESSING ACTUAL RED-HOT IRON AGAINST THE FOREHEAD.
OF COURSE, THE MARK IT LEAVES CAN'T BE EASILY ERASED.
BUT HIS FOREHEAD IS UNBLEMISHED...
DOCTORS, MEDICINE ...?
UNLESS EVERYTHING WORKED OUT JUST SO, IT WOULDN'T HEAL THAT WELL.
STARE...
...WHAT?! DON'T LOOK AT ME!
NOTHING.
I WAS JUST FEELING SORRY FOR YOU.
LUCIEN, TOO... THE FIRST THING HE REMEMBERS FIVE YEARS AGO WAS BEING COVERED IN BLOOD...
WELL, DON'T!
...BUT THERE'S NOT A SINGLE SCAR ON HIM.

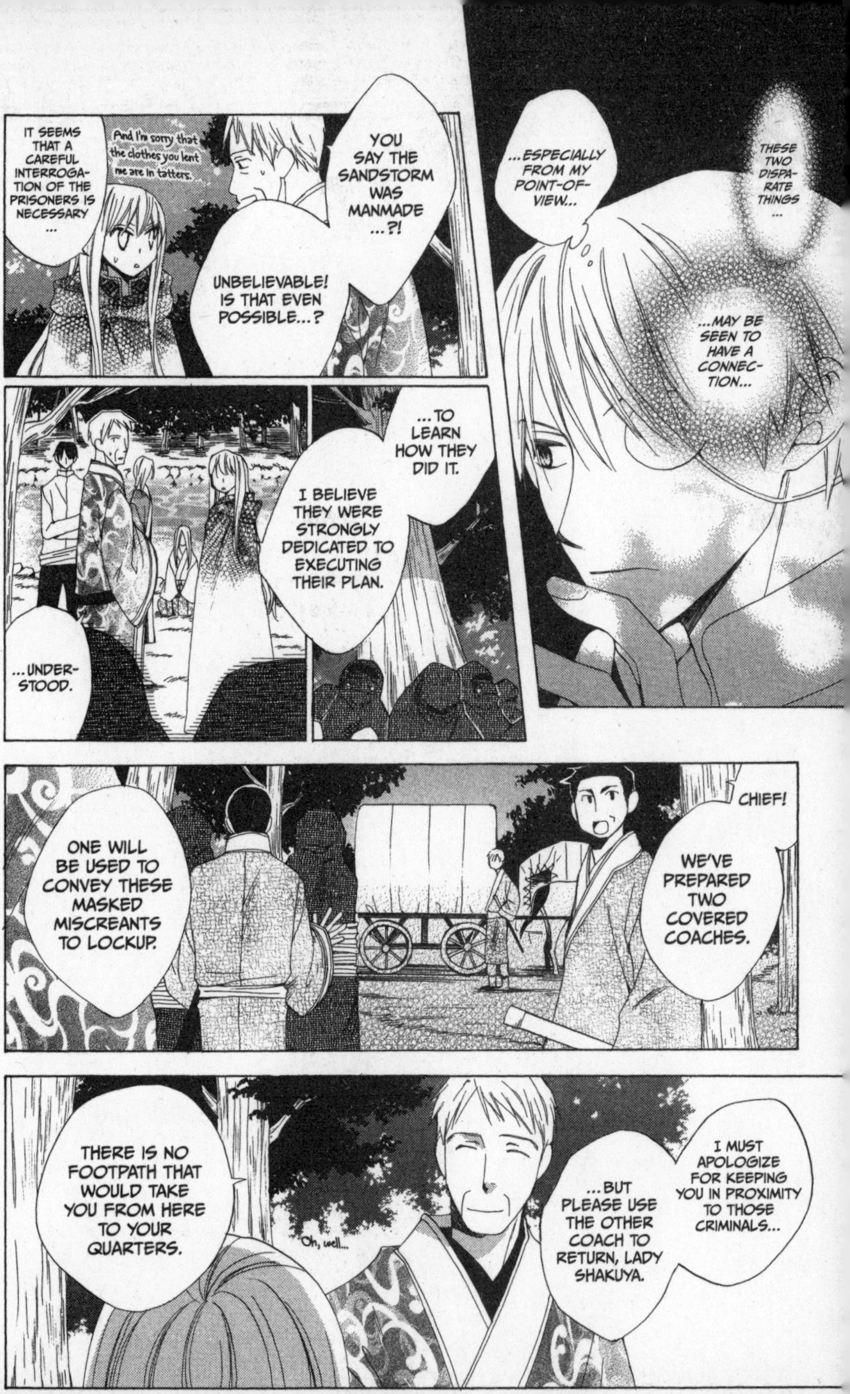
...ESPECIALLY FROM MY POINT-OF-VIEW...
THESE TWO DISPARATE THINGS ...
...MAY BE SEEN TO HAVE A CONNECTION...
YOU SAY THE SANDSTORM WAS MANMADE ...?!
And I'm sorry that the clothes you lent me are in tatters.
IT SEEMS THAT A CAREFUL INTERROGATION OF THE PRISONERS IS NECESSARY ...
UNBELIEVABLE! IS THAT EVEN POSSIBLE...?
...TO LEARN HOW THEY DID IT.
I BELIEVE THEY WERE STRONGLY DEDICATED TO EXECUTING THEIR PLAN.
...UNDERSTOOD.
CHIEF!
WE'VE PREPARED TWO COVERED COACHES.
ONE WILL BE USED TO CONVEY THESE MASKED MISCREANTS TO LOCKUP.
I MUST APOLOGIZE FOR KEEPING YOU IN PROXIMITY TO THOSE CRIMINALS...
...BUT PLEASE USE THE OTHER COACH TO RETURN, LADY SHAKUYA.
Oh, well...
THERE IS NO FOOTPATH THAT WOULD TAKE YOU FROM HERE TO YOUR QUARTERS.

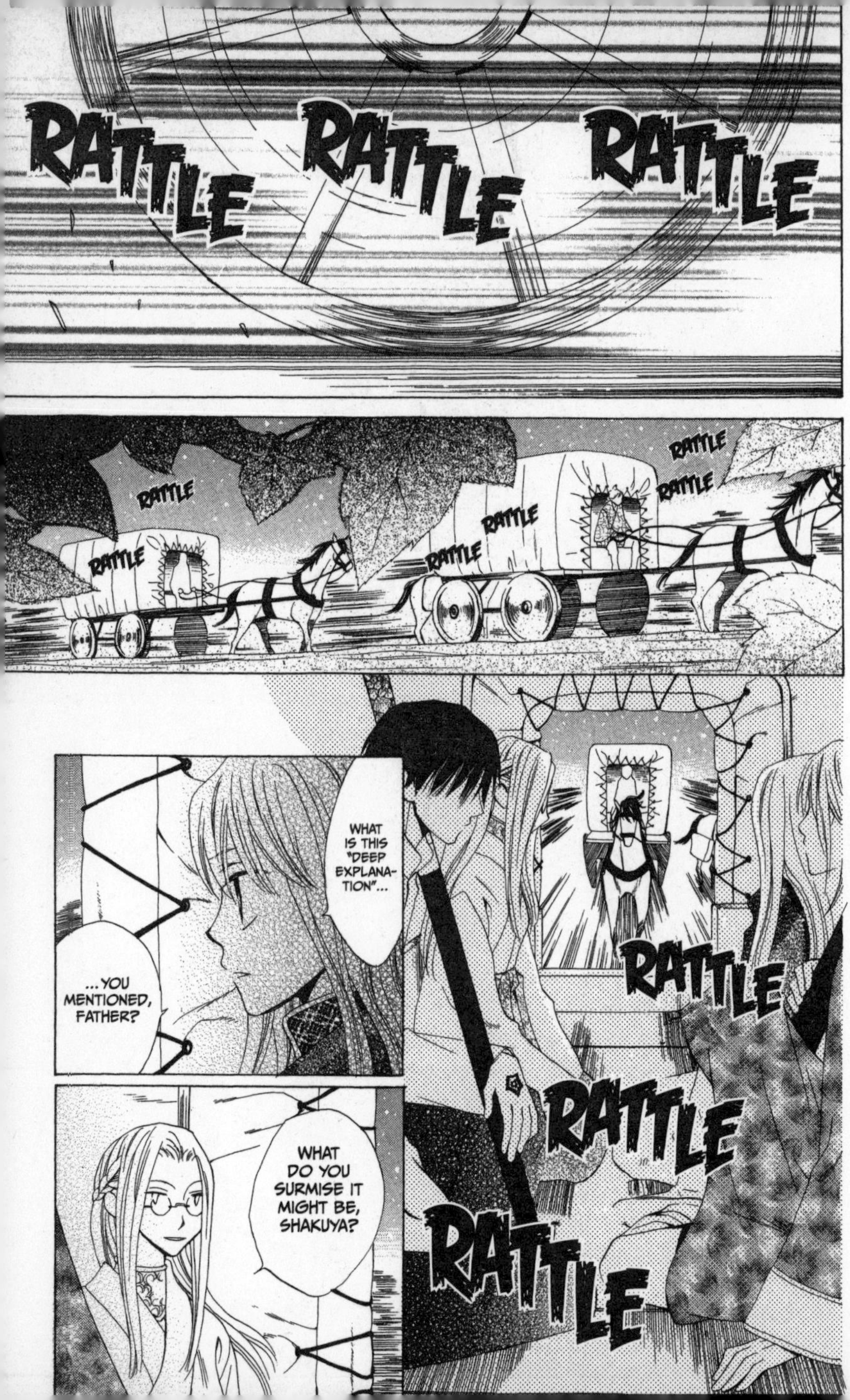
RATTLE RATTLE RATTLE
RATTLE
RATTLE
RATTLE
RATTLE
RATTLE
RATTLE
RATTLE
RATTLE
RATTLE
WHAT IS THIS "DEEP EXPLANATION"...
...YOU MENTIONED, FATHER?
WHAT DO YOU SURMISE IT MIGHT BE, SHAKUYA?

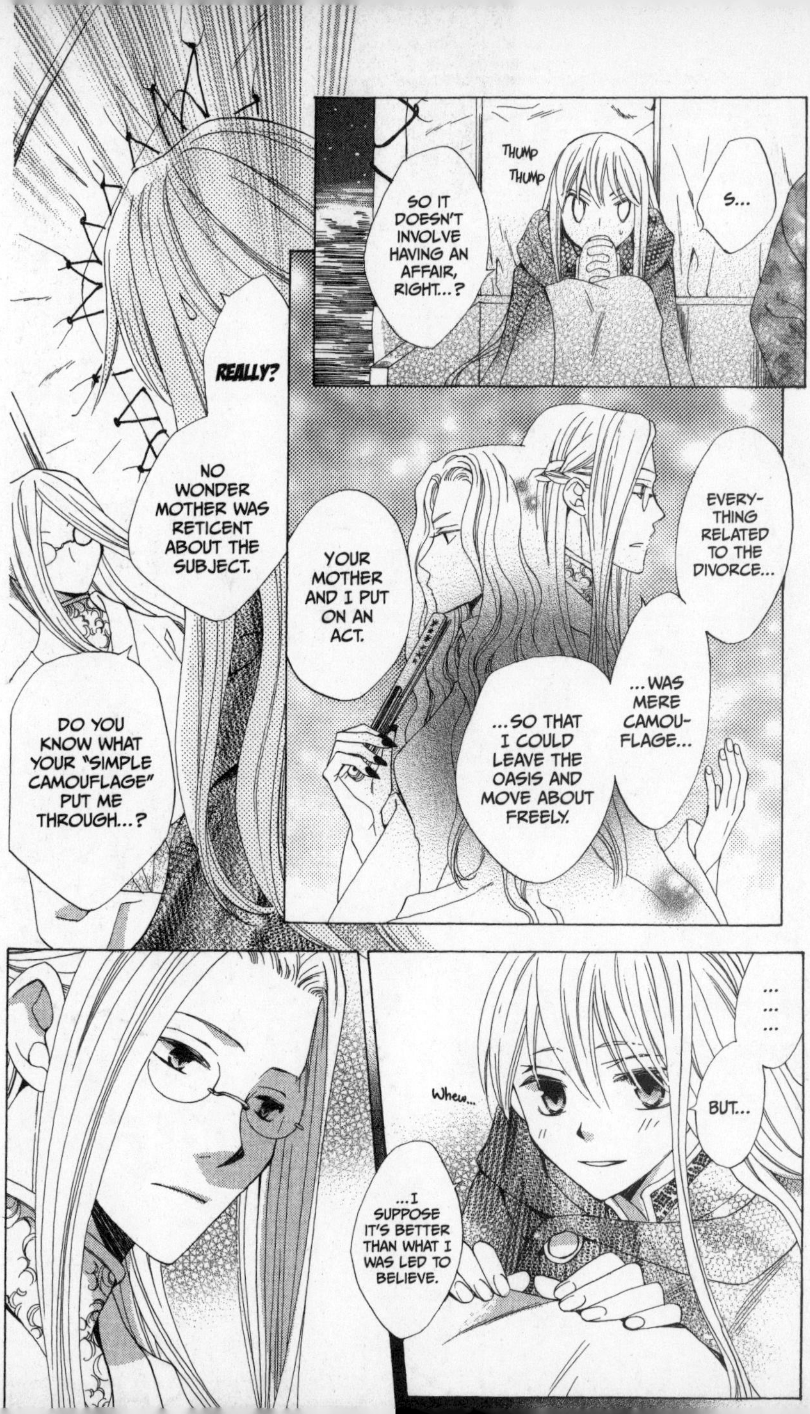
S...
THUMP THUMP
SO IT DOESN'T INVOLVE HAVING AN AFFAIR, RIGHT...?
EVERY-THING RELATED TO THE DIVORCE...
...WAS MERE CAMOU-FLAGE...
...SO THAT I COULD LEAVE THE OASIS AND MOVE ABOUT FREELY.
YOUR MOTHER AND I PUT ON AN ACT.
REALLY?
NO WONDER MOTHER WAS RETICENT ABOUT THE SUBJECT.
DO YOU KNOW WHAT YOUR "SIMPLE CAMOUFLAGE" PUT ME THROUGH...?
...
...
...
BUT...
Whew...
...I SUPPOSE IT'S BETTER THAN WHAT I WAS LED TO BELIEVE.

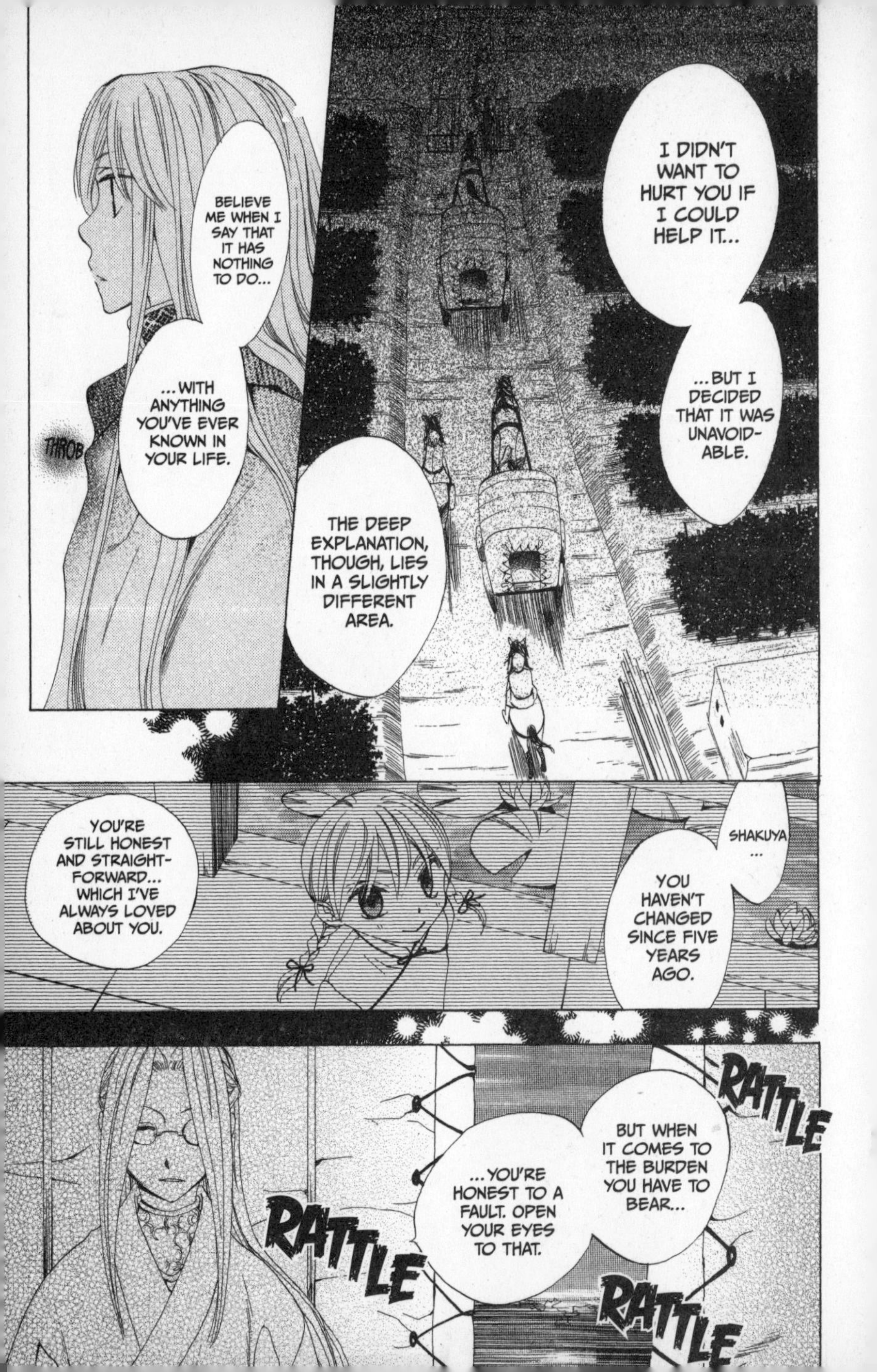
I DIDN'T WANT TO HURT YOU IF I COULD HELP IT...
...BUT I DECIDED THAT IT WAS UNAVOID-ABLE.
THE DEEP EXPLANATION, THOUGH, LIES IN A SLIGHTLY DIFFERENT AREA.
BELIEVE ME WHEN I SAY THAT IT HAS NOTHING TO DO...
...WITH ANYTHING YOU'VE EVER KNOWN IN YOUR LIFE.
THROB
SHAKUYA...
YOU HAVEN'T CHANGED SINCE FIVE YEARS AGO.
YOU'RE STILL HONEST AND STRAIGHT-FORWARD... WHICH I'VE ALWAYS LOVED ABOUT YOU.
RATTLE
BUT WHEN IT COMES TO THE BURDEN YOU HAVE TO BEAR...
...YOU'RE HONEST TO A FAULT. OPEN YOUR EYES TO THAT.
RATTLE
RATTLE

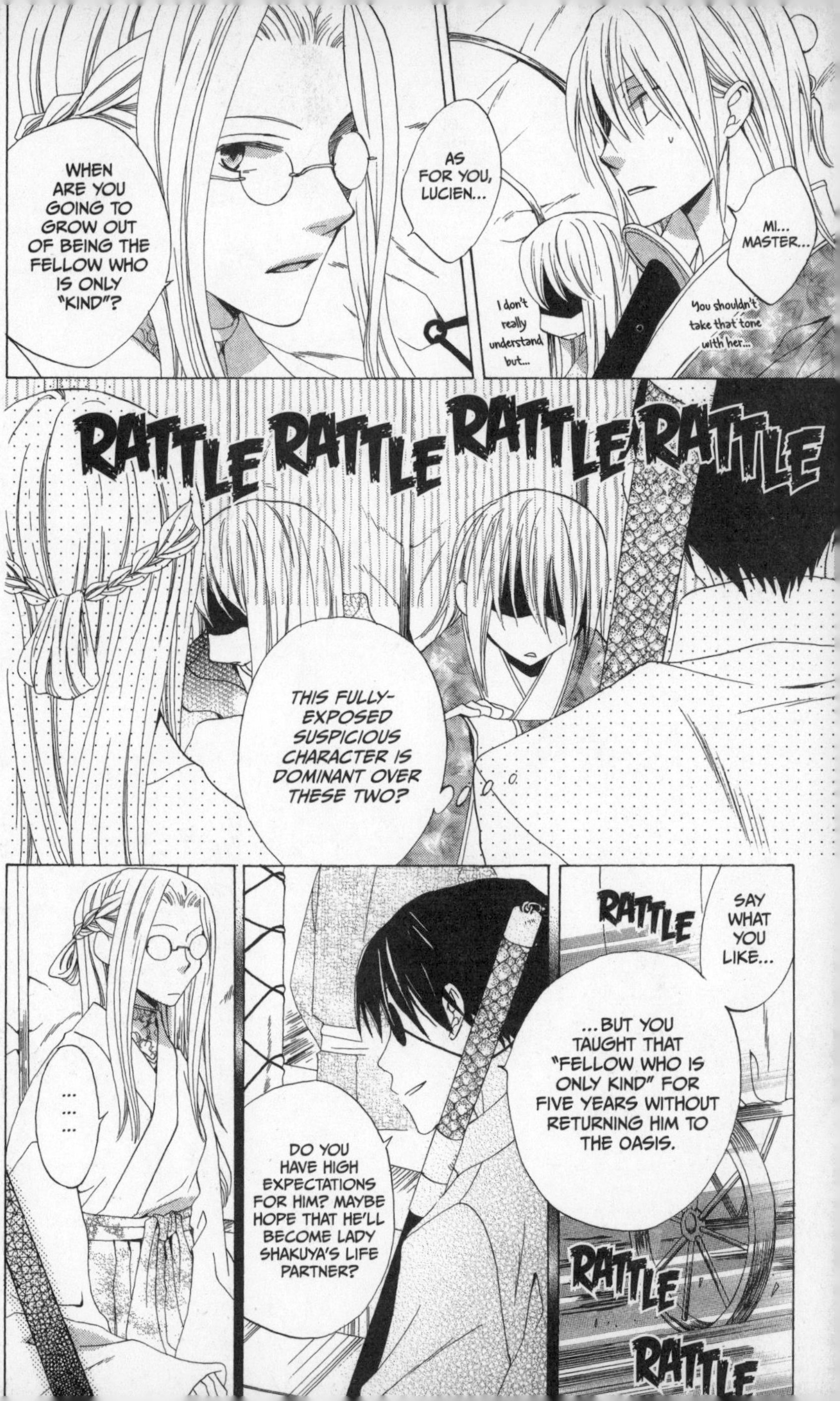
MI... MASTER...
You shouldn't take that tone with her...
I don't really understand but...
AS FOR YOU, LUCIEN...
WHEN ARE YOU GOING TO GROW OUT OF BEING THE FELLOW WHO IS ONLY "KIND"?
RATTLE RATTLE RATTLE RATTLE
THIS FULLY-EXPOSED SUSPICIOUS CHARACTER IS DOMINANT OVER THESE TWO?
RATTLE
SAY WHAT YOU LIKE...
...BUT YOU TAUGHT THAT "FELLOW WHO IS ONLY KIND" FOR FIVE YEARS WITHOUT RETURNING HIM TO THE OASIS.
RATTLE
RATTLE
DO YOU HAVE HIGH EXPECTATIONS FOR HIM? MAYBE HOPE THAT HE'LL BECOME LADY SHAKUYA'S LIFE PARTNER?
... ...

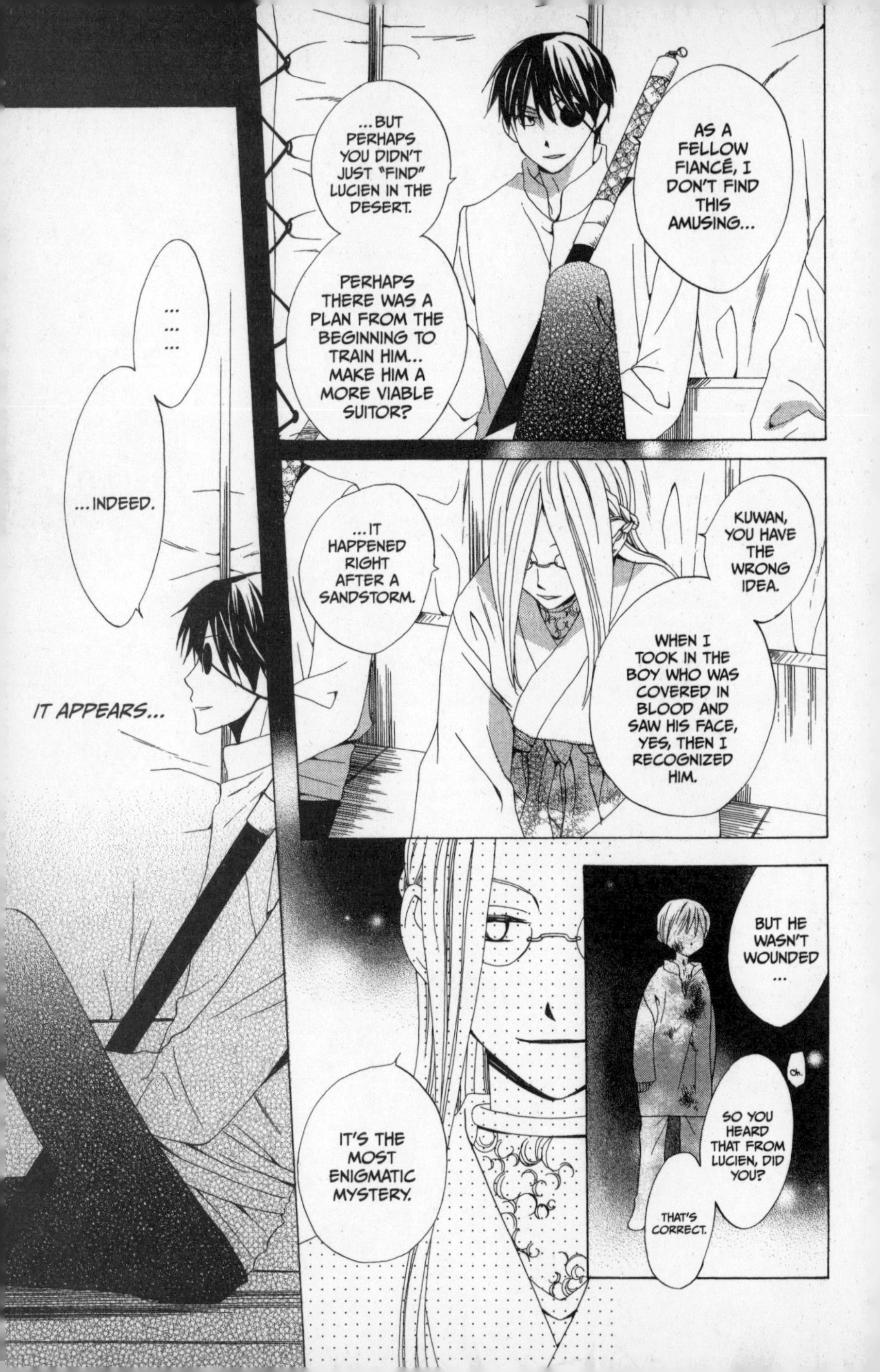
AS A FELLOW FIANCÉ, I DON'T FIND THIS AMUSING...
...BUT PERHAPS YOU DIDN'T JUST "FIND" LUCIEN IN THE DESERT.
PERHAPS THERE WAS A PLAN FROM THE BEGINNING TO TRAIN HIM... MAKE HIM A MORE VIABLE SUITOR?
KUWAN, YOU HAVE THE WRONG IDEA.
WHEN I TOOK IN THE BOY WHO WAS COVERED IN BLOOD AND SAW HIS FACE, YES, THEN I RECOGNIZED HIM.
...IT HAPPENED RIGHT AFTER A SANDSTORM.
BUT HE WASN'T WOUNDED...
Oh.
SO YOU HEARD THAT FROM LUCIEN, DID YOU?
THAT'S CORRECT.
IT'S THE MOST ENIGMATIC MYSTERY.
...
...
...
...INDEED.
IT APPEARS...

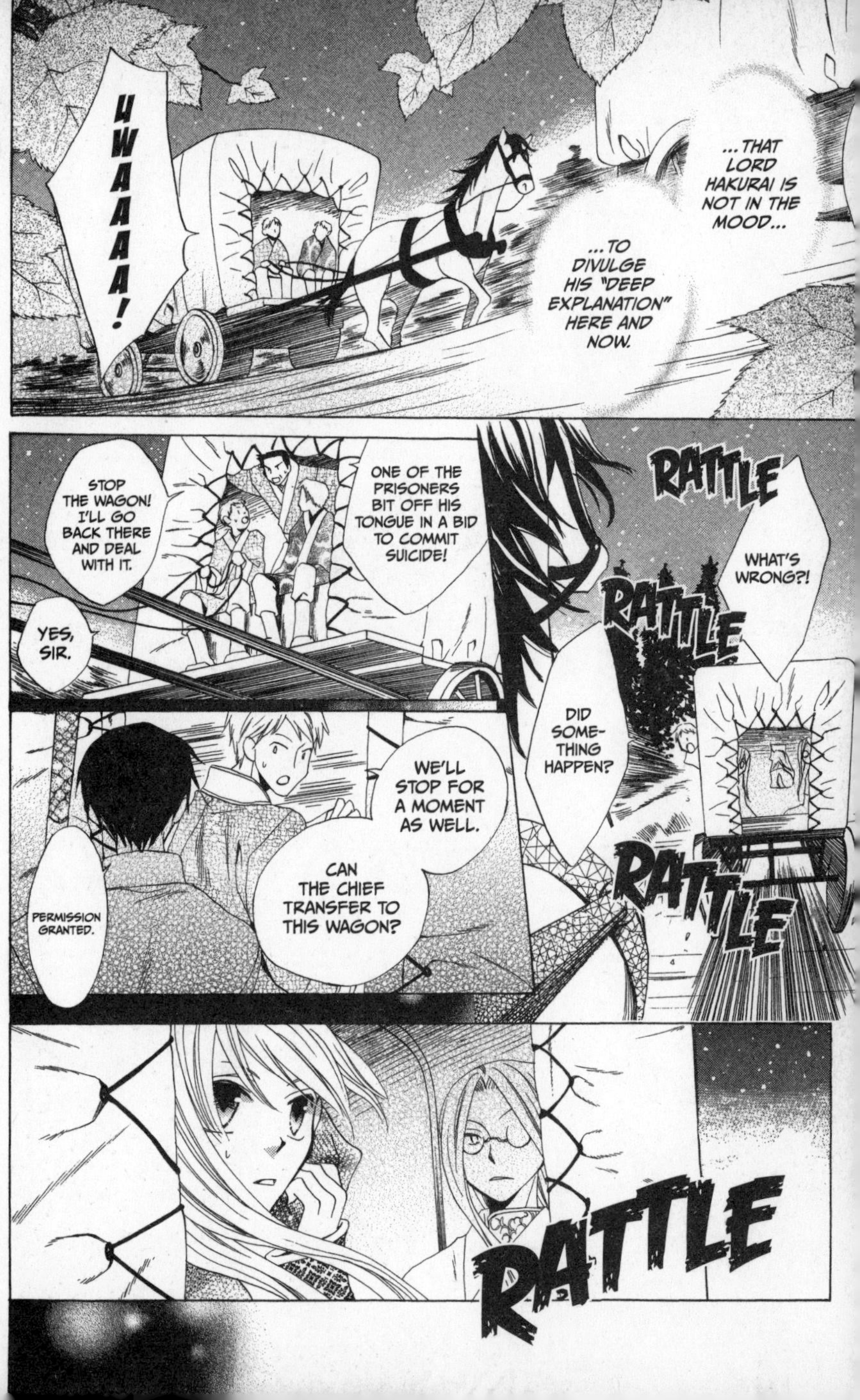
...THAT LORD HAKURAI IS NOT IN THE MOOD...
...TO DIVULGE HIS "DEEP EXPLANATION" HERE AND NOW.
UWAAAAA!
RATTLE
WHAT'S WRONG?!
RATTLE
DID SOME-THING HAPPEN?
RATTLE
RATTLE
ONE OF THE PRISONERS BIT OFF HIS TONGUE IN A BID TO COMMIT SUICIDE!
STOP THE WAGON! I'LL GO BACK THERE AND DEAL WITH IT.
YES, SIR.
WE'LL STOP FOR A MOMENT AS WELL.
CAN THE CHIEF TRANSFER TO THIS WAGON?
PERMISSION GRANTED.
RATTLE

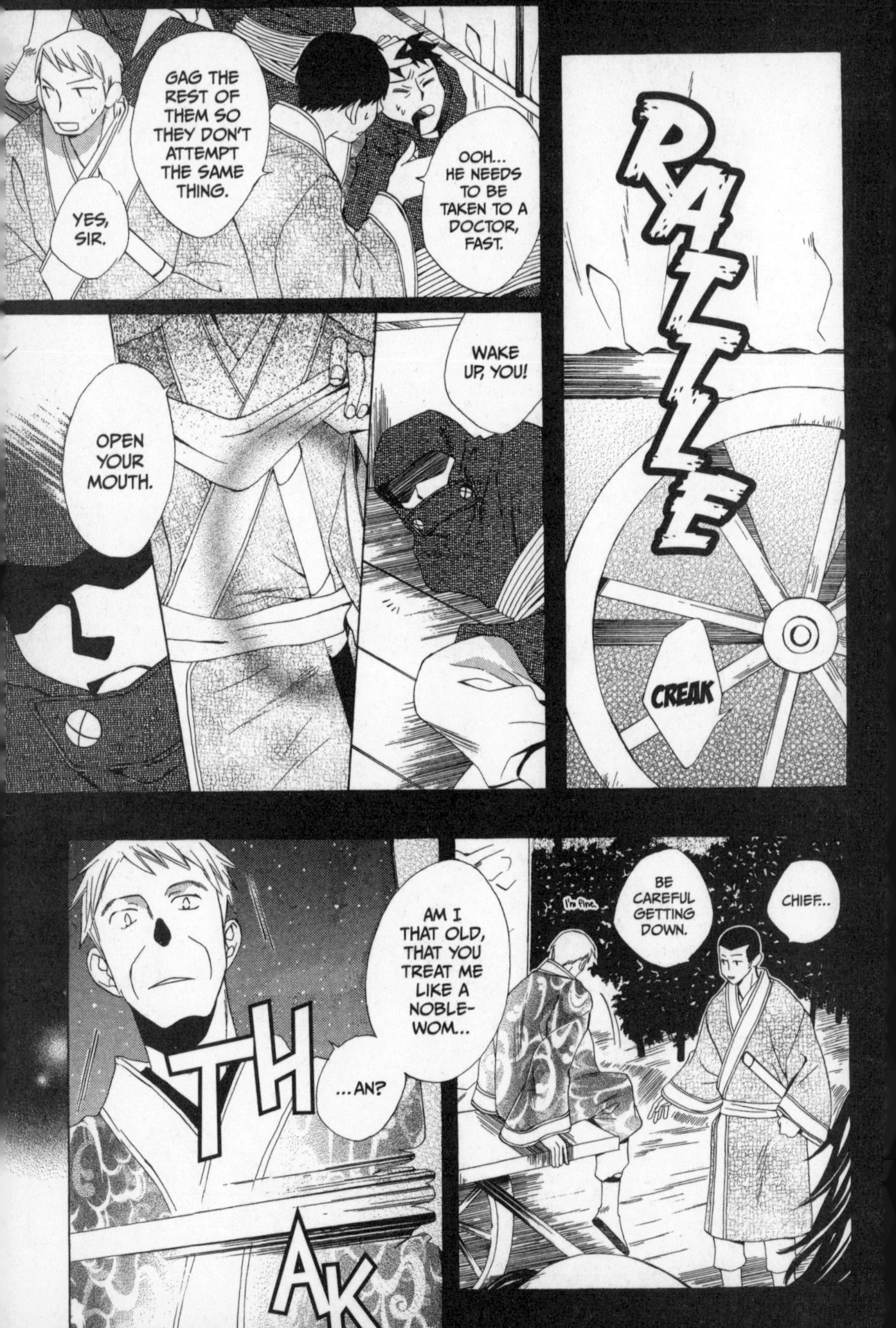

RATTLE
CREAK
OOH... HE NEEDS TO BE TAKEN TO A DOCTOR, FAST.
GAG THE REST OF THEM SO THEY DON'T ATTEMPT THE SAME THING.
YES, SIR.
WAKE UP, YOU!
OPEN YOUR MOUTH.
CHIEF...
BE CAREFUL GETTING DOWN.
I'm fine.
AM I THAT OLD, THAT YOU TREAT ME LIKE A NOBLE-WOM...
...AN?
THWACK

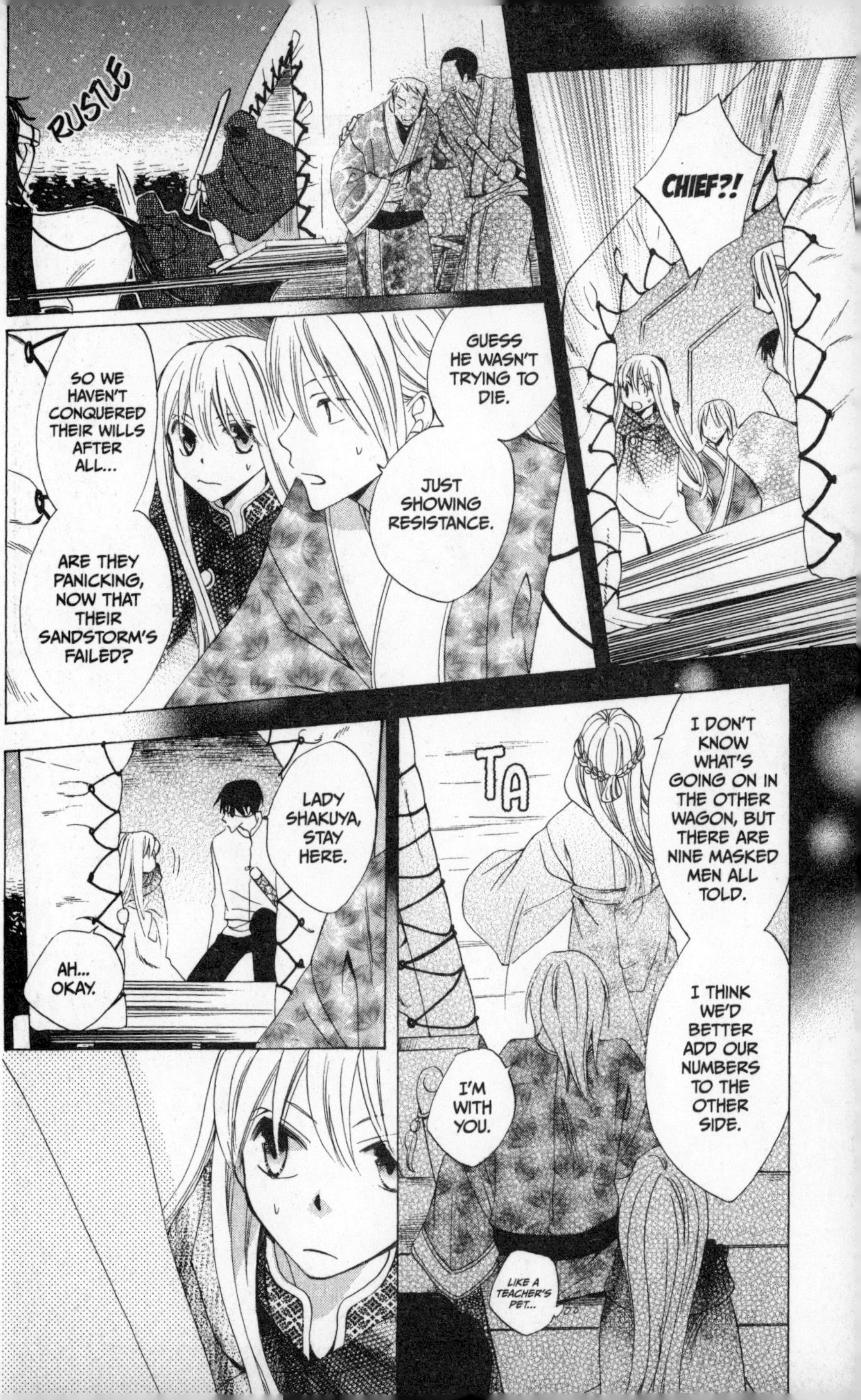
CHIEF?!
RUSTLE
GUESS HE WASN'T TRYING TO DIE.
JUST SHOWING RESISTANCE.
SO WE HAVEN'T CONQUERED THEIR WILLS AFTER ALL...
ARE THEY PANICKING, NOW THAT THEIR SANDSTORM'S FAILED?
I DON'T KNOW WHAT'S GOING ON IN THE OTHER WAGON, BUT THERE ARE NINE MASKED MEN ALL TOLD.
TA
I THINK WE'D BETTER ADD OUR NUMBERS TO THE OTHER SIDE.
I'M WITH YOU.
LIKE A TEACHER'S PET...
LADY SHAKUYA, STAY HERE.
AH... OKAY.

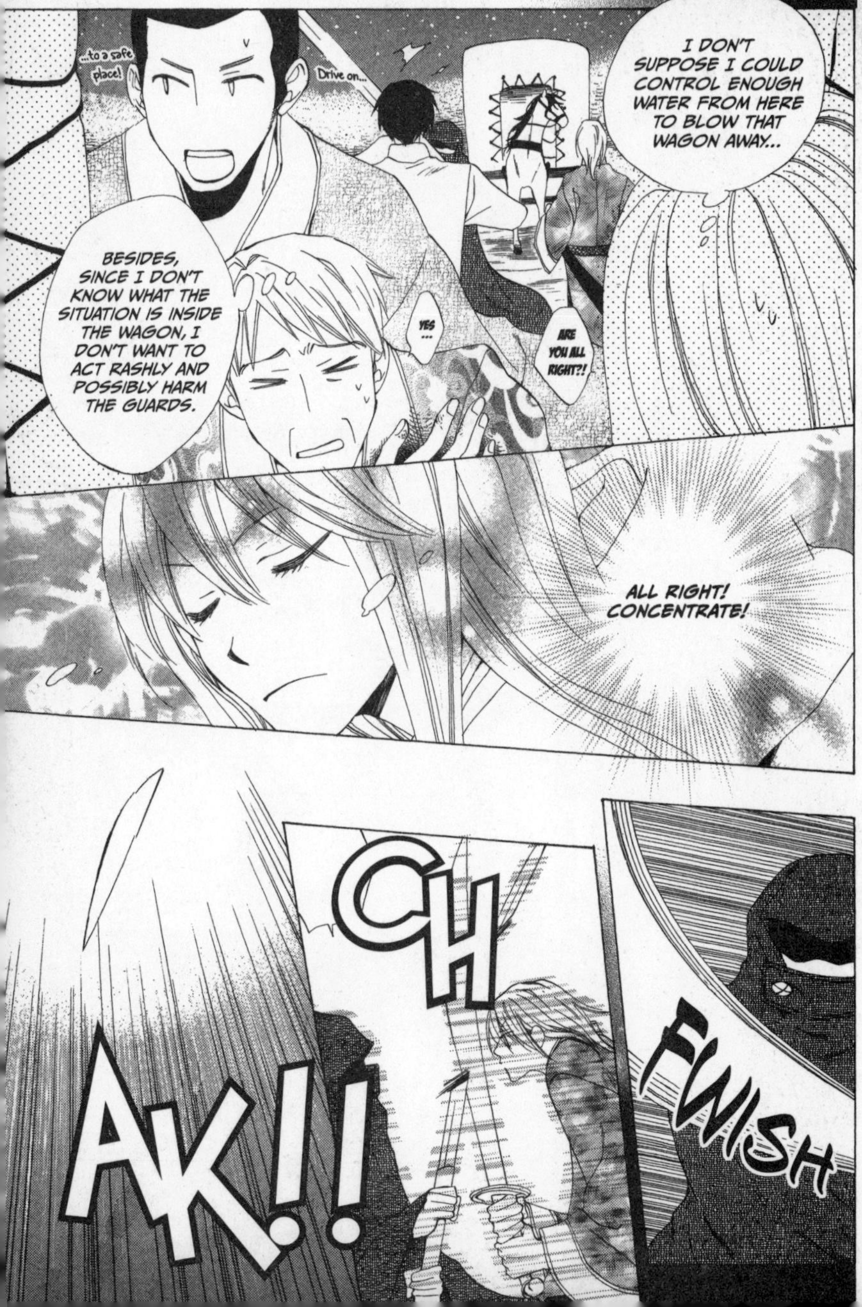
I DON'T SUPPOSE I COULD CONTROL ENOUGH WATER FROM HERE TO BLOW THAT WAGON AWAY...
ARE YOU ALL RIGHT?!
YES...
Drive on...
...to a safe place!
BESIDES, SINCE I DON'T KNOW WHAT THE SITUATION IS INSIDE THE WAGON, I DON'T WANT TO ACT RASHLY AND POSSIBLY HARM THE GUARDS.
ALL RIGHT! CONCENTRATE!
FWISH
CH
AK!!

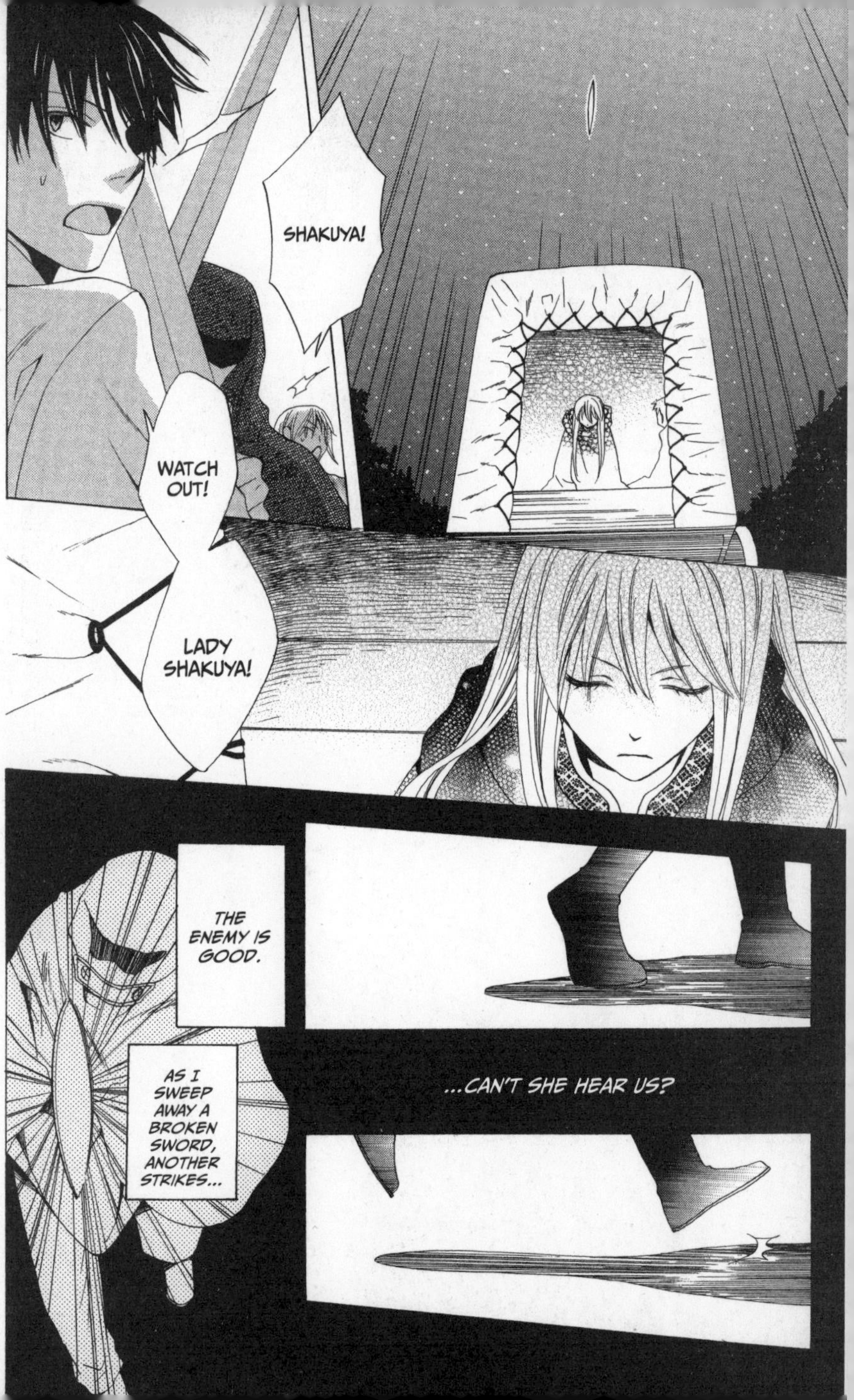
SHAKUYA!
WATCH OUT!
LADY SHAKUYA!
...CAN'T SHE HEAR US?
THE ENEMY IS GOOD.
AS I SWEEP AWAY A BROKEN SWORD, ANOTHER STRIKES...

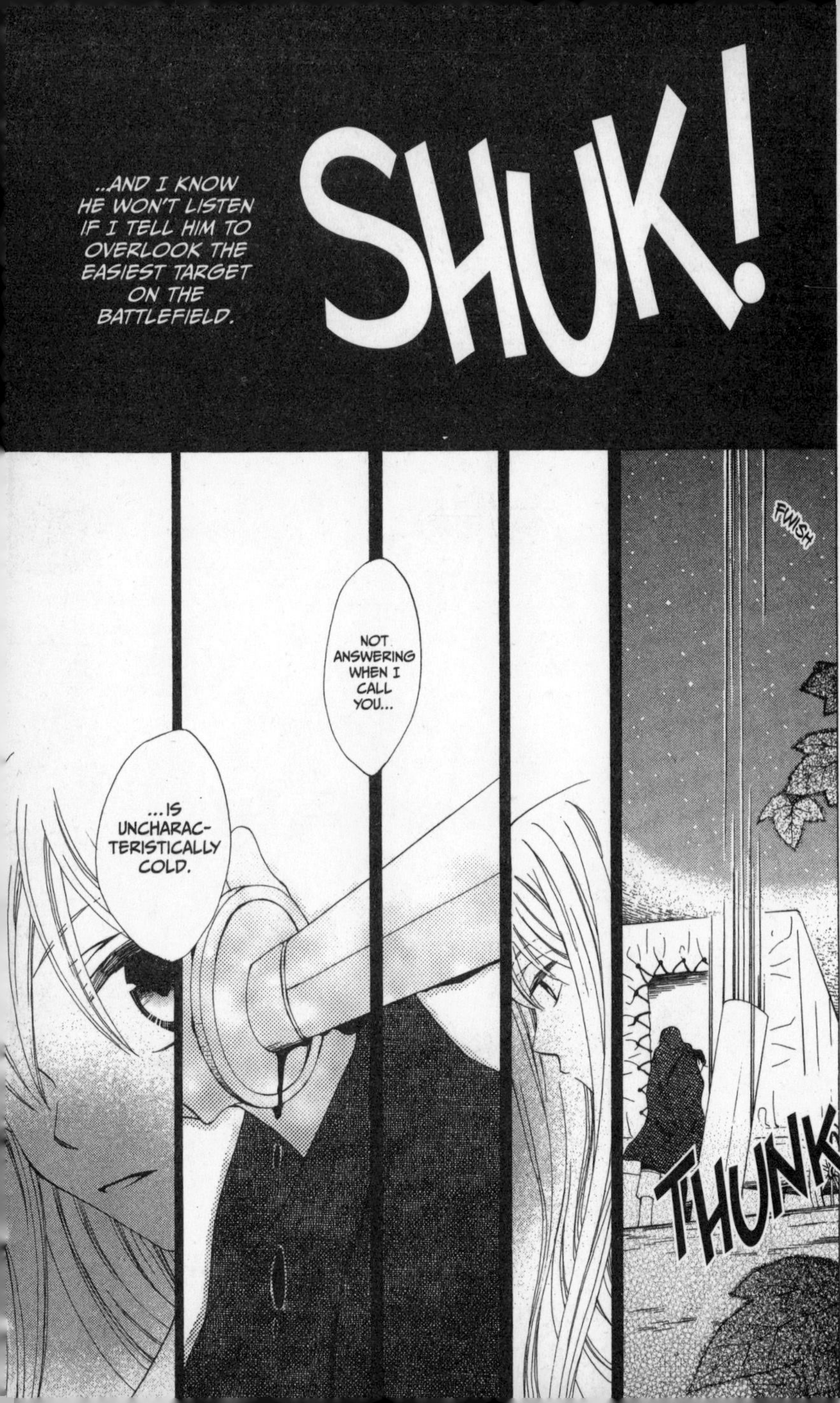
SHUK!
...AND I KNOW HE WON'T LISTEN IF I TELL HIM TO OVERLOOK THE EASIEST TARGET ON THE BATTLEFIELD.
FWISH
THUNK
NOT ANSWERING WHEN I CALL YOU...
...IS UNCHARAC-TERISTICALLY COLD.

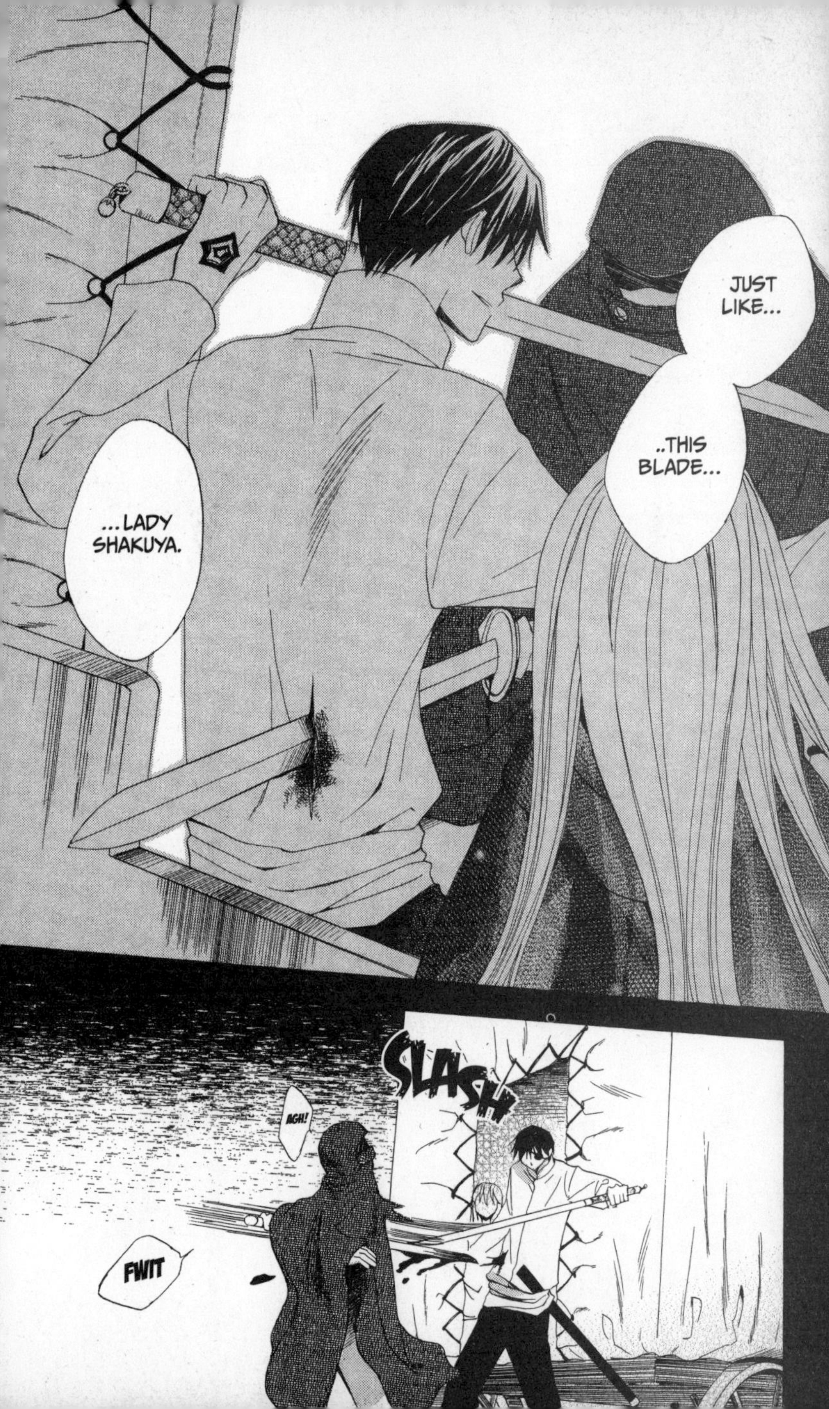
JUST LIKE...
..THIS BLADE...
...LADY SHAKUYA.
SLASH
AGH!
FWIT

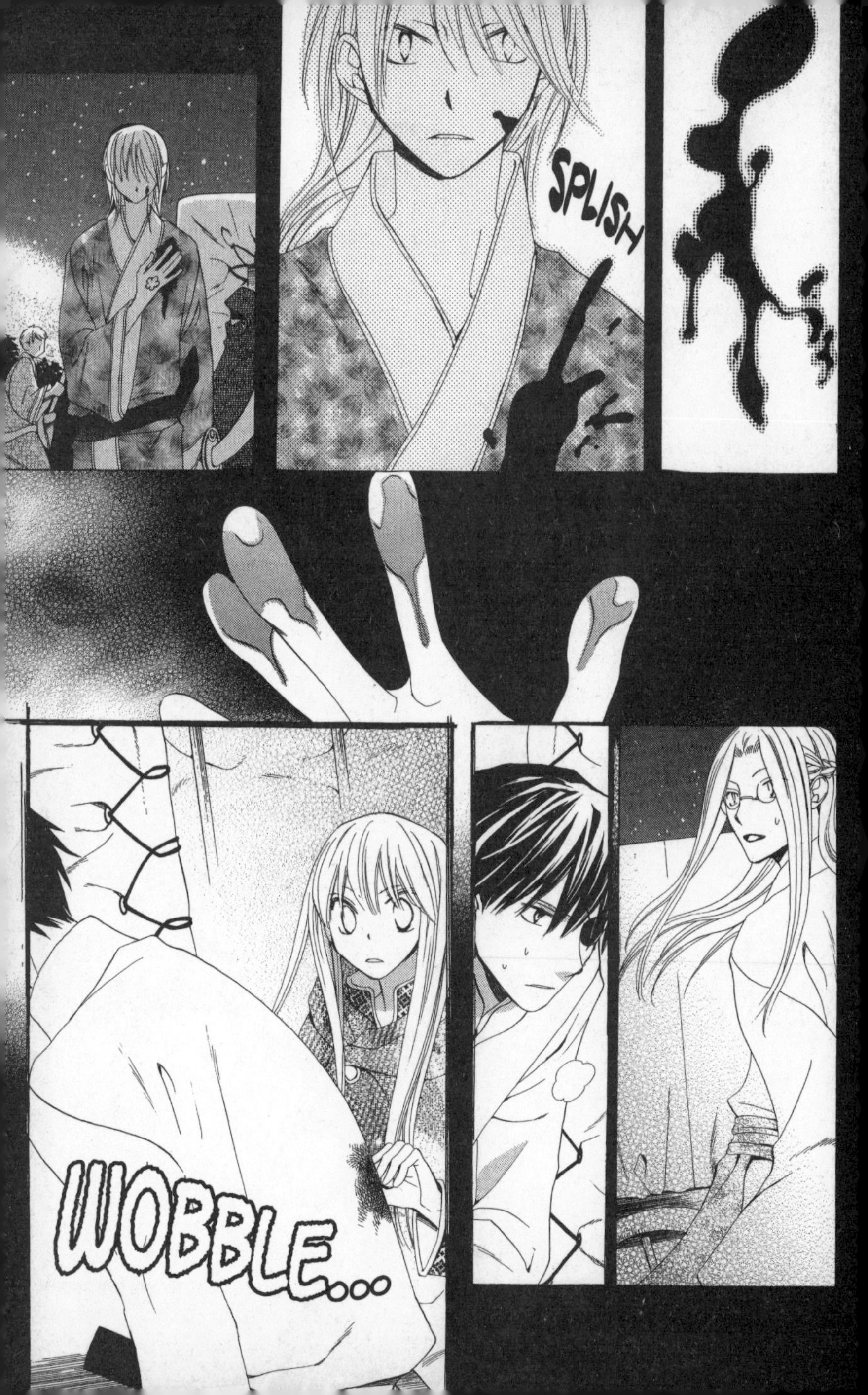
SPLISH
WOBBLE...

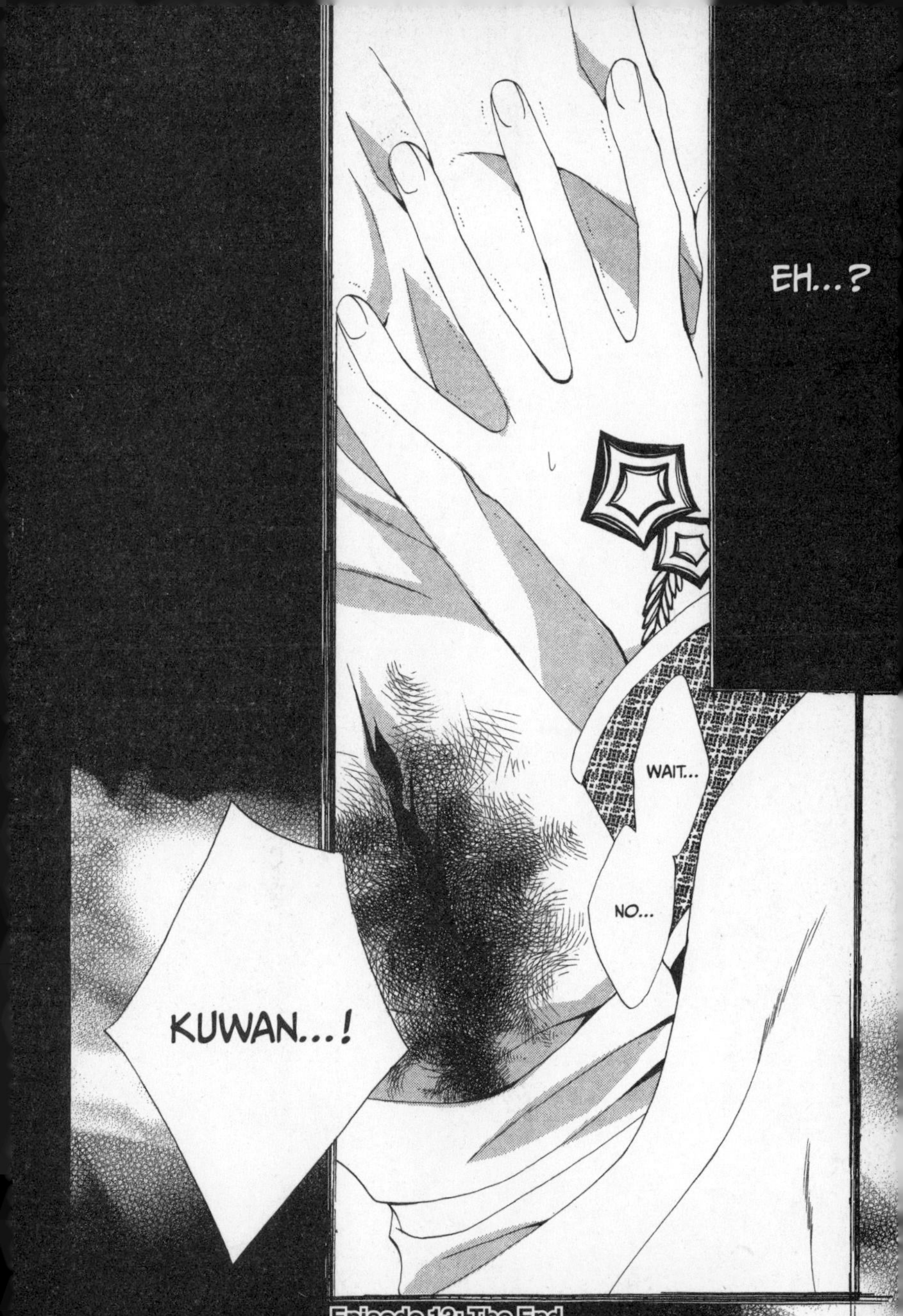
EH...?
WAIT...
NO...
KUWAN...!

Episode 13: The End

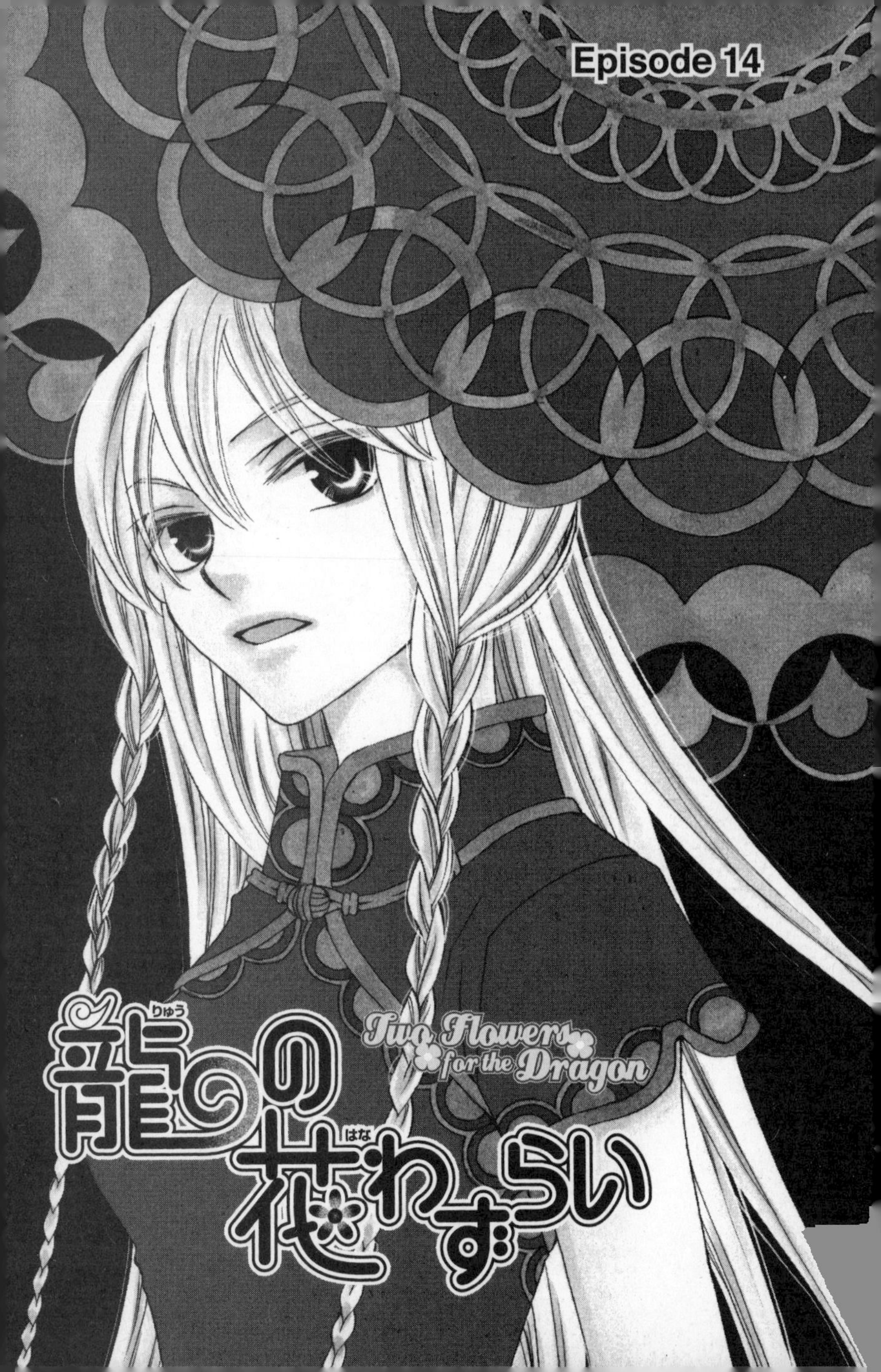
Episode 14
龍の花わずらい
りゅう
はな
Two Flowers for the Dragon

Volume 14 Preview Cut

Is Kuwan okay? was the question that demanded to be answered in this episode, so I had Shakuya being unusually meek here.

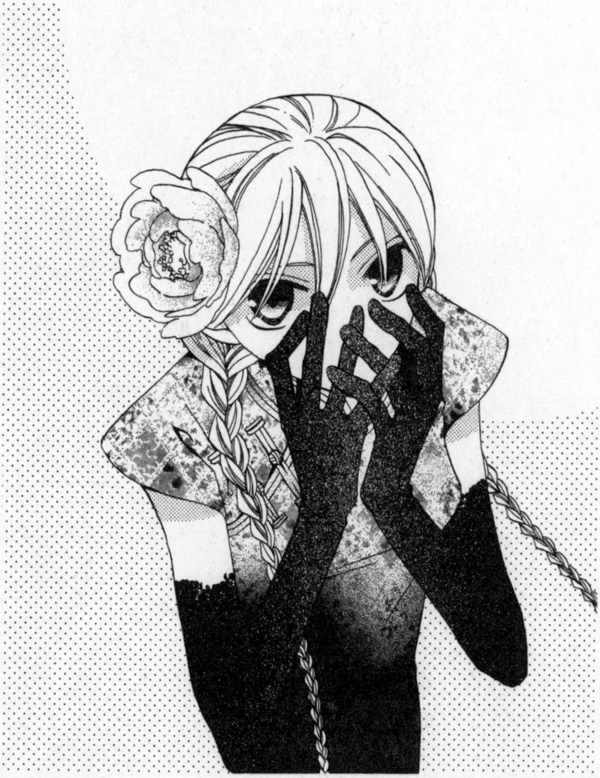

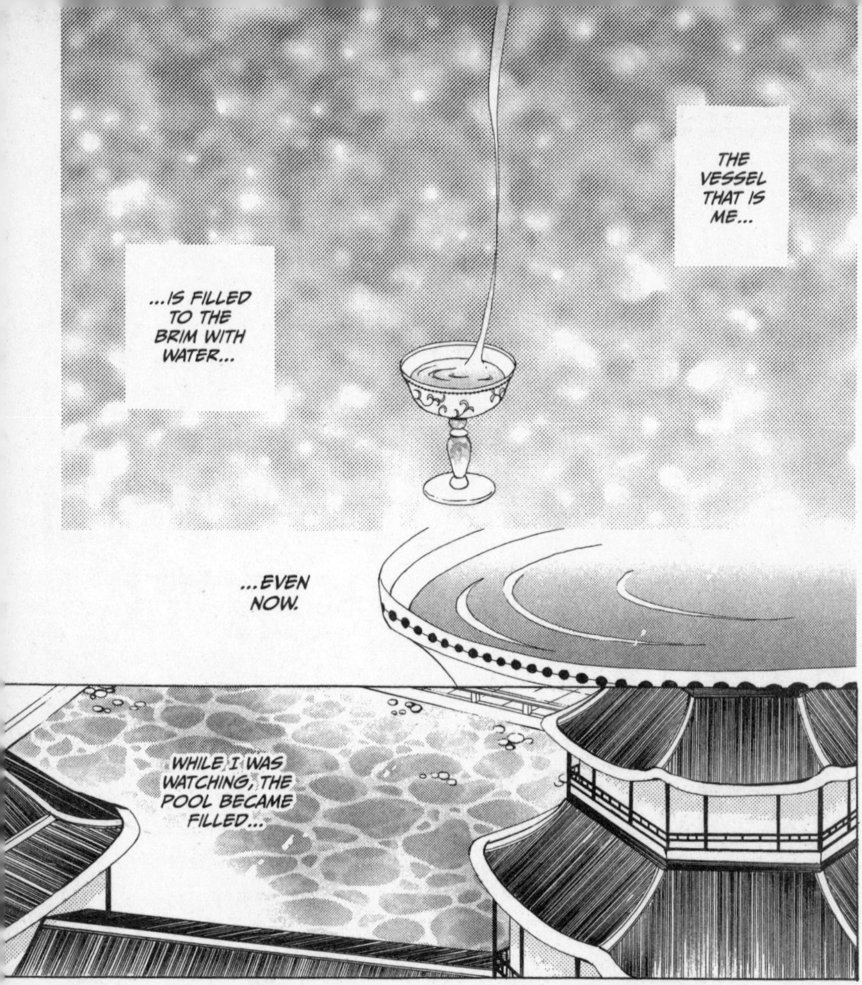
THE VESSEL THAT IS ME...
...IS FILLED TO THE BRIM WITH WATER...
...EVEN NOW.
WHILE I WAS WATCHING, THE POOL BECAME FILLED...

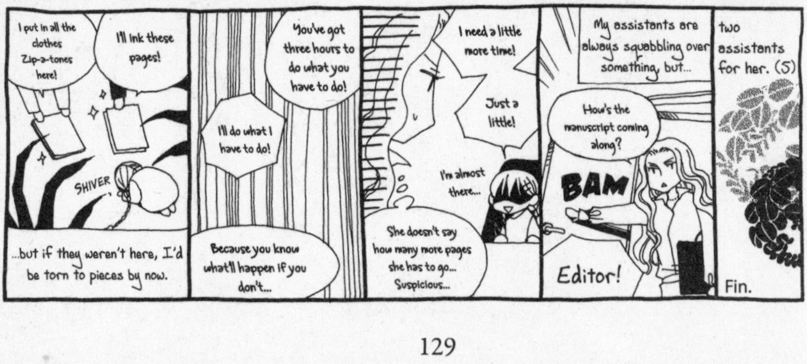
two assistants for her. (5)
Fin.
My assistants are always squabbling over something, but...
How's the manuscript coming along?
BAM
Editor!
I need a little more time!
Just a little!
I'm almost there...
She doesn't say how many more pages she has to go... Suspicious...
You've got three hours to do what you have to do!
I'll do what I have to do!
Because you know what'll happen if you don't...
I'll ink these pages!
I put in all the clothes Zip-a-tones here!
SHIVER
...but if they weren't here, I'd be torn to pieces by now.

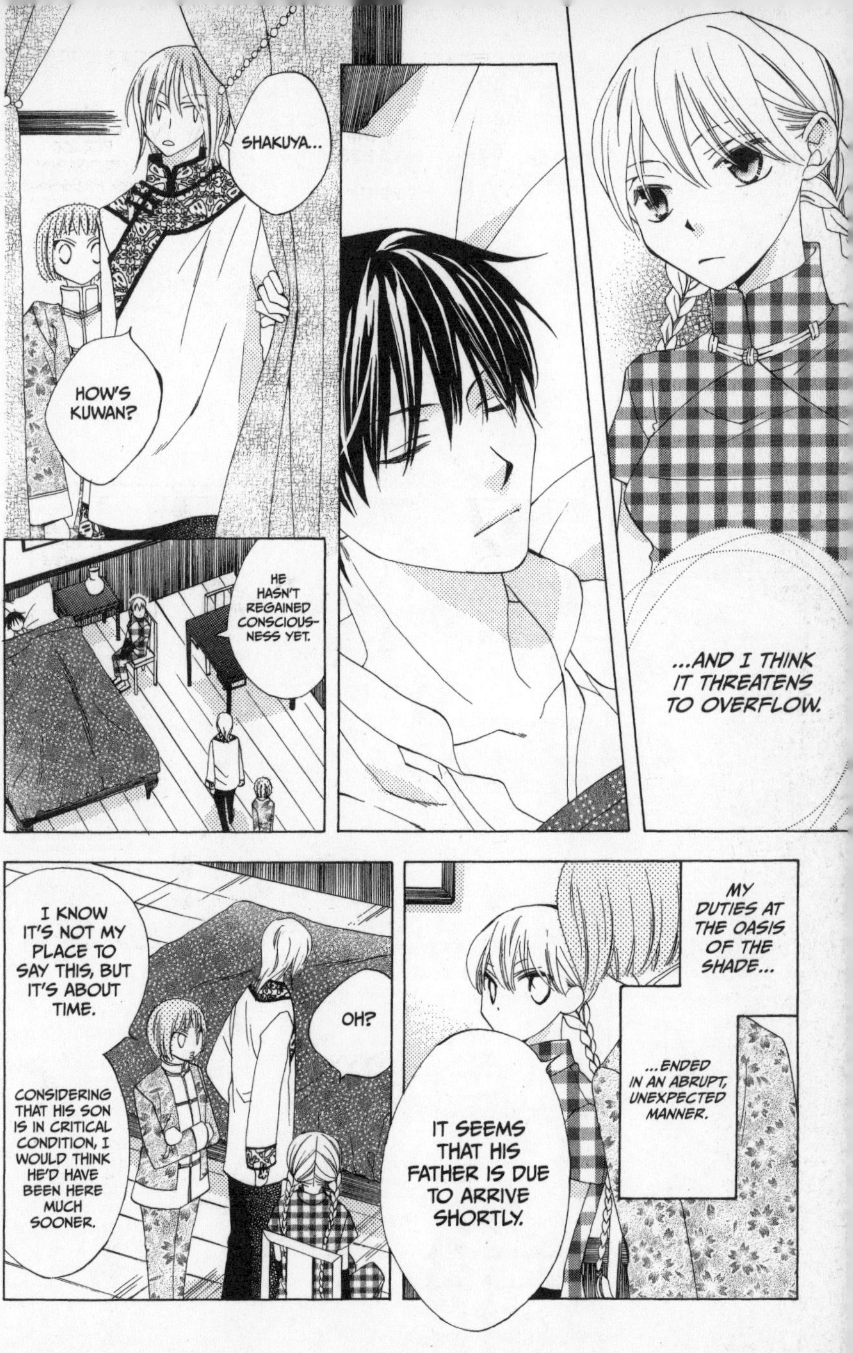
...AND I THINK IT THREATENS TO OVERFLOW.
SHAKUYA...
HOW'S KUWAN?
HE HASN'T REGAINED CONSCIOUSNESS YET.
MY DUTIES AT THE OASIS OF THE SHADE...
...ENDED IN AN ABRUPT, UNEXPECTED MANNER.
IT SEEMS THAT HIS FATHER IS DUE TO ARRIVE SHORTLY.
OH?
I KNOW IT'S NOT MY PLACE TO SAY THIS, BUT IT'S ABOUT TIME.
CONSIDERING THAT HIS SON IS IN CRITICAL CONDITION, I WOULD THINK HE'D HAVE BEEN HERE MUCH SOONER.

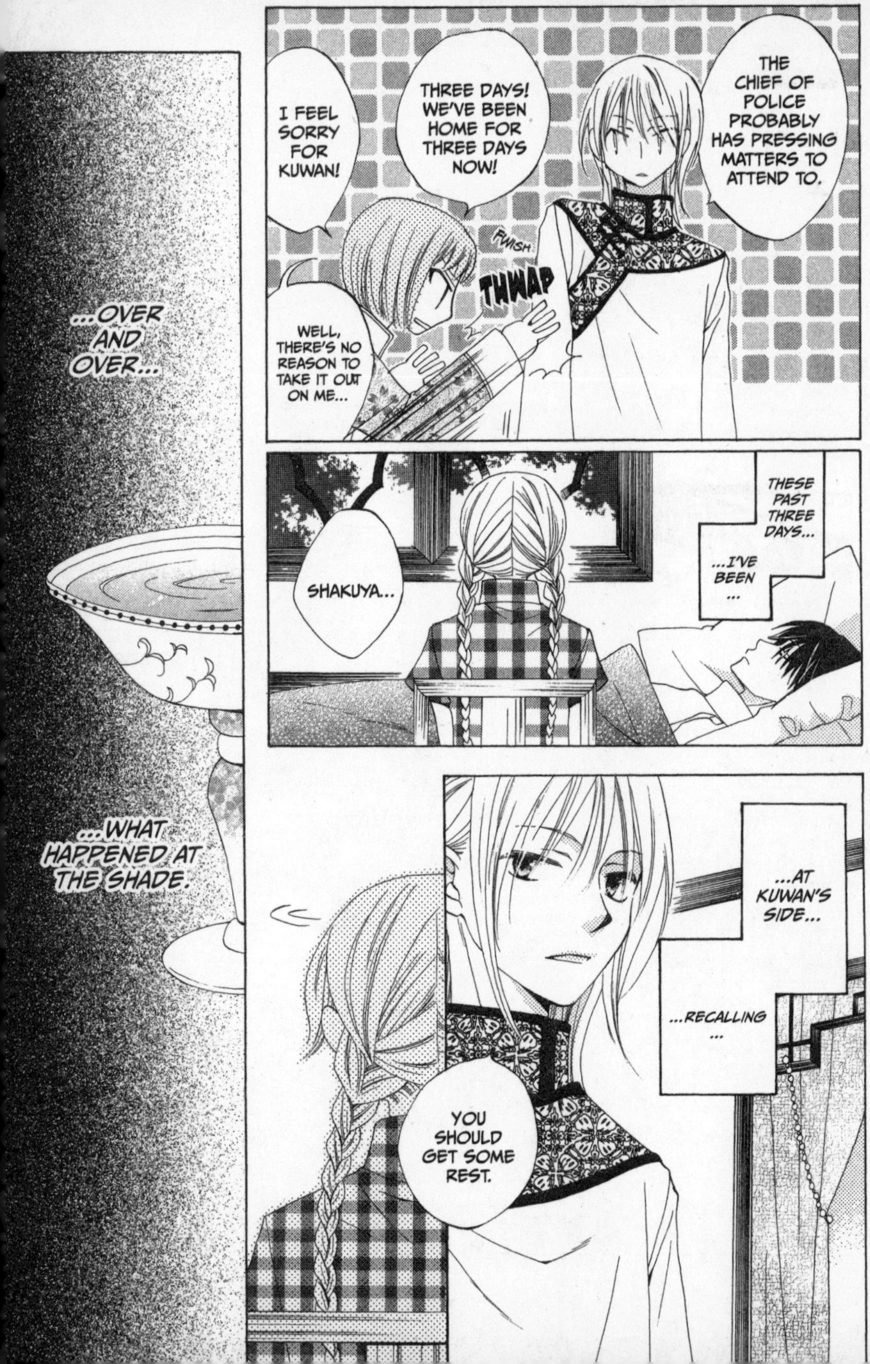
THE CHIEF OF POLICE PROBABLY HAS PRESSING MATTERS TO ATTEND TO.
THREE DAYS! WE'VE BEEN HOME FOR THREE DAYS NOW!
I FEEL SORRY FOR KUWAN!
FWISH
THWAP
WELL, THERE'S NO REASON TO TAKE IT OUT ON ME...
THESE PAST THREE DAYS...
...I'VE BEEN ...
SHAKUYA...
...AT KUWAN'S SIDE...
...RECALLING ...
YOU SHOULD GET SOME REST.
...OVER AND OVER...
...WHAT HAPPENED AT THE SHADE.

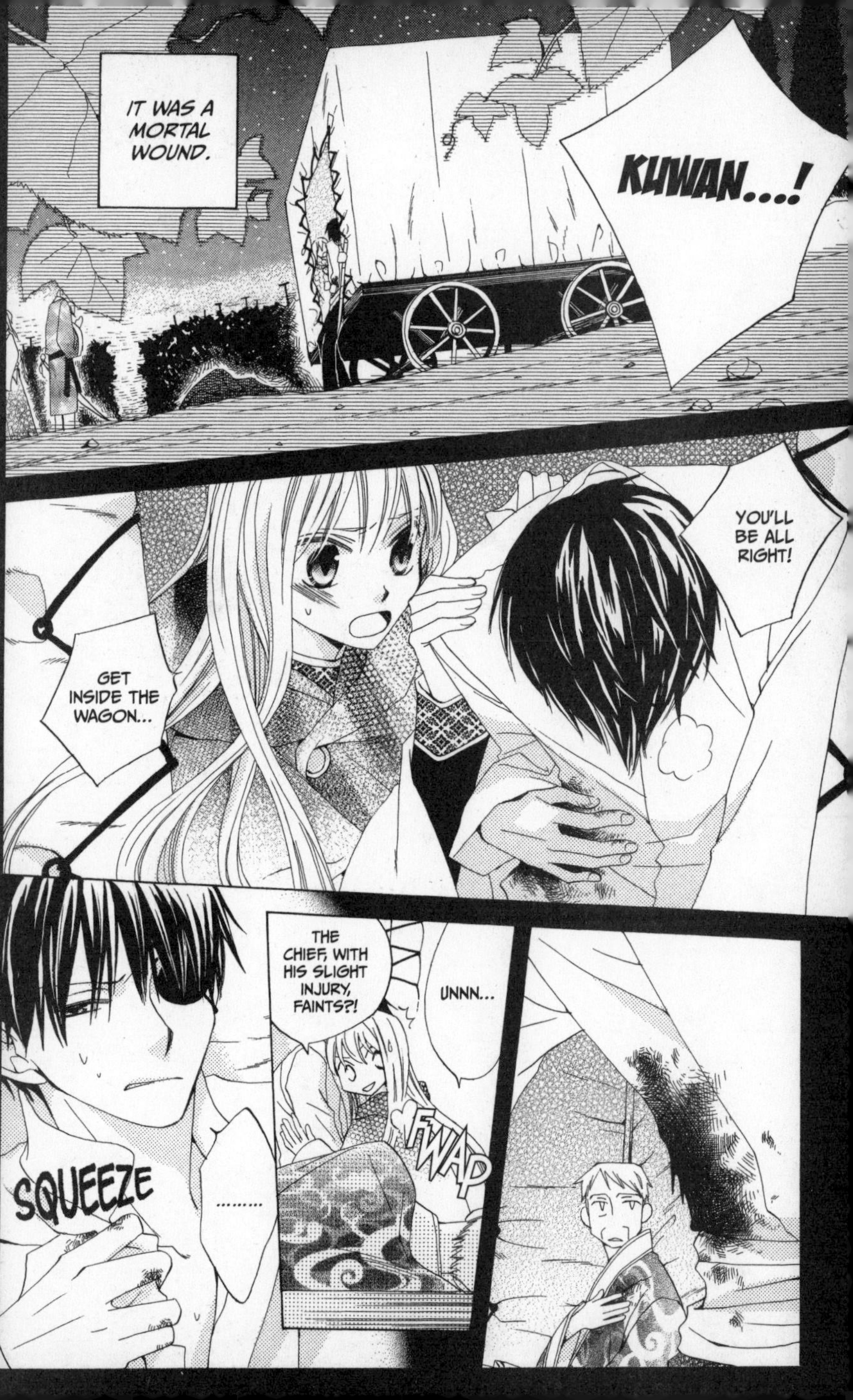
KUWAN...!
IT WAS A MORTAL WOUND.
YOU'LL BE ALL RIGHT!
GET INSIDE THE WAGON...
UNNN...
THE CHIEF, WITH HIS SLIGHT INJURY, FAINTS?!
FWAP
....
SQUEEZE

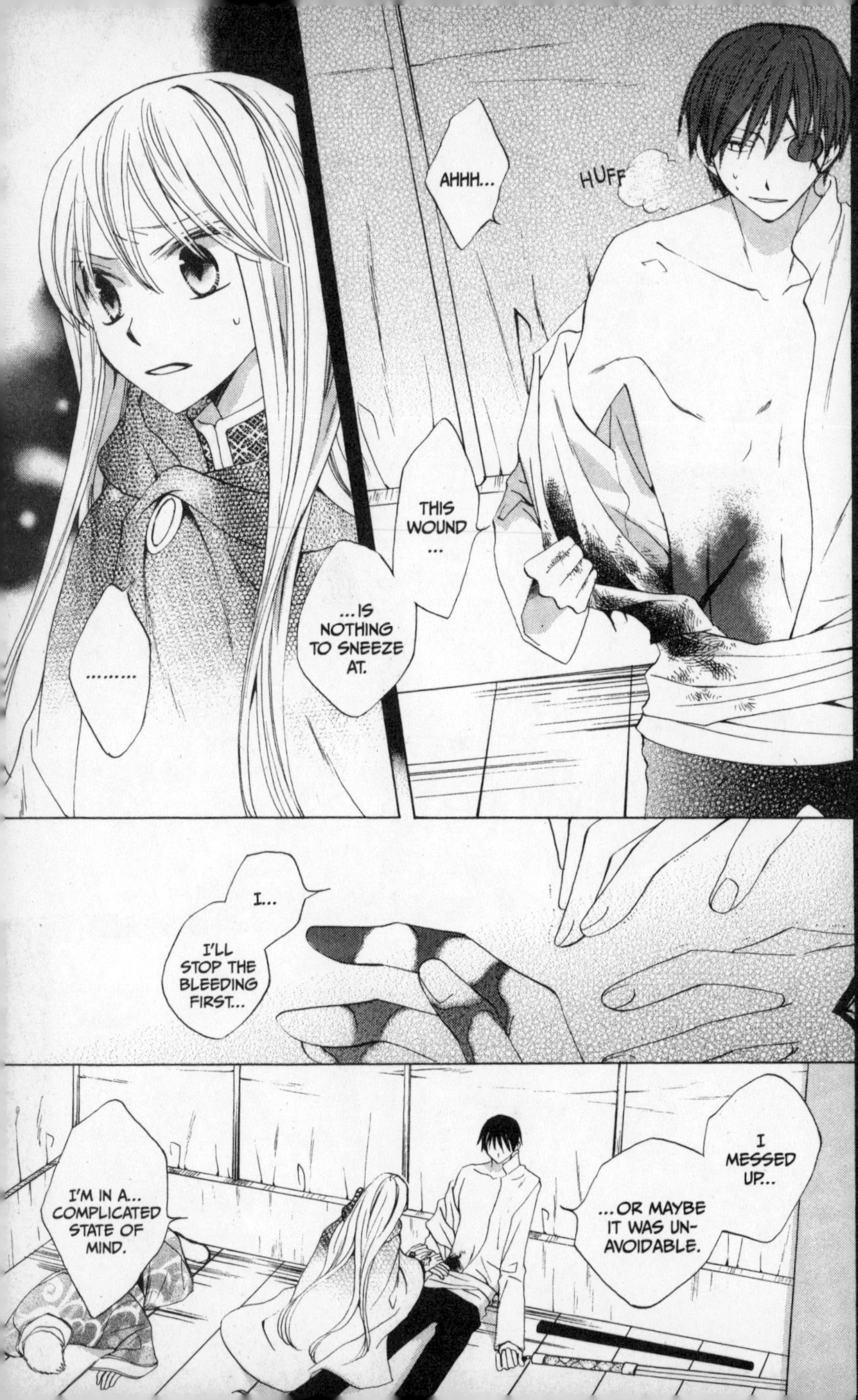
HUFF
AHHH...
THIS WOUND ...
...IS NOTHING TO SNEEZE AT.
....
I...
I'LL STOP THE BLEEDING FIRST...
I MESSED UP...
...OR MAYBE IT WAS UN-AVOIDABLE.
I'M IN A... COMPLICATED STATE OF MIND.

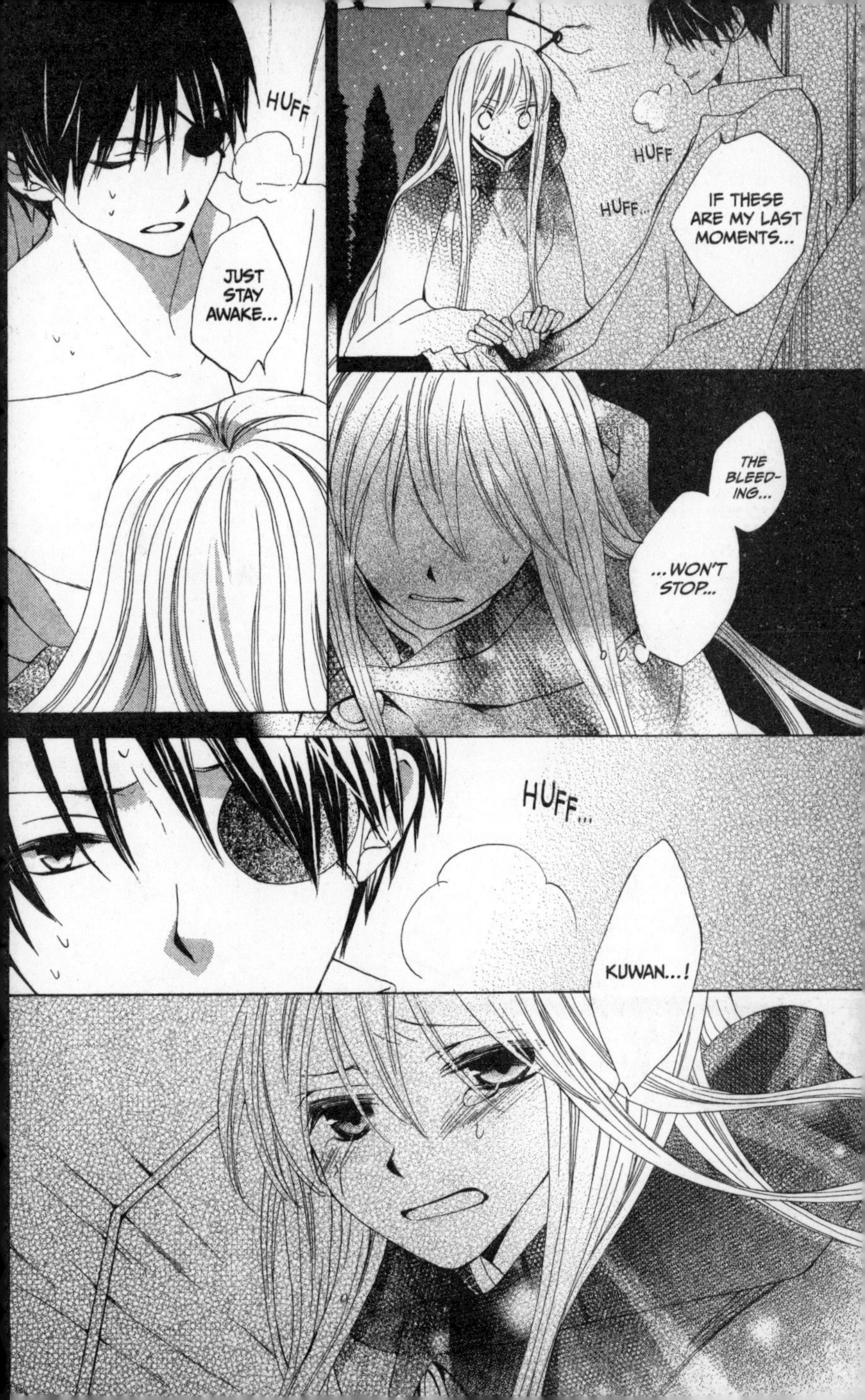
HUFF
IF THESE ARE MY LAST MOMENTS...
HUFF...
HUFF
JUST STAY AWAKE...
THE BLEED-ING...
...WON'T STOP...
HUFF...
KUWAN...!

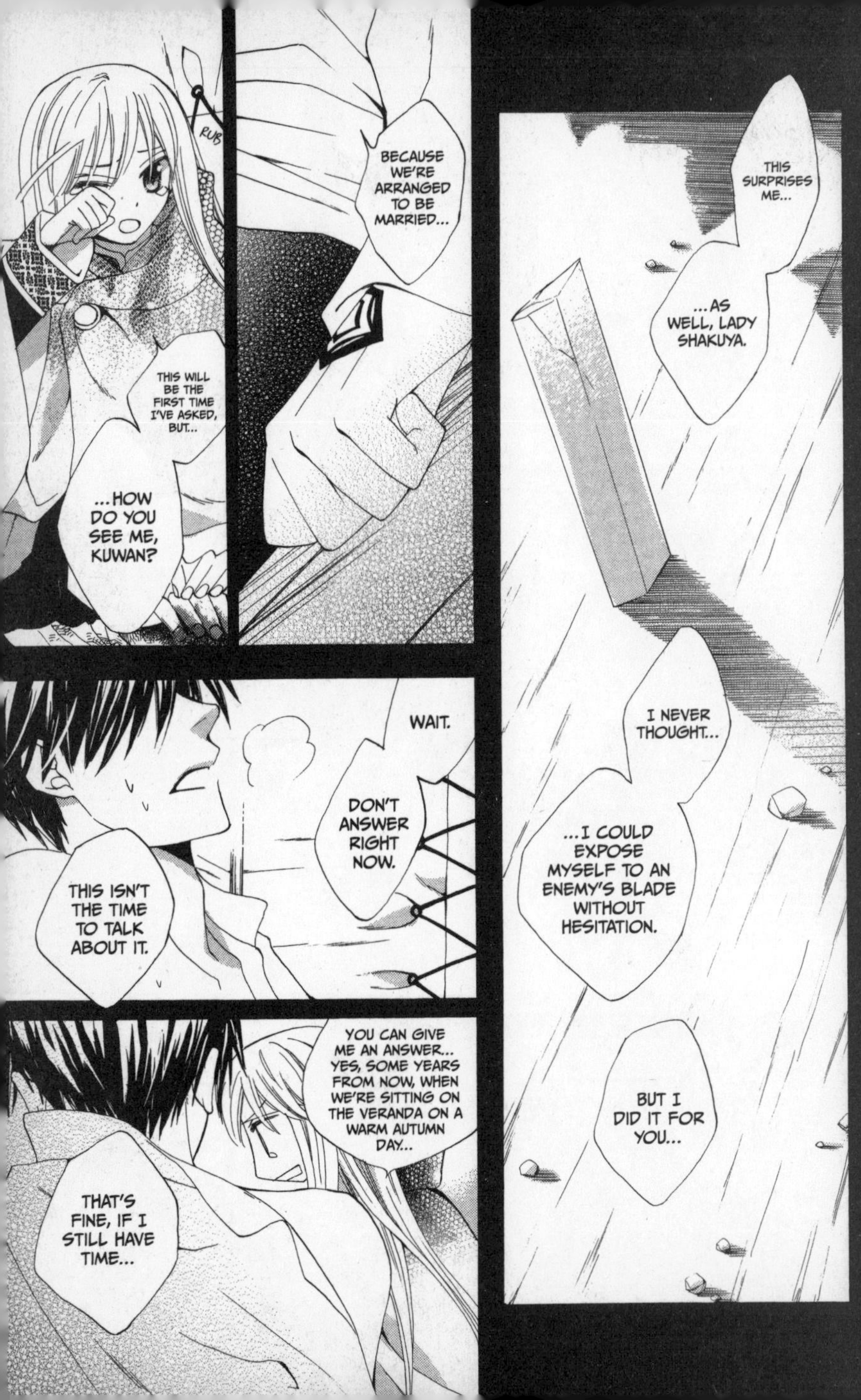
THIS SURPRISES ME...
...AS WELL, LADY SHAKUYA.
I NEVER THOUGHT...
...I COULD EXPOSE MYSELF TO AN ENEMY'S BLADE WITHOUT HESITATION.
BUT I DID IT FOR YOU...
BECAUSE WE'RE ARRANGED TO BE MARRIED...
RUB
THIS WILL BE THE FIRST TIME I'VE ASKED, BUT...
...HOW DO YOU SEE ME, KUWAN?
WAIT.
DON'T ANSWER RIGHT NOW.
THIS ISN'T THE TIME TO TALK ABOUT IT.
YOU CAN GIVE ME AN ANSWER... YES, SOME YEARS FROM NOW, WHEN WE'RE SITTING ON THE VERANDA ON A WARM AUTUMN DAY...
THAT'S FINE, IF I STILL HAVE TIME...

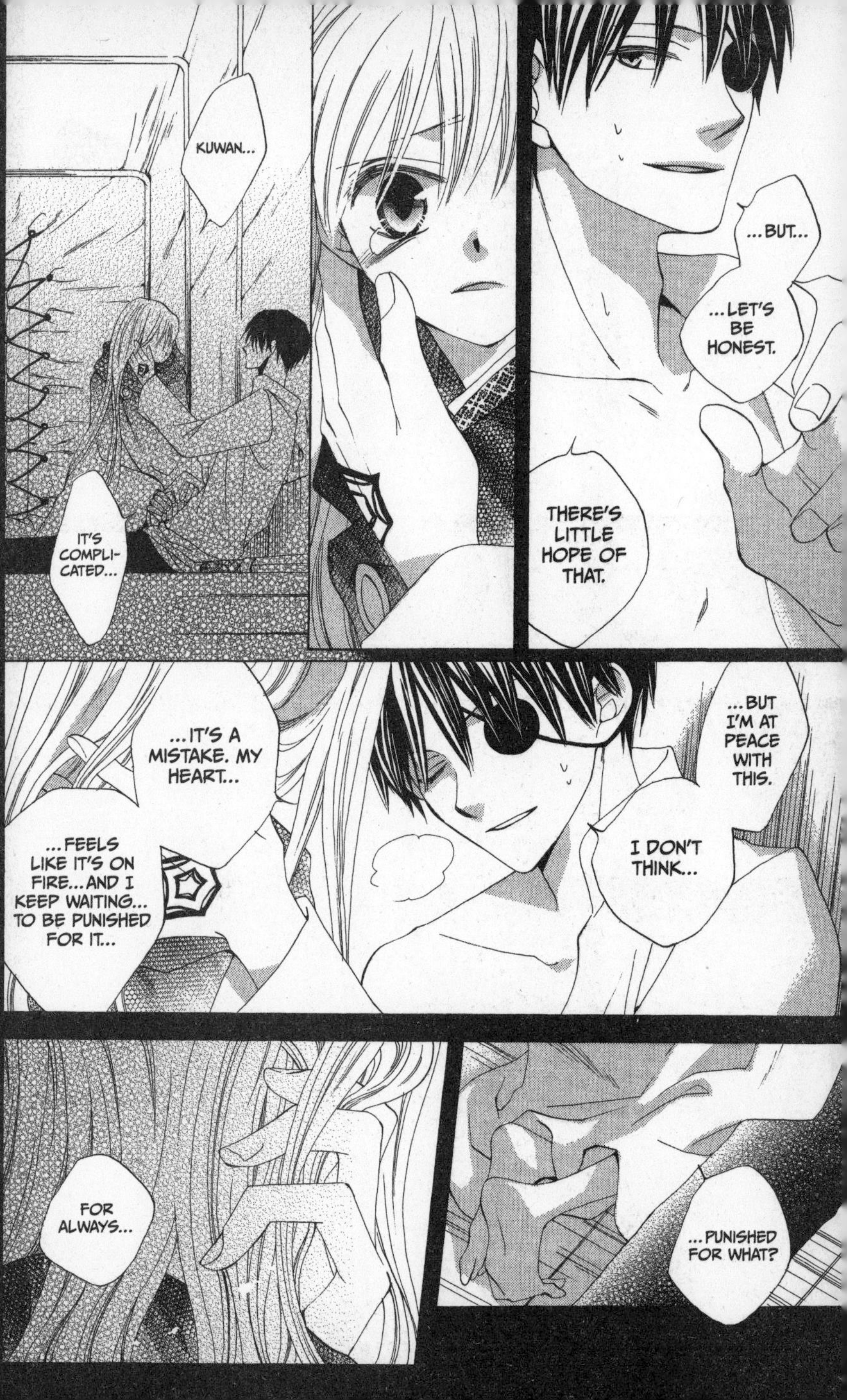
...BUT...
...LET'S BE HONEST.
THERE'S LITTLE HOPE OF THAT.
KUWAN...
IT'S COMPLI-CATED...
...BUT I'M AT PEACE WITH THIS.
I DON'T THINK...
...IT'S A MISTAKE. MY HEART...
...FEELS LIKE IT'S ON FIRE...AND I KEEP WAITING... TO BE PUNISHED FOR IT...
...PUNISHED FOR WHAT?
FOR ALWAYS...

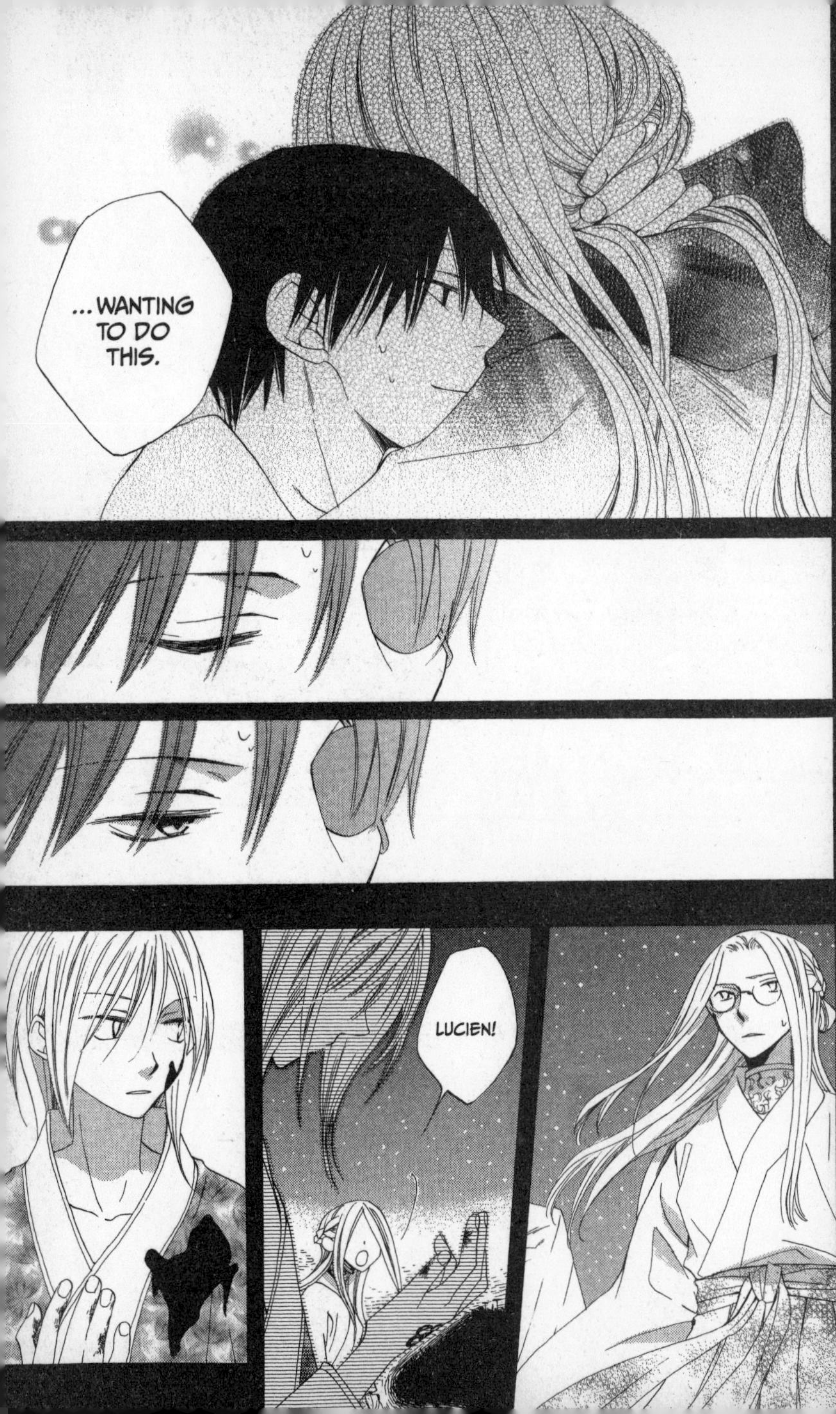
...WANTING TO DO THIS.
LUCIEN!

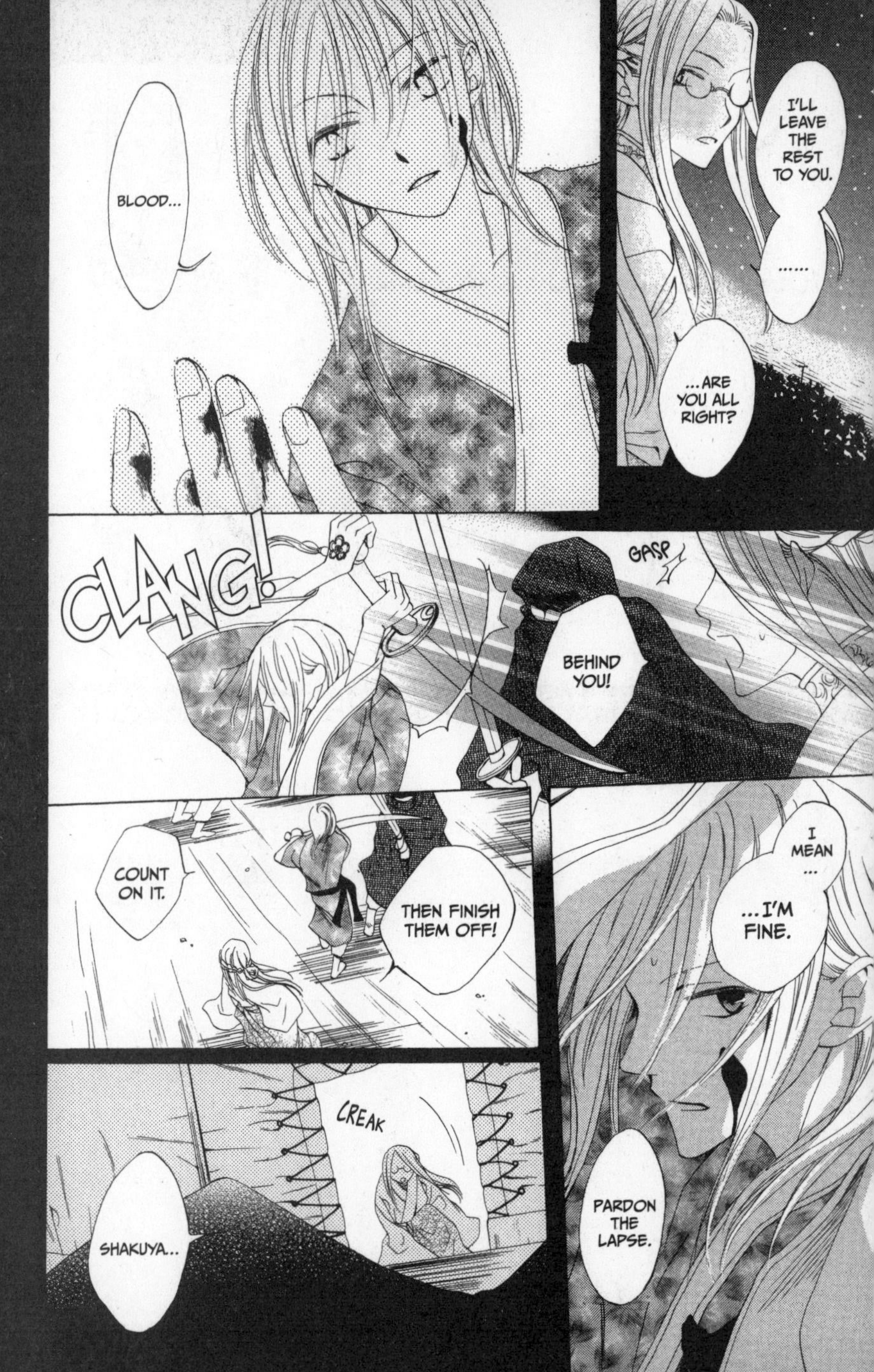
I'LL LEAVE THE REST TO YOU.
......
...ARE YOU ALL RIGHT?
BLOOD...
GASP
CLANG!
BEHIND YOU!
I MEAN ...
...I'M FINE.
PARDON THE LAPSE.
COUNT ON IT.
THEN FINISH THEM OFF!
CREAK
SHAKUYA...

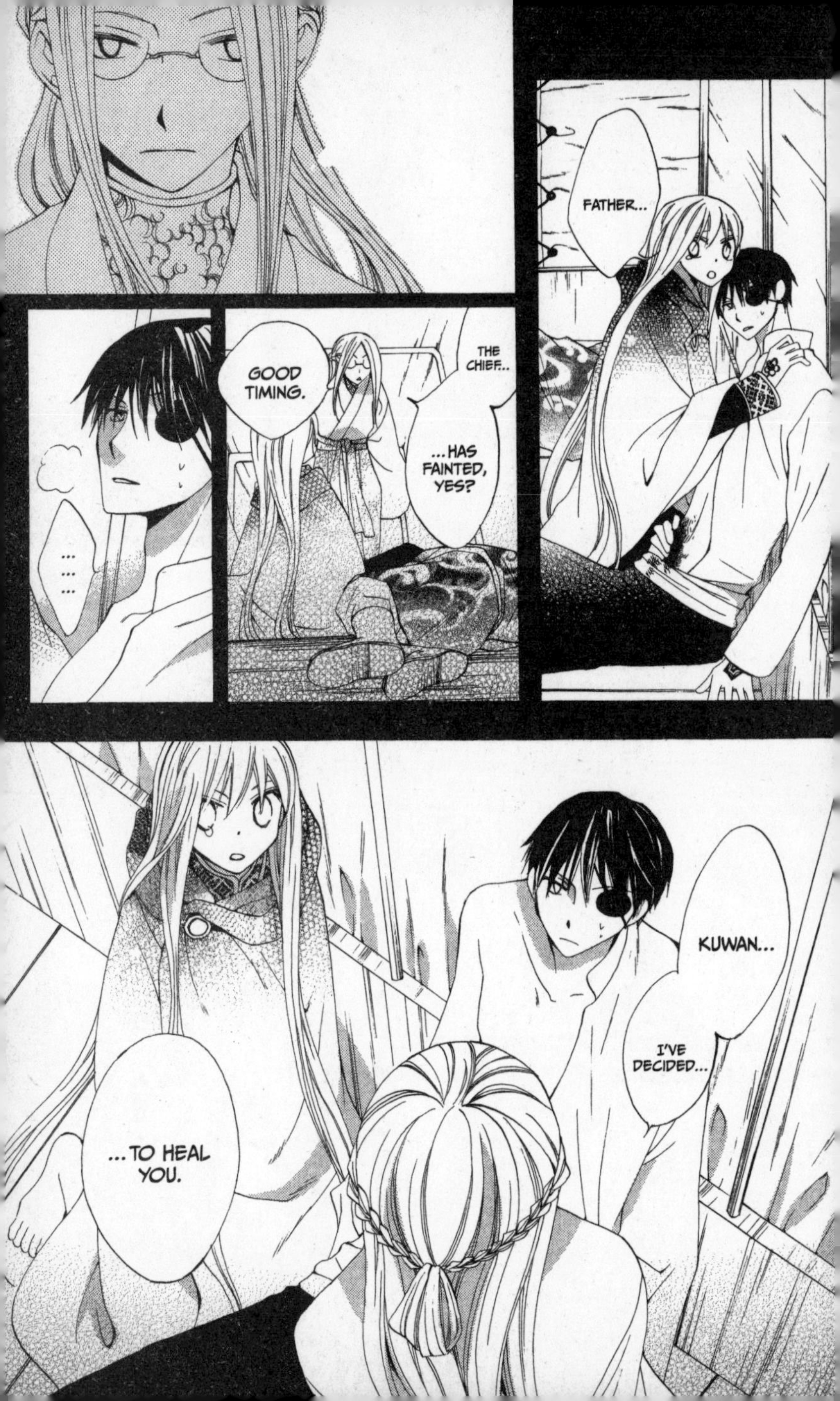
FATHER...
THE CHIEF...
...HAS FAINTED, YES?
GOOD TIMING.
...
...
...
KUWAN...
I'VE DECIDED...
...TO HEAL YOU.

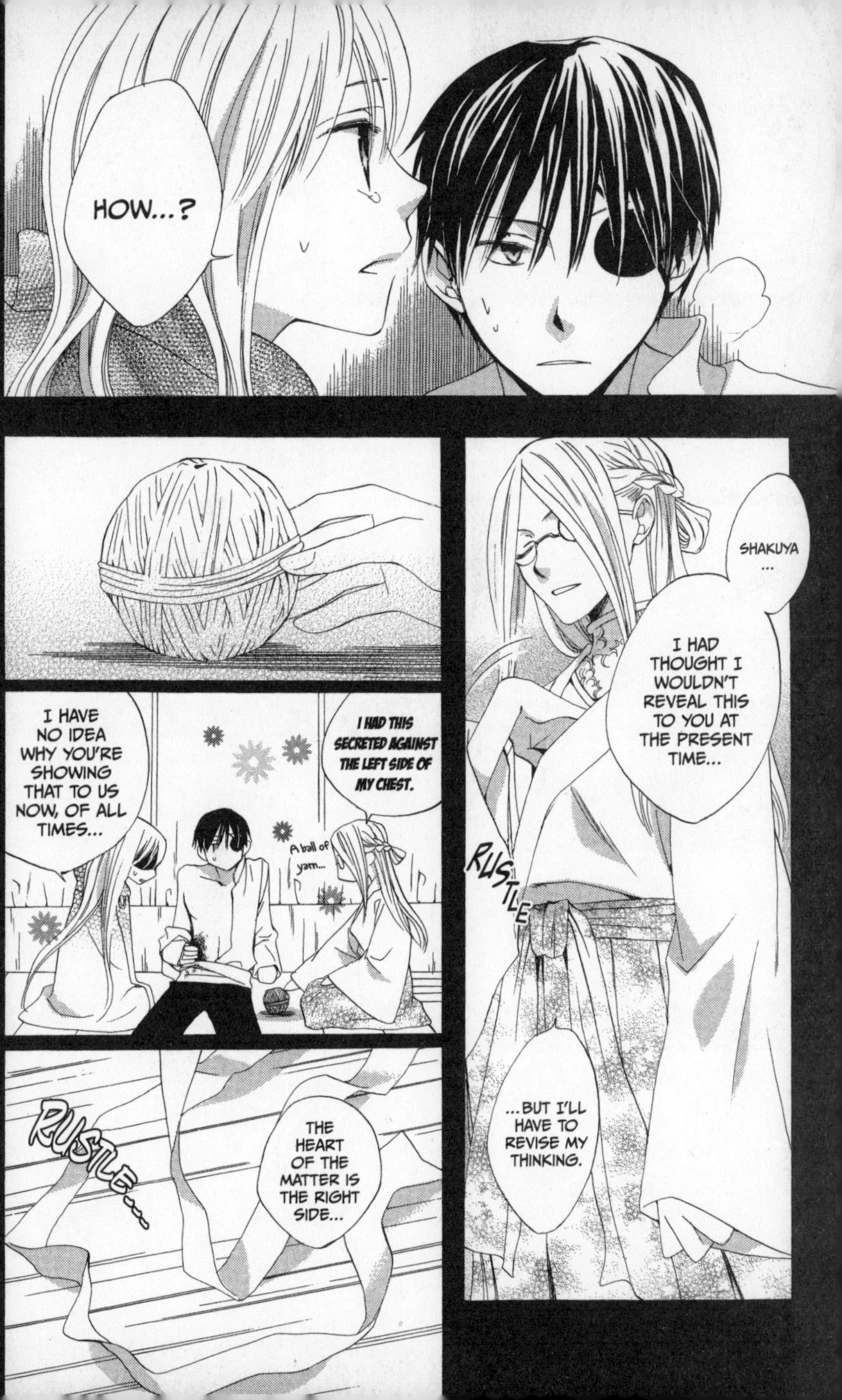
HOW...?
SHAKUYA...
I HAD THOUGHT I WOULDN'T REVEAL THIS TO YOU AT THE PRESENT TIME...
RUSTLE
...BUT I'LL HAVE TO REVISE MY THINKING.
I HAD THIS SECRETED AGAINST THE LEFT SIDE OF MY CHEST.
A ball of yarn...
I HAVE NO IDEA WHY YOU'RE SHOWING THAT TO US NOW, OF ALL TIMES...
THE HEART OF THE MATTER IS THE RIGHT SIDE...
RUSTLE...

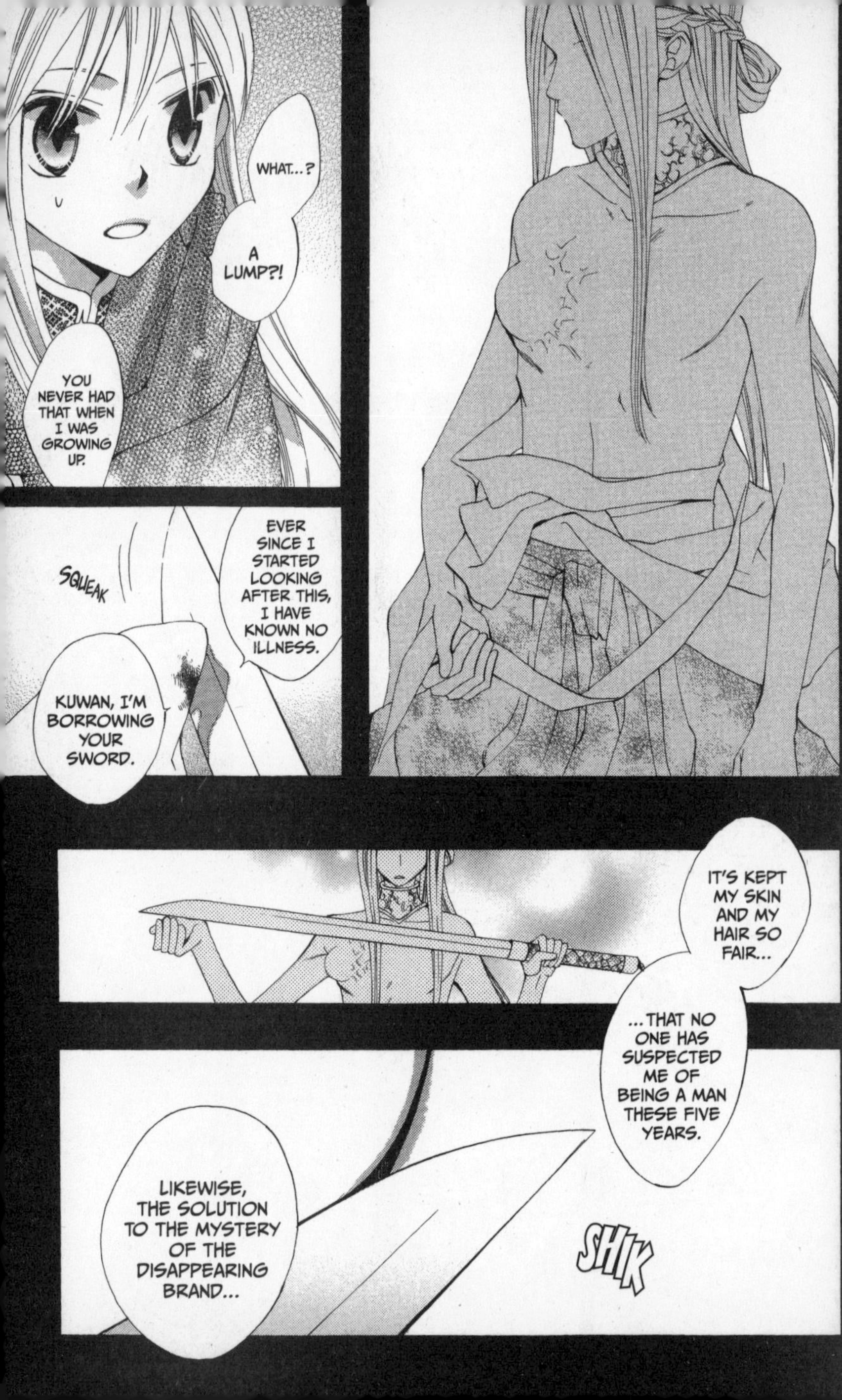
WHAT...?
A LUMP?!
YOU NEVER HAD THAT WHEN I WAS GROWING UP.
EVER SINCE I STARTED LOOKING AFTER THIS, I HAVE KNOWN NO ILLNESS.
SQUEAK
KUWAN, I'M BORROWING YOUR SWORD.
IT'S KEPT MY SKIN AND MY HAIR SO FAIR...
...THAT NO ONE HAS SUSPECTED ME OF BEING A MAN THESE FIVE YEARS.
SHIK
LIKEWISE, THE SOLUTION TO THE MYSTERY OF THE DISAPPEARING BRAND...

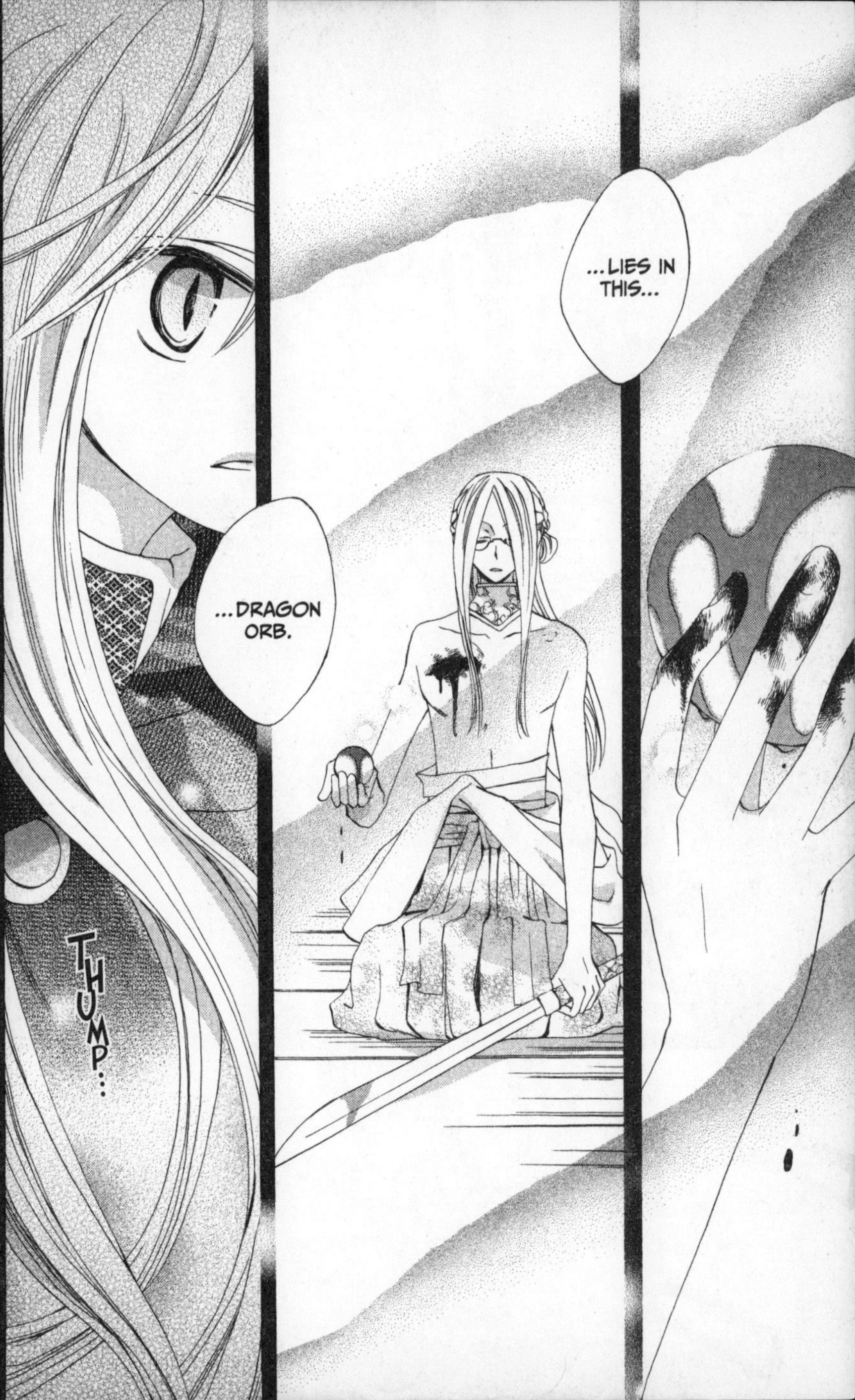
...LIES IN THIS...
...!
...DRAGON ORB.
THUMP...

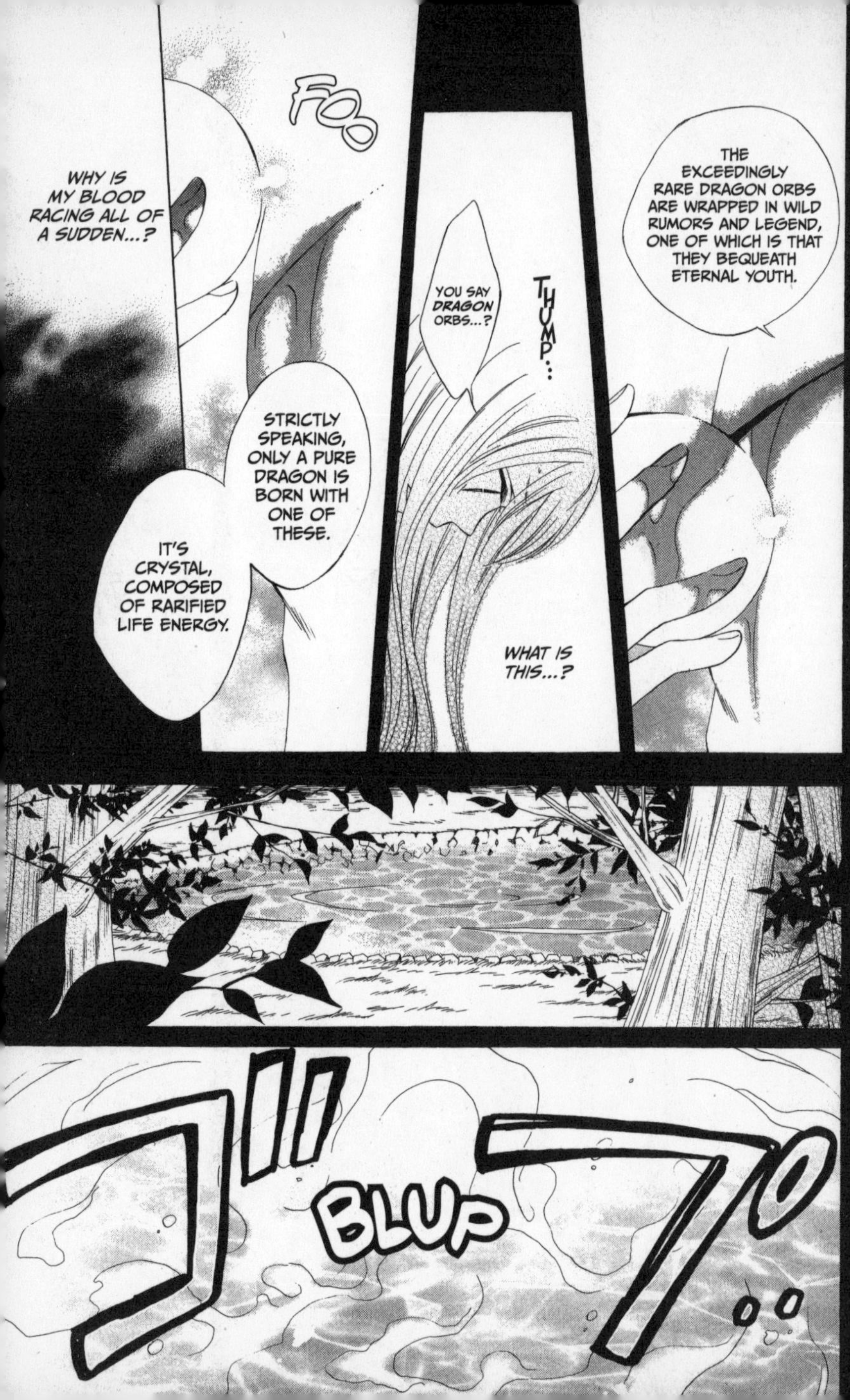
THE EXCEEDINGLY RARE DRAGON ORBS ARE WRAPPED IN WILD RUMORS AND LEGEND, ONE OF WHICH IS THAT THEY BEQUEATH ETERNAL YOUTH.
WHAT IS THIS...?
YOU SAY DRAGON ORBS...?
THUMP...
STRICTLY SPEAKING, ONLY A PURE DRAGON IS BORN WITH ONE OF THESE.
IT'S CRYSTAL, COMPOSED OF RARIFIED LIFE ENERGY.
FOO
WHY IS MY BLOOD RACING ALL OF A SUDDEN...?
BLUP

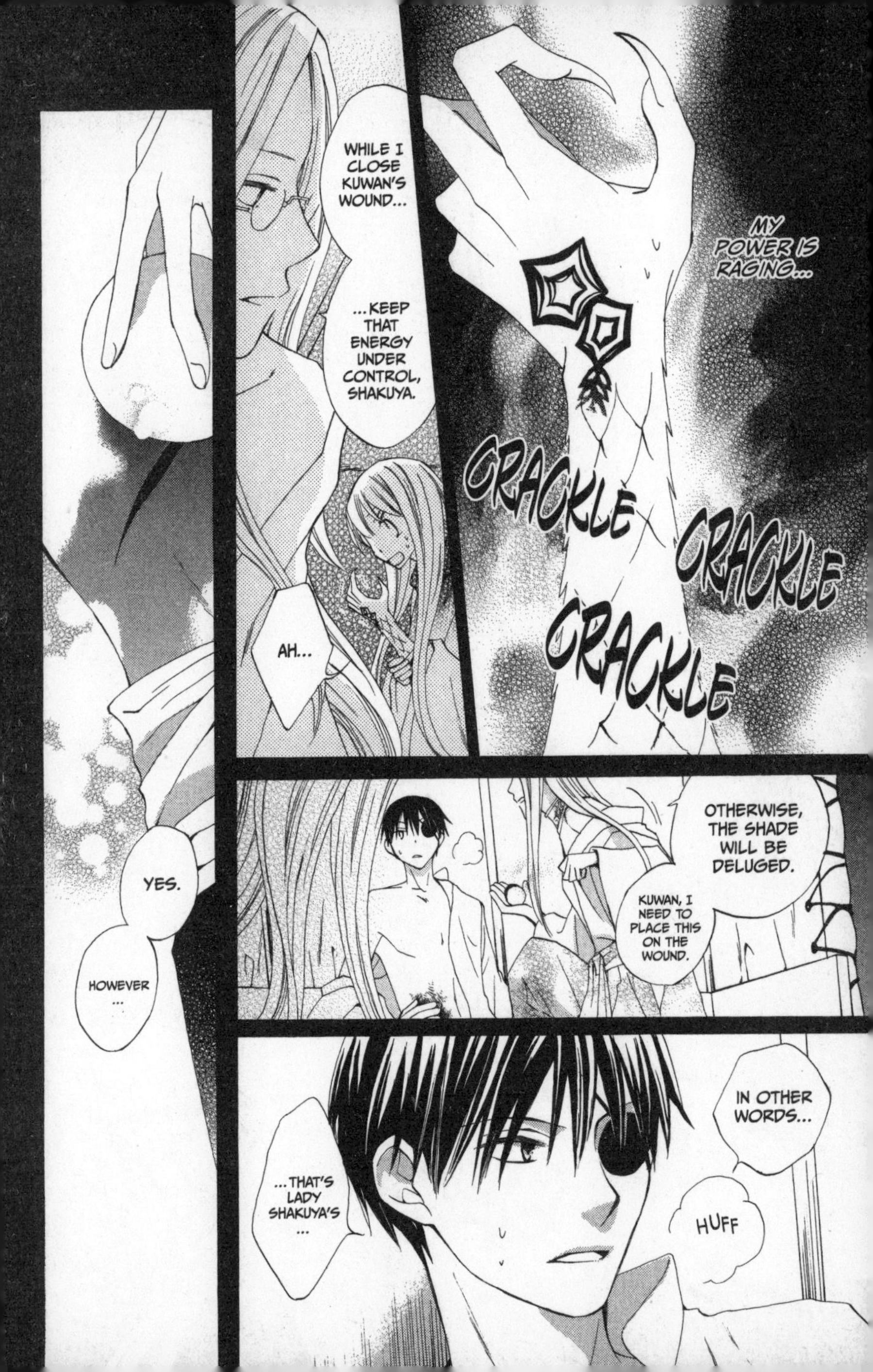
MY POWER IS RAGING...
CRACKLE
CRACKLE
CRACKLE
WHILE I CLOSE KUWAN'S WOUND...
...KEEP THAT ENERGY UNDER CONTROL, SHAKUYA.
AH...
OTHERWISE, THE SHADE WILL BE DELUGED.
KUWAN, I NEED TO PLACE THIS ON THE WOUND.
IN OTHER WORDS...
HUFF
...THAT'S LADY SHAKUYA'S ...
YES.
HOWEVER ...

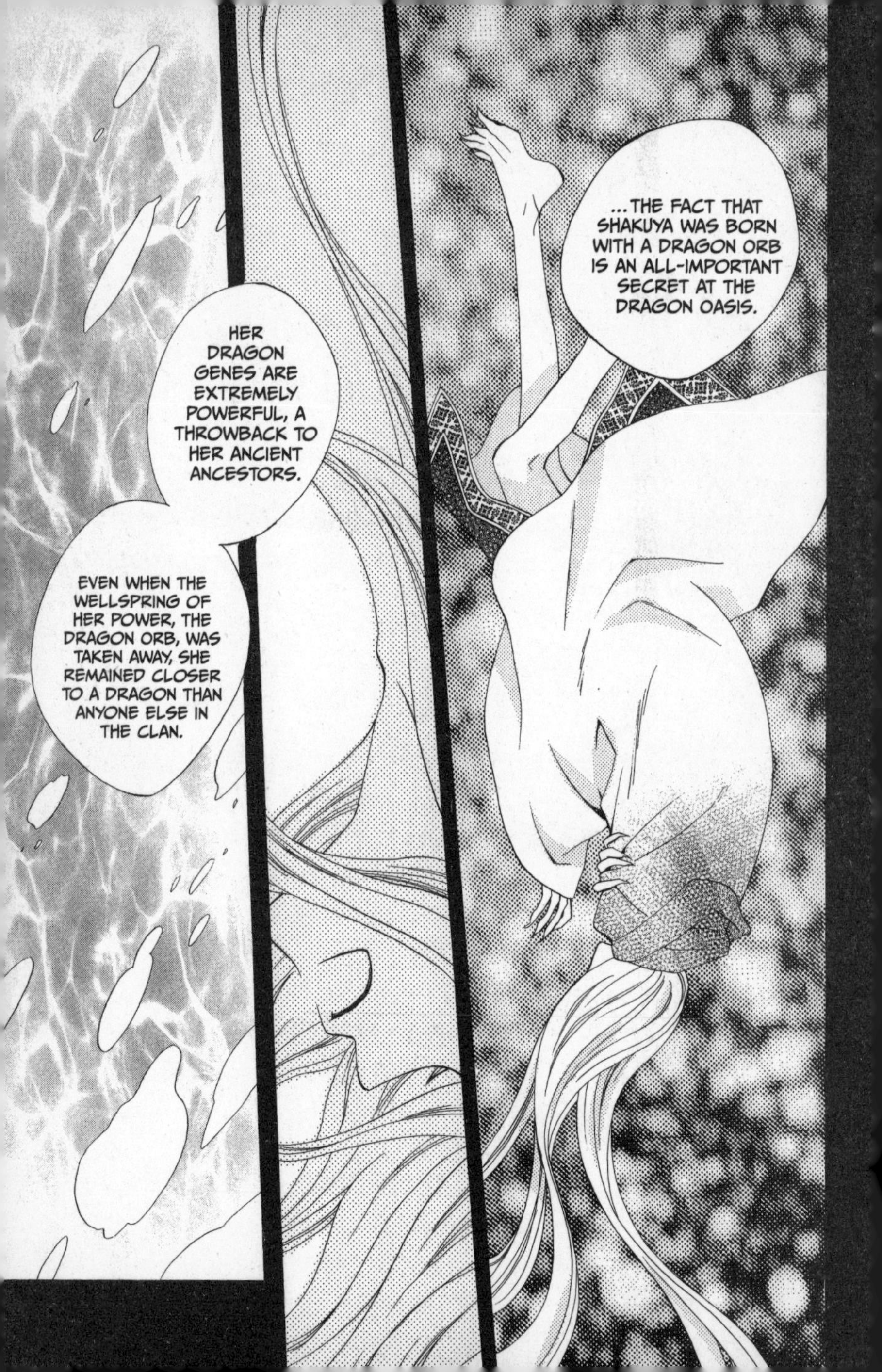
...THE FACT THAT SHAKUYA WAS BORN WITH A DRAGON ORB IS AN ALL-IMPORTANT SECRET AT THE DRAGON OASIS.
HER DRAGON GENES ARE EXTREMELY POWERFUL, A THROWBACK TO HER ANCIENT ANCESTORS.
EVEN WHEN THE WELLSPRING OF HER POWER, THE DRAGON ORB, WAS TAKEN AWAY, SHE REMAINED CLOSER TO A DRAGON THAN ANYONE ELSE IN THE CLAN.

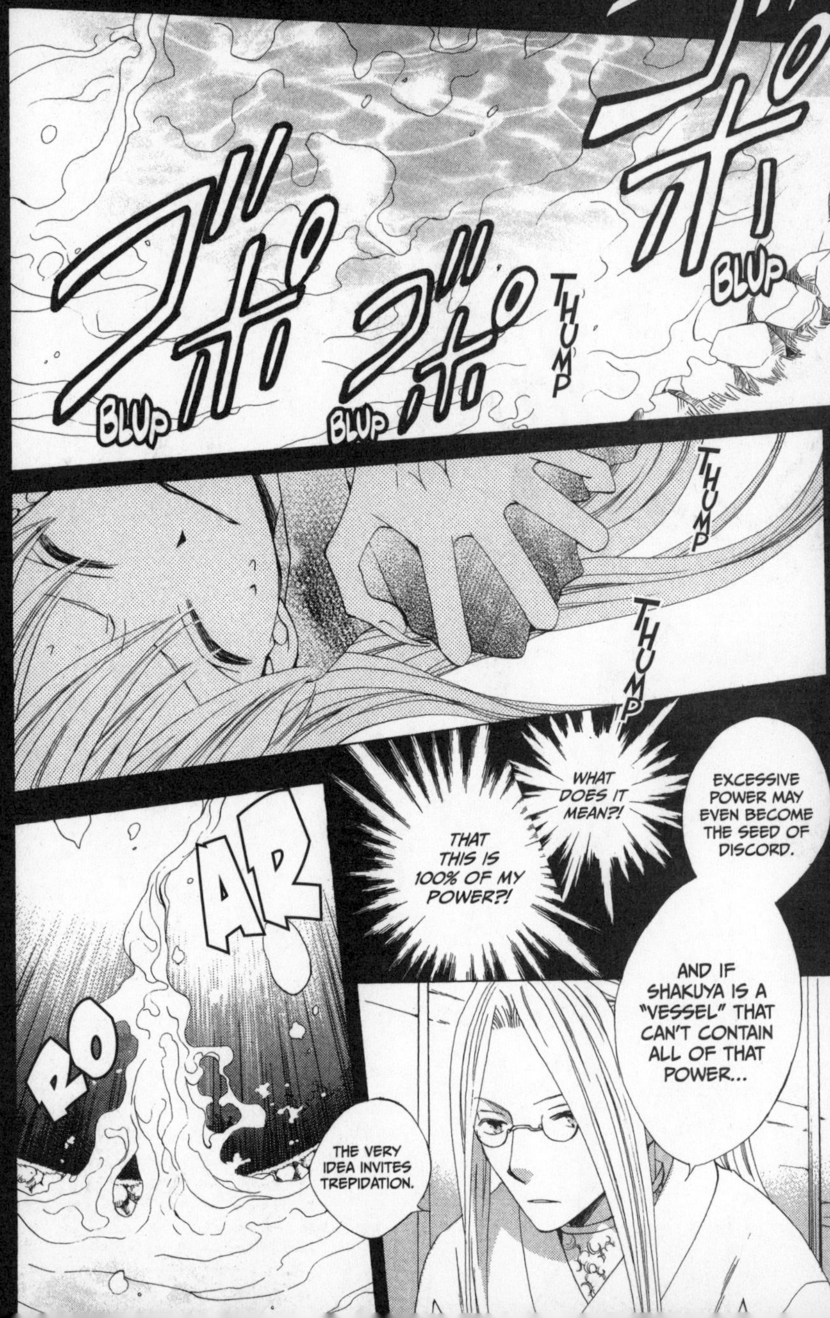
ゴポ
BLUP
THUMP
ゴポ
BLUP
ゴポ
BLUP
THUMP
THUMP
EXCESSIVE POWER MAY EVEN BECOME THE SEED OF DISCORD.
WHAT DOES IT MEAN?!
THAT THIS IS 100% OF MY POWER?!
AND IF SHAKUYA IS A "VESSEL" THAT CAN'T CONTAIN ALL OF THAT POWER...
THE VERY IDEA INVITES TREPIDATION.
ROAR

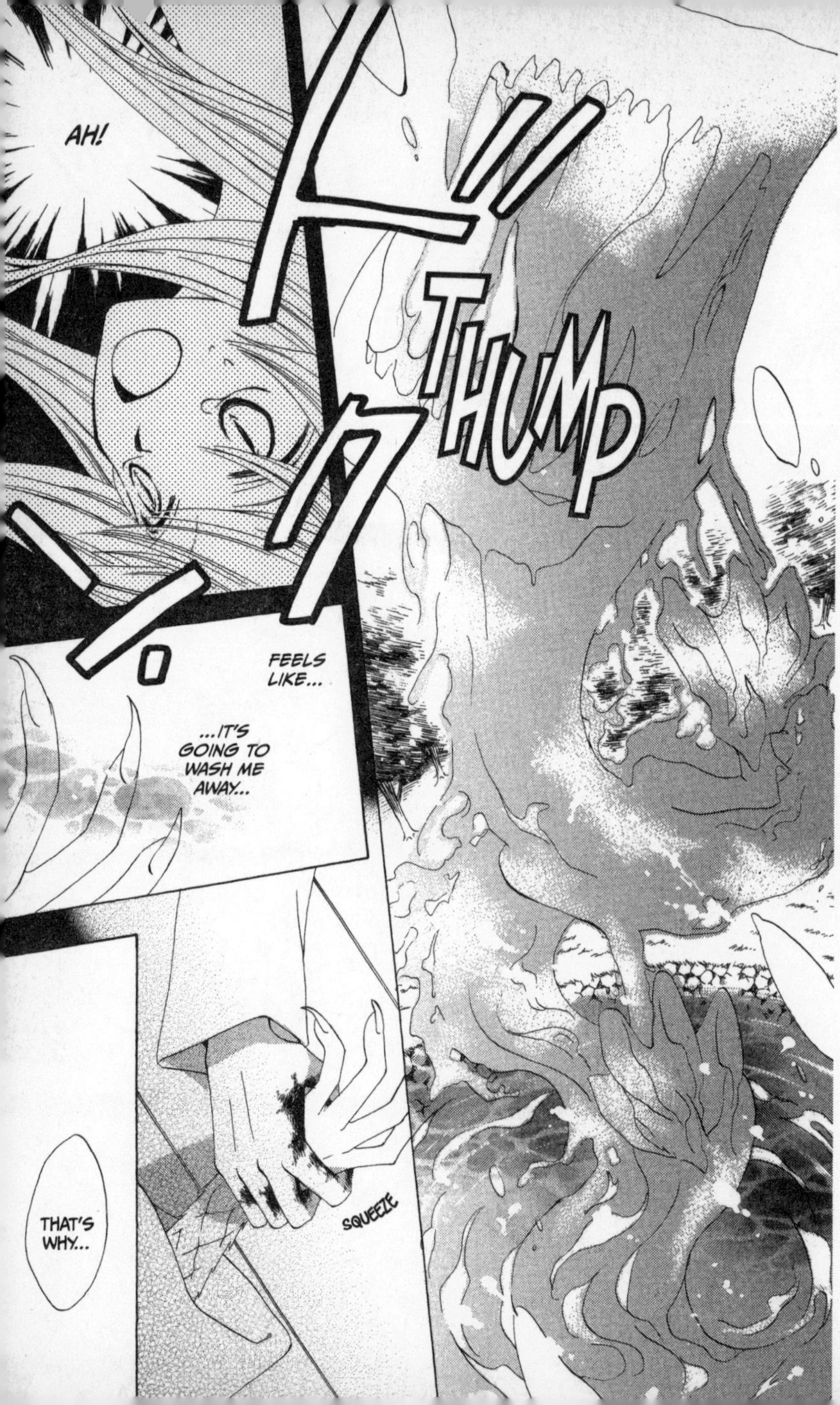
THUMP
AH!
FEELS LIKE...
...IT'S GOING TO WASH ME AWAY...
SQUEEZE
THAT'S WHY...

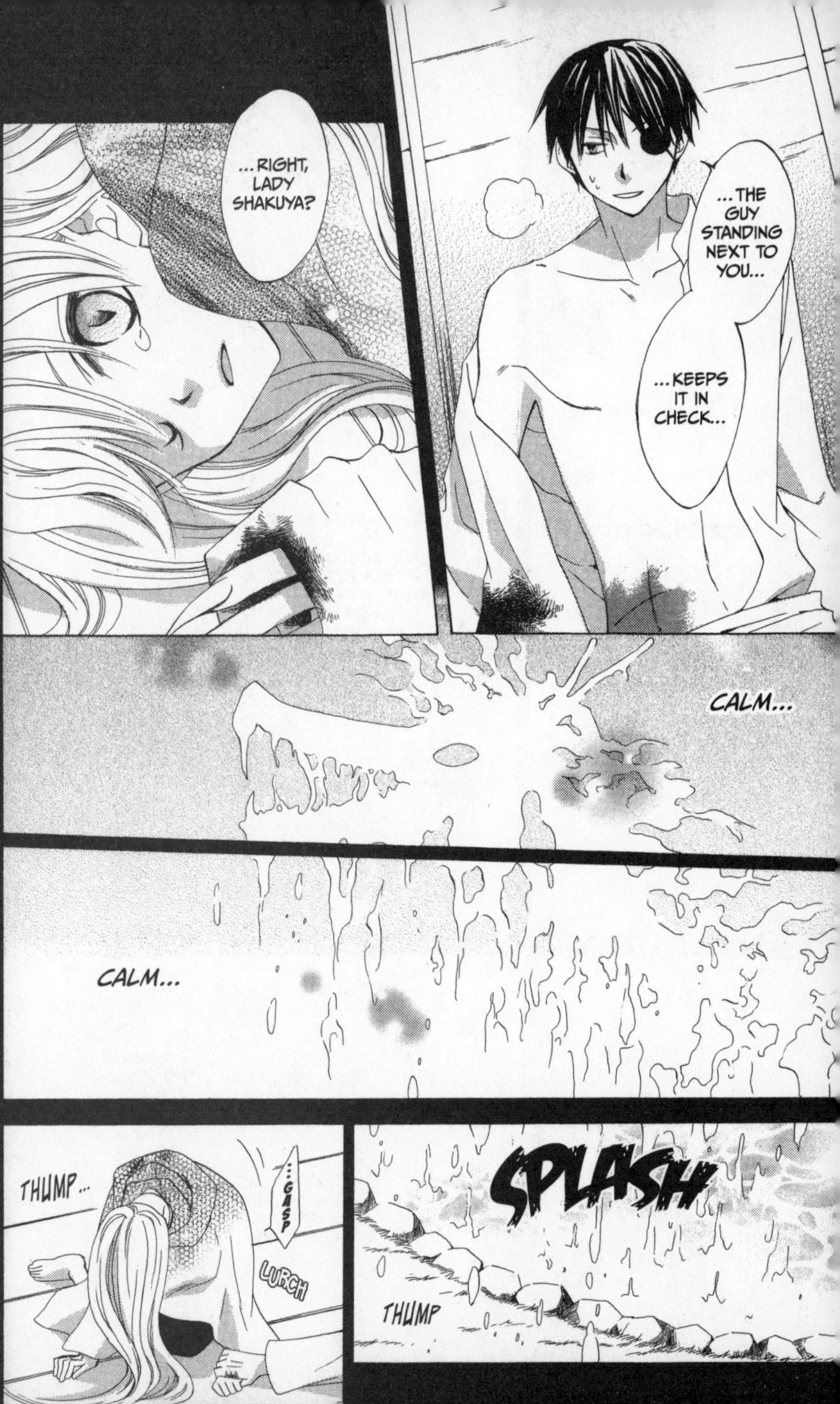
...THE GUY STANDING NEXT TO YOU...
...KEEPS IT IN CHECK...
...RIGHT, LADY SHAKUYA?
CALM...
CALM...
SPLASH
THUMP
THUMP...
...GASP
LURCH

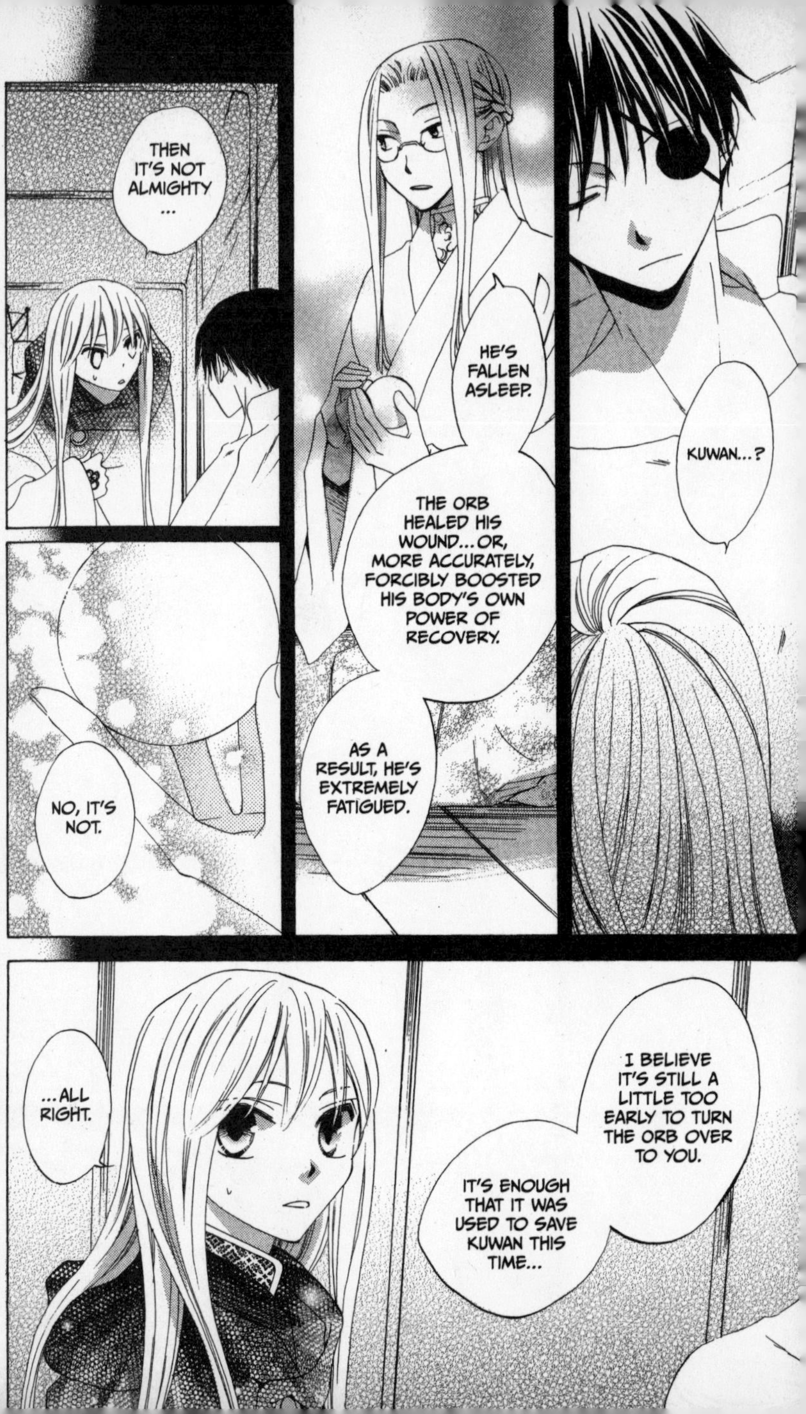
KUWAN...?
HE'S FALLEN ASLEEP.
THE ORB HEALED HIS WOUND...OR, MORE ACCURATELY, FORCIBLY BOOSTED HIS BODY'S OWN POWER OF RECOVERY.
AS A RESULT, HE'S EXTREMELY FATIGUED.
THEN IT'S NOT ALMIGHTY ...
NO, IT'S NOT.
I BELIEVE IT'S STILL A LITTLE TOO EARLY TO TURN THE ORB OVER TO YOU.
IT'S ENOUGH THAT IT WAS USED TO SAVE KUWAN THIS TIME...
...ALL RIGHT.

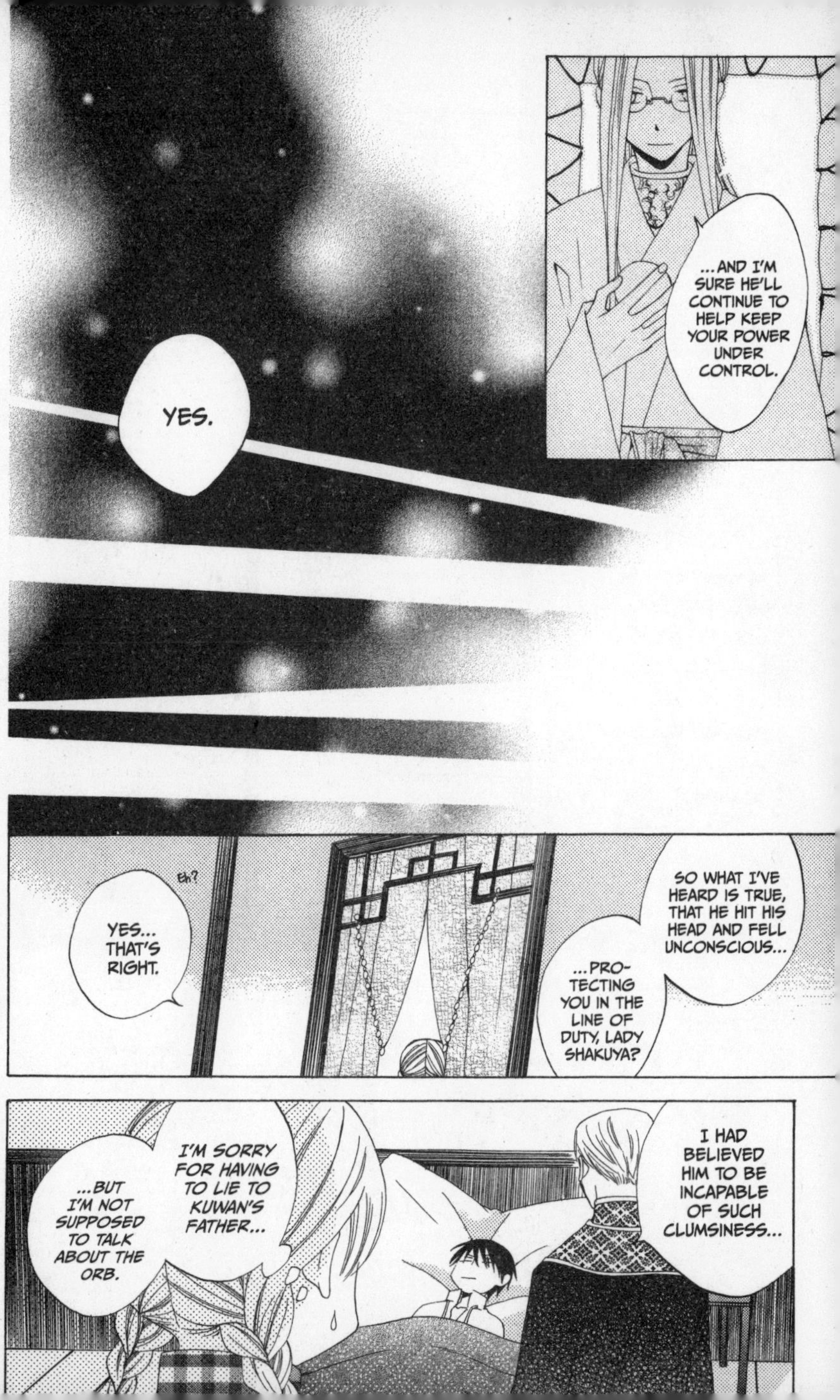
...AND I'M SURE HE'LL CONTINUE TO HELP KEEP YOUR POWER UNDER CONTROL.
YES.
SO WHAT I'VE HEARD IS TRUE, THAT HE HIT HIS HEAD AND FELL UNCONSCIOUS...
...PROTECTING YOU IN THE LINE OF DUTY, LADY SHAKUYA?
Eh?
YES... THAT'S RIGHT.
I HAD BELIEVED HIM TO BE INCAPABLE OF SUCH CLUMSINESS...
I'M SORRY FOR HAVING TO LIE TO KUWAN'S FATHER...
...BUT I'M NOT SUPPOSED TO TALK ABOUT THE ORB.

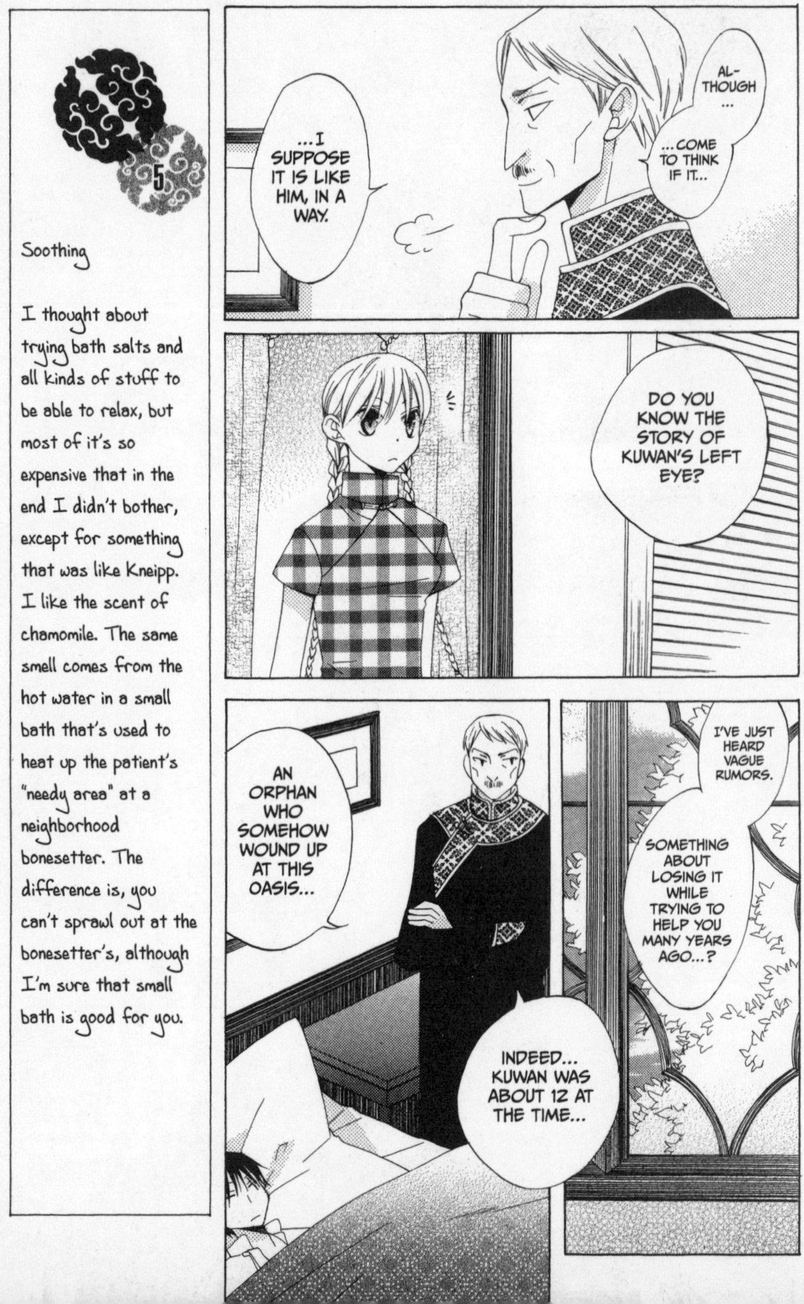
AL-THOUGH...
...COME TO THINK IF IT...
...I SUPPOSE IT IS LIKE HIM, IN A WAY.
DO YOU KNOW THE STORY OF KUWAN'S LEFT EYE?
I'VE JUST HEARD VAGUE RUMORS.
SOMETHING ABOUT LOSING IT WHILE TRYING TO HELP YOU MANY YEARS AGO...?
AN ORPHAN WHO SOMEHOW WOUND UP AT THIS OASIS...
INDEED... KUWAN WAS ABOUT 12 AT THE TIME...

5

Soothing

I thought about trying bath salts and all kinds of stuff to be able to relax, but most of it's so expensive that in the end I didn't bother, except for something that was like Kneipp. I like the scent of chamomile. The same smell comes from the hot water in a small bath that's used to heat up the patient's "needy area" at a neighborhood bonesetter. The difference is, you can't sprawl out at the bonesetter's, although I'm sure that small bath is good for you.

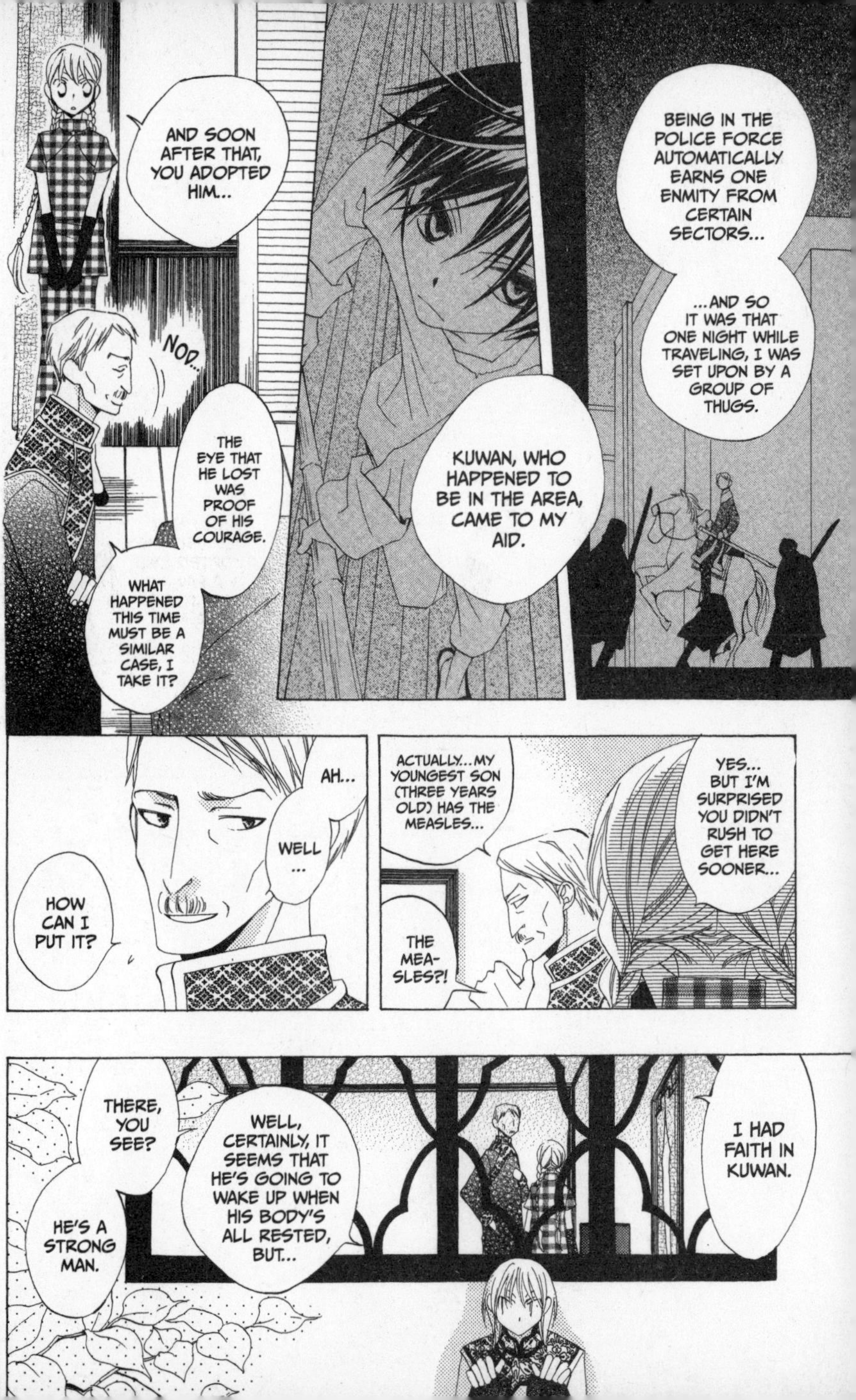
BEING IN THE POLICE FORCE AUTOMATICALLY EARNS ONE ENMITY FROM CERTAIN SECTORS...
...AND SO IT WAS THAT ONE NIGHT WHILE TRAVELING, I WAS SET UPON BY A GROUP OF THUGS.
KUWAN, WHO HAPPENED TO BE IN THE AREA, CAME TO MY AID.
AND SOON AFTER THAT, YOU ADOPTED HIM...
NOD...
THE EYE THAT HE LOST WAS PROOF OF HIS COURAGE.
WHAT HAPPENED THIS TIME MUST BE A SIMILAR CASE, I TAKE IT?
YES... BUT I'M SURPRISED YOU DIDN'T RUSH TO GET HERE SOONER...
ACTUALLY...MY YOUNGEST SON (THREE YEARS OLD) HAS THE MEASLES...
THE MEA-SLES?!
AH...
WELL ...
HOW CAN I PUT IT?
I HAD FAITH IN KUWAN.
WELL, CERTAINLY, IT SEEMS THAT HE'S GOING TO WAKE UP WHEN HIS BODY'S ALL RESTED, BUT...
THERE, YOU SEE?
HE'S A STRONG MAN.

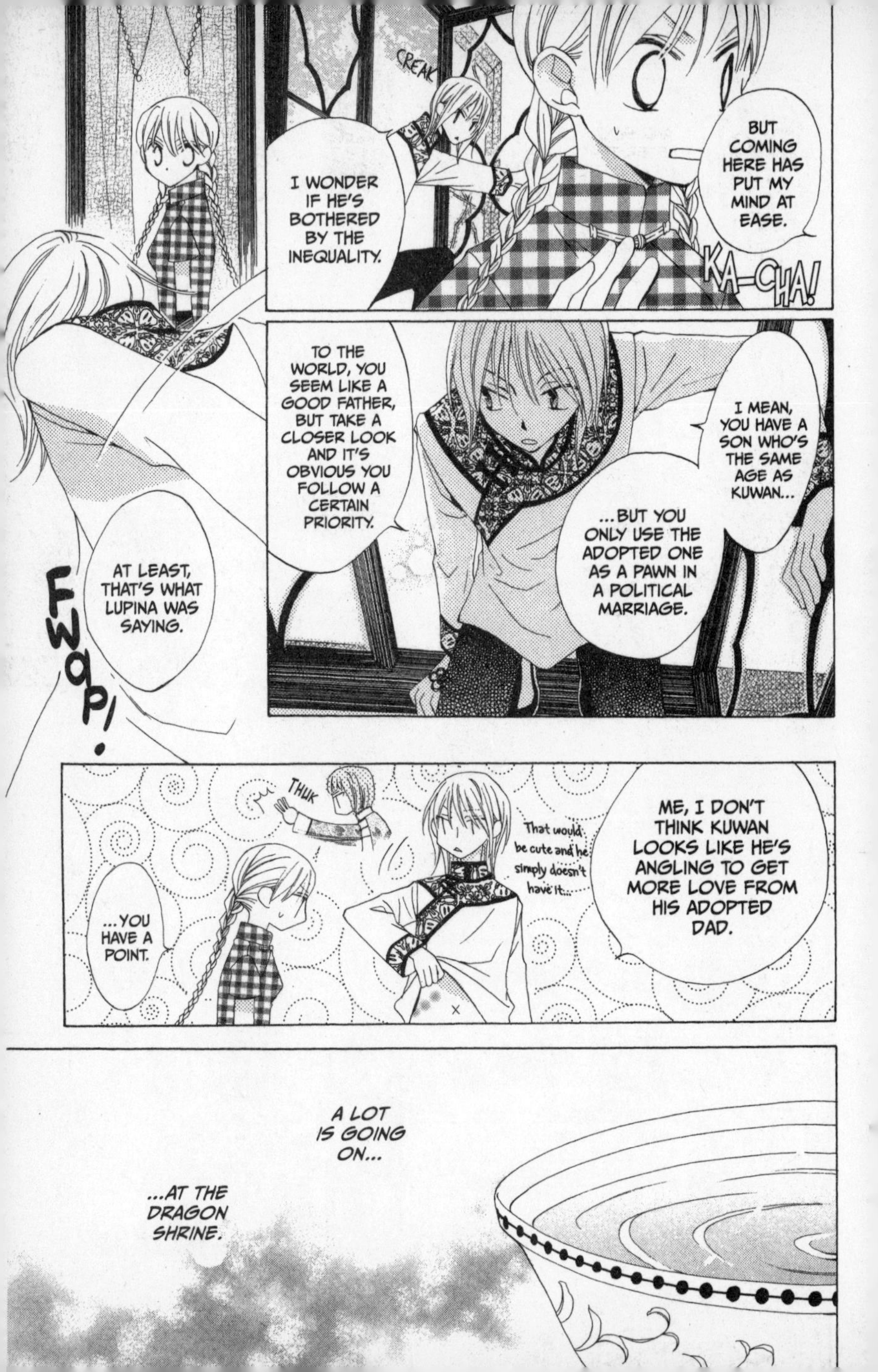
BUT COMING HERE HAS PUT MY MIND AT EASE.
KA-CHA!
CREAK
I WONDER IF HE'S BOTHERED BY THE INEQUALITY.
I MEAN, YOU HAVE A SON WHO'S THE SAME AGE AS KUWAN...
...BUT YOU ONLY USE THE ADOPTED ONE AS A PAWN IN A POLITICAL MARRIAGE.
TO THE WORLD, YOU SEEM LIKE A GOOD FATHER, BUT TAKE A CLOSER LOOK AND IT'S OBVIOUS YOU FOLLOW A CERTAIN PRIORITY.
AT LEAST, THAT'S WHAT LUPINA WAS SAYING.
FWOP!
ME, I DON'T THINK KUWAN LOOKS LIKE HE'S ANGLING TO GET MORE LOVE FROM HIS ADOPTED DAD.
That would be cute and he simply doesn't have it...
THUK
...YOU HAVE A POINT.
A LOT IS GOING ON...
...AT THE DRAGON SHRINE.

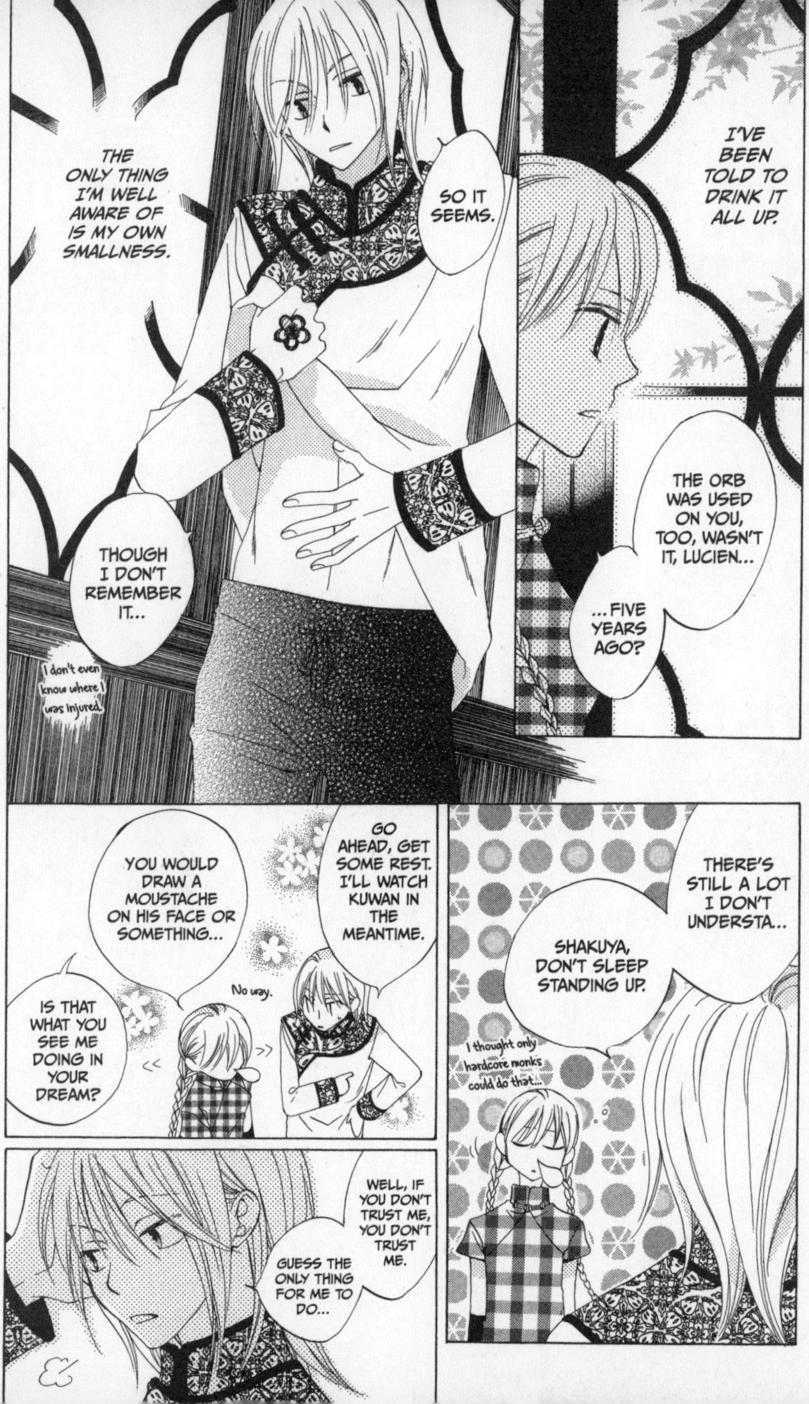
I'VE BEEN TOLD TO DRINK IT ALL UP.
THE ORB WAS USED ON YOU, TOO, WASN'T IT, LUCIEN...
...FIVE YEARS AGO?
SO IT SEEMS.
THE ONLY THING I'M WELL AWARE OF IS MY OWN SMALLNESS.
THOUGH I DON'T REMEMBER IT...
I don't even know where I was injured.
THERE'S STILL A LOT I DON'T UNDERSTA...
SHAKUYA, DON'T SLEEP STANDING UP.
I thought only hardcore monks could do that...
GO AHEAD, GET SOME REST. I'LL WATCH KUWAN IN THE MEANTIME.
YOU WOULD DRAW A MOUSTACHE ON HIS FACE OR SOMETHING...
No way.
IS THAT WHAT YOU SEE ME DOING IN YOUR DREAM?
WELL, IF YOU DON'T TRUST ME, YOU DON'T TRUST ME.
GUESS THE ONLY THING FOR ME TO DO...

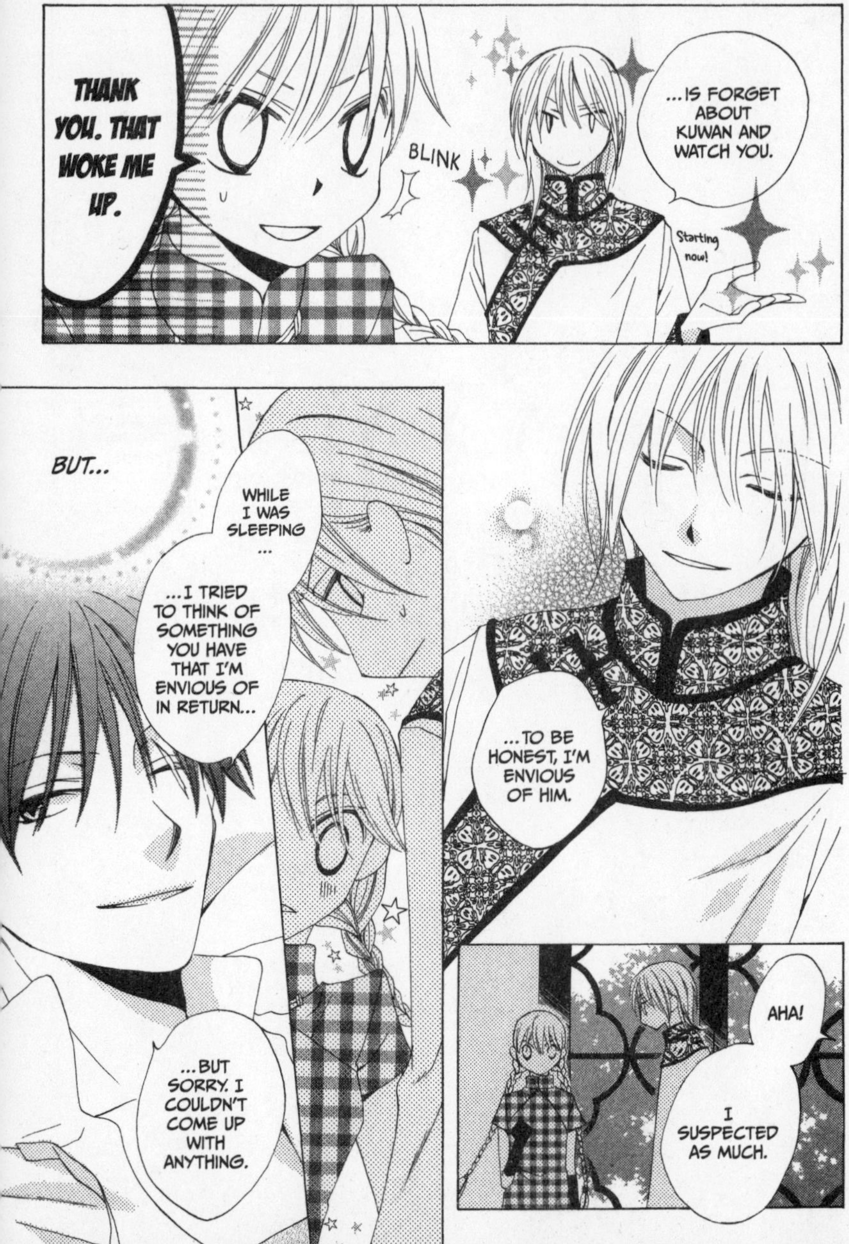
...IS FORGET ABOUT KUWAN AND WATCH YOU.
Starting now!
BLINK
THANK YOU. THAT WOKE ME UP.
...TO BE HONEST, I'M ENVIOUS OF HIM.
AHA!
I SUSPECTED AS MUCH.
BUT...
WHILE I WAS SLEEPING...
...I TRIED TO THINK OF SOMETHING YOU HAVE THAT I'M ENVIOUS OF IN RETURN...
...BUT SORRY. I COULDN'T COME UP WITH ANYTHING.

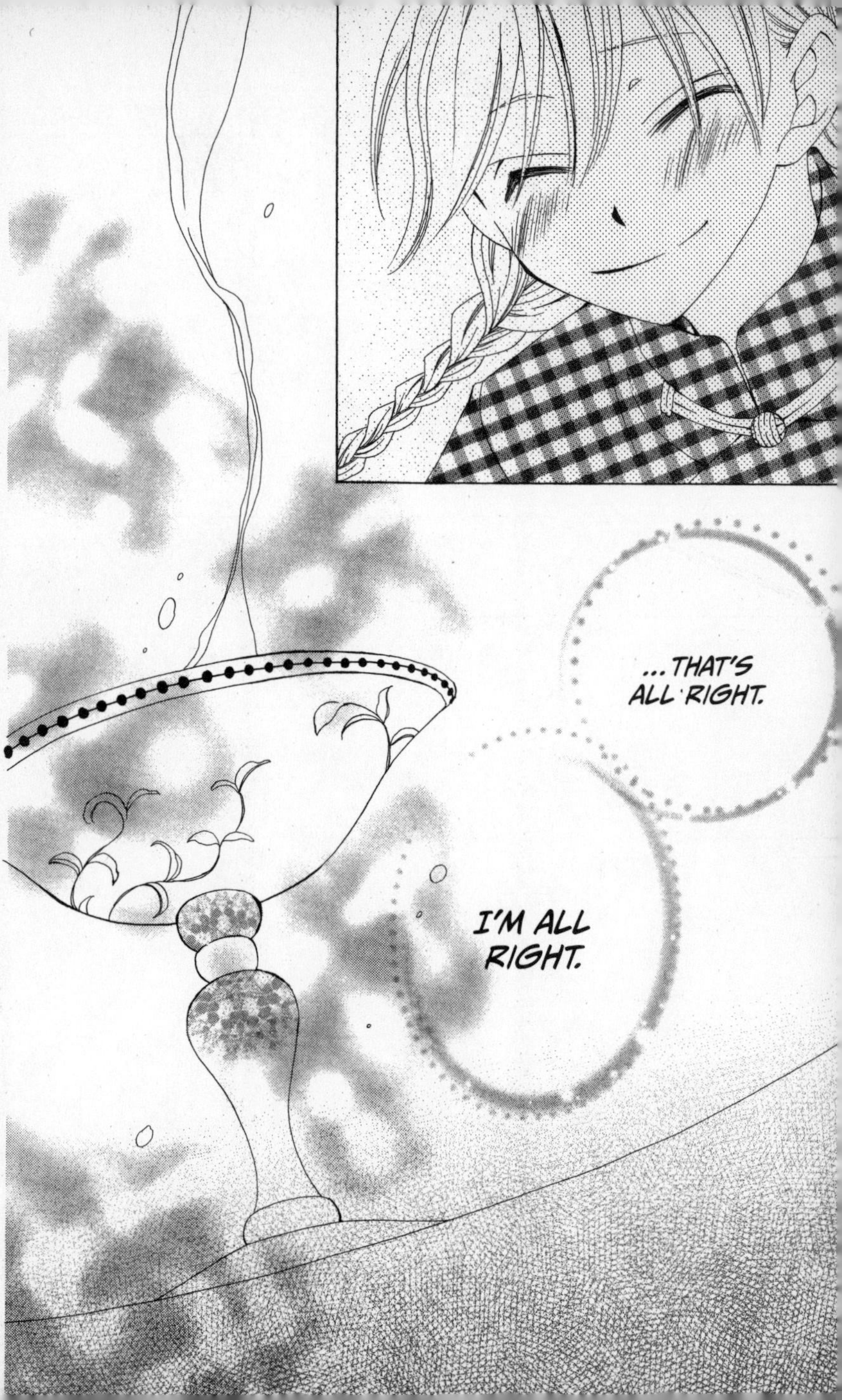
...THAT'S ALL·RIGHT.
I'M ALL RIGHT.

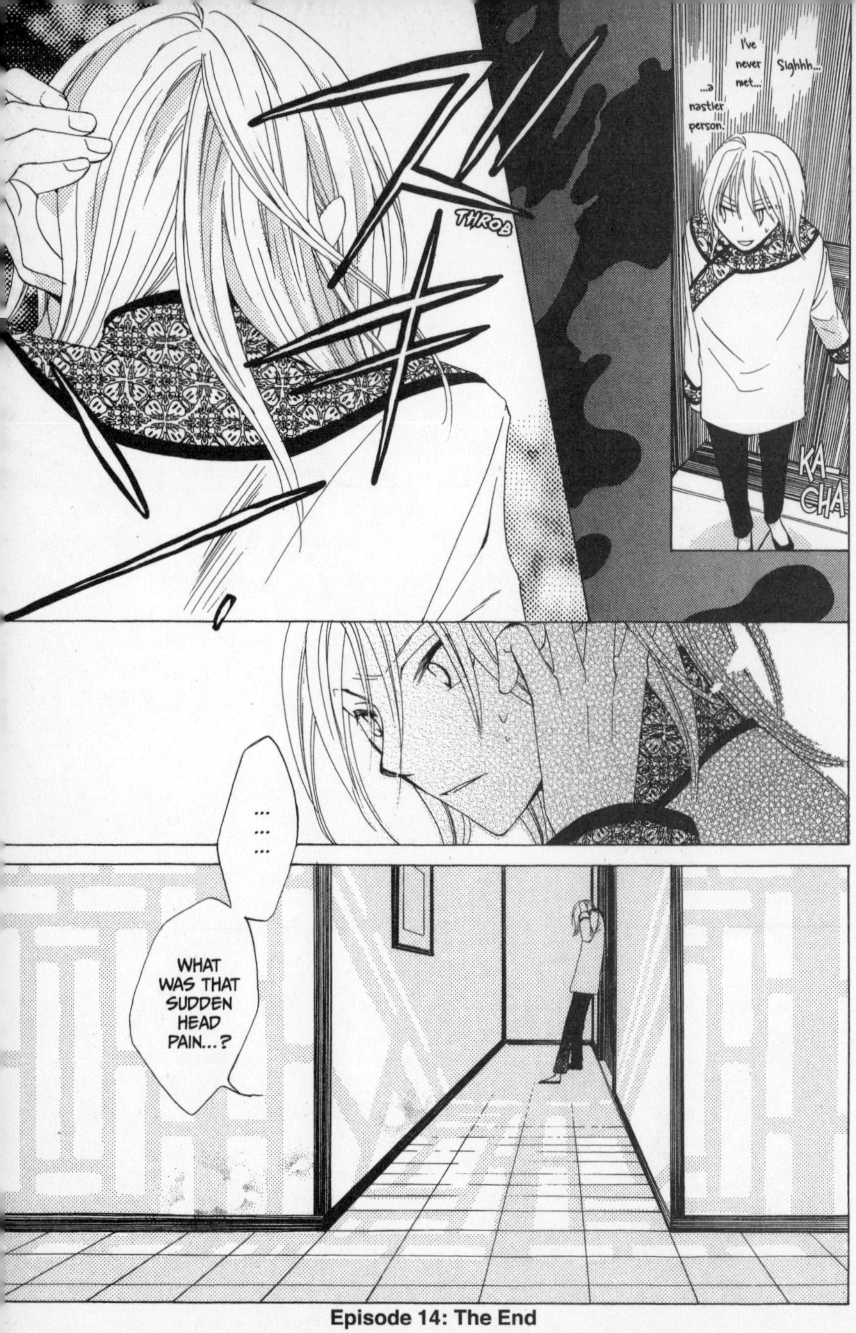
Sighhh...
I've never met...
...a nastier person.
KA-CHA
THROB
......
WHAT WAS THAT SUDDEN HEAD PAIN...?

Episode 14: The End

Double Crown Preview Cut

The one on the left is a girl and...well, I don't want to give away the plot. This is my third published story since my debut and it's done-in-one.

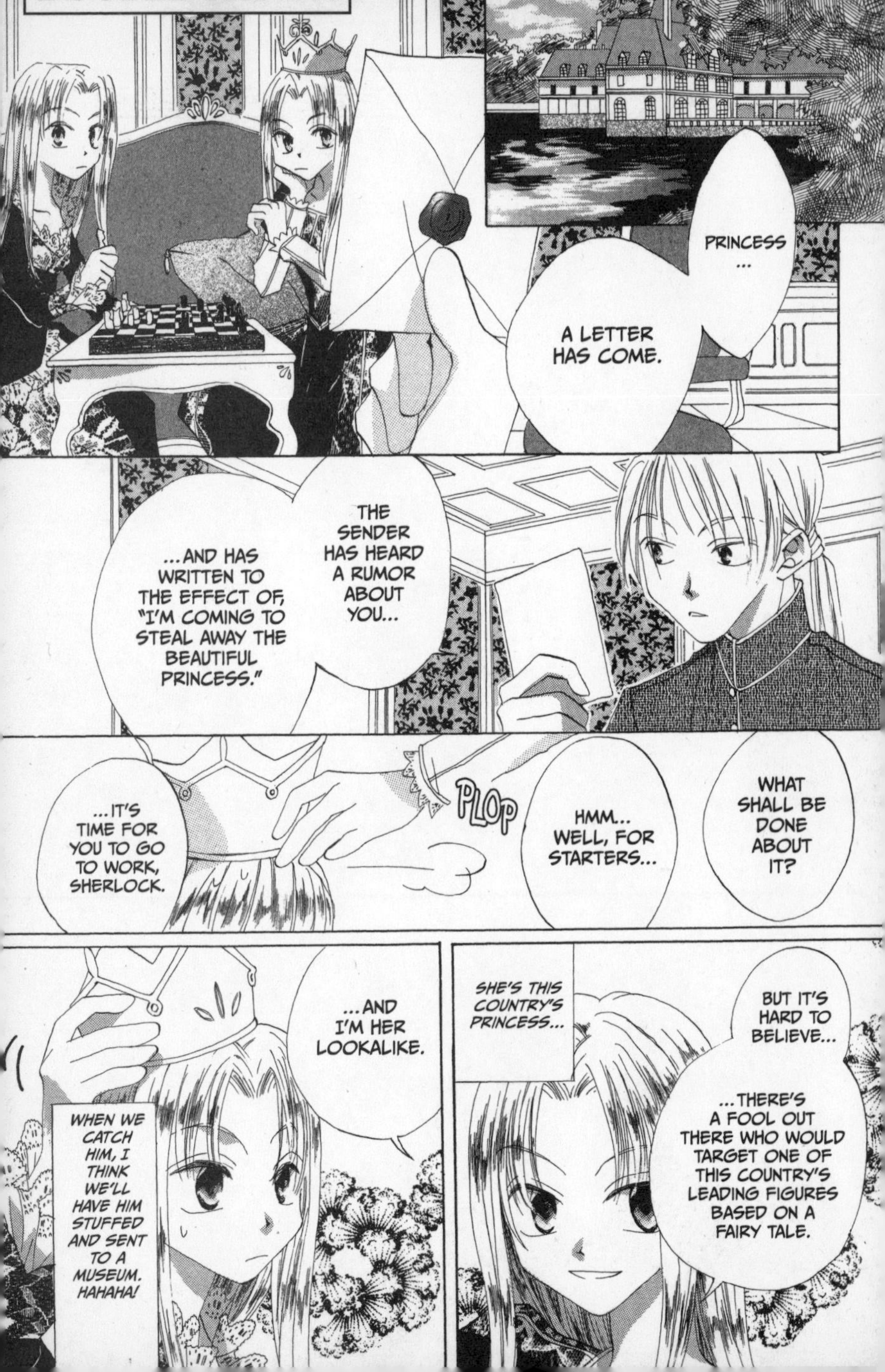
PRINCESS ...
A LETTER HAS COME.
THE SENDER HAS HEARD A RUMOR ABOUT YOU...
...AND HAS WRITTEN TO THE EFFECT OF, "I'M COMING TO STEAL AWAY THE BEAUTIFUL PRINCESS."
WHAT SHALL BE DONE ABOUT IT?
HMM... WELL, FOR STARTERS...
PLOP
...IT'S TIME FOR YOU TO GO TO WORK, SHERLOCK.
BUT IT'S HARD TO BELIEVE...
...THERE'S A FOOL OUT THERE WHO WOULD TARGET ONE OF THIS COUNTRY'S LEADING FIGURES BASED ON A FAIRY TALE.
SHE'S THIS COUNTRY'S PRINCESS...
...AND I'M HER LOOKALIKE.
WHEN WE CATCH HIM, I THINK WE'LL HAVE HIM STUFFED AND SENT TO A MUSEUM. HAHAHA!

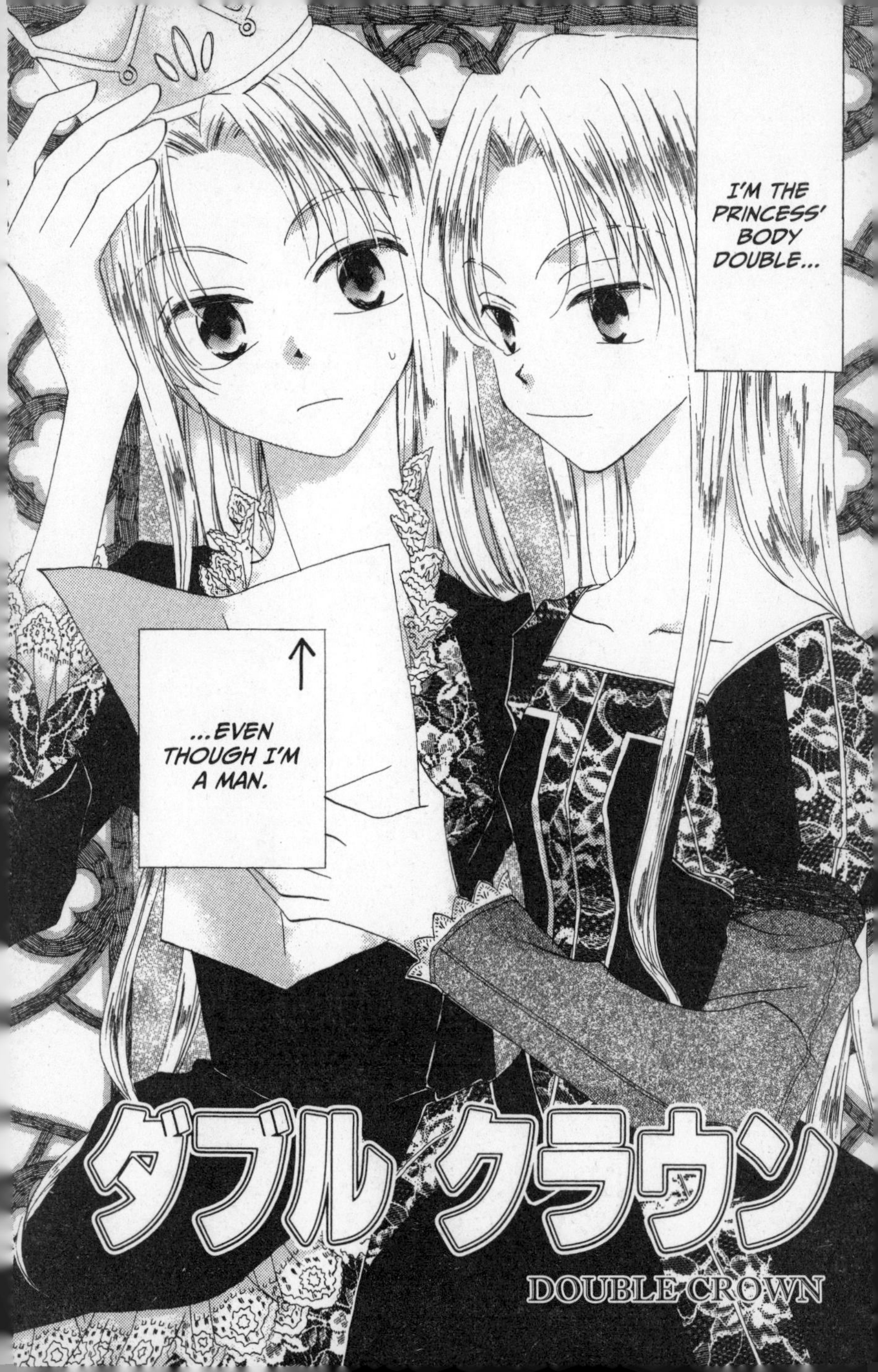
I'M THE PRINCESS' BODY DOUBLE...
...EVEN THOUGH I'M A MAN.
ダブルクラウン
DOUBLE CROWN

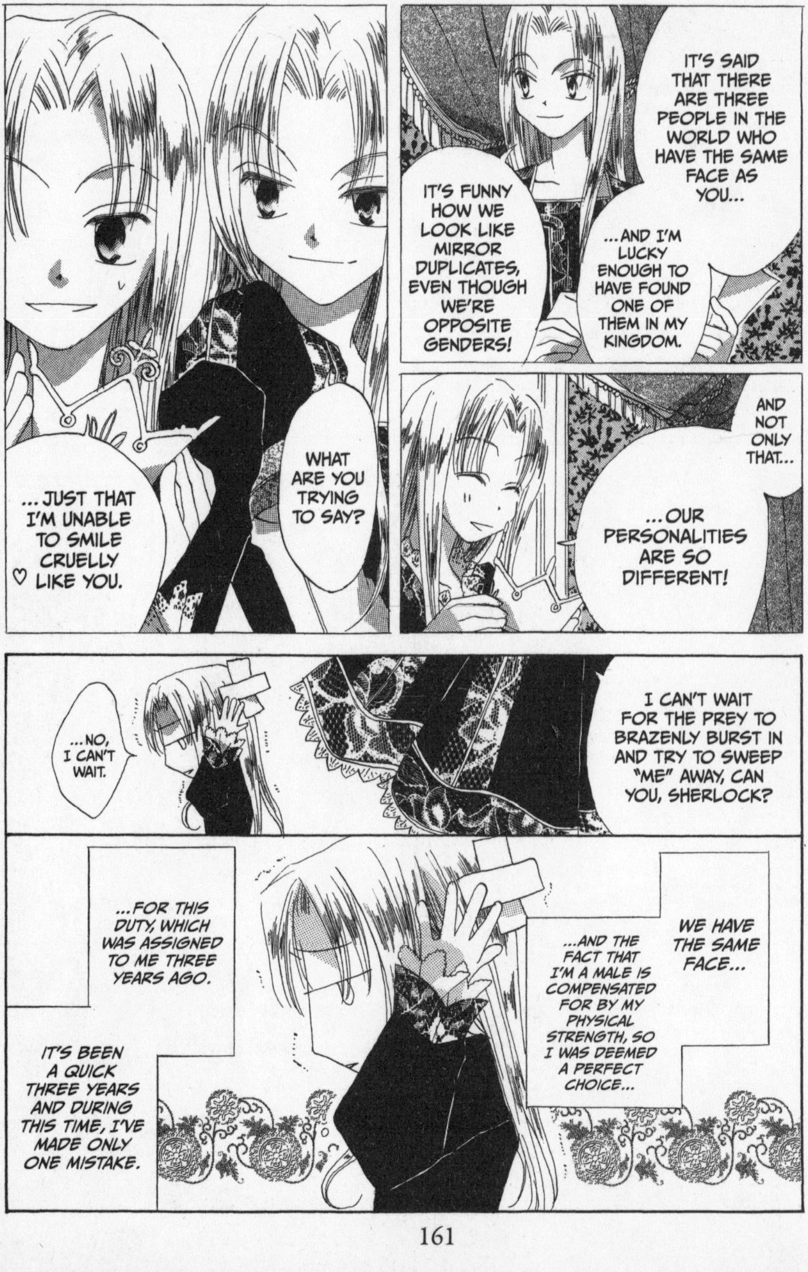
IT'S SAID THAT THERE ARE THREE PEOPLE IN THE WORLD WHO HAVE THE SAME FACE AS YOU...
...AND I'M LUCKY ENOUGH TO HAVE FOUND ONE OF THEM IN MY KINGDOM.
IT'S FUNNY HOW WE LOOK LIKE MIRROR DUPLICATES, EVEN THOUGH WE'RE OPPOSITE GENDERS!
AND NOT ONLY THAT...
...OUR PERSONALITIES ARE SO DIFFERENT!
WHAT ARE YOU TRYING TO SAY?
...JUST THAT I'M UNABLE TO SMILE CRUELLY ♡ LIKE YOU.
I CAN'T WAIT FOR THE PREY TO BRAZENLY BURST IN AND TRY TO SWEEP "ME" AWAY, CAN YOU, SHERLOCK?
...NO, I CAN'T WAIT.
WE HAVE THE SAME FACE...
...AND THE FACT THAT I'M A MALE IS COMPENSATED FOR BY MY PHYSICAL STRENGTH, SO I WAS DEEMED A PERFECT CHOICE...
...FOR THIS DUTY, WHICH WAS ASSIGNED TO ME THREE YEARS AGO.
IT'S BEEN A QUICK THREE YEARS AND DURING THIS TIME, I'VE MADE ONLY ONE MISTAKE.

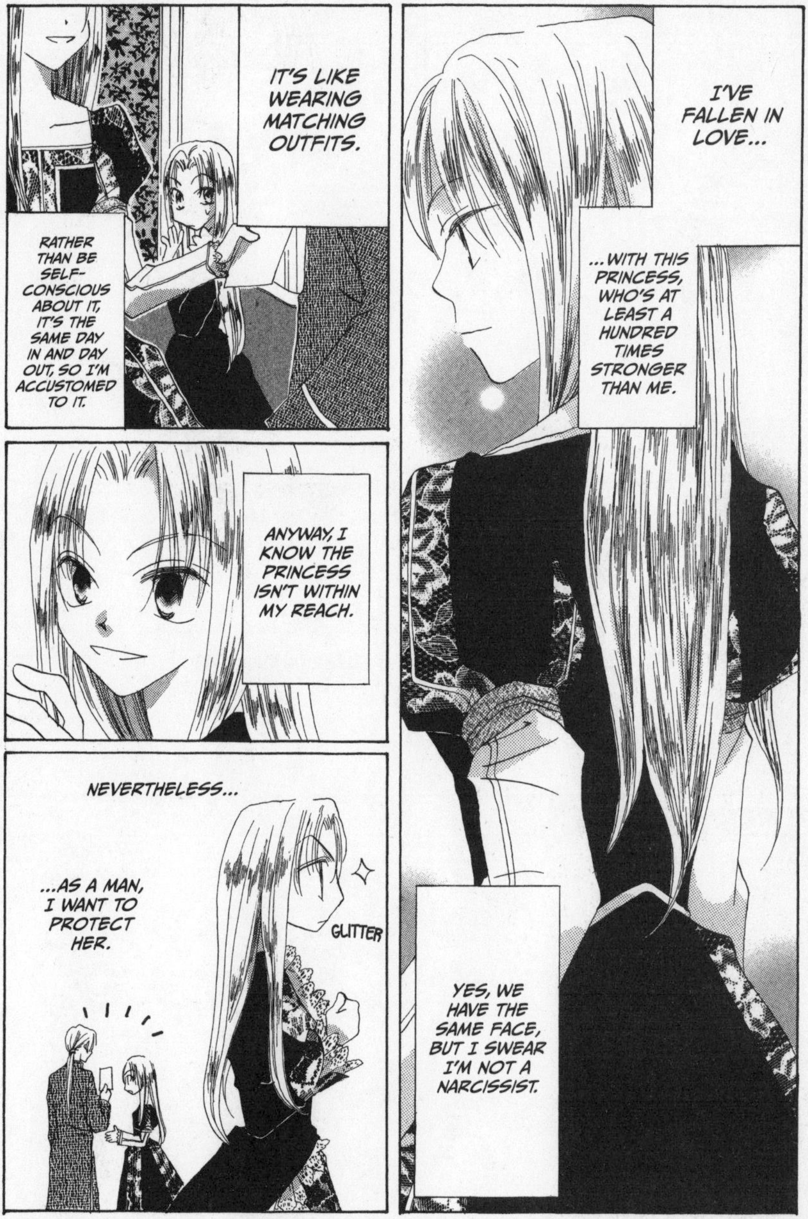
I'VE FALLEN IN LOVE...
...WITH THIS PRINCESS, WHO'S AT LEAST A HUNDRED TIMES STRONGER THAN ME.
YES, WE HAVE THE SAME FACE, BUT I SWEAR I'M NOT A NARCISSIST.
IT'S LIKE WEARING MATCHING OUTFITS.
RATHER THAN BE SELF-CONSCIOUS ABOUT IT, IT'S THE SAME DAY IN AND DAY OUT, SO I'M ACCUSTOMED TO IT.
ANYWAY, I KNOW THE PRINCESS ISN'T WITHIN MY REACH.
NEVERTHELESS...
...AS A MAN, I WANT TO PROTECT HER.
GLITTER

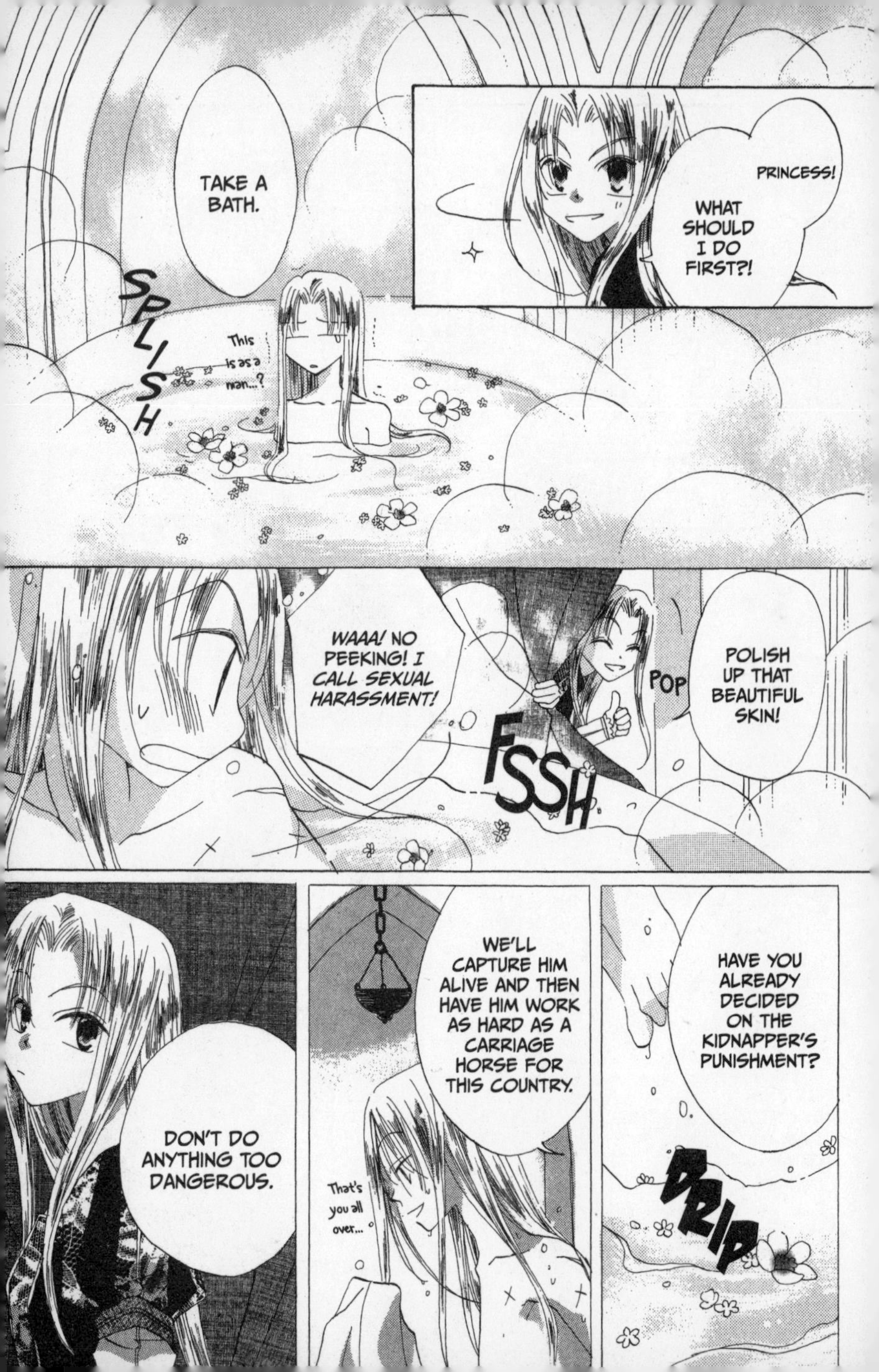
PRINCESS!
WHAT SHOULD I DO FIRST?!
TAKE A BATH.
SPLISH
This is as a man...?
POLISH UP THAT BEAUTIFUL SKIN!
POP
FSSH
WAAA! NO PEEKING! I CALL SEXUAL HARASSMENT!
HAVE YOU ALREADY DECIDED ON THE KIDNAPPER'S PUNISHMENT?
DRIP
WE'LL CAPTURE HIM ALIVE AND THEN HAVE HIM WORK AS HARD AS A CARRIAGE HORSE FOR THIS COUNTRY.
That's you all over...
DON'T DO ANYTHING TOO DANGEROUS.

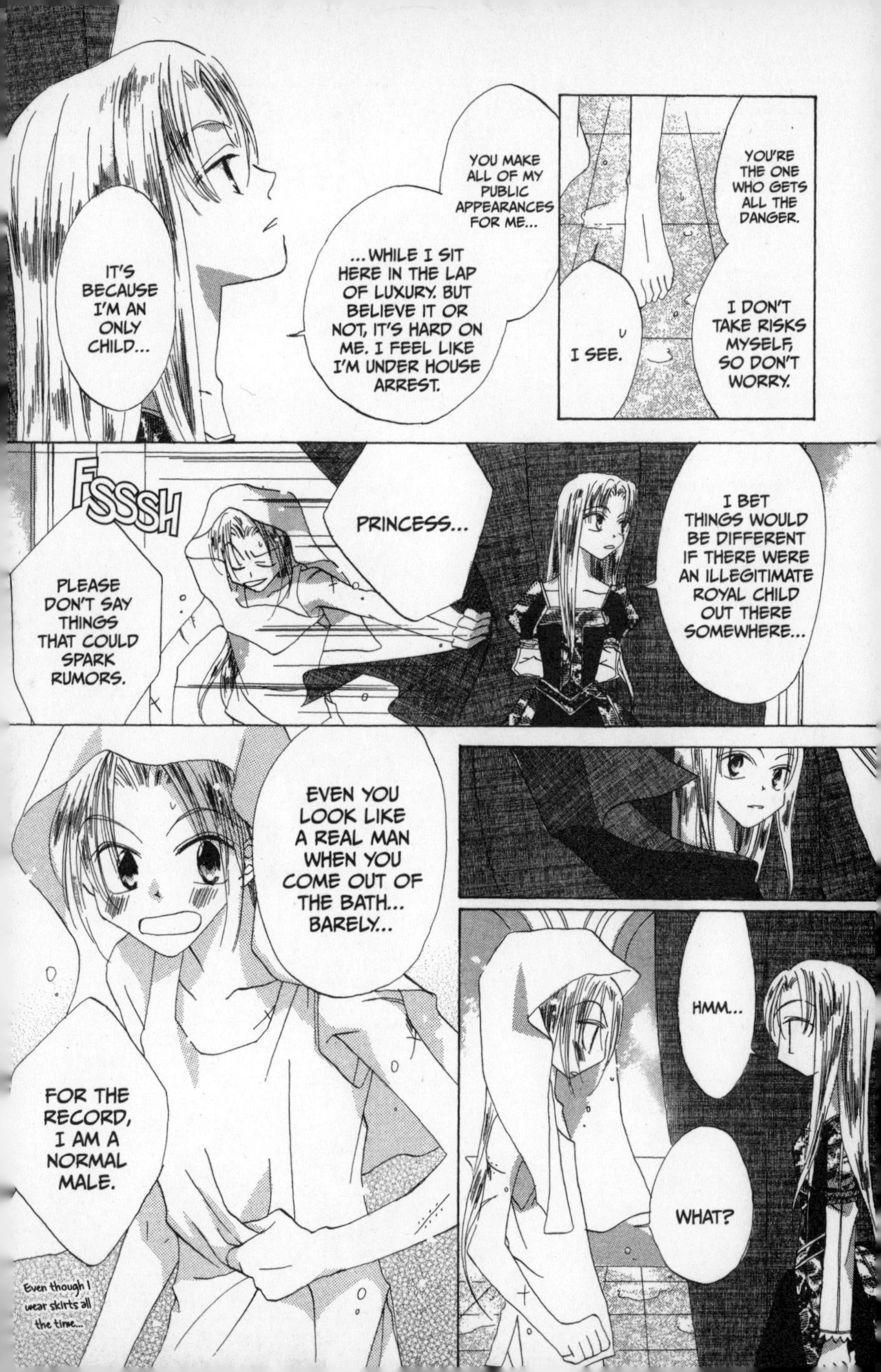
YOU'RE THE ONE WHO GETS ALL THE DANGER.
I DON'T TAKE RISKS MYSELF, SO DON'T WORRY.
I SEE.
IT'S BECAUSE I'M AN ONLY CHILD...
YOU MAKE ALL OF MY PUBLIC APPEARANCES FOR ME...
...WHILE I SIT HERE IN THE LAP OF LUXURY. BUT BELIEVE IT OR NOT, IT'S HARD ON ME. I FEEL LIKE I'M UNDER HOUSE ARREST.
I BET THINGS WOULD BE DIFFERENT IF THERE WERE AN ILLEGITIMATE ROYAL CHILD OUT THERE SOMEWHERE...
PRINCESS...
FSSSH
PLEASE DON'T SAY THINGS THAT COULD SPARK RUMORS.
HMM...
WHAT?
EVEN YOU LOOK LIKE A REAL MAN WHEN YOU COME OUT OF THE BATH... BARELY...
FOR THE RECORD, I AM A NORMAL MALE.
Even though I wear skirts all the time...

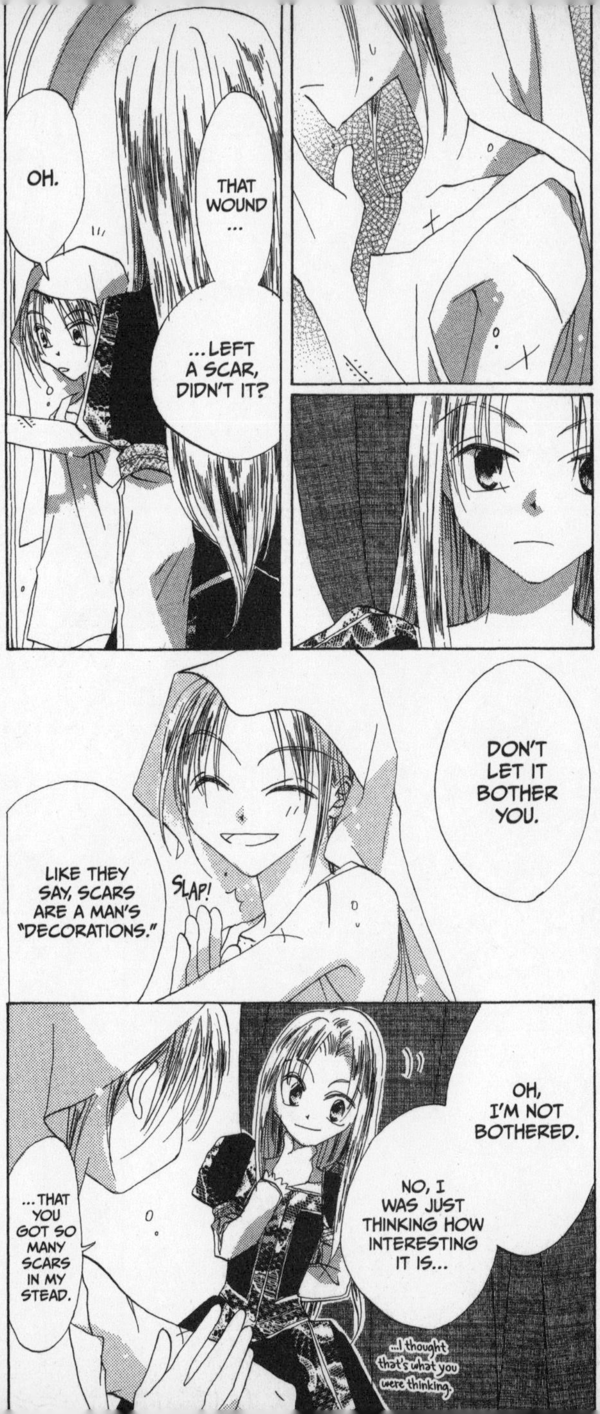
OH.
THAT WOUND ...
...LEFT A SCAR, DIDN'T IT?
DON'T LET IT BOTHER YOU.
SLAP!
LIKE THEY SAY, SCARS ARE A MAN'S "DECORATIONS."
OH, I'M NOT BOTHERED.
NO, I WAS JUST THINKING HOW INTERESTING IT IS...
...THAT YOU GOT SO MANY SCARS IN MY STEAD.
...I thought that's what you were thinking.

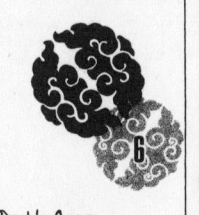

6

Double Crown

I suck at drawing, don't I...? And yet, I remember being confident at the time I was working on the manuscript for this. Subjectivity is scary. Recently, when I feel that something's interesting, I try to get it down on paper without thinking too much about it in order to preserve a sense of freshness. Otherwise, I have the tendency to think about morals or what other people might think when they eventually see the art and this makes me stiffen up. Now, when I reread my older stories, I get the impression that I wasn't stiff at all, but just had a good time drawing. I wonder where this insecurity gap between then and now came from?

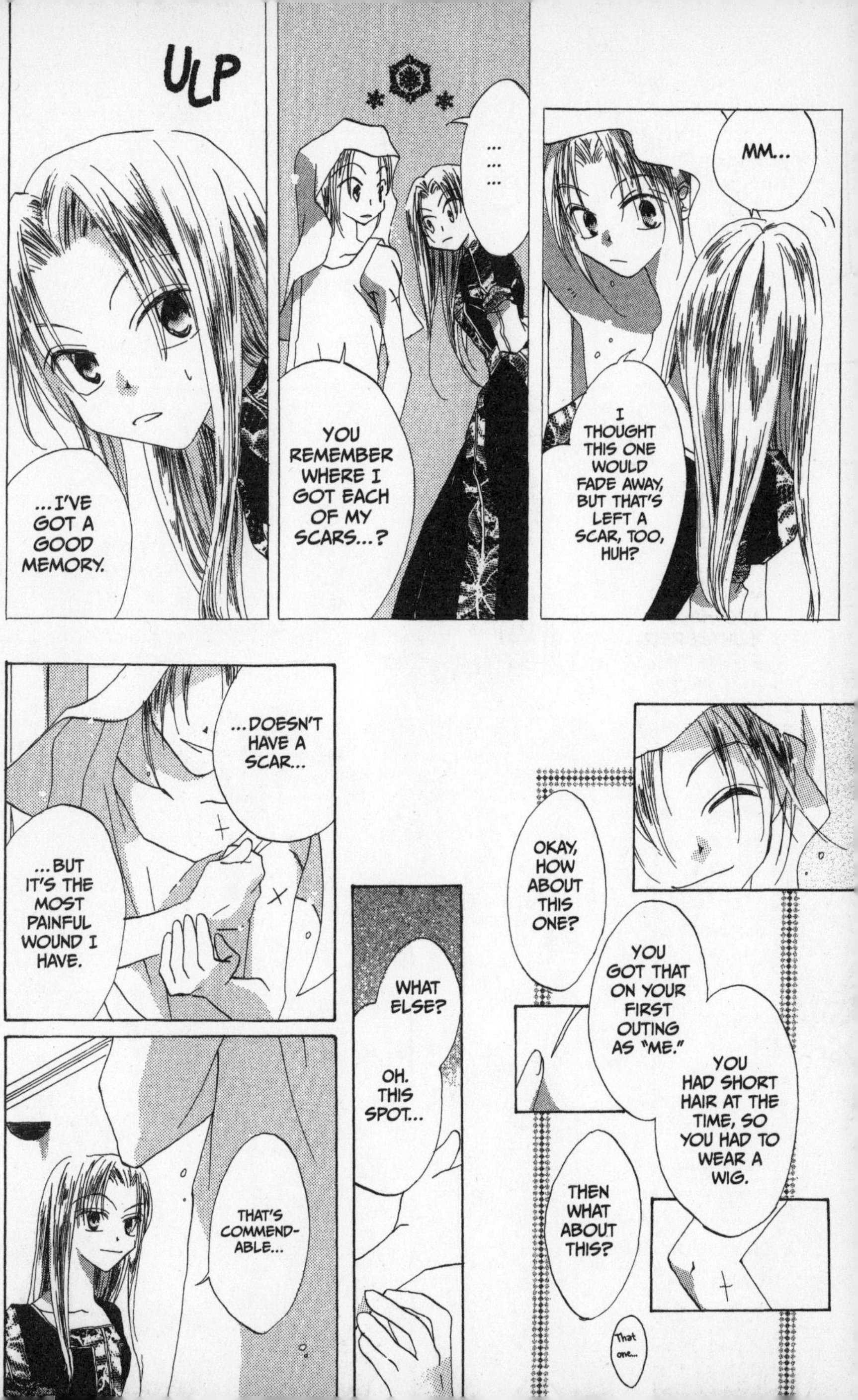
MM...
I THOUGHT THIS ONE WOULD FADE AWAY, BUT THAT'S LEFT A SCAR, TOO, HUH?
...
...
...
YOU REMEMBER WHERE I GOT EACH OF MY SCARS...?
ULP
...I'VE GOT A GOOD MEMORY.
OKAY, HOW ABOUT THIS ONE?
YOU GOT THAT ON YOUR FIRST OUTING AS "ME."
YOU HAD SHORT HAIR AT THE TIME, SO YOU HAD TO WEAR A WIG.
THEN WHAT ABOUT THIS?
That one...
WHAT ELSE?
OH. THIS SPOT...
...DOESN'T HAVE A SCAR...
...BUT IT'S THE MOST PAINFUL WOUND I HAVE.
THAT'S COMMEND-ABLE...

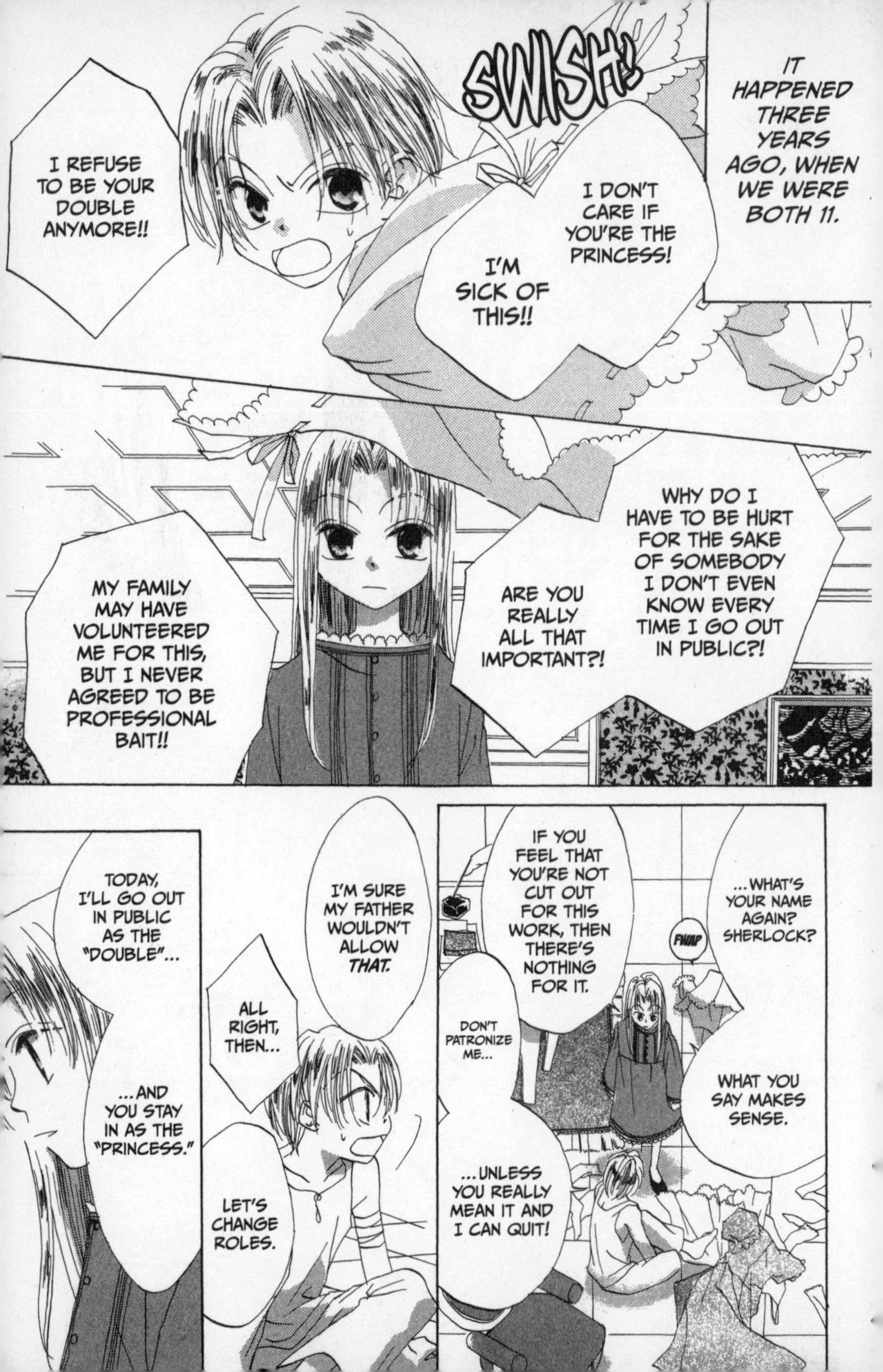
IT HAPPENED THREE YEARS AGO, WHEN WE WERE BOTH 11.
SWISH!
I DON'T CARE IF YOU'RE THE PRINCESS!
I'M SICK OF THIS!!
I REFUSE TO BE YOUR DOUBLE ANYMORE!!
WHY DO I HAVE TO BE HURT FOR THE SAKE OF SOMEBODY I DON'T EVEN KNOW EVERY TIME I GO OUT IN PUBLIC?!
ARE YOU REALLY ALL THAT IMPORTANT?!
MY FAMILY MAY HAVE VOLUNTEERED ME FOR THIS, BUT I NEVER AGREED TO BE PROFESSIONAL BAIT!!
...WHAT'S YOUR NAME AGAIN? SHERLOCK?
FWAP
IF YOU FEEL THAT YOU'RE NOT CUT OUT FOR THIS WORK, THEN THERE'S NOTHING FOR IT.
WHAT YOU SAY MAKES SENSE.
DON'T PATRONIZE ME...
...UNLESS YOU REALLY MEAN IT AND I CAN QUIT!
I'M SURE MY FATHER WOULDN'T ALLOW *THAT.*
ALL RIGHT, THEN...
LET'S CHANGE ROLES.
TODAY, I'LL GO OUT IN PUBLIC AS THE "DOUBLE"...
...AND YOU STAY IN AS THE "PRINCESS."

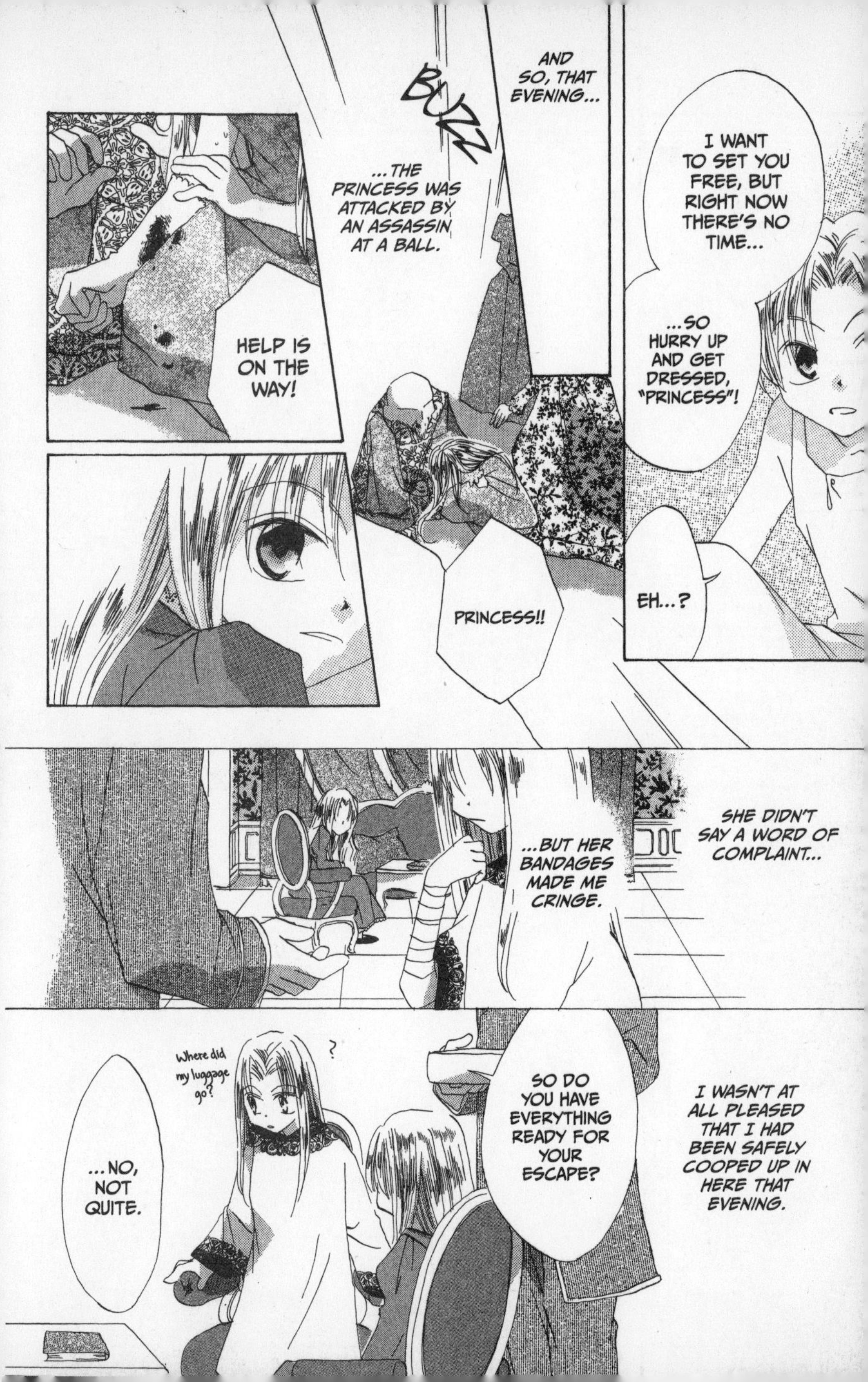
I WANT TO SET YOU FREE, BUT RIGHT NOW THERE'S NO TIME...
...SO HURRY UP AND GET DRESSED, "PRINCESS"!
EH...?
AND SO, THAT EVENING...
BUZZ
...THE PRINCESS WAS ATTACKED BY AN ASSASSIN AT A BALL.
HELP IS ON THE WAY!
PRINCESS!!
SHE DIDN'T SAY A WORD OF COMPLAINT...
...BUT HER BANDAGES MADE ME CRINGE.
I WASN'T AT ALL PLEASED THAT I HAD BEEN SAFELY COOPED UP IN HERE THAT EVENING.
SO DO YOU HAVE EVERYTHING READY FOR YOUR ESCAPE?
?
Where did my luggage go?
...NO, NOT QUITE.

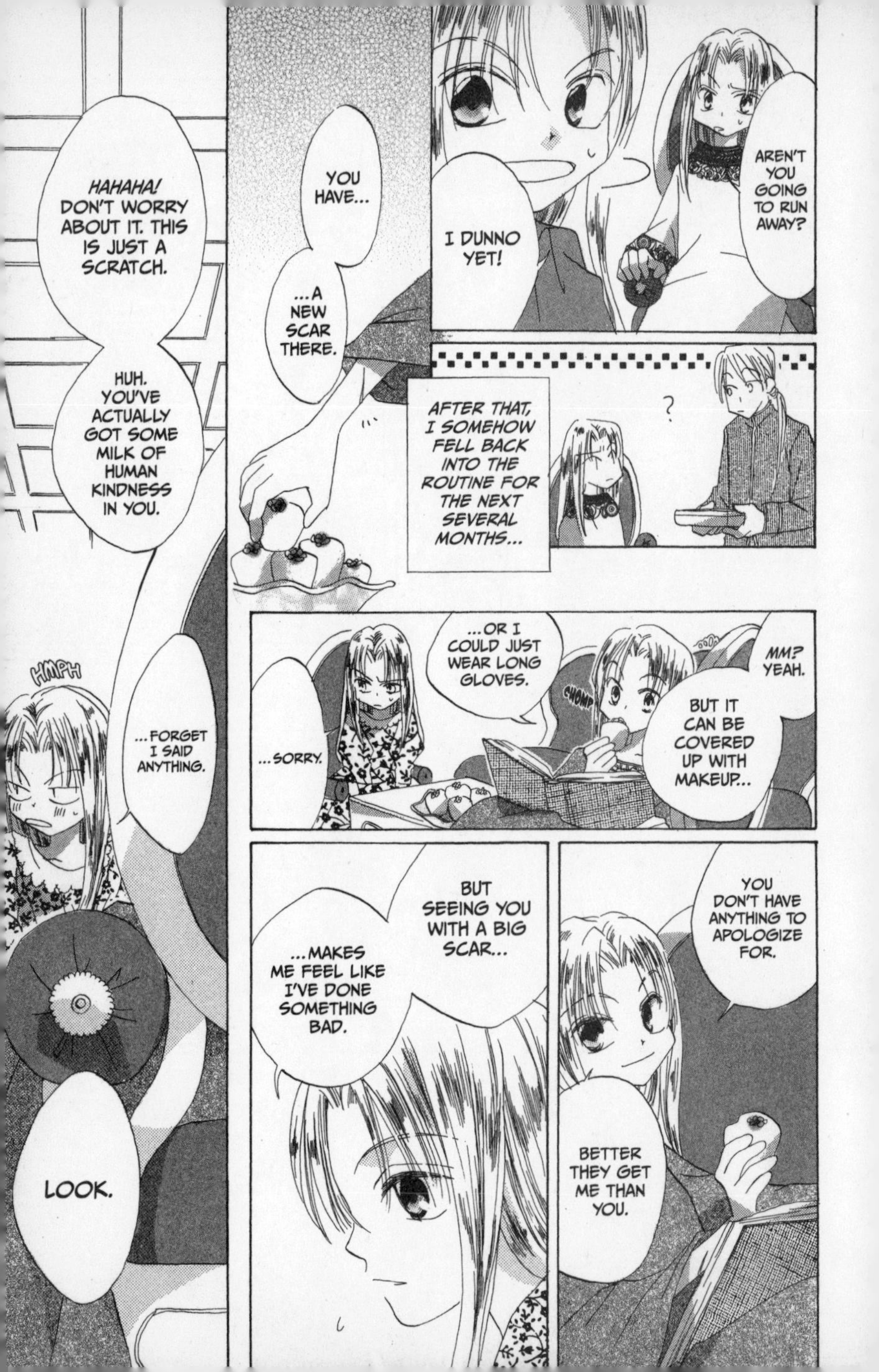
AREN'T YOU GOING TO RUN AWAY?
I DUNNO YET!
AFTER THAT, I SOMEHOW FELL BACK INTO THE ROUTINE FOR THE NEXT SEVERAL MONTHS...
?
MM? YEAH.
BUT IT CAN BE COVERED UP WITH MAKEUP...
CHOMP
...OR I COULD JUST WEAR LONG GLOVES.
...SORRY.
YOU DON'T HAVE ANYTHING TO APOLOGIZE FOR.
BETTER THEY GET ME THAN YOU.
BUT SEEING YOU WITH A BIG SCAR...
...MAKES ME FEEL LIKE I'VE DONE SOMETHING BAD.
YOU HAVE...
...A NEW SCAR THERE.
HAHAHA! DON'T WORRY ABOUT IT. THIS IS JUST A SCRATCH.
HUH. YOU'VE ACTUALLY GOT SOME MILK OF HUMAN KINDNESS IN YOU.
HMPH
...FORGET I SAID ANYTHING.
LOOK.

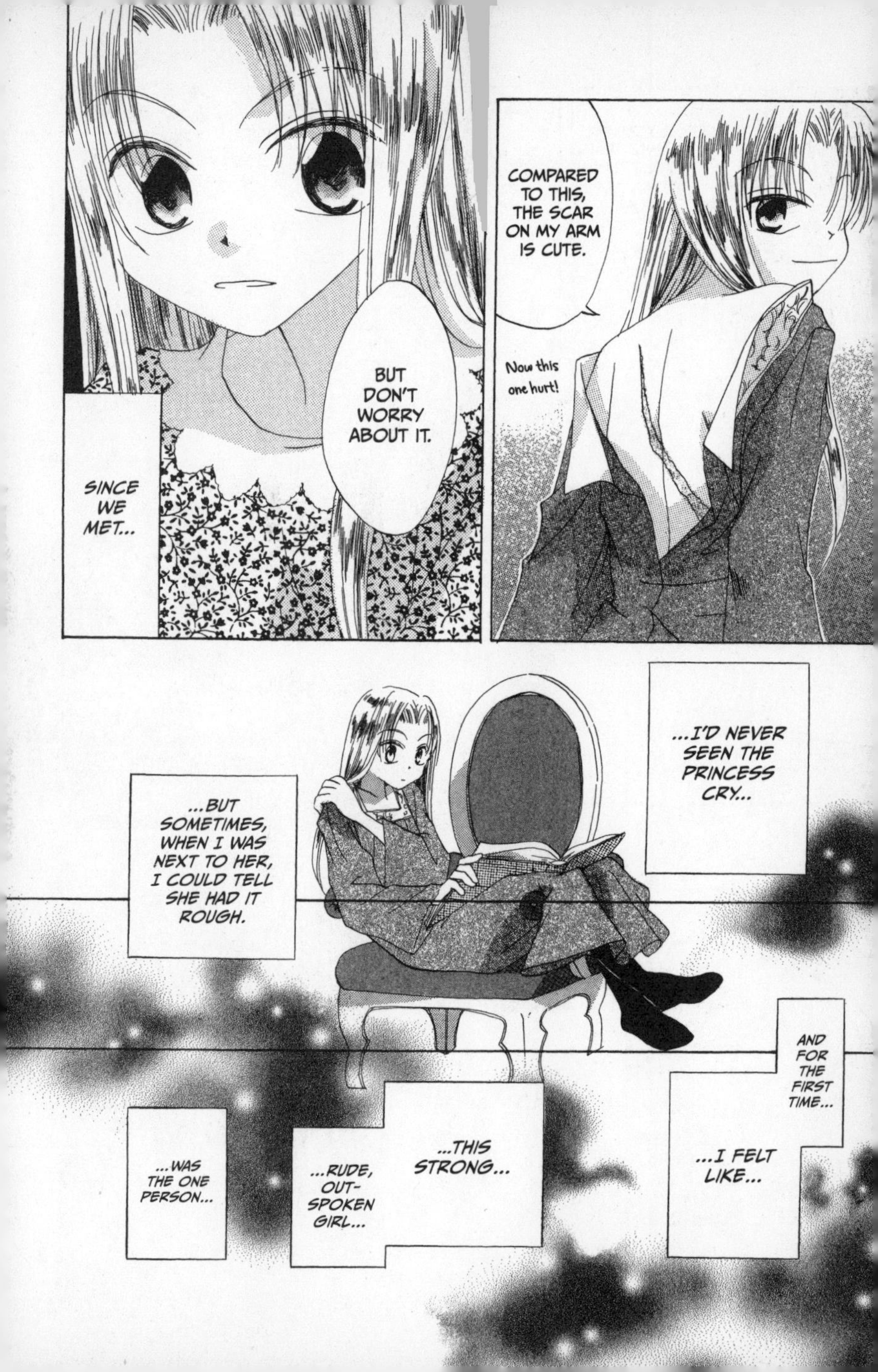
COMPARED TO THIS, THE SCAR ON MY ARM IS CUTE.
Now this one hurt!
BUT DON'T WORRY ABOUT IT.
SINCE WE MET...
...I'D NEVER SEEN THE PRINCESS CRY...
...BUT SOMETIMES, WHEN I WAS NEXT TO HER, I COULD TELL SHE HAD IT ROUGH.
AND FOR THE FIRST TIME...
...I FELT LIKE...
...THIS STRONG...
...RUDE, OUT-SPOKEN GIRL...
...WAS THE ONE PERSON...

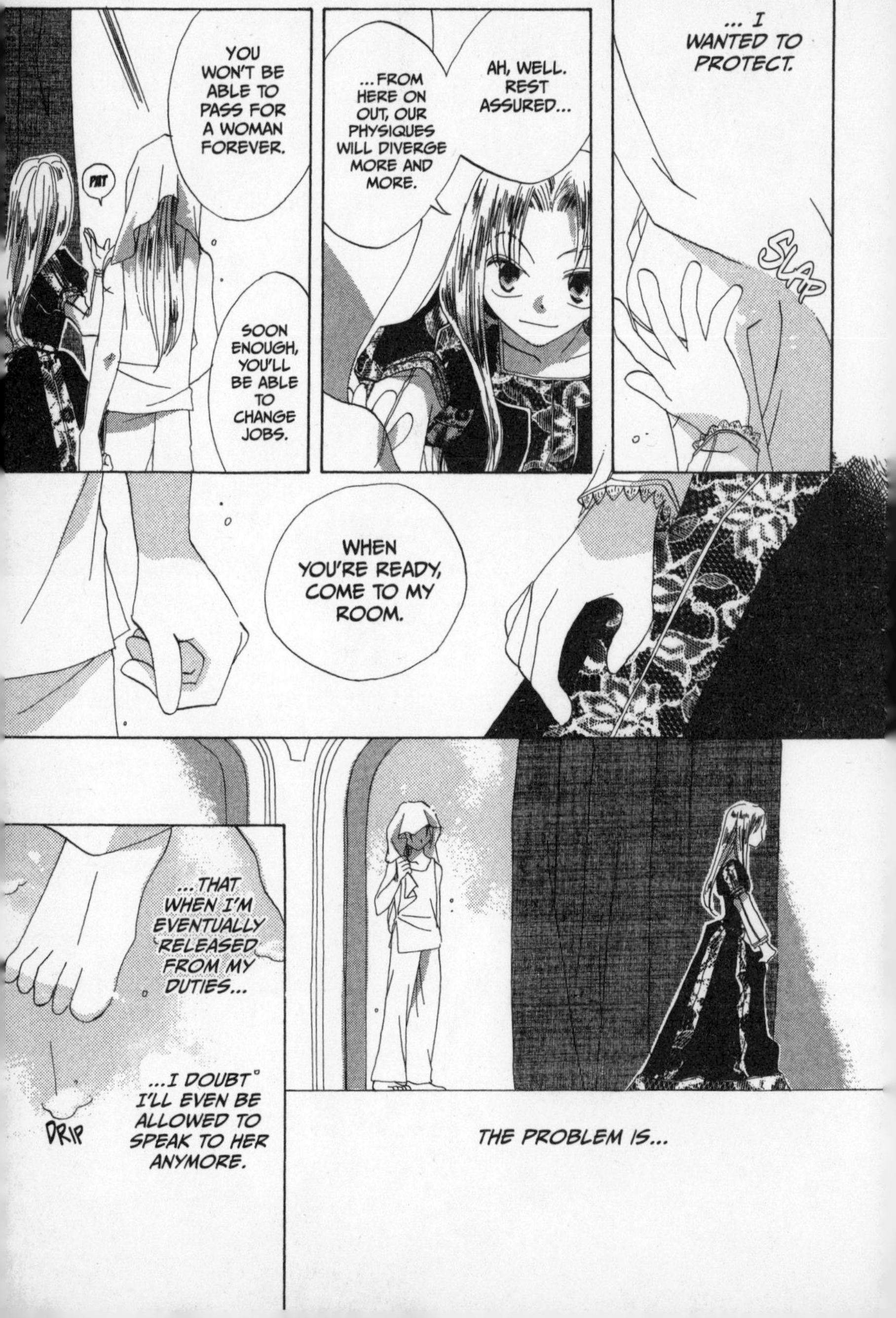
... I WANTED TO PROTECT.
SLAP
AH, WELL. REST ASSURED...
...FROM HERE ON OUT, OUR PHYSIQUES WILL DIVERGE MORE AND MORE.
YOU WON'T BE ABLE TO PASS FOR A WOMAN FOREVER.
PAT
SOON ENOUGH, YOU'LL BE ABLE TO CHANGE JOBS.
WHEN YOU'RE READY, COME TO MY ROOM.
THE PROBLEM IS...
...THAT WHEN I'M EVENTUALLY RELEASED FROM MY DUTIES...
...I DOUBT I'LL EVEN BE ALLOWED TO SPEAK TO HER ANYMORE.
DRIP

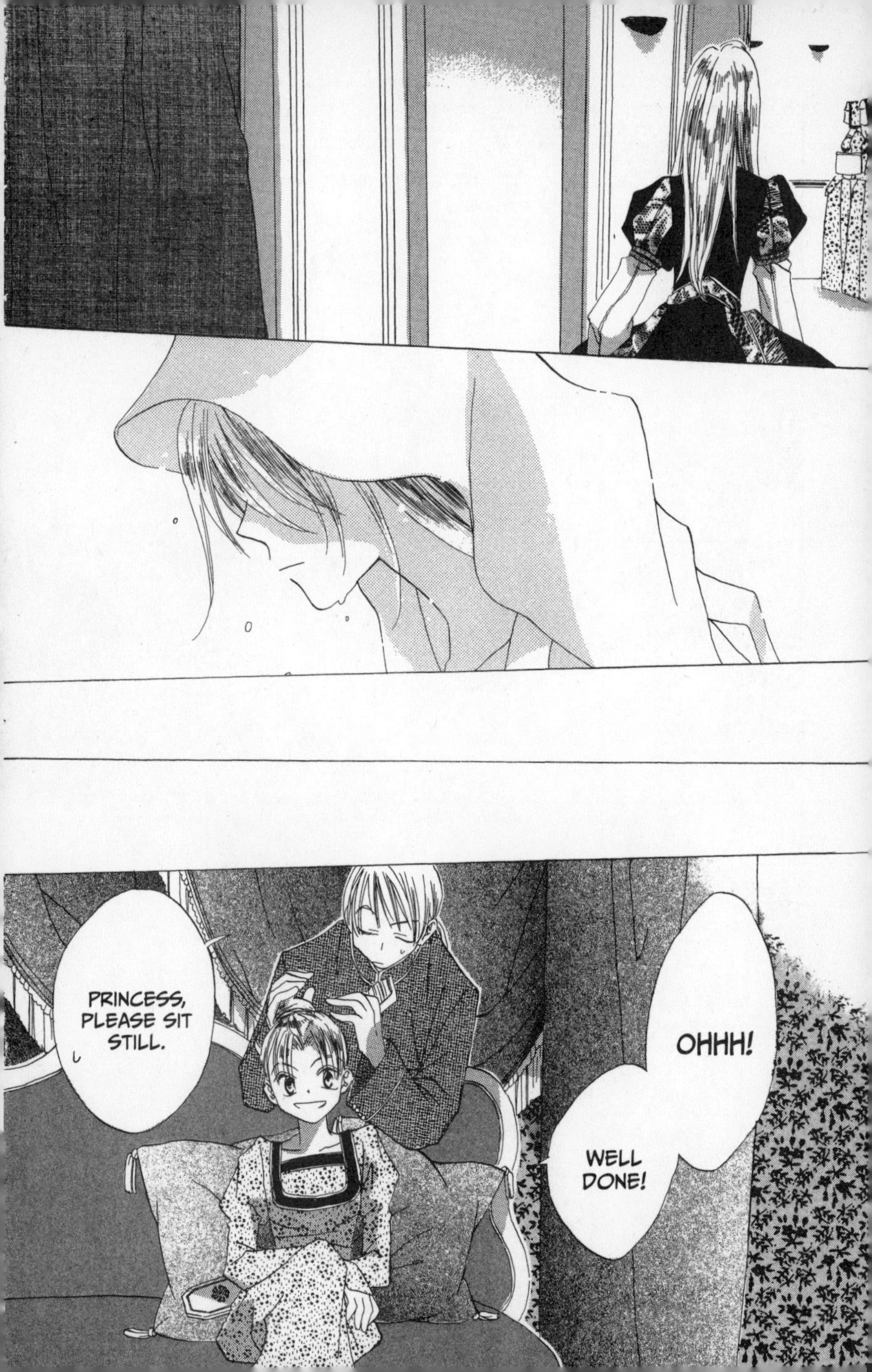
OHHH!
WELL DONE!
PRINCESS, PLEASE SIT STILL.

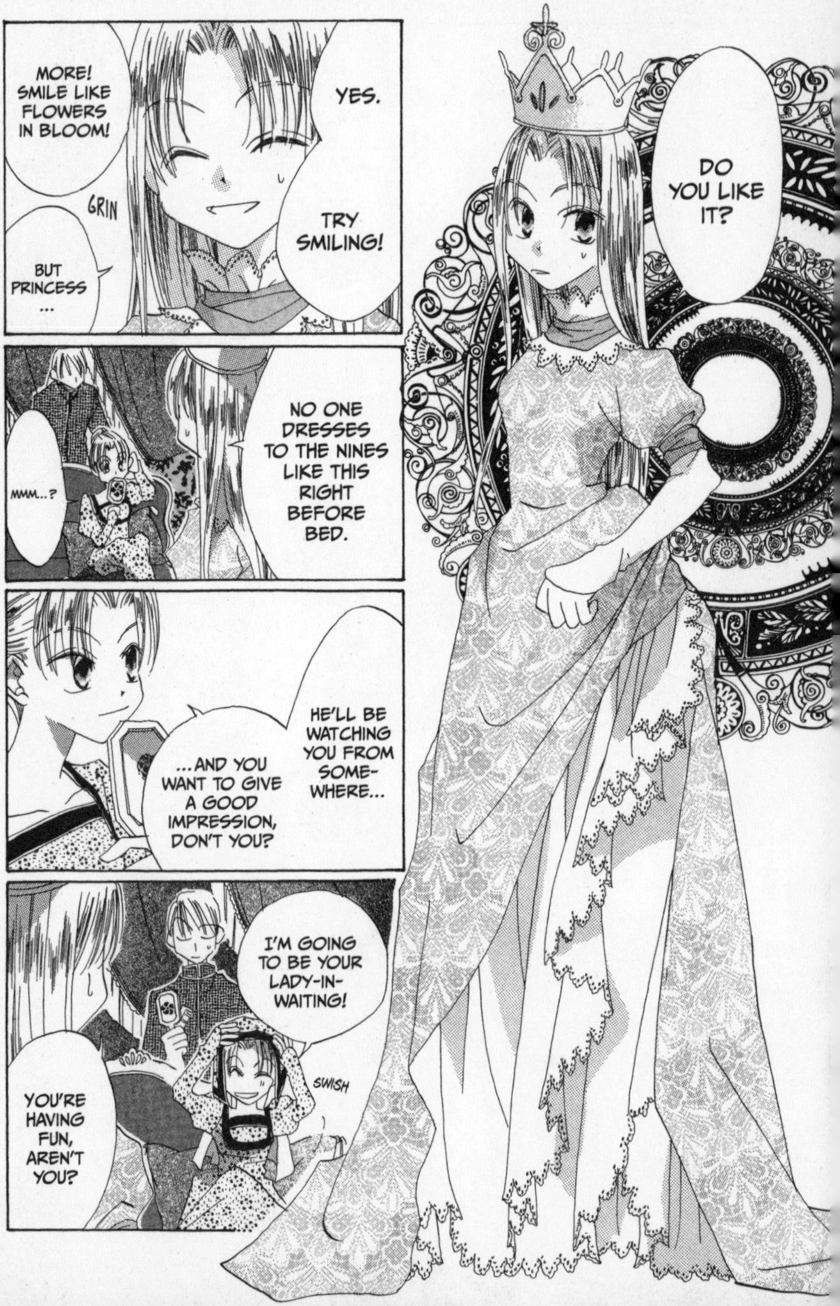
DO YOU LIKE IT?
YES.
TRY SMILING!
MORE! SMILE LIKE FLOWERS IN BLOOM!
GRIN
BUT PRINCESS ...
NO ONE DRESSES TO THE NINES LIKE THIS RIGHT BEFORE BED.
MMM...?
HE'LL BE WATCHING YOU FROM SOME-WHERE...
...AND YOU WANT TO GIVE A GOOD IMPRESSION, DON'T YOU?
I'M GOING TO BE YOUR LADY-IN-WAITING!
SWISH
YOU'RE HAVING FUN, AREN'T YOU?

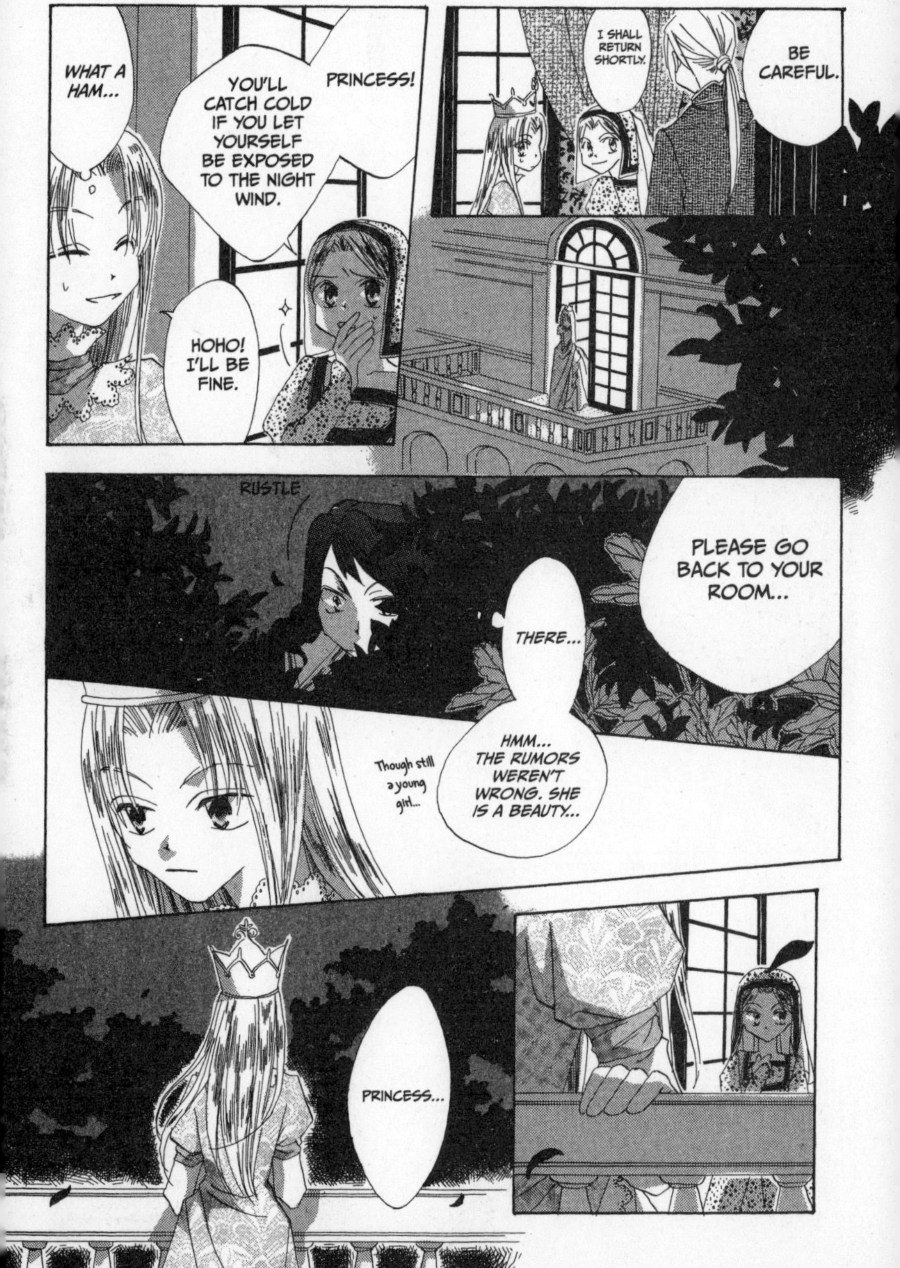
BE CAREFUL.
I SHALL RETURN SHORTLY.
PRINCESS!
YOU'LL CATCH COLD IF YOU LET YOURSELF BE EXPOSED TO THE NIGHT WIND.
WHAT A HAM...
HOHO! I'LL BE FINE.
PLEASE GO BACK TO YOUR ROOM...
RUSTLE
THERE...
HMM... THE RUMORS WEREN'T WRONG. SHE IS A BEAUTY...
Though still a young girl...
PRINCESS...

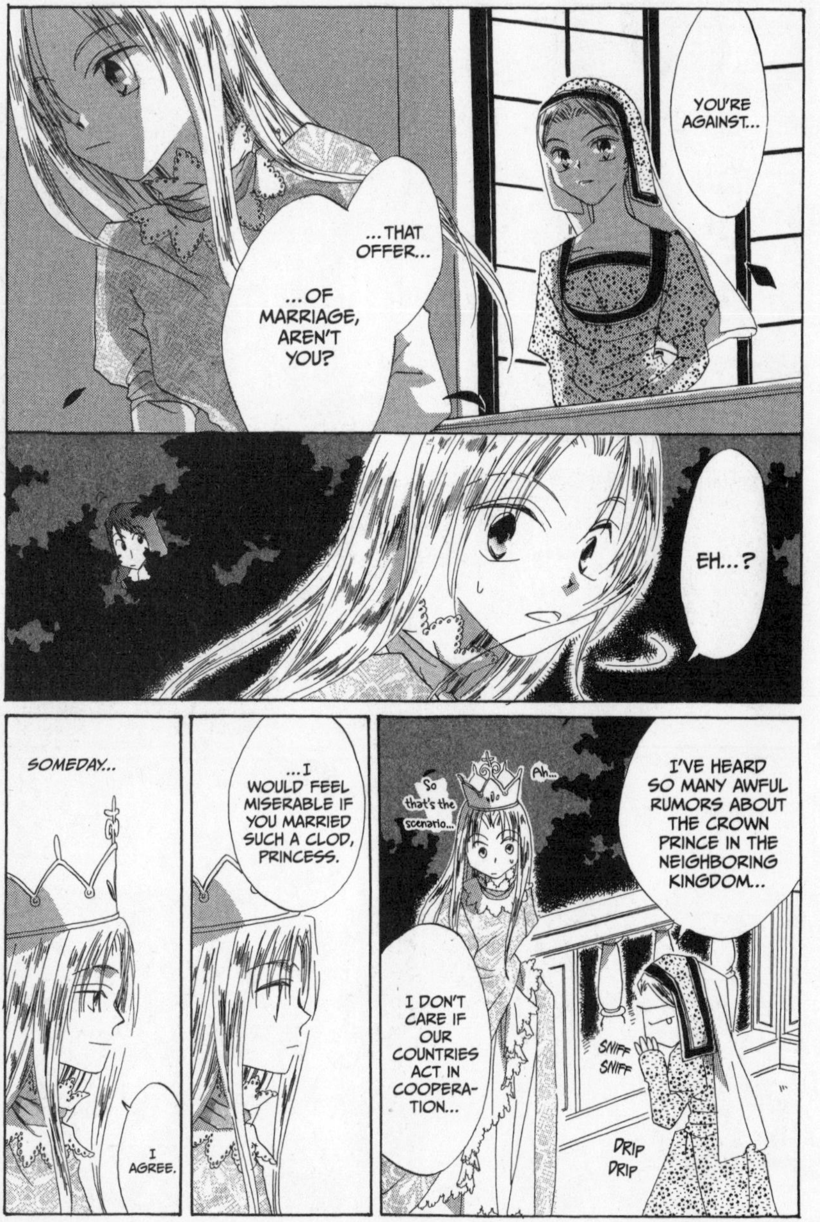
YOU'RE AGAINST...
...THAT OFFER...
...OF MARRIAGE, AREN'T YOU?
EH...?
I'VE HEARD SO MANY AWFUL RUMORS ABOUT THE CROWN PRINCE IN THE NEIGHBORING KINGDOM...
SNIFF SNIFF
DRIP DRIP
Ah...
So that's the scenario...
I DON'T CARE IF OUR COUNTRIES ACT IN COOPERATION...
...I WOULD FEEL MISERABLE IF YOU MARRIED SUCH A CLOD, PRINCESS.
SOMEDAY...
I AGREE.

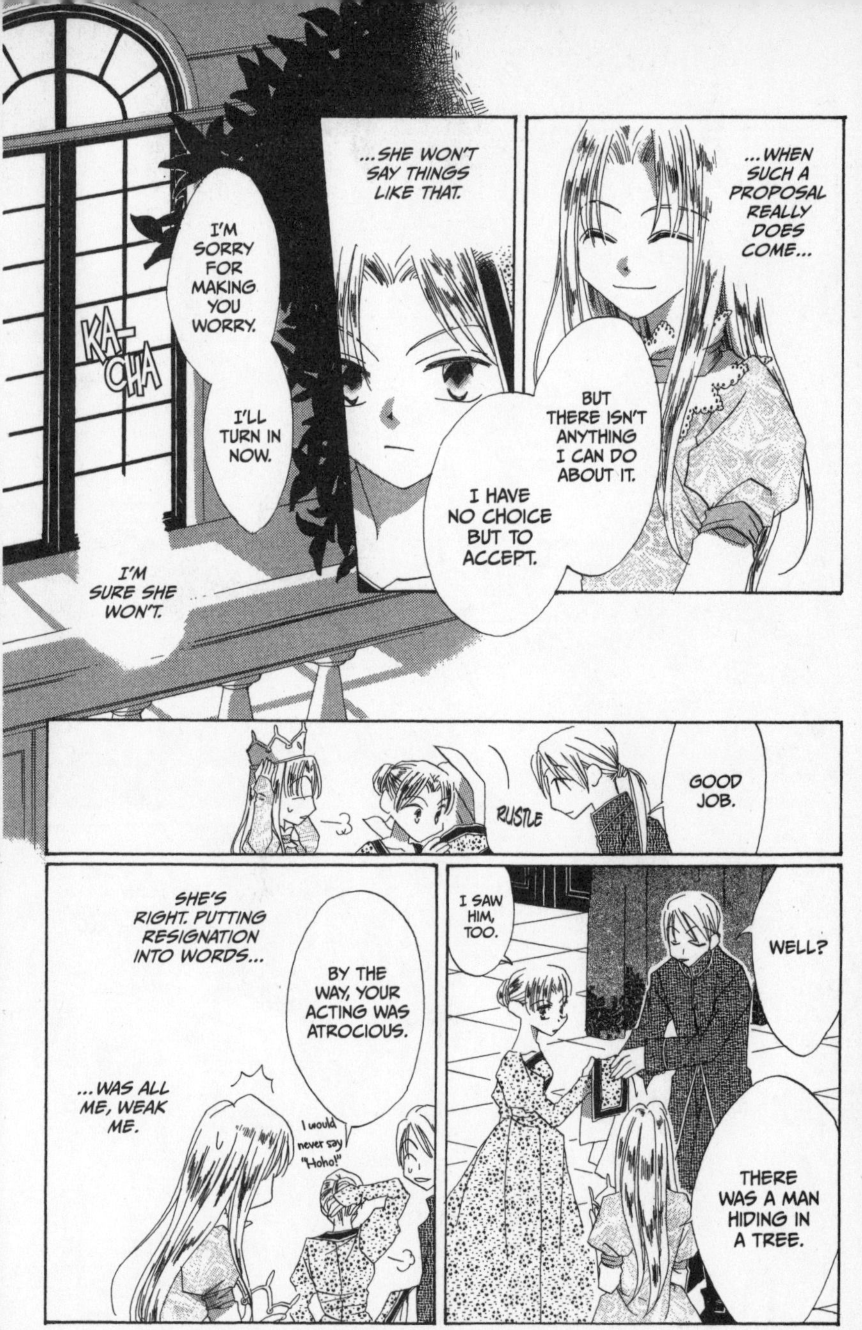
...WHEN SUCH A PROPOSAL REALLY DOES COME...
BUT THERE ISN'T ANYTHING I CAN DO ABOUT IT.
I HAVE NO CHOICE BUT TO ACCEPT.
...SHE WON'T SAY THINGS LIKE THAT.
I'M SORRY FOR MAKING YOU WORRY.
KA-CHA
I'LL TURN IN NOW.
I'M SURE SHE WON'T.
GOOD JOB.
RUSTLE
WELL?
THERE WAS A MAN HIDING IN A TREE.
I SAW HIM, TOO.
SHE'S RIGHT. PUTTING RESIGNATION INTO WORDS...
BY THE WAY, YOUR ACTING WAS ATROCIOUS.
I would never say "Hoho!"
...WAS ALL ME, WEAK ME.

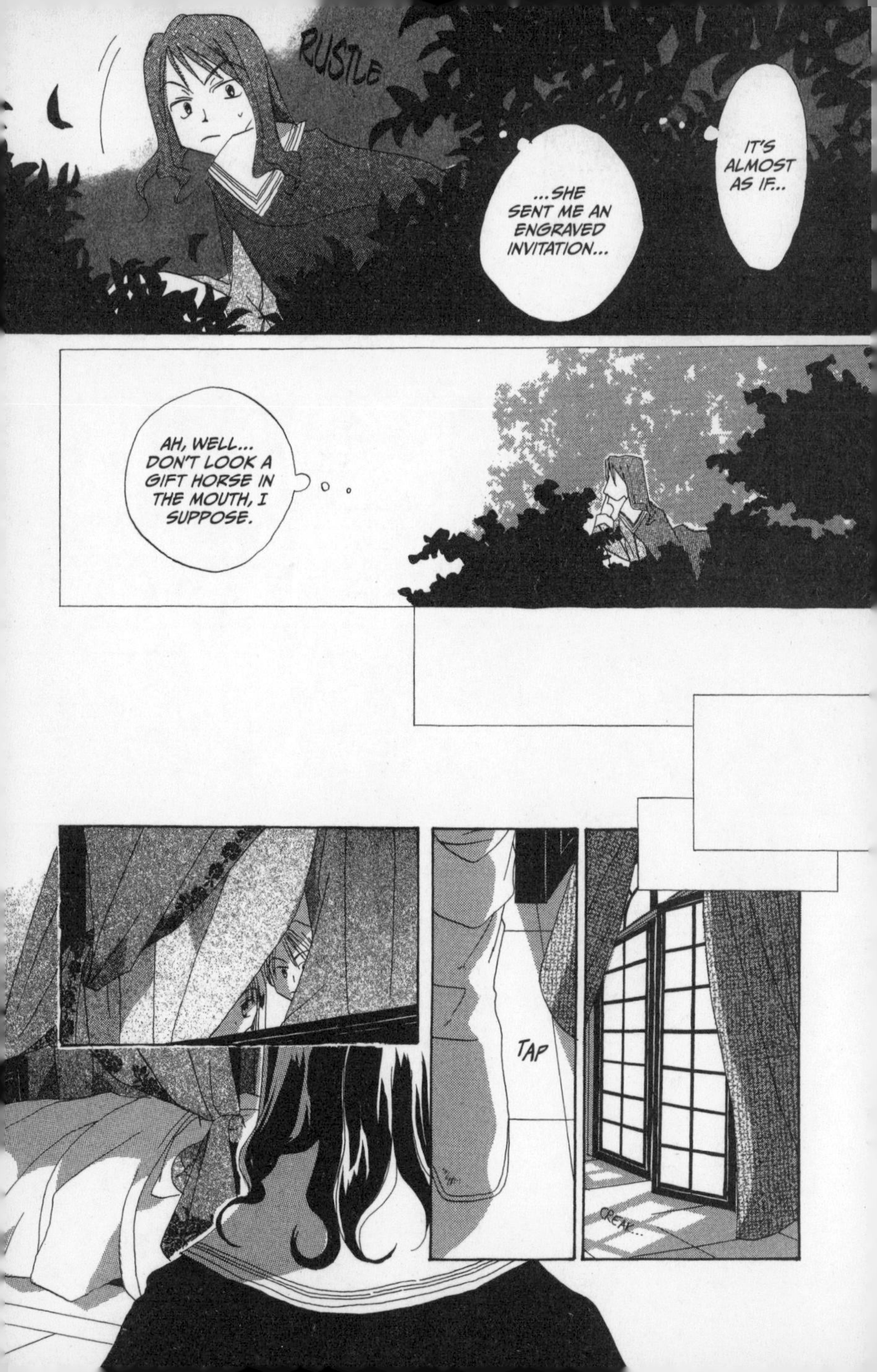
IT'S ALMOST AS IF...
...SHE SENT ME AN ENGRAVED INVITATION...
RUSTLE
AH, WELL... DON'T LOOK A GIFT HORSE IN THE MOUTH, I SUPPOSE.
CREAK...
TAP

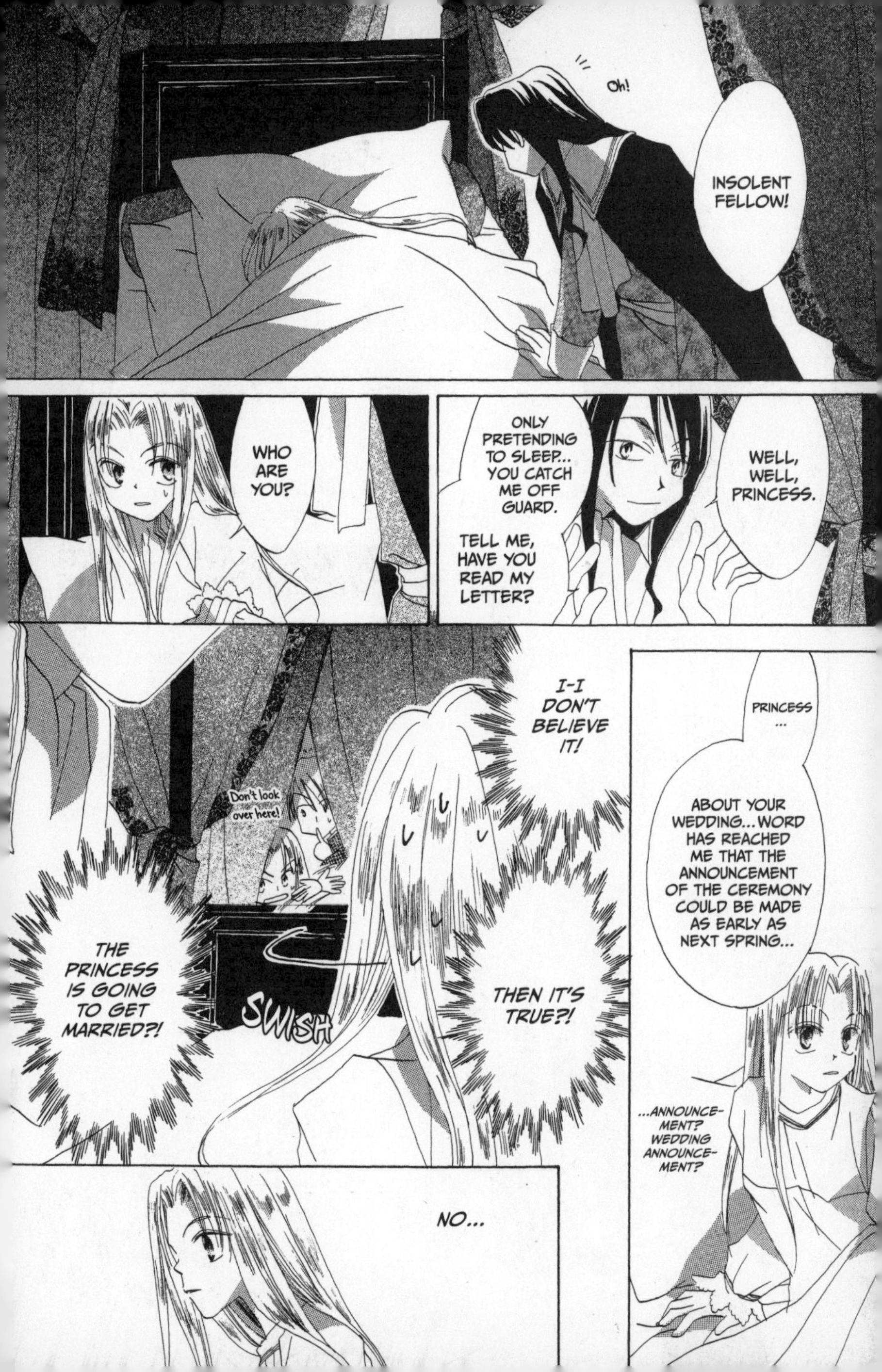
Oh!
INSOLENT FELLOW!
WELL, WELL, PRINCESS.
ONLY PRETENDING TO SLEEP... YOU CATCH ME OFF GUARD.
TELL ME, HAVE YOU READ MY LETTER?
WHO ARE YOU?
PRINCESS ...
ABOUT YOUR WEDDING...WORD HAS REACHED ME THAT THE ANNOUNCEMENT OF THE CEREMONY COULD BE MADE AS EARLY AS NEXT SPRING...
...ANNOUNCE-MENT? WEDDING ANNOUNCE-MENT?
I-I DON'T BELIEVE IT!
THEN IT'S TRUE?!
SWISH
Don't look over here!
THE PRINCESS IS GOING TO GET MARRIED?!
NO...

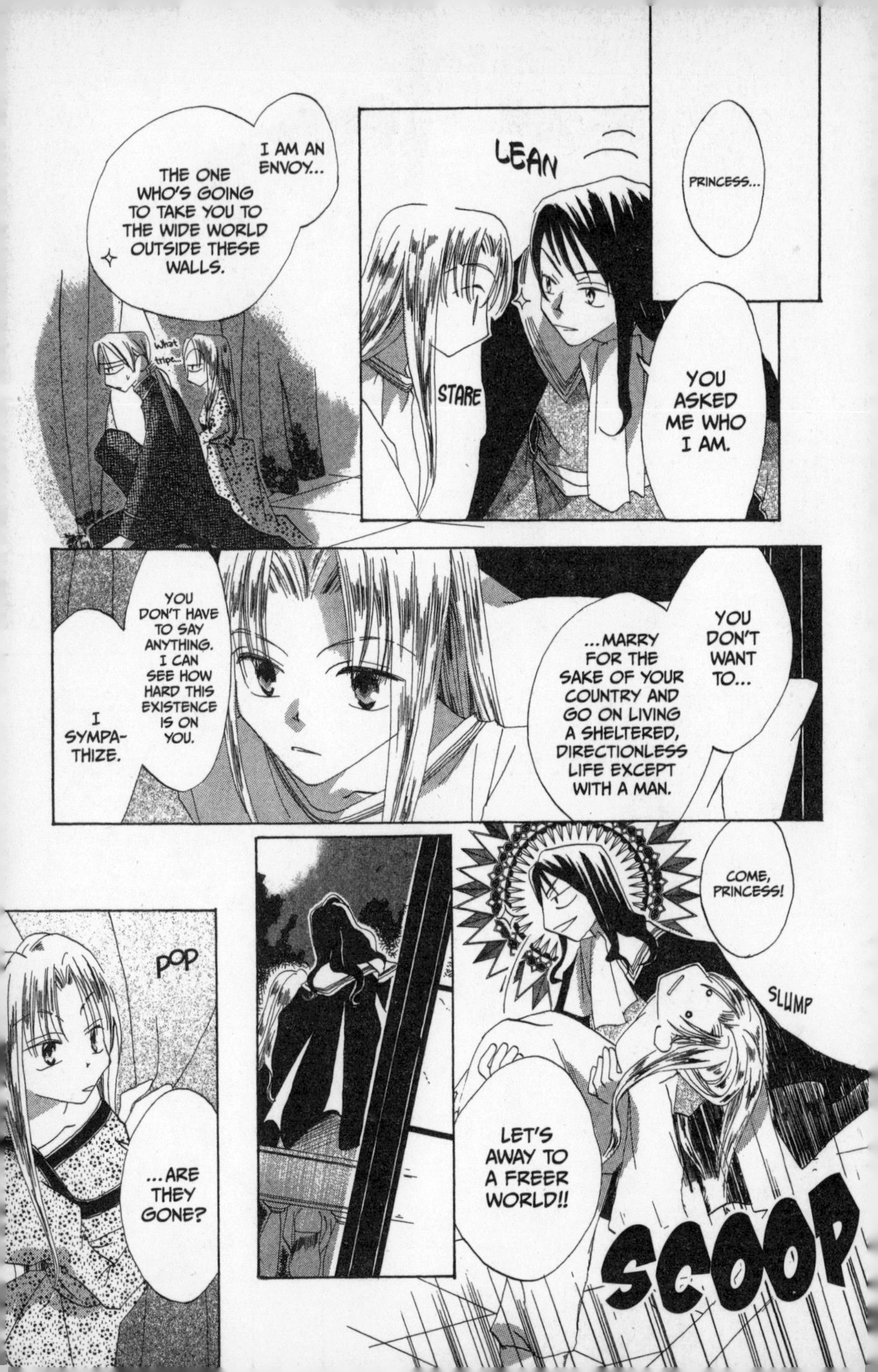
PRINCESS...
LEAN
YOU ASKED ME WHO I AM.
STARE
I AM AN ENVOY...
THE ONE WHO'S GOING TO TAKE YOU TO THE WIDE WORLD OUTSIDE THESE WALLS.
What tripe...
YOU DON'T WANT TO...
...MARRY FOR THE SAKE OF YOUR COUNTRY AND GO ON LIVING A SHELTERED, DIRECTIONLESS LIFE EXCEPT WITH A MAN.
YOU DON'T HAVE TO SAY ANYTHING. I CAN SEE HOW HARD THIS EXISTENCE IS ON YOU.
I SYMPATHIZE.
COME, PRINCESS!
SLUMP
LET'S AWAY TO A FREER WORLD!!
SCOOP
POP
...ARE THEY GONE?

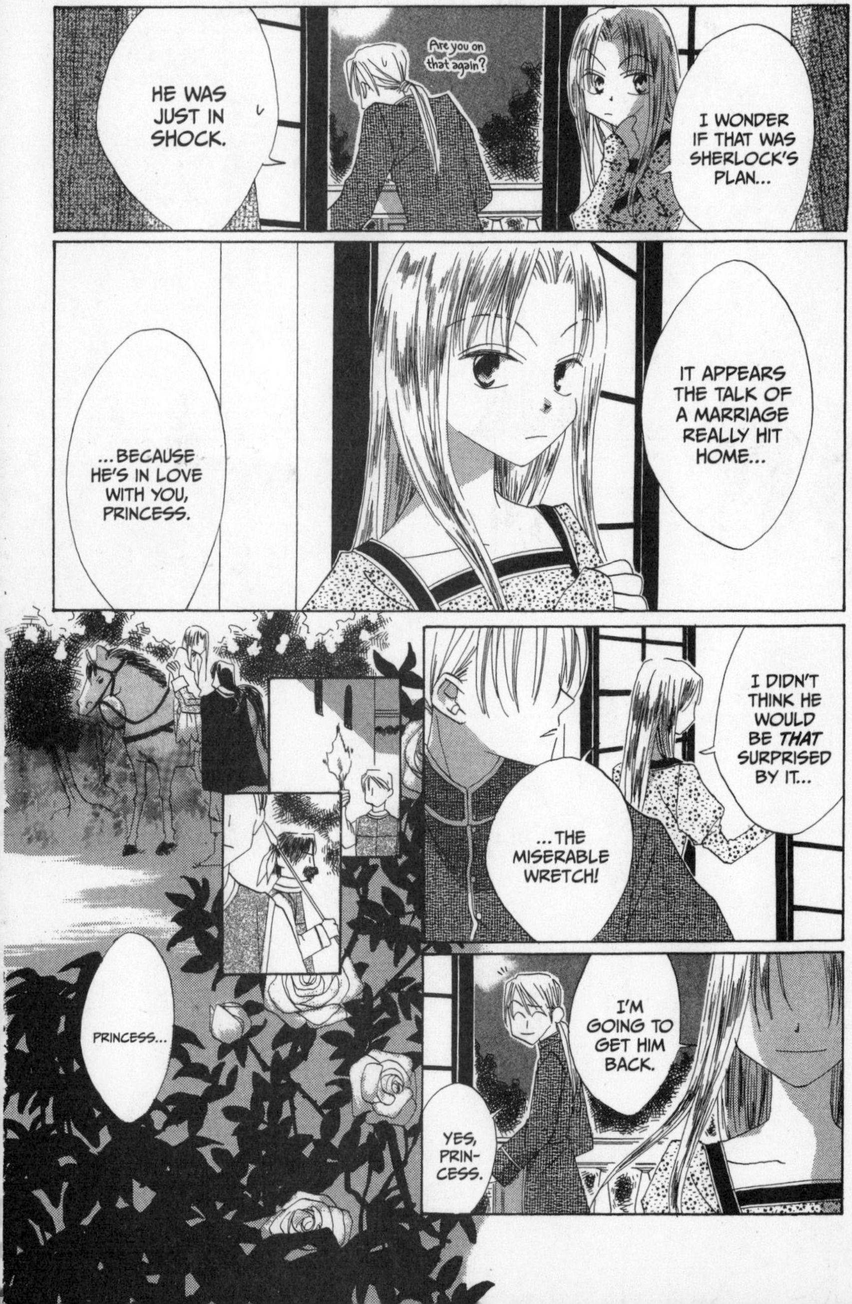
I WONDER IF THAT WAS SHERLOCK'S PLAN...
Are you on that again?
HE WAS JUST IN SHOCK.
IT APPEARS THE TALK OF A MARRIAGE REALLY HIT HOME...
...BECAUSE HE'S IN LOVE WITH YOU, PRINCESS.
I DIDN'T THINK HE WOULD BE *THAT* SURPRISED BY IT...
...THE MISERABLE WRETCH!
I'M GOING TO GET HIM BACK.
YES, PRIN-CESS.
PRINCESS...

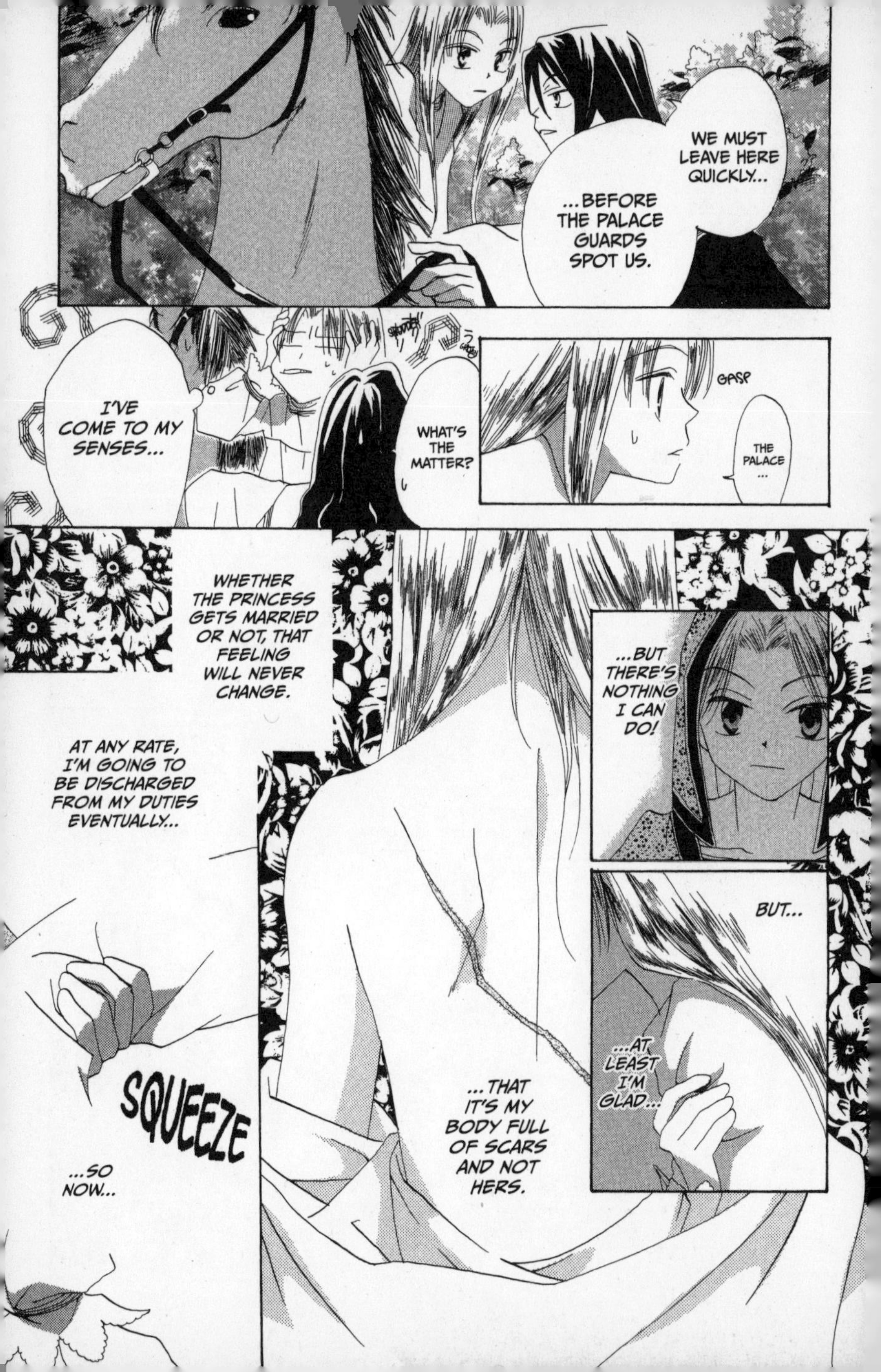
WE MUST LEAVE HERE QUICKLY...
...BEFORE THE PALACE GUARDS SPOT US.
GASP
THE PALACE ...
WHAT'S THE MATTER?
I'VE COME TO MY SENSES...
...BUT THERE'S NOTHING I CAN DO!
BUT...
...AT LEAST I'M GLAD...
...THAT IT'S MY BODY FULL OF SCARS AND NOT HERS.
WHETHER THE PRINCESS GETS MARRIED OR NOT, THAT FEELING WILL NEVER CHANGE.
AT ANY RATE, I'M GOING TO BE DISCHARGED FROM MY DUTIES EVENTUALLY...
SQUEEZE
...SO NOW...

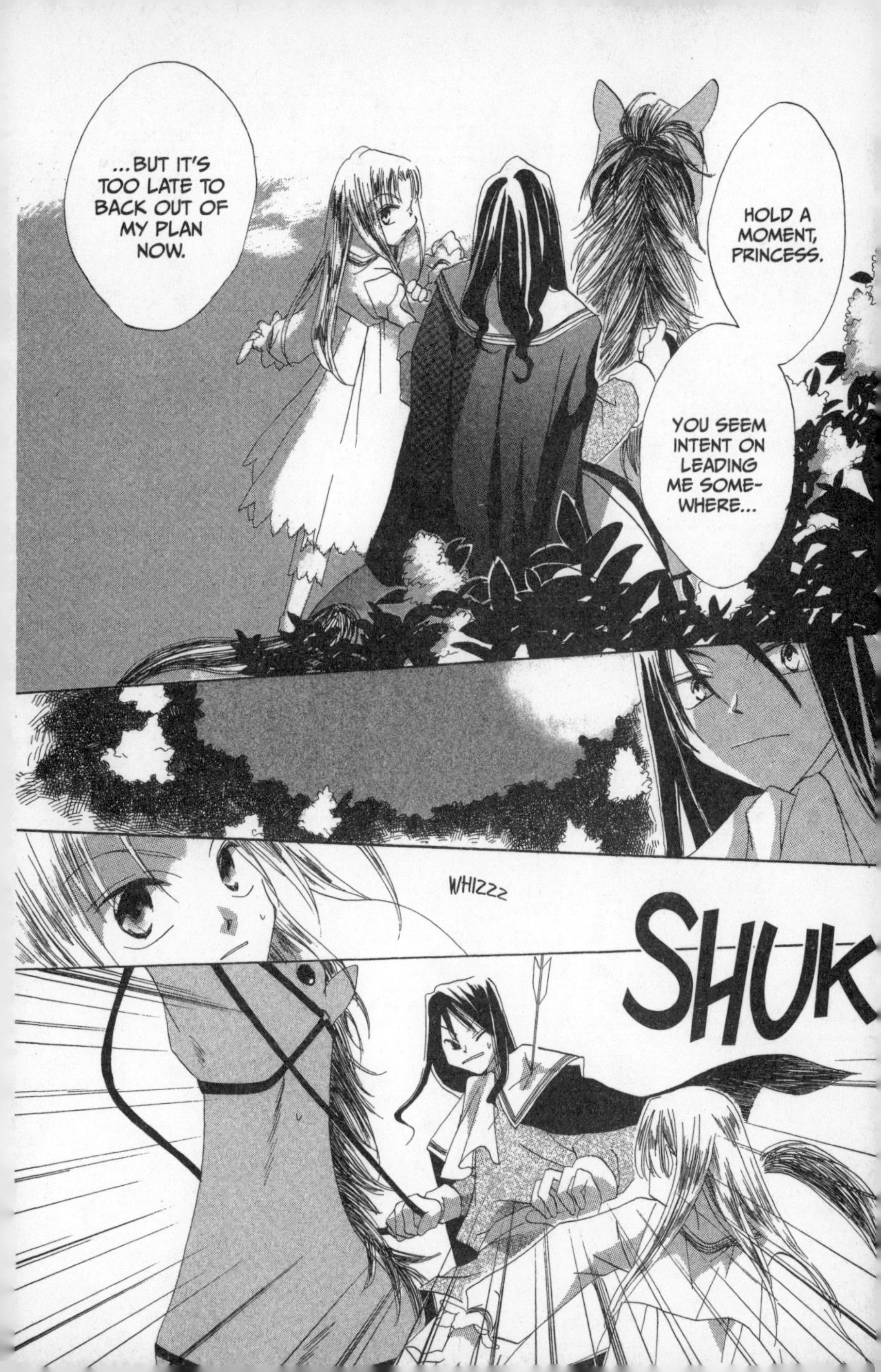
HOLD A MOMENT, PRINCESS.
YOU SEEM INTENT ON LEADING ME SOME-WHERE...
...BUT IT'S TOO LATE TO BACK OUT OF MY PLAN NOW.
WHIZZZ
SHUK

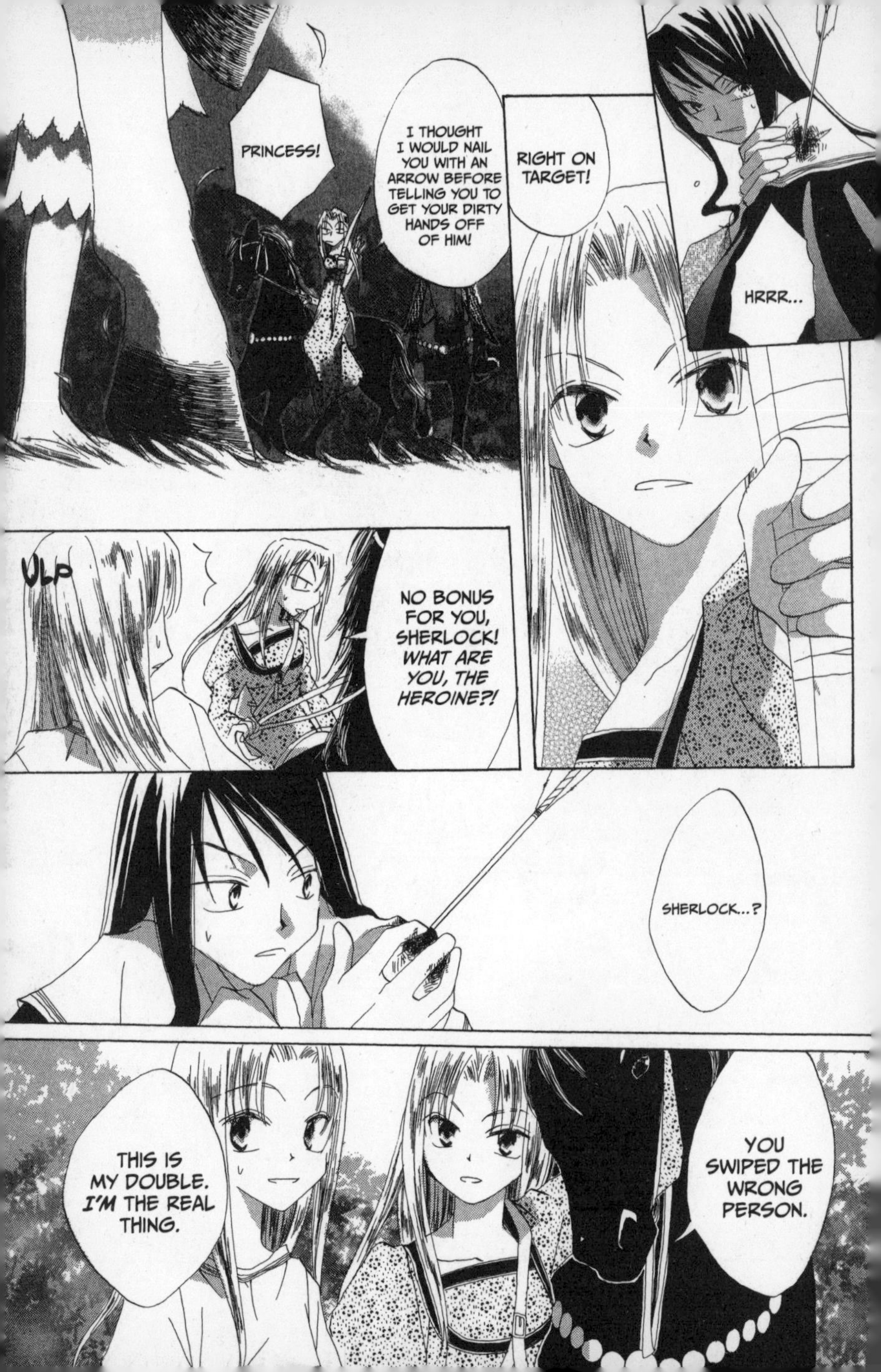
HRRR...
RIGHT ON TARGET!
I THOUGHT I WOULD NAIL YOU WITH AN ARROW BEFORE TELLING YOU TO GET YOUR DIRTY HANDS OFF OF HIM!
PRINCESS!
NO BONUS FOR YOU, SHERLOCK! WHAT ARE YOU, THE HEROINE?!
ULP
SHERLOCK...?
YOU SWIPED THE WRONG PERSON.
THIS IS MY DOUBLE. I'M THE REAL THING.

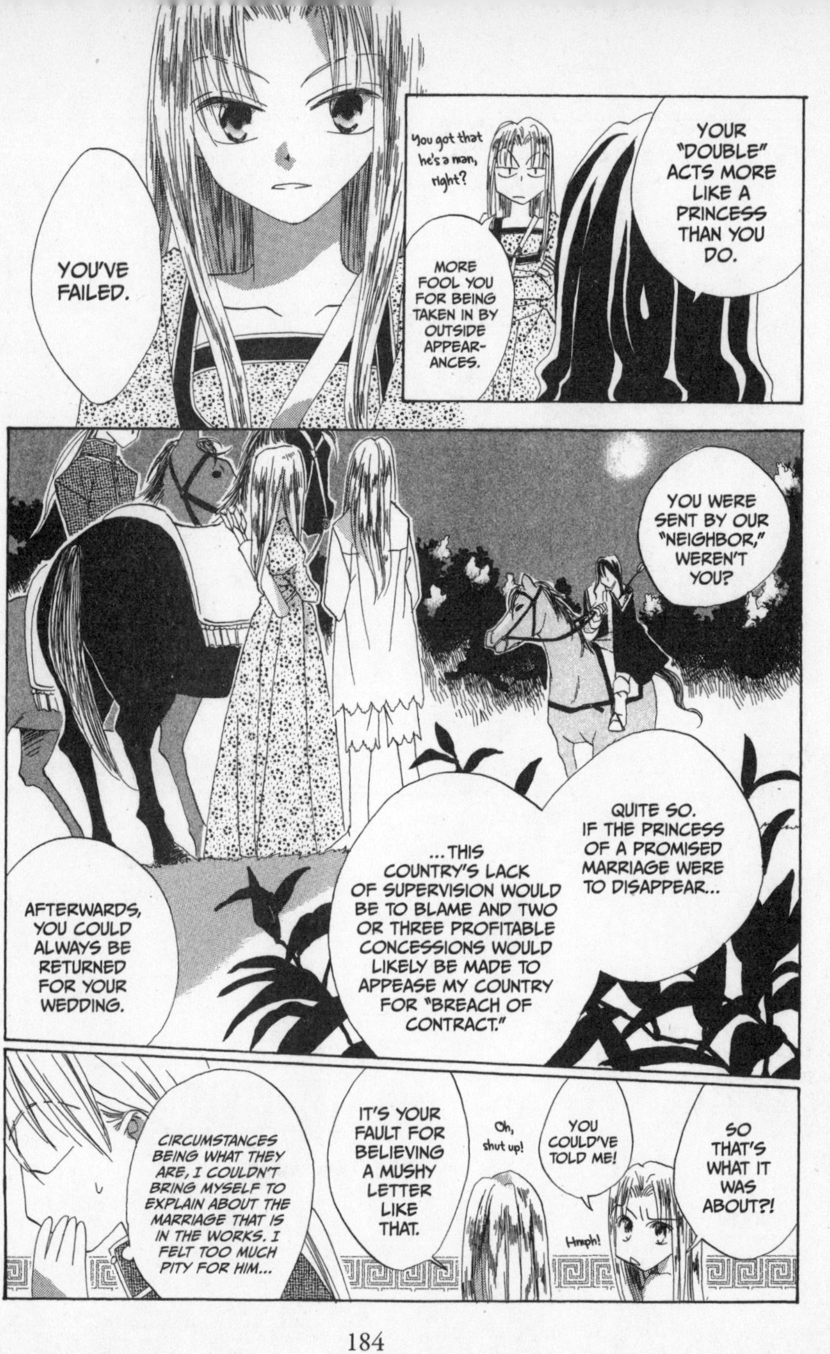
YOUR "DOUBLE" ACTS MORE LIKE A PRINCESS THAN YOU DO.
You got that he's a man, right?
MORE FOOL YOU FOR BEING TAKEN IN BY OUTSIDE APPEAR-ANCES.
YOU'VE FAILED.
YOU WERE SENT BY OUR "NEIGHBOR," WEREN'T YOU?
QUITE SO. IF THE PRINCESS OF A PROMISED MARRIAGE WERE TO DISAPPEAR...
...THIS COUNTRY'S LACK OF SUPERVISION WOULD BE TO BLAME AND TWO OR THREE PROFITABLE CONCESSIONS WOULD LIKELY BE MADE TO APPEASE MY COUNTRY FOR "BREACH OF CONTRACT."
AFTERWARDS, YOU COULD ALWAYS BE RETURNED FOR YOUR WEDDING.
SO THAT'S WHAT IT WAS ABOUT?!
YOU COULD'VE TOLD ME!
Hmph!
Oh, shut up!
IT'S YOUR FAULT FOR BELIEVING A MUSHY LETTER LIKE THAT.
CIRCUMSTANCES BEING WHAT THEY ARE, I COULDN'T BRING MYSELF TO EXPLAIN ABOUT THE MARRIAGE THAT IS IN THE WORKS. I FELT TOO MUCH PITY FOR HIM...

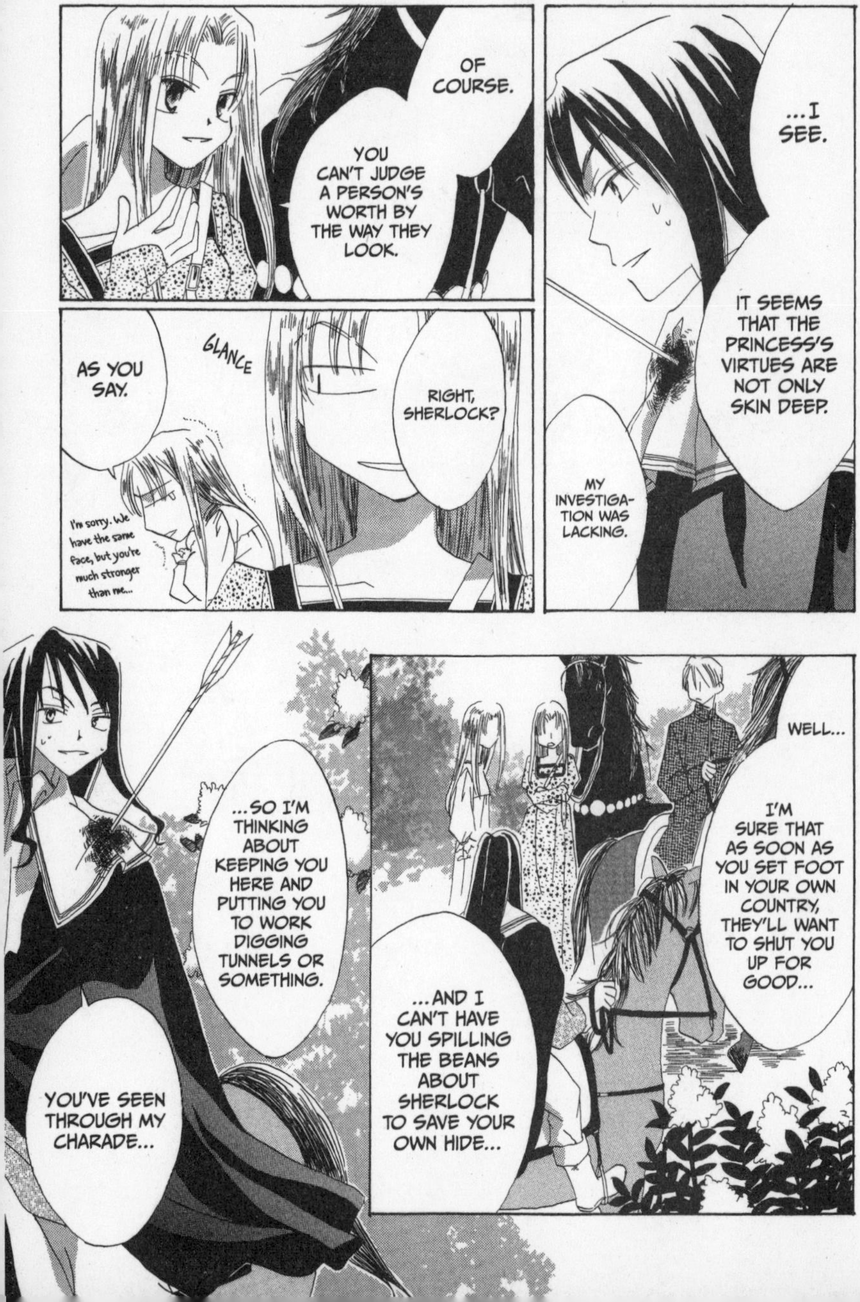
...I SEE.
IT SEEMS THAT THE PRINCESS'S VIRTUES ARE NOT ONLY SKIN DEEP.
MY INVESTIGATION WAS LACKING.
OF COURSE.
YOU CAN'T JUDGE A PERSON'S WORTH BY THE WAY THEY LOOK.
RIGHT, SHERLOCK?
GLANCE
AS YOU SAY.
I'm sorry. We have the same face, but you're much stronger than me...
WELL...
I'M SURE THAT AS SOON AS YOU SET FOOT IN YOUR OWN COUNTRY, THEY'LL WANT TO SHUT YOU UP FOR GOOD...
...AND I CAN'T HAVE YOU SPILLING THE BEANS ABOUT SHERLOCK TO SAVE YOUR OWN HIDE...
...SO I'M THINKING ABOUT KEEPING YOU HERE AND PUTTING YOU TO WORK DIGGING TUNNELS OR SOMETHING.
YOU'VE SEEN THROUGH MY CHARADE...

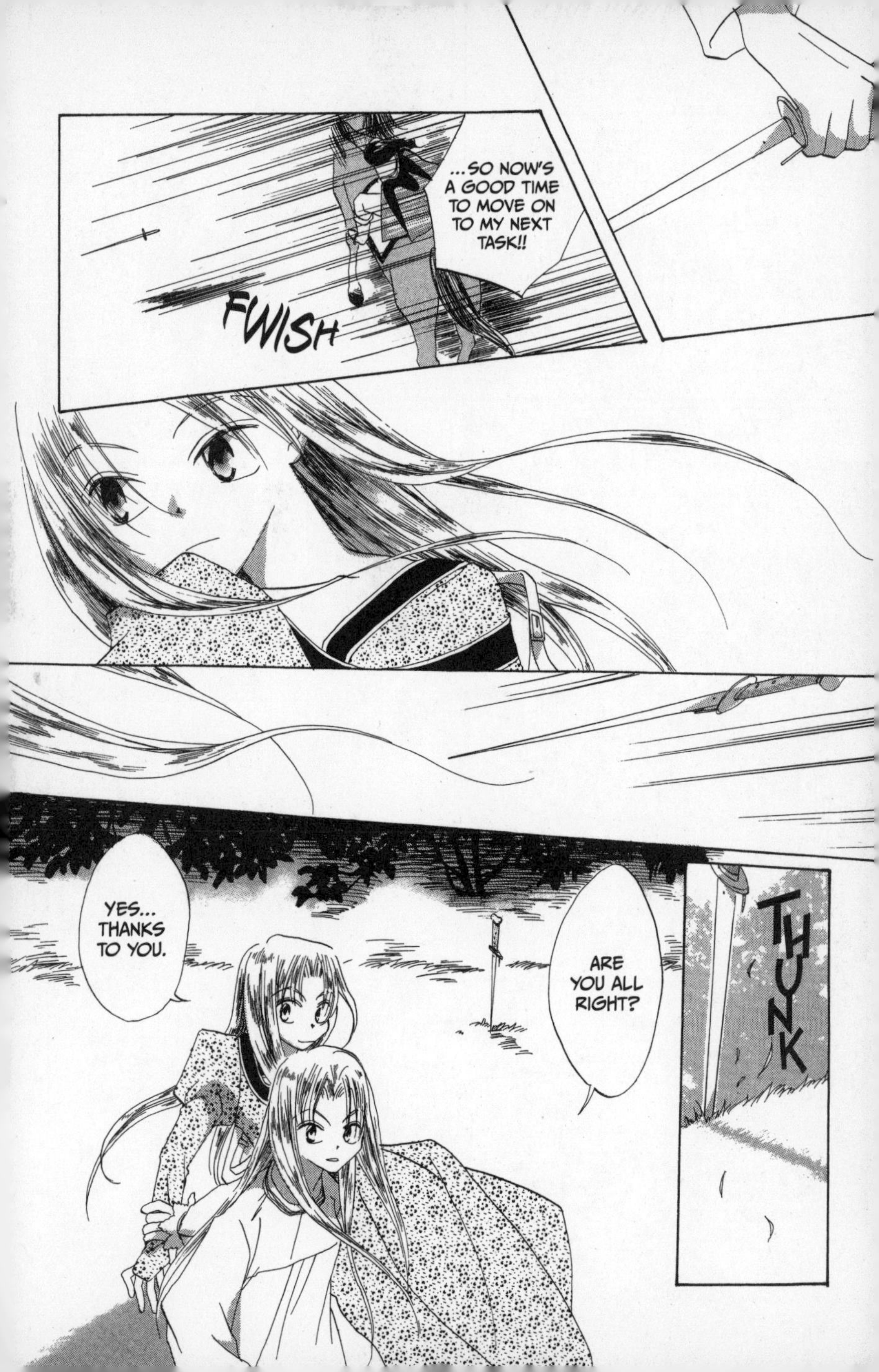
...SO NOW'S A GOOD TIME TO MOVE ON TO MY NEXT TASK!!
FWISH
THUNK
ARE YOU ALL RIGHT?
YES... THANKS TO YOU.

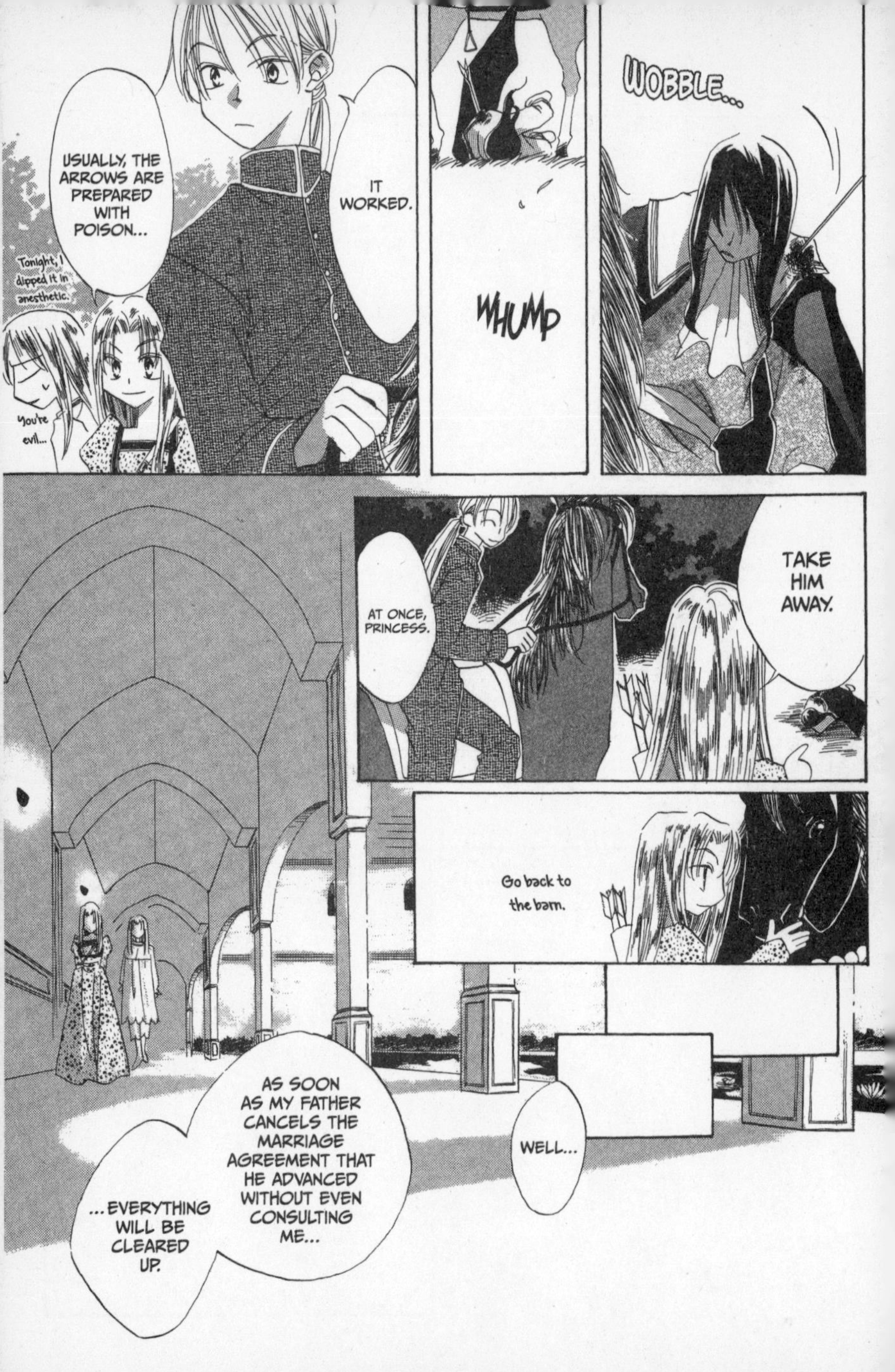
WOBBLE...
WHUMP
IT WORKED.
USUALLY, THE ARROWS ARE PREPARED WITH POISON...
Tonight, I dipped it in anesthetic.
You're evil...
TAKE HIM AWAY.
AT ONCE, PRINCESS.
Go back to the barn.
WELL...
AS SOON AS MY FATHER CANCELS THE MARRIAGE AGREEMENT THAT HE ADVANCED WITHOUT EVEN CONSULTING ME...
...EVERYTHING WILL BE CLEARED UP.

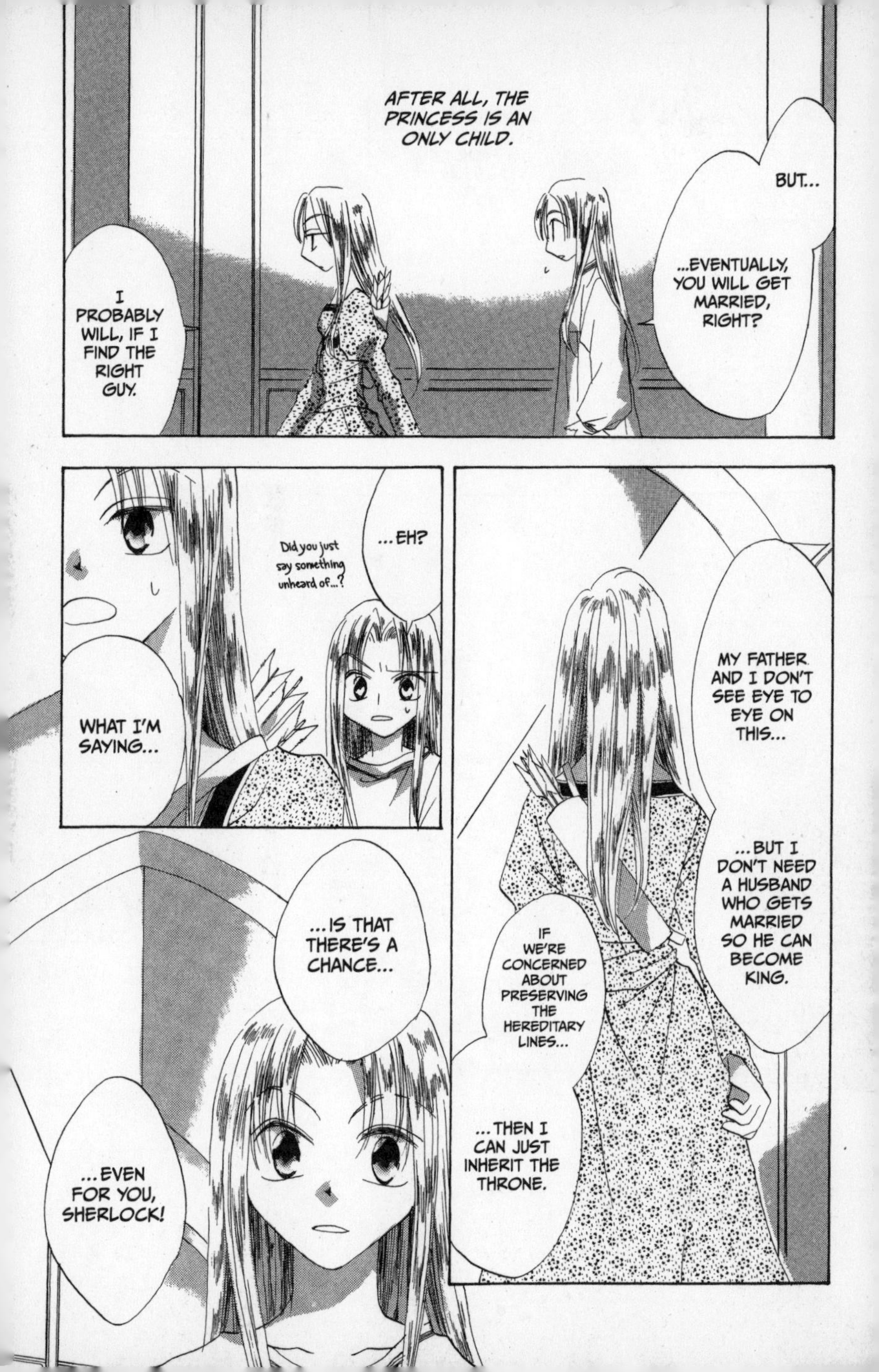
BUT...
...EVENTUALLY, YOU WILL GET MARRIED, RIGHT?
AFTER ALL, THE PRINCESS IS AN ONLY CHILD.
I PROBABLY WILL, IF I FIND THE RIGHT GUY.
MY FATHER AND I DON'T SEE EYE TO EYE ON THIS...
...BUT I DON'T NEED A HUSBAND WHO GETS MARRIED SO HE CAN BECOME KING.
IF WE'RE CONCERNED ABOUT PRESERVING THE HEREDITARY LINES...
...THEN I CAN JUST INHERIT THE THRONE.
...EH?
Did you just say something unheard of...?
WHAT I'M SAYING...
...IS THAT THERE'S A CHANCE...
...EVEN FOR YOU, SHERLOCK!

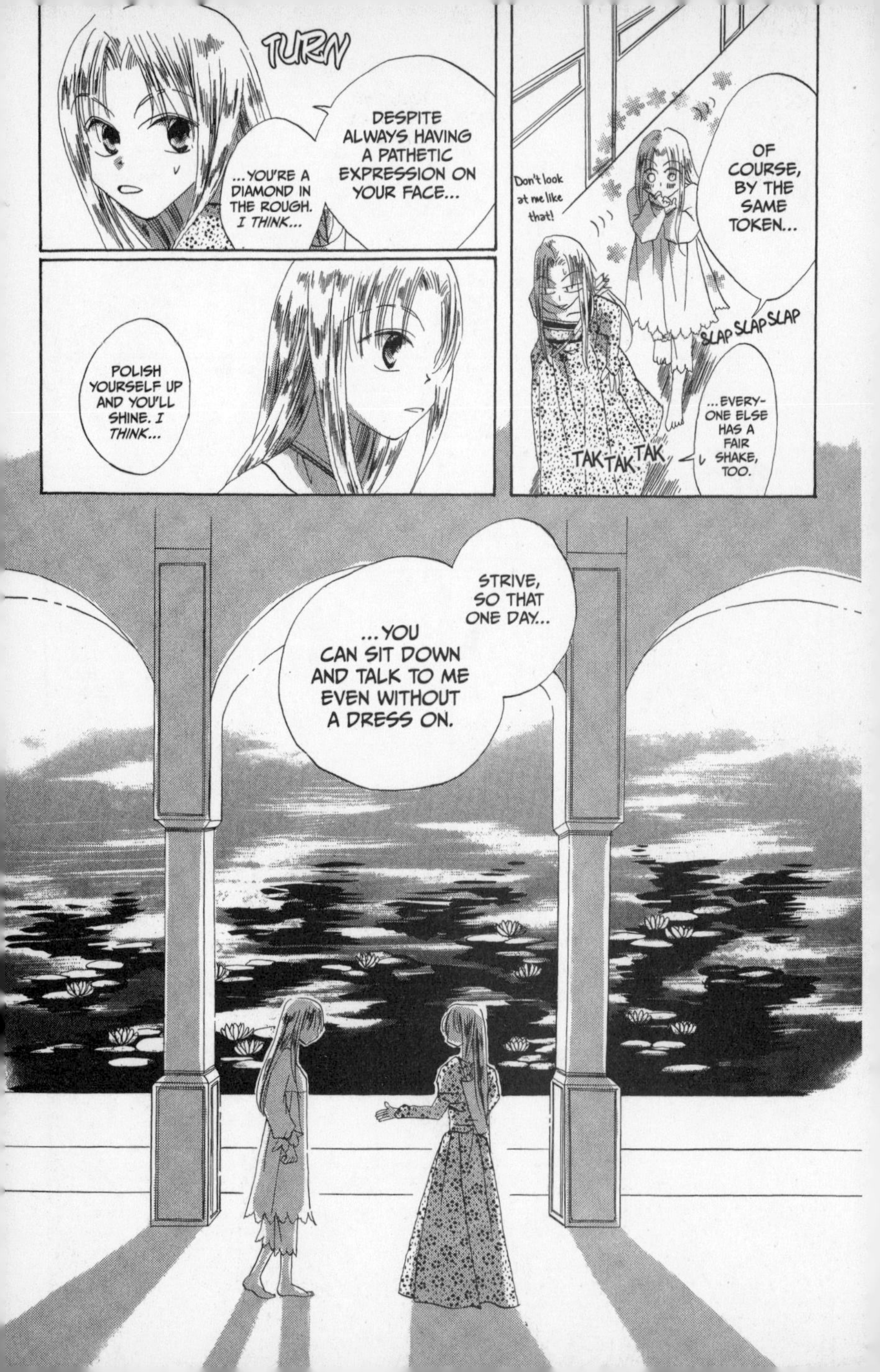
OF COURSE, BY THE SAME TOKEN...
Don't look at me like that!
SLAP SLAP SLAP
...EVERY-ONE ELSE HAS A FAIR SHAKE, TOO.
TAK TAK TAK
TURN
DESPITE ALWAYS HAVING A PATHETIC EXPRESSION ON YOUR FACE...
...YOU'RE A DIAMOND IN THE ROUGH. I THINK...
POLISH YOURSELF UP AND YOU'LL SHINE. I THINK...
STRIVE, SO THAT ONE DAY...
...YOU CAN SIT DOWN AND TALK TO ME EVEN WITHOUT A DRESS ON.

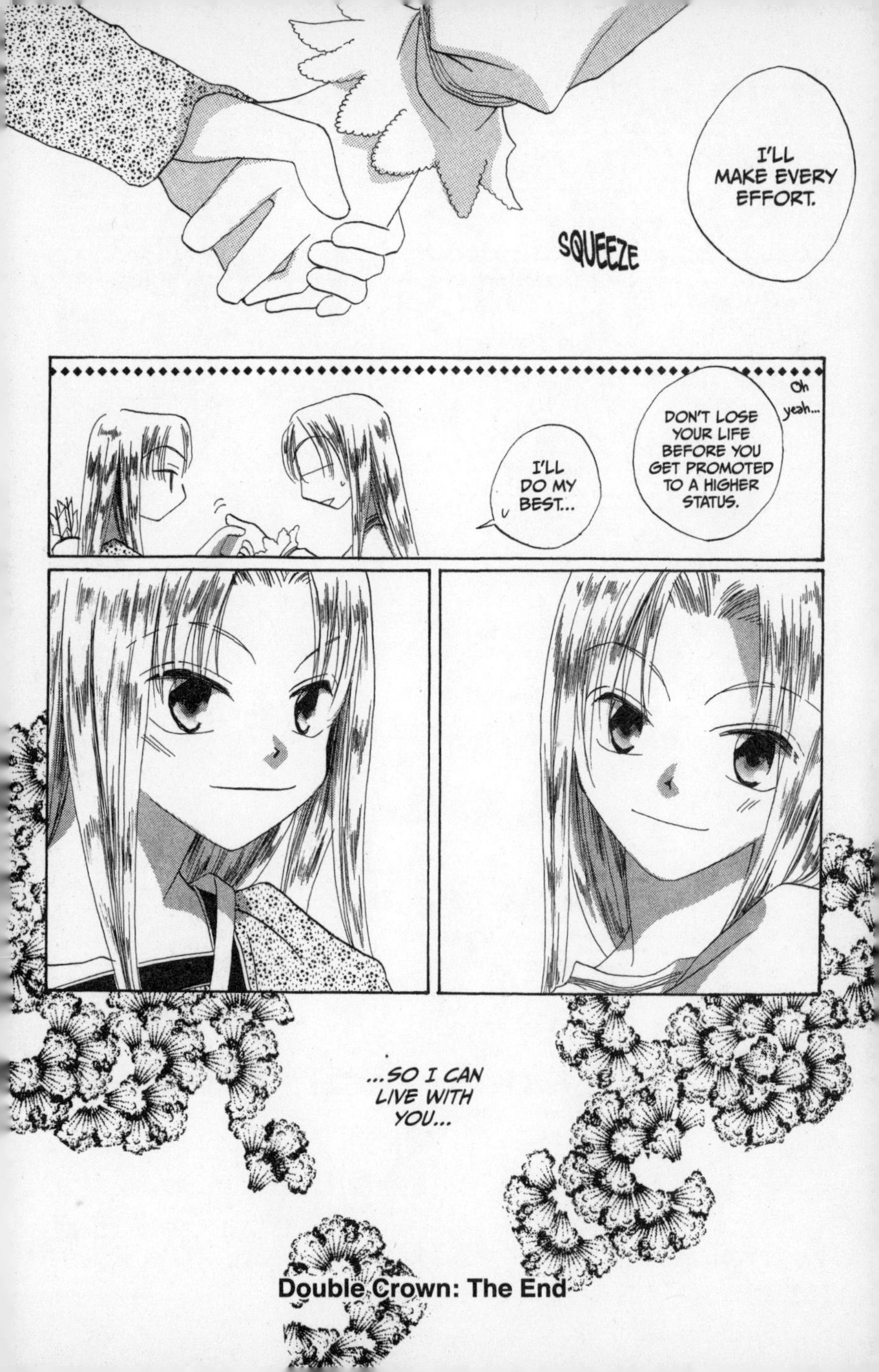
I'LL MAKE EVERY EFFORT.
SQUEEZE
Oh yeah...
DON'T LOSE YOUR LIFE BEFORE YOU GET PROMOTED TO A HIGHER STATUS.
I'LL DO MY BEST...
...SO I CAN LIVE WITH YOU...
Double Crown: The End

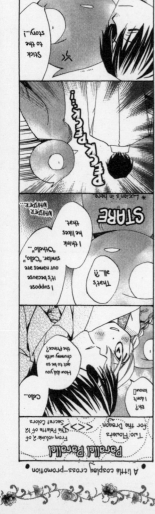

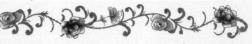

Afterword

I'm sorry that I'm unable to reply, but if you'd like to share your thoughts about "Two Flowers," by all means, please send them to:

Nari Kusakawa
c/o CMX
888 Prospect St.
Suite 240
La Jolla, CA 92037

My website, with announcements about my work, etc, is:

http://lotus.her.jp/
(current as of August 2008)

I want to thank: all of you for reading this; my editor, the publishing company and the stores for stocking this; my family, relatives and friends; the liquor store that lets me make my copies; Kaoru Sashi-sama and Baku Yumitsuki-sama.
I appreciate all of you.

December 2006

A little cosplay cross-promotion

Parallel Parallel
Two Flowers for the Dragon
From volume 2 of The Palette of 12 Secret Colors
Cello...
How did you get to be so chummy with the Prince?
Eh? I don't know
I suppose it's because our names are similar. "Cello," "Othello"...
That's all...?!
I think he likes that.
WHISPER WHISPER...
STARE
* Lucian's in here.
PECK PECK...!
Stick to the story...!
KKKKK...
Heh.
Your face alone is enough comic relief.

P9-DCG-261

By Nari Kusakawa. The tattoo signifying Kuwan has expanded to fill Shakuya's arm. What has given him the upper hand? Meanwhile, the handmaids wonder why Shakuya's gloves are getting longer. Lucien starts to piece together memories from his youth; has a dangerous part of the past returned to haunt him? Shakuya has a hard time reconciling the difference between Lucien the boy and Lucien the man. Will the resurrected past hurt their chances of a romance in the future?

Volume 4

Two Flowers for the Dragon

FINALLY, LUCIEN'S MEMORIES RETURN! AVAILABLE IN MAY!

Sheldon Drzka – Translation and Adaptation
Zack Giallongo – Lettering
Larry Berry – Design
Jim Chadwick – Editor

ISBN: 978-1-4012-1905-5

DC Comics, a Warner Bros. Entertainment Company.

TWO FLOWERS FOR THE DRAGON Volume 3, published by WildStorm Productions, an imprint of DC Comics. 888 Prospect St. #240, La Jolla, CA 92037. English Translation © 2009. All Rights Reserved. English translation rights in U.S.A. And Canada arranged with HAKUSENSHA, INC., through Tuttle-Mori Agency, Inc., Tokyo. CMX is a trademark of DC Comics. The stories, characters, and incidents mentioned in this magazine are entirely fictional. Printed on recyclable paper. WildStorm does not read or accept unsolicited submissions of ideas, stories or artwork. Printed in Canada.

RYU NO HANAWAZURAI by Nari Kusakawa © 2007 Nari Kusakawa. All rights reserved. First published in Japan in 2007 by HAKUSENSHA, INC., Tokyo.

Jim Lee Editorial Director **John Nee** Senior VP—Business Development
Hank Kanalz VP—General Manager, WildStorm **Paul Levitz** President & Publisher
Georg Brewer VP—Design & DC Direct Creative **Richard Bruning** Senior VP—Creative Director
Patrick Caldon Executive VP—Finance & Operations **Chris Caramalis** VP—Finance
John Cunningham VP—Marketing **Terri Cunningham** VP—Managing Editor **Alison Gill** VP—Manufacturing
David Hyde VP—Publicity **Paula Lowitt** Senior VP—Business & Legal Affairs
Gregory Noveck Senior VP—Creative Affairs **Sue Pohja** VP—Book Trade Sales
Steve Rotterdam Senior VP—Sales & Marketing **Cheryl Rubin** Senior VP—Brand Management
Jeff Trojan VP—Business Development, DC Direct **Bob Wayne** VP—Sales